EUROPE ENLARGED

A handbook of education, labour and welfare regimes in Central and Eastern Europe

Edited by Irena Kogan, Michael Gebel and Clemens Noelke

This edition published in Great Britain in 2008 by

The Policy Press
University of Bristol
Fourth Floor
Beacon House
Queen's Road
Bristol BS8 1QU
UK

Tel +44 (0)117 331 4054
Fax +44 (0)117 331 4093
e-mail tpp-info@bristol.ac.uk
www.policypress.org.uk

© The Policy Press 2008

British Library Cataloguing in Publication Data
A catalogue record for this book is available from the British Library.

Library of Congress Cataloging-in-Publication Data
A catalog record for this book has been requested.

ISBN 978 1 84742 064 0 hardcover

The right of Irena Kogan, Michael Gebel and Clemens Noelke to be identified as editors
of this work has been asserted by them in accordance with the 1988 Copyright, Designs
and Patents Act.

Cover design by Robin Hawes.
Front cover: image kindly supplied by Alamy Images.
Printed and bound in Great Britain by MPG Books, Bodmin.

Contents

List of tables and figures   vi
List of abbreviations   xii
Notes on contributors   xiv
Acknowledgements   xvii

Introduction   **1**
Walter Müller

One   **Education systems of Central and Eastern European countries**   **7**
Irena Kogan
Cohort succession and education attainment   7
Basic level of education   11
Secondary level of education   13
Tertiary level of education   22
Conclusion   30

Two   **Labour markets in Central and Eastern Europe**   **35**
Michael Gebel
Economic development   35
Labour market dynamics   41
Labour market institutions   52
Conclusion   59

Three   **Social protection, inequality and labour market risks in Central and Eastern Europe**   **63**
Clemens Noelke
Social policy under communism   64
Rising wealth, inequality and poverty   68
Institutional reform trends and outcomes   76
Social protection against labour market risks   80
Active labour market policy   86
Conclusion   89

Four   **Bulgaria**   **97**
Dobrinka Kostova
Education system   98
Labour market   109
Welfare regime   116

Five	**Czech Republic**	**123**
	Jana Straková	
	Education system	124
	Labour market	134
	Welfare regime	143

Six	**Estonia**	**151**
	Ellu Saar and Kristina Lindemann	
	Education system	152
	Labour market	162
	Welfare regime	171

Seven	**Hungary**	**183**
	Erzsébet Bukodi and Péter Róbert	
	Education system	183
	Labour market	194
	Welfare regime	202

Eight	**Latvia**	**213**
	Ilze Trapenciere	
	Education system	214
	Labour market	224
	Welfare regime	232

Nine	**Lithuania**	**241**
	Meilute Taljunaite	
	Education system	242
	Labour market	253
	Welfare regime	261

Ten	**Poland**	**268**
	Anna Baranowska	
	Education system	269
	Labour market	278
	Welfare regime	286

Eleven	**Romania**	**295**
	Cristina Mocanu	
	Education system	295
	Labour market	305
	Welfare regime	313

Twelve   **Slovakia**   **323**
Ján Košta and Rastislav Bednárik
Education system   323
Labour market   333
Welfare regime   341

Thirteen   **Slovenia**   **353**
Angela Ivančič
Education system   354
Labour market   363
Welfare regime   369

Index   **379**

List of tables and figures

Tables

1.1	Age of selection in secondary schools and the number of programmes at the secondary level	14
1.2	Upper-secondary schools in CEE countries	16
1.3	The predominant form of organisation of VET	22
1.4	The proportion of students enrolled in private institutions or proportion of private institutions at the tertiary level	28
2.1	GDP per capita in CEE countries, 1990	36
2.2	Weighted privatisation index and private sector share in GDP in CEE countries, 1990-2007	39
2.3	Labour force participation rate by gender, 1990 and 2006	44
2.4	Flexible employment forms in 2006	48
2.5	Unemployment rates in 2006	50
2.6	Unemployment rates by education level in 2006	52
2.7	Employment protection legislation	55
2.8	Key figures of industrial relations in CEE countries	57
3.1	Levels and trends of material welfare	70
3.2	Distribution of income and unemployment risks	72
3.3	Poverty rates and long-term unemployment	74
3.4	Social protection expenditure and financing	79
3.5	Unemployment insurance benefits for reference individual 2006/07	85
4.1	Labour force participation rate by age group, 1990-2006	112
4.2	Characteristics of the unemployment benefit system in Bulgaria, 1995-2007	117
5.1	Primary and lower-secondary education in the Czech Republic	125
5.2	Upper-secondary education in the Czech Republic	127
5.3	Tertiary education in the Czech Republic	128
5.4	Labour force participation rate by age group, 1990-2006	137
5.5	Unemployment rate by level of education, 2001-06	140
5.6	Unemployment rate by region, 2006	141
5.7	Wage and benefits levels, 1990-2005 (% average wage)	145
6.1	Labour force participation rate (%) by age cohort, 1990-2006	165
6.2	Expenditure on social protection for the unemployed in Estonia	172
6.3	Unemployment benefit in Estonia	174
6.4	Percentage of children enrolled in pre-school institutions by age	176
7.1	Description of the education system	184
7.2	Number of education institutions by type of schools	193

7.3	Labour force participation rate by age groups, 1990-2006	198
7.4	Unemployment rates by education level, 1993-2004	200
7.5	Labour force participation rates and LFS unemployment rates by NUTS-2 level of region, 1993 and 2004	201
7.6	Two indicators on temporal change of the role of ALMP in employment policy, 1999-2003	203
7.7	Description of unemployment insurance since the mid-1990s	204
7.8	Proportion of children younger than two enrolled in nurseries, 1995-2004	206
7.9	Regular social assistance, average number and ratio of recipients, average monthly amount per capita (in HUF), 2000-04	208
8.1	Labour force participation rate by age cohort, 1990-2006	228
8.2	Characteristics of the Latvian unemployment benefit system	234
8.3	Minimum wage in Latvia (in LVL), as of 1 January in respective year	236
8.4	Age group specific pre-school enrolment rates (1997-2005)	237
9.1	Total number of education establishments and number of non-public schools in Lithuania	252
9.2	Labour force participation rate (%) by age cohort, 1990-2006	257
9.3	Characteristics of the unemployment benefit system in Lithuania	262
9.4	Pre-school establishments and enrolment (end of year estimates)	265
10.1	Secondary enrolment rates by type of school in Poland (%), 1990-2005	275
10.2	Proportion of students attending tuition and free of charge courses in Poland, 1995-2002 (column %)	279
10.3	Labour force participation rate by age group, 1990-2006	283
11.1	Pupil achievement in reading, mathematics and science, PISA results for 2006	303
11.2	Labour force participation rate by age cohort, 1990-2006	309
11.3	Characteristics of the unemployment benefit system, 1998-2005	316
11.4	Pre-school education in Romania, 1990-2005	317
11.5	The value of child allowance relative to net average wage, 1994-2005	318
11.6	The share of in-kind income from own agricultural produce as a percentage of gross total household income, 1998-2005	319
12.1	Changes in main groups of population influencing the labour force, 1990-98	337
12.2	Labour force participation rate (%) by age group, 1990-2006	337
12.3	Characteristics of graduate practice programme	342
12.4	Number of receivers of unemployment benefit	343
12.5	Development of gross monthly minimum wage, relative to gross average wage	345

12.6 Age-specific enrolment rate children aged 3-5 (percentages enrolled within age group), 1989-2005   346
12.7 Development of kindergartens in Slovakia (absolute figures), 1989-2006   346
12.8 Main cash benefits for children in Slovakia, 2001 and 2005   347
12.9 Social assistance in Slovakia, 1995-2005   348
13.1 Labour force participation rate by age cohort, 1990-2006   365
13.2 Changing payment duration of income restitution payments   371
13.3 Trends in the percentage of unemployed receiving financial assistance by age group, 1997-2005   372
13.4 Pre-primary enrolments (net rates, percentage of population aged 3-6) in organised childcare, 1989-2005   373

Figures

1.1   Percentage with lower-secondary education or less (ISCED 0-2) by cohort, 2002   8
1.2   Percentage with upper-secondary or post-secondary non-tertiary education (ISCED 3-4) by cohort, 2002   9
1.3   Percentage with tertiary education (ISCED 5-6) by cohort, 2002   10
1.4   Percentage of people aged 18-24 not in education with only lower-secondary education in 2002   12
1.5   General upper-secondary education enrolments (gross ratios, percentage of population aged 15-18), 1989-2005   18
1.6   Vocational/technical secondary education enrolments (gross ratios, percentage of population aged 15-18), 1989-2005   19
1.7   Secondary education options in the CEE countries in the mid-1990s   20
1.8   Higher education enrolments (gross population ratios, percentage of population aged 19-24), 1989-2005   23
1.9   Proportion of women among students (ISCED 5-6) as percentage of the total students at this level, 1998-2004   24
1.10 Enrolment by fields of study (%), 2004   25
1.11 The proportion of tertiary educated people aged 25-29, by type of tertiary education, 2001   27
1.12 Financial aid to students in the form of scholarships and loans, as a percentage of total public expenditure on tertiary education, 2002   29
2.1   Real GDP in CEE countries, 1989-2007   37
2.2   Employment by sector in CEE countries   42
2.3   Labour force participation rate (%) by age cohort, 1990 and 2006   45
3.1   Expenditure on passive and active labour market policies as a percentage of GDP, 2005   87

3.2   Expenditure on different types of ALMPs as a percentage of
      GDP, 2005   88
4.1   The contemporary Bulgarian education system, 1998   100
4.2   Enrolment by type of school in Bulgaria (%)   102
4.3   Proportion of females by type of school in Bulgaria   103
4.4   School-aged population by levels of education and type of
      school on the upper-secondary level (%), 1993-98   104
4.5   Enrolment in tertiary education by selected fields of study (%)   106
4.6   Percentage of females in tertiary education by fields of study   107
4.7   Proportion of public and private institutions in Bulgaria (%),
      2004/05   108
4.8   GDP growth, 1989-2006   110
4.9   Labour force participation rate (age group 15-64), 1990-2006   111
4.10 Unemployment rates, 1990-2006   113
5.1   The Czech education system   126
5.2   Enrolment by type of school in the Czech Republic (%)   129
5.3   Graduates of basic and secondary schools by type of continuing
      studies, 1998/99   130
5.4   Enrolment in education and training at the (upper) secondary
      level (%)   131
5.5   Enrolment in tertiary education by field of study (%)   133
5.6   GDP growth, 1991-2006   135
5.7   Labour force participation rate (age group 15-64), 1990-2006   137
5.8   Unemployment rates, 1990-2006   139
6.1   The Estonian system of education since the mid-1990s   154
6.2   Enrolment by type of school of school-age population in
      Estonia (%)   156
6.3   Transitions in the Estonian education system in 1998   157
6.4   Proportion of females in various school types in Estonia,
      1995-2005   157
6.5   Number of students in different types of higher education,
      1993/94-2005/06   159
6.6   Enrolment in tertiary education by field of study (%)   160
6.7   Percentage of females per field of study   161
6.8   Proportion and number of students paying tuition fees and
      receiving state support, 1993/94-2005/06   161
6.9   GDP growth in Estonia, 1989-2006   163
6.10 Labour force participation rate (age group 15-64), 1990-2006   165
6.11 Flows from and into employment (000s), 1992-2005   166
6.12 Unemployment rates, 1990-2006   167
6.13 Unemployment rate (%) of different age groups, 1993-2005   168
6.14 Number of youth (absolute numbers) by job search time periods,
      1997-2005   169

7.1	The Hungarian system of education	187
7.2	Number of students entering the school system by level of education, 1989-2004	188
7.3	Proportion of women among full-time students at secondary and tertiary level, 1990-2004	189
7.4	Enrolment in education and training at the (upper)- secondary level (%), 1990-2004	190
7.5	Enrolment in tertiary education by field of study (%)	192
7.6	GDP growth, 1989-2006	195
7.7	Labour force participation rate (age group 15-64), 1990-2006	197
7.8	Unemployment rates, 1990-2006	199
8.1	The Latvian educational system	215
8.2	Enrolment by type of school (%)	218
8.3	Graduates of basic and secondary schools of 1998 by type of continuing studies	219
8.4	School-age population by levels of education and type of school on the upper-secondary level (%)	220
8.5	Enrolment in tertiary education by field of study (%)	222
8.6	GDP growth, 1989-2006	226
8.7	Sectoral share of employed (%), 1990-2005	227
8.8	Labour force participation rate (age group 15-64), 1990-2006	228
8.9	Unemployment rates, 1992-2006	229
9.1	The Lithuanian education system after 1990	244
9.2	Enrolment by type of school in Lithuania (%)	247
9.3	Flowcharts for the further education of graduates from different education institutions (%), 1998	247
9.4	Proportion of women in various school types, 1996-2006	248
9.5	Students in vocational schools by stage of studies (%)	249
9.6	Proportion of graduates from post-secondary education by field of study	251
9.7	GDP growth, 1991-2006	254
9.8	Sectoral share of employed, 1990-2005	256
9.9	Labour force participation rate (age group 15-64), 1990-2006	257
9.10	Unemployment rates, 1991-2006	258
10.1	The Polish education system, 2000	272
10.2	The structure of enrolment (%) by type of school in Poland, 1950-2004	274
10.3	Enrolment in tertiary education (%) by field of study in Poland, 1990-2004	277
10.4	Proportion of females in tertiary education by selected fields of study in Poland, 1990-2004	278
10.5	GDP growth, 1991-2006	280
10.6	Labour force participation rate (age group 15-64), 1990-2006	282

10.7   Unemployment rates, 1990-2006   285
11.1   The Romanian education system   297
11.2   School-aged population by levels of education and type of
        school (%)   300
11.3   Enrolment in education and training at the (upper)-secondary
        level (%)   302
11.4   Tertiary education enrolment by group of specialisation (%)   304
11.5   GDP growth, 1990-2006   306
11.6   Labour force participation rate (age group 15-64), 1990-2006   308
11.7   Unemployment rates, 1991-2006   310
12.1   The Slovak education system   325
12.2   Enrolment by type of school in Slovakia   328
12.3   Transitions in the Slovak educational system in 2005   328
12.4   Enrolment in upper-secondary education in Slovakia   329
12.5   Enrolment in tertiary education by field of study (%)   331
12.6   The proportion of women in tertiary education (excluding PhD
        students), 1995-2005   332
12.7   GDP growth, 1989-2006   334
12.8   Labour force participation rate (age group 15-64), 1990-2006   336
12.9   Unemployment rates, 1991-2006   338
13.1   The Slovenian education system, 1996-2004   356
13.2   Enrolment (% of total students enrolled) by type of school in
        Slovenia   358
13.3   Enrolment in initial secondary education by type of programme
        (%), 1994/95-2004/05   360
13.4   Enrolment in tertiary education by field of study (%)   362
13.5   GDP growth, 1991-2006   363
13.6   Labour force participation rate (age group 15-64), 1990-2006   365
13.7   Unemployment rates, 1990-2006   367

List of abbreviations

ALMP   Active labour market policy
CEE   Central and Eastern European
GDP   Gross domestic product
ECTS   European Credit Transfer System
EPL   Employment protection legislation
ETF   European Training Foundation
EU   European Union
Eurostat Statistical office of the European Union
GMI   Guaranteed minimum income
GVA   Gross value added
ILO   International Labour Organization
IMF   International Monetary Fund
ISCED   International Standard Classification of Education
LFS   Labour Force Survey
MLS   Minimum living standard
NUTS   Nomenclature of Territorial Units for Statistics
OECD   Organisation for Economic Co-operation and Development
OMC   Open method of coordination
PISA   Programme for International Student Assessment
PPP   Purchasing power parity
PPS   Purchasing power standards
SME   Small and medium-sized enterprise
TIMMS   Trends in International Mathematics and Science Study
UNICEF   United Nations International Children's Emergency Fund
VET   Vocational education and training

BG   Bulgaria
CZ   Czech Republic
DE   Germany
EE   Estonia
ES   Spain
GDR   German Democratic Republic
GR   Greece
HU   Hungary
IT   Italy
LV   Latvia
LT   Lithuania
PL   Poland

PT	Portugal
RO	Romania
SE	Sweden
SFRY	Socialist Federal Republic of Yugoslavia
SI	Slovenia
SK	Slovakia
UK	United Kingdom
USSR	Union of Soviet Socialist Republics
EEK	Estonian kroon
HUF	Hungarian forint
LTL	Lithuanian litas
LVL	Latvian lats
PLN	Polish złoty
SKK	Slovak koruna
n.a.	not applicable
–	missing

Notes on contributors

Anna Baranowska is Research Associate in the Labour Market Division of the Department of Economic Analysis and Forecasts at the Ministry of Labour and Social Policy in Poland and a PhD student at the Warsaw School of Economics. Her research interests cover labour markets and demography.

Rastislav Bednárik is Senior Researcher in the Institute of Labour and Family Research, Bratislava (Slovak Republic) and Assistant Professor at universities in Trnava and Nitra. He is interested in problems of social protection, labour market and sociological research methodology.

Erzsébet Bukodi is Research Officer at the Centre for Longitudinal Studies, Institute of Education, University of London, UK. Her research interests include educational inequalities, trends in intergenerational mobility, different aspects of life-course analysis and the relationship between social and cultural stratification.

Michael Gebel is Researcher at the Mannheim Centre for European Social Research (MZES), University of Mannheim, Germany. His main research interests are labour economics, educational inequality and the dynamics of school-to-work transition.

Angela Ivančič is Senior Researcher at the Slovenian Institute for Adult Education in Ljubljana, Slovenia. Her research work is mainly focused on areas such as patterns of participation of adults in lifelong learning, lifelong learning and the labour market, workplace literacy, labour market careers and social exclusion.

Ján Košta is Senior Researcher at the Institute of Economic Research, Slovak Academy of Sciences, Bratislava (Slovakia). His main research interests are in the area of education, labour markets and social policy.

Irena Kogan is Professor of Sociology at the University of Bamberg and external fellow at the Mannheim Centre for European Social Research (MZES), Germany. Her main research interests include school-to-work transitions, social stratification, immigration and inequality in comparative perspective.

Dobrinka Kostova is Head of the Department of Labour and Social Policy at the Institute of Sociology at the Bulgarian Academy of Sciences. Her main interests are in the field of Eastern European transformation, employment risks and management of intercultural relations.

Kristina Lindemann is affiliated with the Institute of International and Social Studies and the Department of Social Stratification of Tallinn University, Estonia. Her research interests are education, labour markets, youth, transition from school to work and ethnical stratification.

Cristina Mocanu is Researcher at the National Scientific Research Institute for Labour and Social Protection, Bucharest, Romania. Her main research interests include education, labour markets and social protection.

Walter Müller is Professor-Emeritus at the University of Mannheim, Germany. He has published extensively in the areas of social stratification and labour market development, in particular on social inequality in educational participation and attainment, the role of education for job allocation and social mobility, the development of self-employment in advanced economies and on class cleavages in political party preferences.

Clemens Noelke is Researcher at the Mannheim Centre for European Social Research (MZES), University of Mannheim, Germany. His scientific interests include comparative labour market research, specifically labour market entry dynamics and the labour market consequences of structural change.

Péter Róbert is Associate Professor at the Department of Sociology, Faculty of Social Sciences, ELTE University, Budapest, Hungary. He is also Senior Researcher at the TÃRKI Social Research Institute. His research interests include social stratification and mobility with a special focus on educational inequalities and life-course analysis. He also researches lifestyle differentiation and attitudes toward social inequalities.

Ellu Saar is Professor of Social Sciences at the Tallinn University and Senior Researcher at the Institute of International and Social Studies, Estonia. She has published extensively in the areas of social stratification, job mobility and transitions in youth.

Jana Straková is Senior Researcher at the Department of Sociology of Education and Stratification at the Institute of Sociology of the Czech Academy of Sciences. Among her main research interests are educational inequalities. She is a member of the Institute for Social and Economical

Analyses where she is engaged in educational research leading to recommendations for educational policy.

Meilute Taljunaite is Head of the Department of Sociology of Business and Education at the Institute for Social Research and a Professor at the Vilnius Pedagogical University, Lithuania. She deals with EU citizenship and European social integration, gender policy and migration.

Ilze Trapenciere is professor at the Institute of Philosophy and Sociology, in Riga, Latvia. Her main research interests are society, population, policy, and labour market.

Acknowledgements

This book, a comparative analysis of education systems, labour markets and welfare regimes in ten Central and Eastern European countries, stems from a project running at the Mannheim Centre for European Social Research (MZES), Germany. It has been generously supported by a grant from the Volkswagen Foundation for the period from 2006-2009, which we gratefully acknowledge.

This volume became possible only through the collaborative effort of many people. First and foremost, we are grateful for the contributions of the various authors included in this collection, contributing their local expertise. We would also like to thank Franz Kraus from the Research Archive Eurodata at the MZES for help in obtaining empirical data for Table 3.5. Special thanks are reserved to Stefanie Heyne, Julie Gast, Romina Müller, Elena Boldin and Milena Zaimova for their excellent research and editorial assistance. Also, thanks to Ben Davidson, Thomas Walker and Joseph Wilde-Ramsing for polishing the English of this book; Laura Greaves and the editorial team of the Policy Press for their patient work, assistance and cooperativeness. While working on this book MZES provided a stimulating environment – warm thanks to everybody who contributed to the discussions on this book.

Mannheim Centre for European Social Research (MZES)   *Irena Kogan*
University of Mannheim   *Michael Gebel*
May 20, 2008   *Clemens Noelke*

Introduction

Walter Müller

In May 2004, the European Union (EU) experienced the largest expansion in its history when it accepted 10 new member states, among them eight Central and Eastern European (CEE) countries. Two other CEE countries, Bulgaria and Romania, joined the enlarged EU in January 2007. The enlargement put an end to the painful division of the European continent and enhanced prospects of sharing Europe's rich cultural heritage in peace. At the same time, enlargement has increased the cultural heterogeneity, social disparities and economic imbalances within the EU, exemplified, for instance, by the below-average living standards and above-average unemployment rates in some of the new member states.

In modern societies, education systems, labour markets and the welfare state constitute core factors of the international competitive position of a society and of the living conditions of the population. These institutions also constitute the backbone of social stratification within a society. Accession to the EU thus raises a question about the implications of the new social order for social stratification and the living conditions in Eastern Europe. To answer this and related questions, it is necessary to come to a deeper understanding of the nature of the stratification processes, which are known to be shaped by countries' institutional structures, primary among which are the education system, the labour market and the welfare state (Kerckhoff, 1996; Müller and Shavit, 1998; DiPrete, 2002).

While much progress has been made with respect to the comparative analysis of education systems and labour markets in Western industrialised countries, systematic descriptions and analyses of these institutions and related systems of welfare support in CEE countries are still lacking. Hence, the main goal of this handbook is to describe the education systems, labour markets and welfare states in the CEE countries and to provide a set of theory-driven, comprehensive and comparable indicators illustrating these institutions. In a nutshell, the handbook is intended to provide policy makers with the tools to assess the structural and institutional changes in CEE countries and scholars with a possibility to apply the proposed indicators to their analytic research.

Education, labour markets and welfare states in CEE countries: comparative focus

With the transition to capitalism, education qualifications have become the key resource determining individual labour market outcomes in CEE countries. Individual education attainment is constrained by the choices that the education system allows, i.e., by the institutional structure of education and training systems in terms of education curricula, streams, tracks and pathways, as well as the rules governing access to particular types of training. Differences in individuals' choice of education degree and the role of the education system in this choice are well understood in Western countries (see, for example, Erikson and Jonsson, 1996; Breen and Goldthorpe, 1997; Breen and Jonsson, 2000). Furthermore, education degrees are the central determinants of labour market entry and subsequent labour market careers. Hence, a central concern of this book is to describe systematic differences in the education systems of CEE countries, focusing on those dimensions that past research has identified to be central for subsequent labour market outcomes (Müller and Shavit, 1998; Müller and Gangl, 2003). Chapter One by Irena Kogan discusses the vertical dimension of the education system, i.e., the different levels of education attainment distinguished within the education system, as well as the central dimensions of differentiation within levels, drawing on a set of theoretically derived, comparable indicators. The stratification of the education system at the secondary level is described in terms of the extent to which the school population is sorted early in the school career into tracks of different curricula and different scholastic demands with different opportunities and barriers for progression up the education ladder. Furthermore, the differentiation between general and vocational tracks, the organisation of vocational training as well as the degree of standardisation and quality differentiation at the secondary level is discussed. At the tertiary level, the focus is on the field-of-study differentiation, institutional segmentation, standardisation and quality differentiation of university education, as well as its openness for various strata of a country's population.

Individual labour market outcomes are affected by the country-specific economic and labour market situations, as well as the institutional setting of the labour market. It is therefore important to know whether cross-country differences exist with regard to economic context, labour market dynamics and institutional settings in the CEE countries. Chapter Two by Michael Gebel begins with a short overview of the economic context of transformation, identifying important contextual factors such as the diversity of existing initial conditions and institutional economic reforms. An examination of trends and cross-country differences in labour market dynamics of the 10 CEE countries follows. The focus lies on sectoral employment reallocation, changes in labour force participation rates and unemployment dynamics, with a specific focus on youth. Additionally, aspects such as the role of employment in the informal sector and the incidence of flexible employment forms like labour contracts with limited duration and part-time work are examined. Then, the nature of labour market institutions CEE countries adopted after the transition is discussed. Earlier research has singled out the dimensions of labour market regulations and industrial relations. Indicators like union density and the degree of centralisation/coordination are also illuminated. In terms of the above-mentioned dimensions, the chapter provides comparable quantitative indicators for 10 CEE countries and, where possible, across time.

Under socialism, workers enjoyed economic security through de facto guaranteed lifetime employment and access to a variety of benefits and social services through the workplace. With the transition to capitalism, job security effectively ended, and workers were exposed to new social risks, especially unemployment and loss of labour market income. Although the initial transition crisis had been overcome by the time of EU accession, unemployment, poverty and other forms of exclusion have become permanent threats to individual welfare and social cohesion in CEE countries. Chapter Three by Clemens Noelke seeks to trace the impact of the transition on individual welfare by drawing on a variety of institutional and structural indicators comparable across countries and time. It focuses particularly on the emerging labour market risks, unemployment and poverty, how these are distributed across the population, and what policy measures have been taken to protect individuals from these risks. The chapter begins by outlining the system of social protection under socialism in light of the reform challenges that the transition to capitalism posed to social policy makers. This is followed by an overview of levels and trends of material welfare in CEE countries since the transition, as well as a description of how income, unemployment and poverty risks are distributed over the population. Furthermore, the development of welfare states in CEE countries in response to these new risks is discussed. Here, the focus is on the development and consequences of active and passive labour market policies in CEE countries, as these have become the central means to help individuals cope with unemployment.

Detailed descriptions of the selected countries' institutional structures

Comparative chapters describing the education systems, labour markets and welfare production regimes of the 10 CEE countries are followed by country chapters in which experts from the respective countries describe the main contours of their countries' education and training systems, including linkages to the labour market, labour market structure and regulations and the provision of both formal and informal welfare support. An important component of each country chapter is the illumination of the historical background and the specific national conditions for the institutional choices in the transformation years in order to improve our understanding of why, despite pressures towards uniformity during the socialist period, the countries developed diverse institutional options in the post-socialist reforms. To this end, each country chapter starts with a short description of the historical background and the specific national conditions for the institutional choices in the transformation years.

The second part of each country chapter is devoted to the country's education system. A short historical overview of the education system after the Second World War is followed by a more detailed description of the education provisions in the 1990s and the new millennium. Analyses of the education systems at the secondary and tertiary levels along the dimensions outlined in the corresponding comparative chapter are presented. These are accompanied by a series of indicators for education systems including, where possible, a temporal dimension.

The third part of each country chapter considers the development of key labour market indicators and institutions over time. Trends in key labour market indicators like employment and unemployment rates for specific subgroups are discussed from a country-specific perspective to gain detailed insight into the transition process. Furthermore, the authors consider aspects of regional variation and minority ethnic groups if it is an important issue in the country. Then, the evolution of labour market institutions is described from a qualitative perspective and combined with additional quantitative indicators. The description of labour market institutions includes country-specific aspects of labour market regulation and industrial relations.

The fourth and final part of the country chapters includes a description of welfare regimes (Kaufmann, 1999) with a focus on protection mechanisms against labour market risks faced by youth and young adults. First, the relative importance and types of active as well as passive labour market policies are described from a historical perspective, with a brief description of existing social assistance schemes. Second, the distribution of child-rearing tasks between states and families are depicted. Third, the relative importance of intergenerational transfers in cushioning youth labour market entry difficulties is assessed.

References

Breen, R. and Goldthorpe, J. (1997) 'Explaining educational differentials: towards a formal rational action theory', *Rationality and Society*, vol 9, pp 275-305.

Breen, R. and Jonsson, J. (2000) 'Analysing educational careers: A multinominal transition model', *American Sociological Review*, vol 65, pp 754-72.

DiPrete, T.A. (2002) 'Life course risks, mobility regimes, and mobility consequences: a comparison of Sweden, Germany and the United States', *American Journal of Sociology*, vol 108, pp 267-309.

Erikson, R. and Jonsson, J. (1996) 'Explaining class inequality in education: the Swedish test case', in R. Erikson and J. Jonsson (eds) *Can education be equalized? The Swedish case in comparative perspective*, Boulder, CO: Westview Press, pp 1-63.

Kaufmann, F.-X. (2000) 'Towards a theory of the welfare state', *European Review – An Interdisciplinary Journal of the Academia Europea. Special Issue: The Future of the Welfare State,* vol 8, pp 291-312.

Kerckhoff, A.C. (1996) 'Building conceptual and empirical bridges between studies of educational and labour force careers', in A.C. Kerckhoff (ed) *Generating social stratification: toward a new research agenda*, Boulder, CO: Westview Press, pp 37-56.

Müller, W. and Gangl, M. (2003) 'The transition from school to work: a European perspective', in W. Müller and M. Gangl (eds) *Transition from education to work in Europe: the integration of youth into EU labour markets*, Oxford: Oxford University Press, pp 1-22.

Müller, W. and Shavit, Y. (1998) 'The institutional embeddedness of the stratification process: a comparative study of qualifications und occupations in thirteen countries', in Y. Shavit and W. Müller (eds) *From school to work: a comparative study of educational qualifications und occupational destinations*, Oxford: Clarendon Press, pp 1-48.

ONE

Education systems of Central and Eastern European countries

Irena Kogan

Education is a crucial determinant of individual life chances and the main predictor of young people's labour market outcomes. The individual endowment of education resources is certainly shaped by the institutional structure of education and training systems. The aim of this chapter is to discuss the main contours of the education systems in Central and Eastern European (CEE) countries and to shed light on the options offered within countries' education systems that might have an impact on labour market entry chances.

An education system has many dimensions and can be characterised by a great number of different indicators. This chapter deliberately focuses on those that are relevant to the job allocation process. It starts with the description of the vertical dimension of the education system and examines the distribution of various age cohorts among different levels of education attainment. Then, the structure of the basic level of education in CEE countries is discussed. At the secondary level of education stratification and track differentiation are the main focus. The present arrangements at the upper-secondary level are considered and compared with those existing before the transition period. Meaningful indicators on enrolment in general, and for technical and vocational tracks are presented. This is followed by an explanation of the organisation of vocational training. At the tertiary level the focus is on the field-of-study differentiation, standardisation, quality differentiation and openness of higher education. The chapter provides comparable indicators for all of the above-mentioned dimensions for the 10 CEE countries and, where possible, complements it with the temporary variation (e.g. the development of institutions over time).

Cohort succession and education attainment

The dramatic growth in education participation and changes in the education and training systems may be studied through the comparison of various birth cohorts. So we start with an analysis of education expansion in CEE countries by looking at the education attainment of successive age cohorts in 2002.

Figure 1.1 shows the proportions of cohort members with only lower-secondary education or less, which corresponds to the International Standard Classification of Education (ISCED) 0-2 (for more on ISCED and its problems for comparative research see Schneider and Kogan, 2008). Figure 1.2 presents the proportion with upper-secondary and post-secondary non-tertiary education (ISCED 3-4). Finally in Figure 1.3 one can find the proportion of individuals with tertiary education (ISCED 5-6) by age cohort. In each figure four age cohorts are shown. The oldest cohort was born just before, during or just after the Second World War and was in compulsory education during the economically difficult early post-war years. The second cohort was in compulsory education at the end of the 1950s and in the 1960s. The second youngest cohort entered schooling from the late 1970s until the perestroika period. The youngest cohort was in the education system roughly during the period when political reforms and the transition to the market economy started.

Figure 1.1: Percentage with lower-secondary education or less (ISCED 0-2) by cohort, 2002

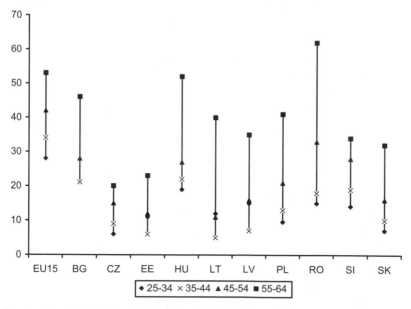

Source: Eurostat (2003)

For all countries, we find a dramatic decline in the proportions of the lower-educated (see Figure 1.1). In the Czech Republic, Estonia and to some degree also in Slovakia, the proportion of individuals with basic education is quite low already for the cohort of children born just before, during or just after the Second World War. Romania, Hungary and Bulgaria, on the other hand, boast markedly high shares of the least educated in this cohort. The education policies of the communist regimes strongly fostered education beyond the elementary level. The effect of these policies is particularly evident in the first post-war cohort, for which the figures indicate a very substantial decline in the proportion of the lower-educated. This decline is particularly pronounced in Lithuania, Hungary and Romania. In the Czech Republic and Slovenia it is, on the other hand, less evident. Education expansion also affected the last socialist cohort, above all in the Baltic countries, but is less manifest for the first transition cohort. Furthermore, in the Baltic countries a larger proportion of the youngest cohort are found among the lower-educated than was the case among the last socialist cohort. In Bulgaria these proportions are roughly equal.

Figure 1.2: Percentage with upper-secondary or post-secondary non-tertiary education (ISCED 3-4) by cohort, 2002

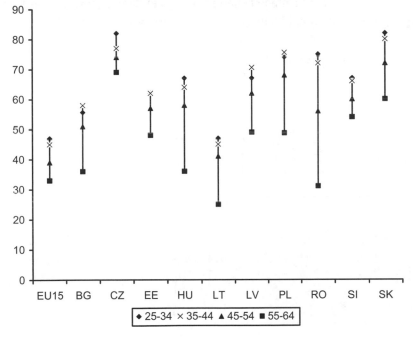

Source: Eurostat (2003)

The particularly low share of the lower-educated in the Czech Republic is achieved due to the extremely high rates of upper-secondary education attainment. This is evident from Figure 1.2, which depicts the proportion of individuals with upper-secondary and post-secondary non-tertiary education by cohort. In Slovakia and Slovenia more than 50% of the population possessed upper-secondary education in the Second World War cohort.

Education expansion at the upper-secondary level was very impressive, particularly in Hungary, Romania, Poland, Bulgaria and Lithuania, where the proportion of individuals with full secondary education in the first post-Second World War cohort increased by about 15% compared to the earlier cohort. As in the earlier analyses, here we also see that the proportion of individuals with upper-secondary education for the transformation cohort is not higher than for the last socialist cohort in Estonia. It is even lower in Latvia, Bulgaria and Poland.

Overall in CEE countries, the communist regimes often pushed for polytechnic qualifications at the upper-secondary level, but did not invest in university or other types of tertiary education. That is why, except for Lithuania and perhaps Poland, Slovenia, Latvia and Bulgaria we hardly see any substantial growth in the proportion of tertiary educated. Surprisingly there was very little expansion at the tertiary level during the early transition period. Moreover, in some countries, such as Estonia, Latvia and Lithuania, the proportion of those educated at the tertiary level is even lower or at least equal among the most recent cohort as compared to their predecessors.

Figure 1.3: Percentage with tertiary education (ISCED 5-6) by cohort, 2002

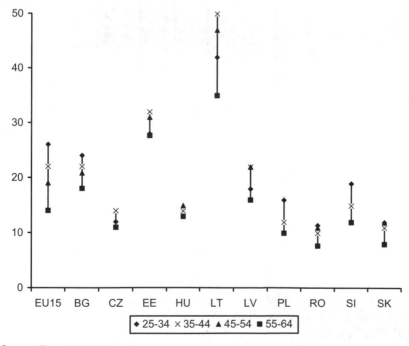

Source: Eurostat (2003)

The lack of obvious education expansion, once we look at the proportion of individuals who have attained tertiary education qualifications, may have various reasons. The youngest cohort, who reached the age to enter tertiary education immediately after the start of the reforms, was either not prepared for academic studies, did not have the means for such education in the turbulent transformation years, or the tertiary education system was not yet able to offer more places for students in these years. It might well be that the increase in tertiary education participation, which is discussed further below, has not yet resulted in higher levels of tertiary education attainment, which is depicted in Figure 1.3, as the truly post-transformation cohort is not found there.

After establishing these general patterns of education attainment in the cohort analyses, let us continue with a description of the education landscape in CEE countries after 1990. In particular, this chapter will now focus on the three major levels of education systems already shown in the figures above: primary and lower-secondary education (or the basic level of education), (upper)-secondary and post-secondary non-tertiary education and tertiary education.

Basic level of education

During the communist period, most of the CEE countries followed the Soviet model of a single and uniform school covering the whole period of compulsory education, comprising primary and lower-secondary education (Cerych, 1997). Unlike the Scandinavian model, although quite similar in structure, basic schools of Soviet origin were very uniform and quite rigid, as a result of extreme centralisation and ideological control (Kotásek, 1996). After 1990, the basic level of education covering the whole compulsory period was largely maintained. Nowadays there is no clear boundary between primary and lower-secondary education in the majority of CEE counties, as there is only one school type with quite a heterogeneous pupil population in terms of their ability and motivation, continuing more or less until the end of compulsory schooling. In some countries (e.g. Poland) a distinction between primary and lower-secondary schools seems to be somewhat more pronounced, since after primary education pupils are transferred into a different school of lower-secondary education. This has, however, no separate tracks and teaches all students practically the same curriculum. In some countries (e.g. Romania) there exist parallel systems of schools offering compulsory education in a single institution and others where basic and lower-secondary education is provided in different schools. In another group of countries, including the Czech and Slovak Republics and Hungary, the transition from primary and secondary education is also the point at which some pupils can select a qualitatively different type of secondary school, the gymnasium, which clearly diverges in its curriculum and ability requirements. Institutional disintegration at the lower-secondary level is a markedly new phenomenon in the above-mentioned countries, as well as Russia, Belarus and Croatia. In these countries, following competitive examinations, pupils could enter new multi-year secondary schools (a gymnasium or lyceum) with a strong academic orientation. This trend towards elite-type education represents a revival of pre-communist patterns, similar to the model of German-speaking countries (Kotásek, 1996; Cerych, 1997). But even in the countries that inherited the Austrian-Hungarian education tradition, only a minority of pupils (as many as 10% in the Czech Republic and Hungary) are selected to follow a separate track early, whereas the majority continue in a uniform-type school.

Figure 1.4: Percentage of people aged 18-24 not in education with only lower-secondary education in 2002

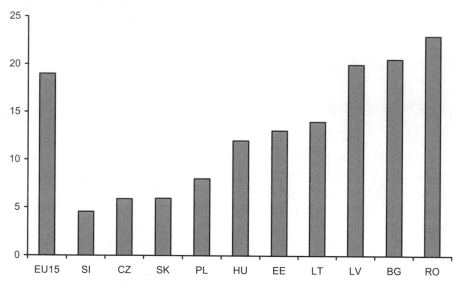

Source: Eurostat (2003)

Normally pupils proceed to (upper)-secondary education after basic schooling. Some pupils leave schooling at this level. These early school leavers are individuals who are bound to experience particular difficulties when trying to enter into employment, since they often lack the basic skills, be they general or vocational, to find skilled employment. Interestingly enough, the proportion of early school leavers in the majority of CEE countries is lower than the EU15 average (see Figure 1.4). Only in Bulgaria and Romania do more than 20% of young people leave education at the lower-secondary level. Slovenia, the Czech Republic, Slovakia and Poland, on the other hand, rank among the countries with the lowest incidence of low qualification, with less than 6.5% of school leavers possessing only lower-secondary education.

Secondary level of education

The secondary stage of education serves several aims. On the one hand, it selects and prepares students for higher education. On the other hand, it has to prepare some students for the jobs in the labour market that usually do not require higher education. All CEE countries offer these two options in their institutional arrangements, but with different levels of involvement of young people and different degrees of success.

Earlier research has singled out the following dimensions in the set-up of education systems at the secondary level as being relevant to further education attainment and the outcomes of the education–job allocation process: (1) the stratification of education systems or the extent to which the pupils are sorted early on in their school careers into tracks of different curricula, with different scholastic demands, and with different opportunities and barriers for progression up to the high end of the education ladder (Allmendinger, 1989); (2) the relative advantages of systems organised to provide largely general education versus those equipping school leavers with vocational skills (Allmendinger, 1989; Kerckhoff, 1996, 2000; Shavit and Müller 1998, 2000a); (3) the form of organisation of vocational training, either based in schools or as a combination of training and working (Allmendinger, 1989; Shavit and Müller, 1998, 2000a; Kerckhoff, 2000; Ryan 2001); and (4) the degree of standardisation of education provisions, i.e., the degree to which the quality of education meets the same standards nation-wide (Allmendinger, 1989).[1]

Stratification and school track differentiation

At the secondary level all education systems split up the student population in segments that follow different tracks or courses of study. This is necessary because students have both different abilities and career preferences. Research shows that the earlier students are assigned to different tracks, the more likely they will end up with different kinds and levels of knowledge, competences and qualifications (Baumert et al, 2007). One advantage of such segmentation is that teaching and learning in groups of homogeneous ability and school performance is more effective. On the other hand, these apparent advantages can be counterbalanced by the negative consequences of stigmatisation that students in low-achievement tracks endure. This is particularly true, since pupils from lower-class and minority families are overrepresented in low-achievement tracks, which contributes overall to the persistence of educational inequality (Erikson and Jonsson, 1996).

As described above, the first serious education decision, the selection of a gymnasium, is taken in Hungary, the Czech Republic and Slovakia at the ages of 10-11 (see Table 1.1). Two years later, pupils are also faced with a similar decision to transfer to a shorter-duration gymnasium. Early selection is to some degree associated with a larger number of options or programmes at the secondary level, which is evident from the last column of Table 1.1. Interestingly enough, early tracking and an increase in the options available at the secondary level was reintroduced in these countries in the framework of the post-socialist reforms, and makes these countries similar to the other countries of Central Europe (Germany, Switzerland, Lichtenstein and Austria).

Table 1.1: Age of selection in secondary schools and the number of programmes at the secondary level

	Gymnasium	General vs. vocational	Earliest age of selection	Number of programmes
Bulgaria		14	14	3
Czech Republic	11,13	15	11	5
Estonia		15	15	3
Hungary	10,12	14	10	4
Latvia		14-16	14	3-5
Lithuania		14	14	3
Poland		15	15	3
Romania		14-15	14	3
Slovakia	10,12	15	10	5
Slovenia		15	15	5

Source: This information is based on country-specific chapters

Unlike in their German-speaking neighbours, pupils in the Czech Republic, Hungary and Slovakia who do not select or are not selected by gymnasia can continue in a single-structure school, which formally offers similar prospects for tertiary education as gymnasia. In reality, however, graduates of selective gymnasia have higher transition rates to tertiary education and are, on average, better equipped with the skills and knowledge to succeed there, as the two types of schools clearly differ in the quality of education (see country-specific chapters for details). Kotásek (1996) mentions, for example, that in the Czech Republic the basic school ceases to be comprehensive and instead gradually turns into something similar to the German *Hauptschule*, with all the consequences that this involves for pupils, curricula and the social and pedagogical climate.

A further education decision with serious implications for education careers is taken in CEE countries at the ages of 14-16. At this point, pupils and their families decide whether to proceed in the general academic or technological tracks, or to switch to vocational education. The latter option is considered to be a second choice and is associated with students of a lower level of academic achievement with more limited labour market prospects (Arum und Shavit, 1995; Shavit and Müller, 2000b).

General versus vocational education

During the socialist era, the school structure and curricula at the upper-secondary level were divided between general and various vocational tracks (Titma and Saar, 1995; Saar, 1997). The curricula of vocational programmes were narrowly defined, focusing closely on the specific occupations for which young people were trained. Vocational education was provided in accordance with scrupulously calculated manpower planning and, in a way, emulated the pattern of overspecialisation found in the economy as a whole (Roberts, 1998; Strietska-Ilina, 2001; Matějů and Simonová, 2003). Students' choices for education and training programmes were restricted to well-specified training places, provided by state enterprises. Except for the former Yugoslavia, the transition from school to work was smooth, as young people were often assigned to their first workplace, which was supported by employers and secured for all school leavers, virtually irrespective of their level of education.

All CEE countries now provide a mix of tracks in their education systems, with more general and more vocational orientation (see Table 1.2 for an overview). In fact, practically all CEE countries have maintained a tripartite system of upper-secondary education, which existed both during the communist and earlier periods: general secondary schools, technical secondary schools and vocational schools, including apprenticeship programmes (Kotásek, 1996; Koucký, 1996; Cerych, 1997)[2].

The general tracks have, as a rule, been academically more demanding and have as their main goal the preparation of students for subsequent entry into higher tertiary education. In Central European countries general tracks preserved their traditional name of *gymnasium* or *lyceum*. In the Baltic countries and Bulgaria these schools were set up as a part of the 'full secondary schools' and offered only a two-year superstructure on top of compulsory schooling (Kotásek, 1996).

Table 1.2: Upper-secondary schools in CEE countries

	Secondary general			Secondary technical			Secondary vocational		
	1	2	3	1	2	3	1	2	3
PL	General lyceum	4	M	Secondary technical	4/5	T + M	Basic vocational	2/3	SW
							+ follow-up course	3	M
	Technical lyceum	4	M	Post-secondary technical	M+2/3	HT	Vocational lyceum	4	SW + M
HU	Gymnasium	4/5	M	Sec. tech. type A	5	M + T	Vocational	3	SW
		(8/6)	M					1/2	-SW
				Sec. tech. type B	4	SW + T			
				Sec. tech. type C	4	M + T			
CZ	Gymnasium	4/5	M	Secondary technical	4/5	T + M	Sec. vocational	2/3	SW
		(8/7/6)	M		2/3	-T	+ follow-up course	2	M
	Technical/ Commercial lyceum	4	M	Post-secondary technical	M+3/4	HT	Sec. vocational integrated	4	SW + M
								4/5	SW + M
									SW + T
SK	Gymnasium	4/5	M	Secondary technical	4/5	T + M	Vocational	1	-SW
		(8)	M		2/3	-T	Sec. vocational	2/3	SW
							+ follow-up course	2	M
							Sec. vocational	4	SW + M
							Vocational	1	-SW

Table 1.2: Upper-secondary schools in CEE countries (continued)

	Secondary general			Secondary technical			Secondary vocational		
	1	2	3	1	2	3	1	2	3
SI	Gymnasium	4	M	Secondary technical	4/5	T + M	Sec. vocational + follow-up course	2/3 2	M
RO	*Lycée*	4/5	M	Secondary technical	4	T + M	Sec. vocational foremen training	2/3 2	SW T
BG	Complete general sec. (grades 9-12)	4	M	Secondary technical	4	T + M	Sec. vocational	1/2/3	SW
LT	Complete general sec. (grades 10-12) Gymnasium	3 4	M M	Post-secondary colleges		HT	Sec. vocational	3	SW
LV	Complete general Sec. (grades 10-12)	3	M	Secondary technical	4	T + M	Sec. vocational	2/3	SW
EE	Gymnasium	3	M	Post-secondary colleges	4/5 2/3	HT	Sec. vocational	2/3 2	SW SW + M

Notes: Column 1 refers to type/name/stream of school, 2 to number of years, 3 to type of certificate. Certificates: M= school leaving examination (*Abitur*), T= technician examination (all fields of national economy, administration, services), -T= lower level of T, HT= higher technician examination, SW = skilled worker examination, -SW = lower level of SW. Abbreviations: sec. = secondary, tech. = technical.
Source: Kotásek (1996).

Higher-level vocational or technological tracks cater for more practically orientated students and offer a mix of general and vocational subjects. They prepare pupils for middle-level professions in various branches of industry, agriculture, commerce, public administration, culture, artistic production, health services and teaching, as well as for entry to tertiary education.

The fact that the final examination (*maturita*) gives pupils the right to attend any kind of institution at the tertiary level has helped to put these schools on an equal footing with general secondary schools (Kotásek, 1996).

The lower-level vocational tracks usually prepare students for entry into the labour market; they specialise in various occupational areas and are often intended for students who are more capable of doing things practically rather than studying them theoretically[3]. Training in vocational tracks has been delivered either in the form of apprenticeships or in schools either closely or loosely linked to appropriate enterprises (Kotásek, 1996). A more or less pronounced hierarchy evolves between the tracks, particularly since vocational tracks often include more students with weaker cognitive abilities and records of school performance (see the sections on quality differentiation at the secondary level in the country-specific chapters).

Figure 1.5: General upper-secondary education enrolments (gross ratios, percentage of population aged 15-18), 1989-2005

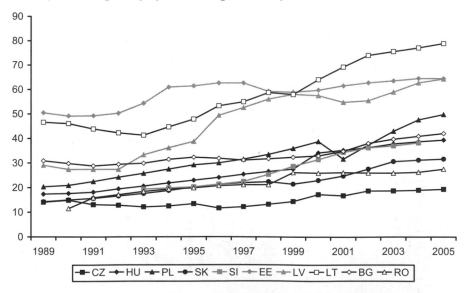

Notes: For the Czech Republic the data for 1989-95 refers to young people aged 14-17, and since 1996 to those aged 15-18; for Hungary and Slovakia for young people aged 14-17; for Poland the data since 2001 refers to young people aged 16-19; for Estonia the data for 1989-95 refers to adolescents aged 16-17, and since 2001 to those aged 16-18; for Latvia to young people aged 16-18; for Lithuania the data for 1989-98 refers to young people aged 16-18, and since 1999 to those aged 17-18.
Source: UNICEF (2007)

Despite the availability of vocational, technological and general tracks in the education systems of all CEE countries, some systems provide more places in tracks that have a general orientation, while other education systems are more vocationally orientated. From Figure 1.5 it is evident that Baltic countries, above all Estonia and Lithuania, have higher enrolments in general tracks and this has been so since 1990. In Latvia general track enrolments increased in the mid-1990s, but had much lower enrolment rates in this type of school in the early 1990s. The Czech Republic, Slovakia and Romania boast, on the other hand, lower enrolments in general education tracks. All in all, an increase in the enrolment of pupils in general tracks is apparent for all CEE countries, with Latvia, Lithuania, Hungary, Poland and Slovenia having more pronounced growth rates.

Figure 1.6: Vocational/technical secondary education enrolments (gross ratios, percentage of population aged 15-18), 1989-2005

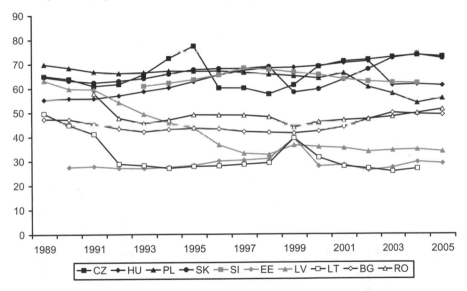

Notes: For the Czech Republic the data for 1989-95 refers to young people aged 14-17, and since 1996 to those aged 15-18; for Hungary and Slovakia for young people aged 14-17; for Poland the data since 2001 refers to young people aged 16-18; for Estonia the data for 1989-95 refers to adolescents aged 16-17, and since 2001 to those aged 16-18; for Latvia to young people aged 16-18; for Lithuania the data for 1989-98 refers to young people aged 16-18, and since 1999 to those aged 17-18.
Source: UNICEF (2007)

A contrary picture with regard to the ranking of countries is observed for secondary education enrolment in vocational/technical tracks (see Figure 1.6). The Baltic countries have the lowest rates of enrolment in these tracks, whereas the Czech Republic, Slovakia, Slovenia and Hungary have more pronounced vocational and technical education sectors. Romania and

Bulgaria lie in between. Some countries experienced a decrease in vocational school enrolment (Lithuania, Latvia, Poland and Romania), whereas in the Czech Republic, Slovakia and Hungary vocational enrolment increased. In Estonia we observe stability, more or less, in vocational and technical enrolment. In Bulgaria a U-shape form in the trend is apparent with vocational education enrolment decreasing until the mid-1990s and increasing further on. In Slovenia an inverted U-shape could be found.

As mentioned above, when it comes to vocational/technical tracks in CEE countries, a meaningful distinction lies in the options available to students on graduation. Technical and upper-level vocational tracks normally end up with a mixture of a matriculation examination and a technical qualification, which gives access to tertiary education (see also Table 1.2). Some technical schools offer post-secondary non-tertiary level education in which students end up with a higher-level technical qualification. Such schools can be found in Poland, the Czech Republic, Lithuania and Estonia. In the Czech and Slovak Republics one type of technical secondary school does not, however, offer unconditional access to tertiary education (via the matriculation examination). Lower-level vocational tracks (without any follow-up courses) normally give school leavers access solely to the labour market and are therefore considered to be educational dead-ends.

Figure 1.7: Secondary education options in the CEE countries in the mid-1990s

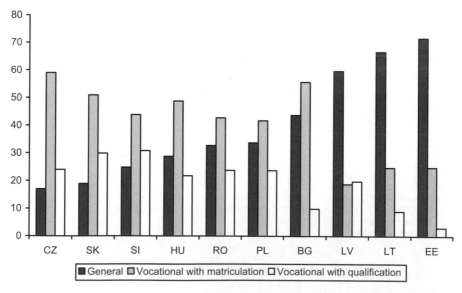

Source: ETF (1998); the information for Slovakia is taken from the country chapter and refers to 1995

Longer-duration vocational schools or vocational schools followed by additional courses, on the other hand, enable students to sit for a matriculation. Figure 1.7 shows that all CEE countries (apart from the Baltic states) have systems that predominantly favour vocational or technical education, but it also confirms that the majority of their pupils leave education with a matriculation certificate. In the Baltic countries the majority of vocational programmes also offer an option for entering tertiary education. Furthermore, analyses presented in the country-specific chapters show that the share of lower-secondary vocational education (without matriculation) has been decreasing in all the countries under discussion since the 1990s. These facts make the secondary education in CEE countries, despite its strong vocational orientation, more open and permeable than similarly organised secondary education systems in German-speaking countries. Even though certain vocational qualifications formally allow access to tertiary education in CEE countries, the participation and success rates of vocational track graduates are usually clearly lower than among graduates from general education tracks (see country-specific chapters).

Organisation of vocational education and training

Further crucial differences within vocational education relate to the form and context in which education and training is provided. Vocational education and training (VET) might be organised in schools and a classroom context. It might also be offered as a combination of learning in schools and practical work in workplaces. In the most explicit way, these two learning environments are combined in the dual-system model, in which a learner has a learning/employment contract as an apprentice with an employer, who commits him or herself to teach the practical side of an occupation or profession either through regular work placements or in special training shops within the firm. Arrangements such as this that work well in Germany, Austria, Switzerland and Denmark require substantial involvement from employers in the provision of training and the setting up of educational programmes.

In the beginning of the privatisation and restructuring processes in CEE countries, which had had their vocational systems organised in the dual system prior to the fall of socialism, employers largely withdrew from the provision of training opportunities as they were not able to maintain the training infrastructure or afford the financing of apprentices. This led to general disarray in the education and training system, and the dismantling of well-established links between schools and enterprises. Overall, elements of enterprise-based apprentice training are now found in the Czech Republic, Slovenia, Hungary and Romania, whereas in the rest of the countries vocational education is mostly carried out under the auspices of schools and workplace learning experiences are much less common (see Figure 1.3). In these countries training is clearly less occupation-specific, but relates rather to broader occupational areas. Some countries (e.g. Poland and Slovakia) operate school-based vocational education together with a much smaller-scale apprenticeship system.

Table 1.3: The predominant form of organisation of VET

	School-based	Dual system
Bulgaria	×	
Czech Republic		×
Estonia	×	
Hungary		×
Latvia	×	
Lithuania	×	
Poland	×	×
Romania		×
Slovakia	×	×
Slovenia	×	×

Source: The information is based on country-specific chapters

Tertiary level of education

Most CEE countries, as well as other European countries, have experienced a strong expansion in the tertiary education sector in recent years. Connected to this, the higher education systems have also become more differentiated through the introduction of new institutional forms (e.g. more practically oriented colleges) or the re-organisation of existing structures (e.g. the upgrading of institutions of higher education to universities). On the one hand, the institutional differentiation and the various reforms have substantially increased the variability of institutional arrangements in tertiary education in CEE countries and in Europe in general. The Bologna process, on the other hand, introduced substantial pressures towards the harmonisation of tertiary education within the European Union (EU). Relevant dimensions of the education system at the tertiary level discussed below are: the horizontal differentiation with regard to the fields of studies and the type of educational institutions (universities versus non-university sector); standardisation and the connected issue of the quality differentiation of tertiary education institutions; and finally, the openness of the education system or the degree of provision of financial support for young people which would allow them to study at the tertiary level.

Education expansion

During the transition period, tertiary education participation substantially increased in all CEE countries, which is evident from Figure 1.8. A surge in tertiary education enrolment is observable for Slovenia, Hungary, Latvia and Poland. Despite its growth, tertiary education enrolment still lags behind in Romania, Bulgaria and Slovakia. Tertiary education expansion occurred not least due to the emergence of private institutions of higher education and the expansion of short, practically oriented programmes at the tertiary level in 'fashionable' areas of specialisation (Cerych, 1997; Roberts, 1998; Micklewright, 1999; Matějů and Simonová, 2003).

Figure 1.8: Higher education enrolments (gross population ratios, percentage of population aged 19-24), 1989-2005

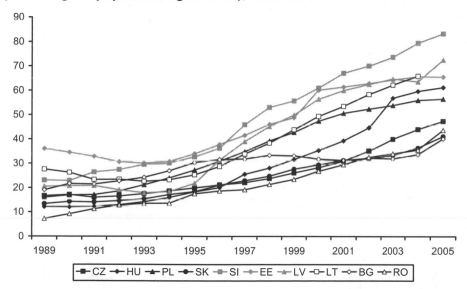

Notes: For the Czech Republic the data for 1989-95 refers to those aged 18-22; 1996-2005 to those aged 19-23; for Hungary data refers to those aged 18-23; for Slovakia - data refers to those aged 18-22, 1989-95 for full-time courses only; for Slovenia data refers to those aged 19-23; data includes all students enrolled at ISCED 5 (also enrolled on post-graduate master's programmes); for Estonia data refers to those aged 19-22; for Latvia and Lithuania data refers to those aged 19-23.
Source: UNICEF (2007)

Gender differences in the access to higher education in CEE countries were eliminated during the socialist period, with women's education attainment eventually surpassing that of men (Simkus and Andorka, 1982; Gerber and Hout, 1995; Saar, 1997; Ganzeboom and Nieuwbeerta, 1999; Micklewright, 1999; Helemäe and Saar, 2003; Matějů et al, 2003). According to Figure 1.9 the proportion of women among students of tertiary education was higher than the proportion of men in all CEE countries except for the Czech Republic and Romania in 1998. The increase in the share of female students is evident for all countries, apart from Bulgaria, where their numbers decreased from 61% in 1998 to 53% in 2004. The proportion of female students remained more or less unchanged in Lithuania (at 60%) and Poland (about 57%). In 2004 women were overrepresented among students in all CEE countries.

Figure 1.9: Proportion of women among students (ISCED 5-6) as percentage of the total students at this level, 1998-2004

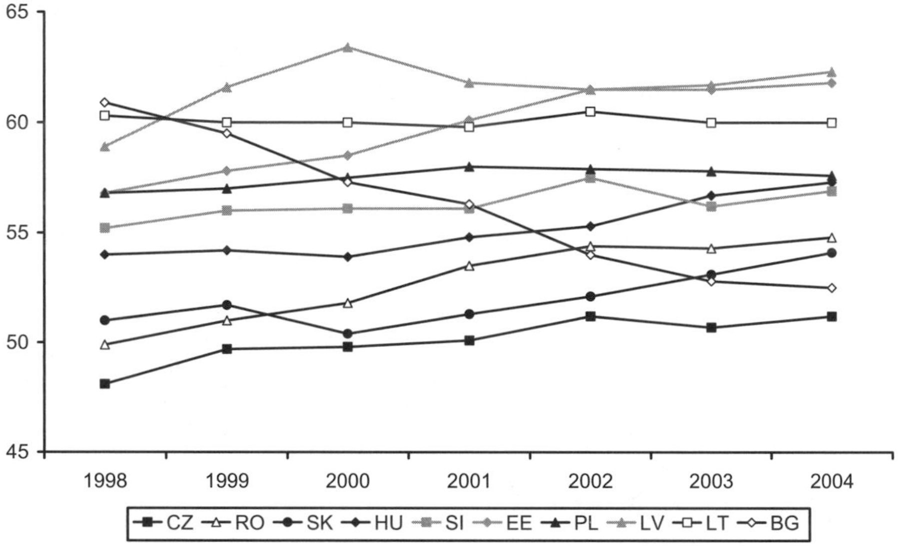

Source: Eurostat (2008a)

Horizontal dimension at the tertiary level: field-of-study differentiation

Higher education in CEE countries has managed to achieve remarkable success in natural sciences and technical education during the post-Second World War period (Cerych, 1997). It should be mentioned that technological (e.g. engineering) education was over-emphasised at the expense of educational opportunities in the humanities and social sciences (Matějů and Simonová, 2003). The proportion of students enrolled in technical fields has decreased since the fall of socialism. In Bulgaria, the decrease was almost 25% between 1970 and 2000. In Estonia it was 33% between 1994 and 2005. A similar drop is also evident in Latvia between 1980 and 2004. In Romania enrolment in technical fields decreased from 70% to 30% between 1990 and 1995, a dramatic fall in such a short period of time. In Hungary, where the proportion enrolled in engineering was not so high, the decrease was less pronounced (from 20% in 1990/91 to 14% in 2003/04).

Student numbers in the social sciences, above all business and law, on the other hand, substantially increased in all CEE countries. In Bulgaria, enrolment in economics increased by almost 10% between 1990 and 2004/05. In Hungary an increase of almost 15% was observed for the same period of time. In Poland the numbers increased by 15% between 1990 and 2001. Twenty per cent more students were counted in the fields of economics and education between 1989/90 and 2004/05 in Romania. And an even more dramatic surge of 45 percentage points in the number of those enrolled in the social sciences were found in Latvia between 1980 and 2004/05.

Figure 1.10 shows the extent of variation between countries in the horizontal dimension of tertiary education. Thirty per cent of students in the Czech Republic and slightly less in Slovakia, Bulgaria and Romania are enrolled in technical fields (engineering, manufacturing and construction, as well as science, mathematics and computing). Health and welfare are more popular in the Czech Republic and Slovakia, and less so in Poland and Latvia. Social sciences, business and law are more popular in Latvia, Romania, Poland, Slovenia and Hungary, but less so in the Czech and Slovak Republics.

Figure 1.10: Enrolment by fields of study (%), 2004

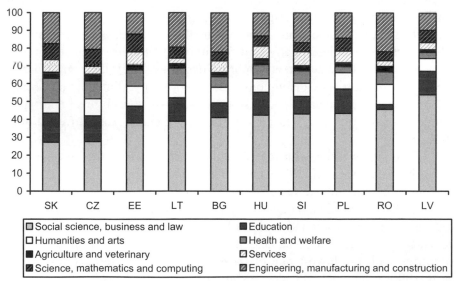

Source: Eurostat (2008a)

With the numerical advantage of females at the tertiary level of education, the issue of gender educational inequalities nowadays is concerned with gender-specific disparities in the choice of the field of study. In nearly all countries far fewer women than men are enrolled in the fields of engineering and architecture, mathematics and computer sciences, while across the board women outnumber men in subjects such as the humanities, social sciences, social work, nursing and the medical (semi-)professions. There exists variation across the countries with regard to the field of study feminisation. The highest proportion of women in typical female fields is found in the Baltic states. In Bulgaria and Romania we find, on the other hand, a relatively high proportion of women in traditionally male technical fields.

Institutional segmentation, standardisation and quality differentiation

Tertiary education in the majority of CEE countries is organised with traditional universities and a non-university sector working in parallel (for similar developments in the EU15, see Müller and Wolbers, 2003). Academically less demanding and less prestigious than conventional universities, non-university institutions of tertiary education (i.e., colleges and polytechnics) can be defined as a second tier of higher education. Still, they provide an opportunity to get an academic degree, and as such they probably attract less able members of privileged groups who are unable to meet the academic demands of the public universities (Shavit et al, 2007). This is particularly true of the professions like business and law, which – since they are rewarding economically and socially – are in great demand, and consequently the universities can be highly selective when recruiting students for them. One could argue then, that colleges and universities in CEE countries are substantially stratified in terms of their status and prestige, as well as the labour market opportunities they offer their graduates. A hierarchy of tertiary institutions, according to Allmendinger (1989), reproduces and perpetuates social stratification, since each level and type of academic institution tends to recruit disproportionally from different social strata.

CEE countries differ with regard to the prominence of the non-university sector in their system of tertiary education. From Figure 1.11 one can see that in countries with higher rates of tertiary education in the early transition period – Lithuania, Estonia and Slovenia – more students in fact attain their degrees in more vocationally oriented programmes. The majority of tertiary educated youth in Romania, and the Czech and Slovak Republics – the countries with the lowest rate of those enrolled at the tertiary level in the early 1990s – attained their degrees in more traditional institutions of higher education.

The expansion of tertiary education has occurred partially due to the introduction of private institutions of higher education. CEE countries differ in the extent to which tertiary education has become open for private providers (see Table 1.4). In the Czech and Slovak Republics almost all students are enrolled in public universities and even in the non-university tertiary sector public institutions largely dominate, particularly in Slovakia. In Romania and Poland more than a quarter of students are enrolled in private universities. In private non-university institutions this proportion is lower and in Romania it is almost negligible.

Figure 1.11: The proportion of tertiary educated people aged 25-29, by type of tertiary education, 2001

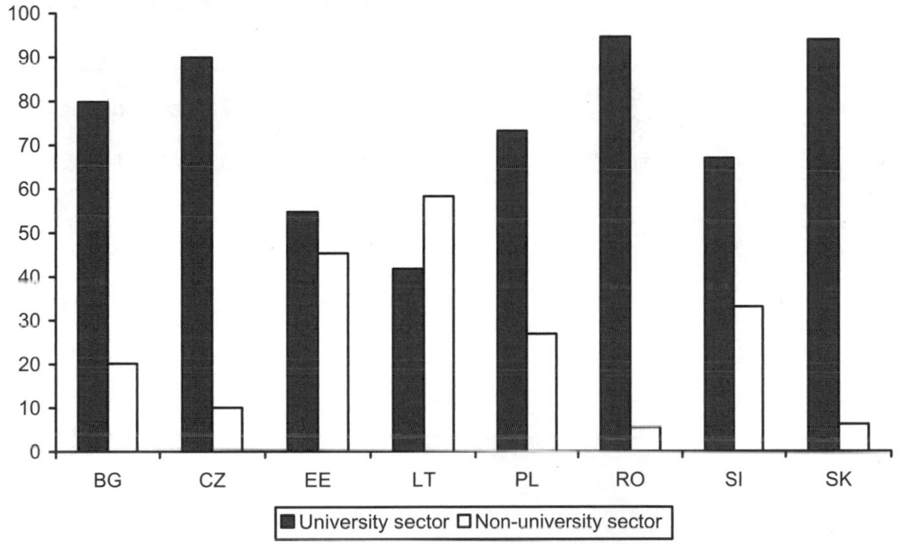

Source: Eurostat (2008b)

In Estonia 20% of students study in private institutions of tertiary education (the data here does not allow for a distinction between colleges and universities). For Bulgaria, Latvia, Lithuania and Slovenia we only have information on the proportion of private institutions of tertiary education and not the number of students enrolled in them. Hence the data is not comparable to the results discussed above. We can see, however, that in Bulgaria less than 10% of tertiary education institutions are private, whereas in Slovenia more than 75% are private. Latvia and Lithuania are in between. In Latvia more private institutions operate in the university sector and fewer in the non-university sector, whereas the opposite picture is evident for Lithuania.

All in all, the expansion of tertiary education, particularly when it comes to the second-tier institutions of higher education, introduced even further variation in the content and quality of training. In other words, it contributed to the decreasing standardisation and growing quality differentiation of various education providers. Recent reorganisation of the university sector according to the Bologna guidelines and the use of the compatible European Credit Transfer System (ECTS) since the early 2000s, on the other hand, contributed to an increase in the standardisation of tertiary education. At the same time, however, the quality differentiation, particularly between the university and college sectors, has persisted. This has led to the initiation of multiple committees responsible for the accreditation of educational providers in CEE countries (see country-specific chapters for details).

Table 1.4: The proportion of students enrolled in private institutions or proportion of private institutions at the tertiary level

	Tertiary university education		Tertiary non-university education		Tertiary education	
	Students	Institutions	Students	Institutions	Students	Institutions
BG						8.6
CZ	1.7		32.1			
EE					20.0	
HU	14.1		20.4			
LV		41.2		34.6		
LT		28.6		40.8		
PL	28.4		17.4			
RO	26.0		3.4			
SK	0.7		6.4			
SI						76.5

Notes: Private education includes either government-sponsored private or independent private. For Czech and Slovak Republics, Estonia, Hungary, Lithuania and Poland the information is for 2002; for Romania 2004 (refers to graduates); for Bulgaria and Lithuania 2004; for Latvia and Slovenia 2006.
Source: OECD (2004) for the Czech and Slovak Republics, Hungary and Poland; country reports for Estonia, Bulgaria, Latvia and Slovenia; Romanian National Institute for Statistics for Romania

Openness of tertiary education

During the socialist period tertiary education was free of charge and students were, as a rule, entitled to scholarships. With the introduction of market economies, this situation has changed. All CEE countries, except for the Czech Republic, Slovenia and Romania[4], have introduced fees at the tertiary level but the amount varies according to the type of university and the type of programme (see country chapters for details). As a rule students in private universities pay fees, while students in public ones pay no fees (e.g. Poland), or students in private universities pay higher fees than the students in the public ones. Among students in the public universities, a lower fee is paid by the more academically successful students (this is particularly pronounced in Bulgaria), and higher fees are paid by part-time students (e.g. Hungary), or students in extra-mural or full-time evening classes (e.g. Poland). The size of fee also varies according to the field of study.

Figure 1.12: Financial aid to students in the form of scholarships and loans, as a percentage of total public expenditure on tertiary education, 2002

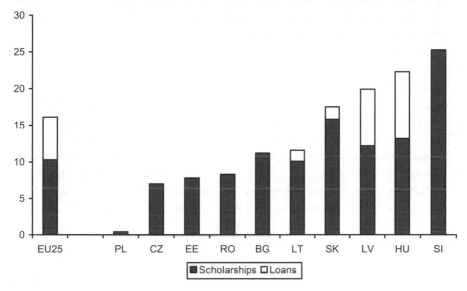

Source: Eurostat (2005)

A system of financial aid to students − in the form of scholarships or both loans and scholarships − operates in all CEE countries, but the amount of support allocated varies across the countries (see Figure 1.12). While Hungary, Latvia, Slovakia and Lithuania offer both scholarships and loans, in the rest of the countries only a system of scholarships is installed. The largest amount of resources (as a percentage of total public expenditure on tertiary education) for student financial aid is allocated in Slovenia, Slovakia, Hungary and Latvia, and this is higher than the average amount directed to student aid in the EU as the whole. In Poland the financial aid offered to students is an almost non-existent item in the budget allocated to tertiary education. In the Czech Republic, Estonia and Romania such expenditure is lower overall than in the EU25. One can expect that in CEE countries that provide a low level of financial aid, students will have to rely on financial support from their families to fund their studies or work in parallel to them. In the latter case, this might result in longer periods of study and possibly lower graduation rates.

Conclusion

Since the early 1990s, CEE countries have without doubt experienced numerous education changes, going hand-in-hand with radical political and economic transformations. In this period, new patterns of education, new types of schools and new institutional structures have emerged. Many of these developments have brought about a certain restoration of pre-communist educational forms; others have been adaptations and assimilations of mainly Western European trends (Cerych, 1997). This chapter has described the structure of the education systems in the CEE countries since the 1990s and explored the central dimensions that might be relevant for the job allocation process.

In summary, we first list the common elements of the post-transformation education systems in CEE countries. Foremost, after 1990 the curricula of general education in all CEE countries were revised, while the curricula of VET courses were broadened (Cedefop, 2001). The latter happened not least due to the increasing importance of the service sector and uncertainty about graduates' job opportunities, demanding flexibility in the skills acquired by leavers from vocational education. Furthermore, the structure of post-secondary education was diversified by the introduction of new post-secondary vocational programmes and the emergence of private institutions. Tertiary education participation has substantially increased, not least due to the emergence of private institutions of higher education and the expansion of short, practically oriented programmes at the tertiary level. The demand for higher education can be attributed, at least partially, to the larger proportion of young people opting for an extension of their studies in order to postpone their labour market entry and to escape youth unemployment, which became a reality in the post-transformation years (ILO, 1999; Róbert, 2002; Róbert and Bukodi, 2005).

Alongside these obvious common elements, post-transformation education institutions to some degree continued to mirror the idiosyncratic historical developments or, in other words, path dependencies of each nation's education system and the different models countries have adopted to prepare young people for adult life. Our analyses clearly showed that in CEE countries geographically and historically closer to Germany or Austria, vocationally oriented secondary education has maintained its dominance over more general curricula (Roberts, 1998). Thus, elements of enterprise-based apprentice training were preserved or re-introduced in the Czech Republic, Slovakia, Hungary and Slovenia, whereas in the Baltic states, Romania and Bulgaria, vocational education has increasingly become school-based.

Overall, the main orientations as well as outcomes of education reforms can be differentiated according to three groups of new EU member states (Cerych, 1997). The first group encompasses Hungary, the Czech and Slovak

Republics, Slovenia and probably also Poland. These countries were a part of the Austro-Hungarian Empire and were hence greatly influenced by the Austrian and, more generally, German education and training systems. These countries, except for Slovenia and Poland, reintroduced early selection in academically prestigious gymnasia, and preserved or reintroduced the dual system of vocational training (although less so in Poland and Slovakia). At the tertiary education level, the developments are more heterogeneous with the Czech and Slovak Republics boasting somewhat lower enrolment rates, whereas the numbers of students enrolling in Slovenia and Poland has soared.

The three Baltic states, Estonia, Latvia and Lithuania, form the second group of countries and have been influenced both by the German and Russian (or Soviet) education traditions. Since their independence in the early 1990s, these countries have established close contacts with Scandinavian countries, so that their education system could be said to combine both Nordic and Central European characteristics. This implies that comprehensive secondary education in these countries also includes elements of school-based vocational education. Higher transition rates to tertiary education are indicated by their towering tertiary education enrolment rates and the expansion of their non-university tertiary sectors.

Finally, Romania and Bulgaria constitute the third group of countries, and are marked by relatively late education expansion and a significant Soviet influence up to the transition period of the 1990s. Their system of secondary education combines both general and vocational elements, whereas tertiary education enrolment lags behind the rest of the CEE countries. Relatively low gender segregation with regard to the choice of the field of study is, however, evident for these two countries.

Müller and Wolbers (2003), in their discussion of the educational landscape of the EU15, suggested that in countries without a system of vocationally oriented training a larger proportion of the youth cohort drops out from the education system immediately after reaching the age at which education is no longer compulsory. It seems that the exceptions the authors found in Western Europe – such as Belgium, Ireland and Greece (countries with small vocational education sectors but low rates of early school leavers) – are not the only ones. In practically all CEE countries, regardless of the level of VET provision, the proportion of early school leavers is lower than in the rest of the EU. The exceptions are Romania and Bulgaria, the two countries in which vocational training provision is at the medium level, but early school leaving rates are comparatively high. Country experts argue that one of the main reasons for the relatively high drop-out rates in these countries is a high proportion of Roma youth, who are often excluded from the education system.

The second central argument put forward by Müller and Wolbers (2003) is that in countries with extensive vocational programmes the demand for tertiary education grows more slowly than in countries with a more pronounced general orientation at the secondary level. This hypothesis is only partially supported by evidence from the CEE countries, in which the system of vocational education appears to be more diverse and also formally more open than the extremely stratified one in the German-speaking neighbour-countries. Overall, however, it could be said that in CEE countries in which a large proportion of young people participate in vocational tracks and in which vocational programmes offer only skilled worker certificates, a smaller proportion of young people proceed to the tertiary level. Examples are the Czech and Slovak Republics, Bulgaria and Romania. However, Hungary and Slovenia do not fit this pattern.

An attempt to find common elements and shared characteristics in the education systems of CEE countries after the transition should not obscure the unique features of each country's system, which are discussed in the single country chapters. Country-specific analyses shed further light on the development of institutions and highlight the trends in each of the above-mentioned sectors of these countries' education systems.

Notes

[1] We will not focus on standardisation at the secondary level here, due to the fact that in all CEE countries the degree of standardisation with regard to certificates is similarly high. Standardisation seems to be higher in the general and technological tracks that end with a matriculation examination, and lower in the vocational tracks offering qualification certificates. For details see country-specific chapters.

[2] Cerych (1997) argues that the tripartite division in upper-secondary education has become much less rigid in the transformation period than it was earlier, with the boundaries between tracks becoming more blurred. A clear sign of this trend is the emergence of integrated schools combining both vocational and advanced technical courses, or the inclusion of more general courses in specialised technical schools.

[3] Although these schools do not imply an automatic entitlement for entry to tertiary education, this can sometimes be attained after an additional two to three years of study (see Table 1.2).

[4] For Slovenia and Romania fees are waived for regular full-time students.

References

Allmendinger, J. (1989) 'Educational systems and labour market outcomes', *European Sociological Review*, vol 5, pp 231-50.

Arum, R. and Shavit, Y. (1995) 'Secondary vocational education and the transition from school to work', *Sociology of Education*, vol 68, pp 187-204.

Baumert, J., Brunner, M., Lüdtke, O. and Trautwein, U. (2007) 'Was messen internationale Schulleistungsstudien? Resultate kumulativer Wissenserwerbsprozesse: Eine Antwort auf Heiner Rindermann', *Psychologische Rundschau*, vol 58, pp 118-28.

Cedefop (2001) *The transition from education to working life. Key data on vocational training in the European Union*, Cedefop Reference Series, Luxembourg: Office for Official Publications of the European Communities.

Cerych, L. (1997) 'Educational reforms in Central and Eastern Europe: processes and outcomes', *European Journal of Education*, vol 32, no 1, pp 75-97.

Erikson, R. and Jonsson, J.O. (1996) 'Explaining class inequality in education: the Swedish test case', in R. Erikson and J.O. Jonsson (eds) *Can education be equalized? The Swedish case in comparative perspective*, Stockholm: Westview Press, pp 1-63.

ETF (European Training Foundation) (1998) *Vocational education and training in Central and Eastern Europe: key indicators*, Luxembourg: Office for Official Publications of the European Communities.

Eurostat (2003) *Education across Europe 2003*, Luxembourg: Eurostat.

Eurostat (2005) *Statistics in Focus 18*, Luxembourg: Eurostat.

Eurostat (2008a) *Data: Education and training*, Luxembourg: Eurostat (http://epp.eurostat.ec.europa.eu).

Eurostat (2008b) *Data: Population*, Luxembourg: Eurostat (http://epp.eurostat.ec.europa.eu).

Ganzeboom, H. and Nieuwbeerta, P. (1999) 'Access to education in six Eastern European countries between 1940 and 1985: results from a cross-national survey', *Communist and Post Communist Studies*, vol 32, pp 339-57.

Gerber, T.P. and Hout, M. (1995) 'Educational stratification in Russia during the Soviet period', *American Journal of Sociology*, vol 101, pp 601-60.

Helemäe, J. and Saar, E. (2003) *Women's employment in Estonia*, Working Paper No 48, Bamberg: University of Bamberg.

ILO (International Labour Organization) (1999) *Employment and labour market policies in transition economies*, Geneva: ILO.

Kerckhoff, A.C. (1996) 'Building conceptual and empirical bridges between studies of educational and labour force careers', in A.C. Kerckhoff (ed) *Generating social stratification: toward a new research agenda*, Boulder, CO: Westview Press, pp 37-56.

Kerckhoff, A.C. (2000) 'Transition from school to work in comparative perspective', in M.T. Hallinan (ed) *Handbook of the sociology of education*, New York: Kluwer, pp 543-74.

Kotásek, J. (1996) 'Structure and organisation of secondary education in Central and Eastern Europe', *European Journal of Education*, vol 31, no 1, pp 25-42.

Koucký, J. (1996) 'Educational reforms in changing societies: Central Europe in the period of transition', *European Journal of Education*, vol 31, no 1, pp 7-24.

Matějů, P. and Simonová, N. (2003) 'Czech higher education still at the crossroads', *Czech Sociological Review* (English Edition), vol 39, no 3, pp 393-410.

Matějů, P., Řeháková, B. and Simonová, N. (2003) 'Transition to university under communism and after its demise. The role of socio-economic background in the transition between secondary and tertiary education in the Czech Republic 1948-1998', *Czech Sociological Review* (English Edition), vol 39, no 3, pp 301-24.

Micklewright, J. (1999) 'Education, inequality and transition', *Economics of Transition,* vol 7, pp 343-76.

Müller, W. and Wolbers, M.H.J. (2003) 'Educational attainment in the European Union: recent trends in qualification patterns', in W. Müller and M. Gangl (eds) *Transition from education to work in Europe: the integration of youth into EU labour markets*, Oxford: Oxford University Press, pp 23-63.

OECD (Organisation for Economic Co-operation and Development) (2004) *Education at a glance*, Paris: OECD.

Róbert, P. (2002) 'Changes over time in transition from school to work in Hungary', Paper presented at the RC28 Annual Conference, Oxford.

Róbert, P. and Bukodi, E. (2005) 'The ffects of the globalization process on the transition to adulthood in Hungary', in H.-P. Blossfeld, E. Klijzing, M. Mills and K. Kurz (eds) *Globalization, uncertainty and youth in society*, London/New York: Routledge, pp 177-214.

Roberts, K. (1998) 'School-to-work transitions in former communist countries', *Journal of Education and Work*, vol 111, pp 221-38.

Ryan, P. (2001) 'The school-to-work transition: a cross-national perspective', *Journal of Economic Literature*, vol 39, pp 34-92.

Saar, E. (1997) 'Transition to tertiary education in Belarus and the Baltic Countries', *European Sociological Review*, vol 13, pp 139-58.

Schneider, S.L and Kogan, I. (2008) 'The International Standard Classification of Education 1997: challenges in the application to national data and the implementation in cross-national surveys', in S.L. Schneider (ed) *The International Standard Classification of Education (ISCED-97): an evaluation of content and criterion validity for 15 European countries*. Mannheim: Mannheimer Zentrum für Europäische Sozialforschung, ppn13-46.

Shavit, Y. and Müller, W. (1998) *From school to work: a comparative study of educational qualifications und occupational destinations*, Oxford: Clarendon Press.

Shavit, Y. and Müller, W. (2000a) 'Vocational secondary education. Where diversion and where safety net?', *European Societies*, vol 2, pp 29-50.

Shavit, Y. and Müller, W. (2000b) 'Vocational secondary education, tracking and social stratification', in M.T. Hallinan (ed) *Handbook of the sociology of education*, New York/Boston: Kluwer Academic/Plenum Publishers, pp 437-52.

Shavit, Y., Ayalon, H., Chachashvili, S. and Menahem, G. (2007) 'Israel: diversification, expansion and inequality in higher education', in Y. Shavit, R. Arum and A. Gamoran (eds) *Stratification in higher education: a comparative study*, Palo Alto: Stanford University Press, pp 39-62.

Simkus, A. and Andorka, R. (1982) 'Educational attainment in Hungary', *American Sociological Review*, vol 47, pp 740-51.

Strietska-Ilina, O. (2001) 'Research on vocational education and training at the crossroads of transition in Central and Eastern Europe', in P. Descy and M. Tessaring (eds) *Training in Europe: second report on vocational training research in Europe 2000 background report (vol 3)*, Cedefop Reference series, Luxembourg: Office for Official Publications of the European Communities, pp 209-311.

Titma, M. and Saar, E. (1995) 'Regional differences in secondary education of the former Soviet Union', *European Sociological Review*, vol 11, no 1, pp 37-58.

UNICEF (United Nations International Children's Emergency Fund) (2007) *TransMONEE 2007 Database*, Florence: UNICEF Innocenti Research Centre (www.unicef-irc.org/publications/pdf/tm2007_features.pdf).

TWO

Labour markets in Central and Eastern Europe

Michael Gebel

This chapter aims to identify key labour market patterns in Central and Eastern European (CEE) countries that have emerged during the transition from state socialism to a market economy and integration into the European Union (EU). Labour market developments can be interpreted as the outcome of interactions between general economic developments and the evolution of specific labour market institutions (Riboud et al, 2002). Both aspects have changed dramatically over the past two decades. First, the transition from socialism to a market economy has induced substantial economic changes. Second, labour law and regulations on industrial relations have been adopted to promote the emergence of capitalism. In the following, we will take a more in-depth look at whether these changes have translated into labour market changes.

The analysis begins with a short overview of the economic context of transformation, identifying important contextual factors such as the diversity of existing initial conditions, the different pathways of privatisation and other institutional economic reforms. An examination of trends and cross-country differences in labour force participation, labour market flexibilisation and unemployment dynamics follows, with a specific focus on the youth demographic group. Finally, the chapter discusses the nature of labour market institutions the CEE countries have adopted since the transition. The central dimensions of employment protection regulations and industrial relations are examined. The entire analysis relies substantially on comparable quantitative indicators and their qualitative evaluation.

Economic development

Initial economic conditions and GDP growth during the transition

The former socialist Eastern European countries experienced significant variation in initial conditions at the outset of the transition period 1988-92 (Ringold, 2005). For example, the Baltic countries were part of the Soviet Union and therefore suffered from an unfavourable set of initial conditions inherited from the social, economic and political activities of the former Soviet regime. In contrast, Central European socialist countries like Poland, the Czech Republic, Hungary and Slovenia had more contact with Western markets, and some market-oriented reforms were already in place before the transition. The variation in initial conditions can be displayed in a simplified manner in terms of gross domestic product (GDP) per capita, measured in current international dollars for reasons of comparability. At the time of the fall of the Iron Curtain, the Czech Republic, Slovenia and Hungary were the wealthiest CEE countries with a GDP per capita twice that of the poorest CEE countries Romania and Bulgaria (Table 2.1). The Baltic countries ranged in the middle despite their disadvantaged position within the former Soviet Union.

Table 2.1: GDP per capita in CEE countries, 1990

	GDP per capita, PPP (in current international $)
Czech Republic	12,006
Slovenia	11,405
Hungary	9,459
Lithuania	9,454
Slovak Republic	8,961
Latvia	7,685
Estonia	7,260
Poland	5,988
Romania	5,520
Bulgaria	5,446

Note: PPP = purchasing power parity.
Source: World Bank (2007)

The fall of the Soviet Block and the transition from command to market economy produced remarkable economic, social and political changes. Figure 2.1 displays the dramatic transformation in CEE countries according to their real GDP development during the first 15 years of transition. Beginning in 1990, real GDP registered a strong decline in real terms in all countries during the first years of transition. This transitional recession peaked in the period 1991-93 and was mainly triggered by the structural changes in the economic system such as the breakdown of trade relations with the countries of the former Soviet Union, the collapse of the old central planning system, extensive price and trade liberalisation, the emergence of product market competition and the abolition of many subsidies. Although all CEE countries experienced an initial downturn, Figure 2.1 shows that the strength of the depression varied. For example, the Baltic countries suffered from the recession more heavily than the other countries because they were hit hardest by the breakdown of trade relations with Soviet Union countries after their independence. They registered a decrease in real GDP of roughly 50% in Latvia (until 1993), 45% in Lithuania (until 1994) and 35% in Estonia (until 1993). A different picture emerges in more Western-oriented countries like Poland and Slovenia, where GDP dropped by only 18% in both countries.

Figure 2.1: Real GDP in CEE countries, 1989-2007

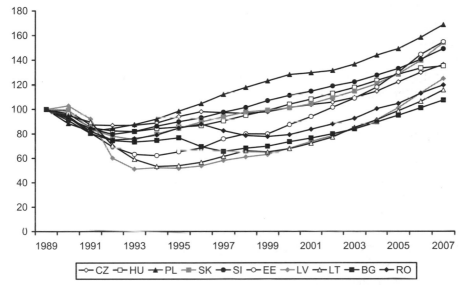

Source: EBRD (2008)

The initial economic contraction was followed by fast growth from 1995 until 1998 in all CEE countries except Romania and Bulgaria. Although the initial recession in Romania and Bulgaria was not as severe as in other areas of CEE, these countries were hit by a second recession at the end of the 1990s due to delayed restructuring. A few countries were able to catch up to their initial 1990 output levels because of fast economic growth; Poland had returned to 1990 levels by 1996 and Slovenia by 1997. Estonia experienced exceptionally good economic performance due to a strict reform process. Despite the acute transition crisis at the beginning of the 1990s, Estonia was able to gradually close the output gap with Hungary and Slovakia, which enjoyed more favourable starting conditions. This recovery after the initial transition crisis creates the typical U-shaped curve in real GDP evolution found in many transition economies (Blanchard, 1997).[1]

The expansion was followed by a short decline in real GDP at the end of the decade. One potential explanation for this later/second collapse in output is the Russian crisis that, in combination with the Asian crisis, induced a serious drying-up of international capital flows to transition countries in particular. This crisis brought a halt to fast growth, but did not reverse the overall upward trend in CEE countries. Nevertheless, even in 2000, real GDP was still at less than 80% of 1990 levels in Bulgaria, Romania, Lithuania and Latvia.

After the brief blip, the economy returned to its positive growth path in 2000. Economic performance remained stable during this preliminary phase of EU accession with high annual growth rates in most CEE countries in the new millennium. This recovery was strong enough to push the real GDP above its 1990 value in many CEE countries with the exception of Romania, Lithuania and Latvia. Overall, Figure 2.1 reveals that all CEE countries reached a positive growth path despite the severe economic and social turbulence in the early 1990s and a temporary setback during the Russian crisis at the end of the 1990s.

Transformation to a market economy

After the fall of the Iron Curtain, a fundamental process of transition from a centrally planned economy to a market economy took place in CEE countries. Some key policy objectives of the transition were common across the region: price and trade liberalisation, macroeconomic stabilisation and rapid privatisation of state enterprises. However, the countries differed widely in their pace, extent and modes of implementation of the transformation approach (Svejnar, 2002; EBRD, 2008). Poland and Hungary profited from early reforms that were already initiated before the official breakdown of socialism. Other countries, like Estonia and the Czech Republic, have undertaken a fast and radical reform process with relative success in regaining macroeconomic stability and increasing economic growth. Countries like Slovenia followed a gradual approach, introducing reforms step by step. Finally, Romania, Bulgaria, Latvia and Lithuania suffered from delayed restructuring. Since the late 1990s, potential and actual EU accession of CEE countries has driven political, economic and social developments, and reforms were subordinated to the EU accession aspirations and demands. The accession policies reinforced the transition process to a market economy and largely eliminated the remnants of socialism (EBRD, 2008). However, Bulgaria and Romania, the latecomers within the round of new EU member countries, are still lacking behind in some fields.

As a first step, most CEE countries forced price liberalisation at the beginning of the transition. The majority of price controls were removed on most food, industrial products and services at the beginning of the 1990s. For example, Poland, Hungary and Slovenia quickly reached almost complete liberalisation of prices, which was combined with currency devaluation

(EBRD, 2008). However, price liberalisation efforts resulted in a huge increase in inflation because relative prices adjusted to relative scarcities. This hyperinflation induced a strong decline in the real value of cash benefits and wages. Efforts directed towards macroeconomic stabilisation, such as tight monetary and fiscal policies, were successful in most countries, and inflation dropped to single-digit numbers at the end of the 1990s (UNICEF, 2007). Tight monetary policy was essential to establishing control over inflation.

In addition to price liberalisation, CEE countries forced the opening of their economies to international competition. Furthermore, many state monopolies were eliminated in order to promote the development of a dynamic private sector and to facilitate competition. Until the breakdown of socialism, firms had been largely protected against the impact of world markets through centrally planned production and distribution and the dominance of producers in the home market (Cazes and Nesporova, 2003). The opening of the national economies to global competition has forced domestic enterprises in transition countries to adjust their production conditions. Again, Poland, Hungary and Slovenia were regional leaders in opening their economies to international markets.

Table 2.2: Weighted privatisation index and private sector share in GDP in CEE countries, 1990-2007

	Privatisation index[a]				Private sector share in GDP[b]			
	1990	1995	2000	2007	1990	1995	2000	2007
BG	1.0	2.5	3.7	4.0	10.0	50.0	70.0	75.0
CZ	1.0	4.0	4.2	4.2	10.0	70.0	80.0	80.0
EE	1.0	4.0	4.2	4.2	10.0	65.0	75.0	80.0
HU	1.5	3.8	4.2	4.2	25.0	60.0	80.0	80.0
LV	1.0	3.0	3.7	4.0	10.0	55.0	65.0	70.0
LT	1.0	3.5	3.7	4.2	10.0	65.0	70.0	75.0
PL	2.5	3.5	3.8	3.8	30.0	60.0	70.0	75.0
RO	1.0	2.3	3.3	3.7	15.0	45.0	60.0	70.0
SK	1.0	3.5	4.2	4.2	10.0	60.0	80.0	80.0
SI	2.0	3.3	3.7	3.7	15.0	50.0	65.0	65.0

Notes: [a] Index represents unweighted average of EBRD index on large-scale privatisation and EBRD index on small-scale privatisation. Both indices range from 1.0 (little private ownership) to 4.5 (standards and performance typical of advanced industrial economies). [b] The underlying concept of private sector includes private registered companies as well as private entities engaged in informal activity if reliable information on informal activity is available.
Source: EBRD (2008)

The central dimension of the transition to a market economy is the degree of privatisation. Privatisation plays a central role in accelerating or delaying the adjustment in the real sector and turnover in labour markets. In the transition economies of CEE, privatisation took place in different modes, ranging from restitution and insider buyouts, management control and strategic investor involvement to mass privatisation schemes and direct sales to foreigners (Riboud et al, 2002). Estonia and Hungary, for example, relied primarily on the direct sale of large and medium-sized companies to foreign investors (Cazes and Nesporova, 2003). In contrast, the Czech Republic, Slovakia and Lithuania opted for mass privatisation through distribution of vouchers to the population. These different modes of privatisation in CEE countries resulted in different privatisation paces. The left part of Table 2.2 reveals that substantial privatisation was already implemented in Poland and Hungary before/at the onset of the transformation. This pattern is in accordance with the high private sector GDP share, which was 30% in Poland and 25% in Hungary in 1990 (see right part of Table 2.2). In contrast, for instance, the Baltic countries had not made much progress towards privatisation in 1990 because they were still part of the former Soviet Union and profited only from the former president Gorbachev's first reforms.

The picture changed dramatically within the first five years of the transition. Substantial progress was made by the Czech Republic and Estonia, both countries achieving roughly Western privatisation standards and a private sector GDP share of 70% and 65%, respectively, in 1995. The other CEE countries also implemented privatisation programmes and increased their private sector GDP share. Countries like Slovenia, and especially Latvia and Romania, were lagging behind in their privatisation efforts. However, these countries were able to catch up in the second half of the 1990s and particularly during the EU pre-accession period at the beginning of the new millennium. In 2007, most of the CEE countries had nearly reached Western European privatisation standards, which has translated into growing private sector GDP shares of between 65% and 80%. Slovenia presents an interesting case in this respect because it was initially (in 1990) a relative leader in privatisation, but was one of the last, along with Romania, to achieve a high degree of privatisation. Slovenia's private GDP share, at 65% in 2007, is also relatively low, comparable only to Romania. All in all, private sector participation has increased significantly over the last decade as the state sector declined. This price and trade liberalisation, combined with other economic, social and political reforms, induced significant changes in the labour market that are studied in detail in the following chapter.

Labour market dynamics

The labour markets of the formerly centrally planned CEE economies were characterised by a system of guaranteed employment and wages that led to high employment rates, no open unemployment and an excess of labour demand over supply (Svejnar, 1999; Cazes and Nesporova, 2003; Rashid et al, 2005). Wages were set centrally and kept largely equal. Unlimited full-time contracts were the norm and secure because dismissals were only allowed for serious misconduct. However, full employment was achieved at the cost of low wages. These low wages had demotivating effects on workers and disturbed the efficient labour allocation, generating a low level of labour productivity. The central planning system created incentives for overstaffing in many sectors due to soft budget constraints. Overstaffing meant that firms were employing more workers than were necessary to produce the given output level, eventually creating another source of low labour productivity. Furthermore, the lack of competition, free markets and free labour movement created serious distortions in the allocation of labour between industries and contributed to the low level of labour productivity.

Socialist Yugoslavia experienced a slightly different situation as its firms were exposed to competition and faced harder budget constraints than in most of the rest of CEE (Rutkowski, 2006). Firms were owned by workers, leading the insider-oriented management to pay higher wages to insiders rather than maximising employment by hiring additional external workers. The result was a high level of open unemployment.

The labour market situation in CEE countries has changed dramatically during the course of transition from socialism to market economies, forcing major labour market adjustments. In the following chapters, we will analyse the labour market dynamics during the transition in more detail in order to identify general temporal trends and cross-country variations.

Sectoral employment dynamics

During the transition, economic structural changes led to redistribution of employment (Boeri and Terrell, 2002). In addition to a general labour reallocation from the public to the private sector, labour resources shifted across economic sectors. The gradual introduction of market mechanisms allowed the misallocation of resources inherited from the previous central planning economy to be redressed, which was characterised by an overdeveloped industry share, large agricultural employment and a less developed service sector. Figure 2.2 shows the general pattern of structural change: the service sector has expanded at the expense of the agriculture sector and, to a somewhat lesser extent, the industrial sector. However, a different pattern with high and slightly increasing agricultural shares can be found in Romania and Bulgaria, indicating a somewhat slower pace of restructuring in these countries.

Around the beginning of the economic transition, a considerable percentage of the workforce was engaged in agriculture. After the de-collectivisation of farms through privatisation, agricultural employment was a source of secondary income and an employment opportunity of last resort for many laid-off workers and pensioners. Thus, agriculture employment might also be interpreted as major coping mechanism during the transition (Jackman and Pauna, 1997). This pattern is reflected in the fact that the high share of subsistence farming translates into low productivity levels in the agricultural sector (European Commission, 2002). Furthermore, many older workers engage in agriculture, and the group of family workers represents a significant employment group in many CEE countries, whereas this group's presence in Western European countries is negligible.

Figure 2.2: Employment by sector in CEE countries

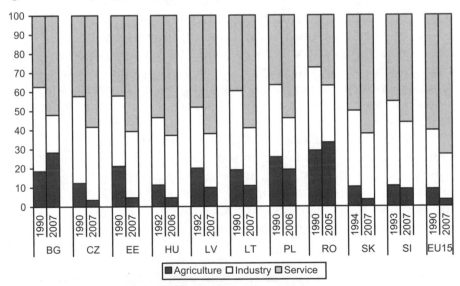

Note: Different start and end years due to limited data availability or comparability.
Source: Latvian data for first year from Eurostat (2008) and for the rest of the countries from ILO (2008); data for the last year from Eurostat (2008)

With the ongoing transition, however, agricultural employment has fallen steadily. This contraction can be explained by the liquidation of the collective and state-owned farms due to privatisation in agricultural industry and international competition. Despite the decrease in employment shares, employment in agriculture is still significantly overrepresented, especially in Poland and Romania.

During socialist times, the industrial sector was characterised by a predominance of large enterprises, especially in the heavy industry and engineering that was developed mostly after the Second World War. The reform process and structural adjustments led to a decline in output and employment in the industrial sector (European Commission, 2002). For example, in Poland there was a decrease in industrial employment shares from 37% in 1990 to 26.9% in 2006. In contrast, the employment share of industry and construction remained fairly stable throughout the entire transition period in Estonia, Hungary and Slovakia. Despite the contraction of industrial employment shares, this sector is significantly higher in CEE than in Western Europe. This is particularly the case in the Czech Republic, Slovenia and Slovakia, where around 33%-38% are employed in the industrial sector. This share still remains significantly above the EU15 average of 23.6%.

The service sector's share of total employment was underdeveloped in socialist times but has been increasing in all CEE countries during the transition years. Thus, the service sector seems to be the driving force in employment creation in the evolving CEE market economies. Despite significant increases, CEE's service sector remained relatively small compared to the EU15 in 2007. The countries with the highest rates of employment in services are Hungary, Slovakia and Estonia, although their share of around 61%-63% is still below the EU15 average.

Labour force participation

The transition period was characterised by a very strong decrease in employment and an increasing mismatch between labour demand and supply. Structural economic change has led to large-scale job destruction, which has not been fully balanced by new job creation. Employment losses were transformed partly into open temporary as well as structural unemployment and partly into official economic inactivity. Indeed, Table 2.3 shows that labour force participation rates of the male population aged 15-64 sharply declined for all CEE countries from an average of 79.9% in 1990 to 71.1% in 2006.[2] Although labour force participation rates have followed a downward trend in all CEE countries, there exists a wide variation between countries. Whereas Bulgaria experienced a large drop of around 16%, male labour force participation remained roughly stable in Slovenia despite the economic transition. In general, the decline in participation rates occurred especially during the first years of the transition. From the mid-1990s on, the decline slowed and even reversed in some countries. Bulgaria and Romania are exceptions to this general recovery trend because they experienced a later start of the decline, which, again, can be interpreted as a sign of delayed restructuring. Furthermore, one can also detect general level differences. For example, in 2006, the range in the level of male labour force participation spanned from only 62.2% in Bulgaria to 77% in the Czech Republic. This pattern reveals that CEE countries have had varying degrees of success in integrating the population into the labour market.

There are different causes for this common drop in participation rates (Cazes and Nesporova, 2003; Rutkowski, 2006). Discouraged workers withdrew from the labour market because they opted for social welfare and/or they engaged in informal sector activities. Others gave up their job search because of the extremely limited job opportunities for their qualifications. Additionally, many potential workers chose to engage in other activities, such as students who prolonged their educational careers or older workers who opted for early retirement schemes that were a popular restructuring instrument.

Table 2.3 reveals additional gender-specific differences in labour force participation trends. As in Western European countries, female participation in the labour force is generally lower than male participation. In 2006, male participation in the labour force in CEE was significantly below the EU15 level whereas the female participation rate was almost the same in the two regions.

Table 2.3: Labour force participation rate by gender, 1990 and 2006

	Male			Female		
	1990	2006	change	1990	2006	change
BG	77.8	62.2	−15.6	72.2	51.6	−20.6
CZ	82.1	77.0	−5.1	74.0	64.4	−9.6
EE	83.1	73.7	−9.4	76.2	64.6	−11.6
HU	74.4	66.6	−7.8	57.3	53.7	−3.6
LV	83.6	72.0	−11.6	75.3	63.1	−12.2
LT	81.7	72.5	−9.2	70.4	66.4	−4.0
PL	79.2	68.2	−11.0	65.1	57.3	−7.8
RO	77.2	66.9	−10.3	61.1	54.4	−6.7
SK	82.5	76.3	−6.2	70.6	62.3	−8.3
SI	76.9	75.6	−1.3	63.3	67.0	3.7
CEE10	79.9	71.1	−8.8	68.6	60.5	−8.1
EU15	80.0	78.3	−1.7	56.1	64.5	8.4

Note: Age group is 15-64.
Source: ILO (2008)

This reveals an underutilisation of male labour resources that can be attributed to the specific restructuring process, which has been biased against manual, less skilled labour, predominantly in heavy industry, that is traditionally male dominated (Rutkowski, 2006). In contrast, female labour force participation is highest in the growing service sector. Furthermore, high female participation was inherited from socialist times when increasing female participation in economic activities was a centrally planned policy aimed at raising overall production levels.[3]

Both female and male participation rates have the same evolution pattern over time: they are decreasing with the exception of female labour force participation in Slovenia. The positive sign in Slovenia coincides with the general pattern of roughly stable male labour force participation. At the regional level, there is no clear gender bias with regard to the decreasing labour force participation. In some countries, like Slovakia, the decrease is stronger for women, whereas in other countries, like Poland, participation by male has seen a greater decline.

Figure 2.3 shows that the youngest age cohort (15-24) suffered a much stronger decline in participation rates than the core workforce (25-54). In all CEE countries the drop in the period from 1990-2005 reached double-digit percentage points.

Figure 2.3: Labour force participation rate (%) by age cohort, 1990 and 2006

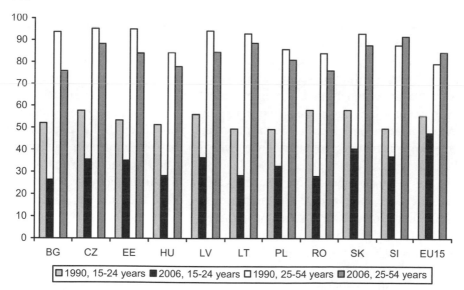

Source: ILO (2008).

Again, there is wide variation between countries. Whereas youth participation in the workforce in Slovenia declined approximately 12 percentage points between 1990 and 2005, the decline for the youth demographic in Romania was about 29 percentage points. In contrast, the middle-age cohort remained at very high average activity rates across the region despite drops in Estonia, Latvia and Bulgaria. In general participation rates are much lower for younger people because a significant portion still participates in education.

The disproportional decrease in youth activity rates can be explained by different factors (O'Higgins, 2004). On the one hand, the decrease is related to the increasing enrolment in higher education. Young people choose higher education to increase their later life chances and because of the anticipated increase in returns on higher education levels (Cazes and Nesporova, 2003). On the other hand, the decreased youth activity rate may also reflect increasing labour market integration problems of the youth demographic. Young people are confronted with an increasingly difficult transition from education to work. They suffer from labour market problems as outsiders due to their lack of work experience. Many young people stop looking for work and withdraw from the labour force because they are discouraged and/or they decide to engage in informal sector activity. Alternatively, they may extend their studies and delay their labour market entry in order to avoid problems integrating into tight labour markets. It remains unclear which of these factors is predominant in explaining the low rate of youth participation in the workforce in CEE countries. Based on a descriptive analysis, O'Higgins (2004) concludes that greater education participation cannot explain the whole decrease in activity rates. The decline in labour force participation is thus also likely to be attributable to the greater discouragement among young people about their prospects in the labour market.

During the transition period a significant part of the economic activity moved to the informal sector. Employment losses in the formal economy were partly compensated by employment growth in the informal sector (Schneider and Burger, 2005). Thus, to gain a more comprehensive picture of labour market processes, one has to take into account the underground economy, i.e., work by individuals who do not participate in the official labour market. The high levels of income tax and social contributions are seen as a motivation for people to work in the informal economy where activities are not taxed. Furthermore, the high degree of government regulation can lead to a substantial increase in labour costs in the official economy and give incentives to move into the shadow economy. Workers who lose their jobs in the formal sector often find alternative incomes in the informal part of the economy. Such work is typically less productive than working in the formal sector, but it offers an alternative that permits many to avoid becoming unemployed and it reduces dependence on public income transfers.

It is very difficult to get accurate information about informal sector activities because most of the individuals engaged in these activities do not wish to be identified. Different approaches are used to measure the size and development of the shadow economy, but regardless of the method used, the informal labour force for the CEE countries during the late 1990s appears to be remarkably high and, unexpectedly, on the increase throughout the transition period.[4] There is significant variation in informal sector sizes and activities between the CEE countries. Estonia has the highest shadow economy labour share, followed by Bulgaria and Latvia with around 30%. Surprisingly, despite the fast economic growth and recovery in Estonia, a large part of the population continues to engage in the shadow economy. The lowest shadow economies are found in Slovakia (16.3%) and the Czech Republic (12.6%). The output share of the so-called 'grey economy' is even larger because informal sector activities and incomes are often underreported in order to avoid taxation (Schneider and Burger, 2005).

Labour market flexibilisation

In socialist times employment meant full-time permanent work contracts. However, the transition saw a shift away from regular full-time wage employment to new, less static employment forms, leading to an increased degree of flexibility in the labour market. Table 2.4 provides a brief overview of three dimensions of flexible employment arrangements as a percentage of total employment. Temporary contracts and part-time employment represent atypical work forms that allow for faster employment adjustments and less costly termination of employment relations. Economic transformation pressed firms to adapt their production patterns and costs to changes in market demand, giving rise to flexible forms of employment (Cazes and Nesporova, 2003, 2007). Self-employment is often considered as another flexible form of work.

There is a wide variation in temporary employment shares between CEE countries. At the lower bound are Romania, Estonia and Slovakia, where flexible employment accounts for less than 5% of total employment. In contrast, the share of employees with temporary contracts was highest in Slovenia and Poland, with 17.1% and 27.3%, respectively. However, there are differences in the workers' assessment of temporary work between the two countries: the share of involuntary temporary employment is much larger in Poland than in Slovenia. The risk of getting a temporary contract is not equally distributed in the population. For example, Baranowska and Gebel (2008) show for most CEE countries that young workers, who lack work experience, seniority and networks, are more likely to find themselves in temporary jobs than the reference group of prime-age workers.

The share of part-time employment is also characterised by a wide spread, with 1.8% in Bulgaria and 9.5% in Lithuania. The comparison with temporary shares shows that there is no clear relationship between these two forms of atypical employment on the aggregate regional level. There are some countries with a positive correlation between temporary and part-time work, such as Poland with high shares and the Slovak Republic with low shares. At the same time, there are other countries that experience a strong negative correlation: Romania has the lowest temporary share and the third highest part-time share, and Slovenia exhibits high temporary employment but low part-time employment. Furthermore, the involuntary nature of part-time employment is more volatile than for temporary work. Whereas, in Slovenia, almost all workers voluntarily choose part-time employment, in Bulgaria part-time employment seems to be a generally undesired form of employment.

Table 2.4: Flexible employment forms in 2006

	TW (% of total employ ment)	% of TW that is involuntary (%)	PT (% of total employ ment)	% of PT that is involuntary (%)	SE (% of total employ- ment)	Percentage of SE that are employers (%)
BG	6.1	65.8	1.8	66.4	11.5	34.1
CZ	8.0	67.8	4.4	17.9	15.3	26.4
EE	2.7	63.3	6.7	21.4	7.9	33.9
HU	6.7	61.4	3.8	25.8	12.1	44.9
LV	7.2	69.2	5.8	38.9	9.7	35.0
LT	4.5	73.9	9.5	35.9	13.1	16.2
PL	27.3	75.9	8.9	29.8	19.4	20.8
RO	1.8	79.0	8.6	55.8	18.3	9.2
SK	5.0	71.7	2.7	16.9	12.5	24.7
SI	17.1	50.3	8.0	6.1	10.4	34.7
EU15	14.8	58.5	20.8	17.7	14.2	33.3

Note: Temporary work (TW), part-time work (PT) and self-employment (SE) as a percentage of the total number of employees aged 15-64.
Source: Eurostat (2008)

Comparisons with Western Europe reveal that part-time work and temporary employment are significantly less prevalent in CEE countries than in the EU15 with the exception of comparably high temporary employment shares for Slovenia and Poland. Part-time work in particular is significantly less prevalent in all candidate countries than in the EU. Lithuania has the highest part-time share with 9.5%, but this compares to 20.8% for the EU15. There could be different reasons for the low amount of part-time arrangements. It may be impossible to afford any reasonable living standard when working part time due to the overall low levels of wages, or employers might prefer to have full-time employees. The European Commission (2002) reports that the adoption of flexible employment forms such as temporary and part-time work seems to be the result of the inability of workers to find full-time and permanent jobs. This is indicated by the high shares of involuntary part-time and limited-duration work that is higher in CEE than in Western European countries. However, one should remember that the comparisons made on the basis of the official statistics are limited to the formal sector, yet the majority of casual and temporary jobs are in the informal sector (Rutkowski, 2006). Since creating irregular jobs in the informal sector is one of the ways to adjust flexibly to changing market conditions, the differences between old and new EU member states in proportion of standard versus 'flexibly adjusted' shares of labour market might be significantly overestimated.

The most commonly used form of flexibility emerging in the new member states is recourse to self-employment (Vaughan-Whitehead, 2004). Table 2.4 shows that self-employment is rather high in most of the CEE countries. Before the transition, self-employment was heavily discouraged through explicit and implicit sanctions, and self-employment was almost exclusively limited to family farming and small businesses (Earle and Sakova, 2000). The share of self-employed workers sharply increased in all the transition countries during the initial period of economic transformation. In 2006, the share of self-employment varies significantly between CEE countries with countries like Estonia and Latvia at the lower bound of around 8%-10%. In Romania and Poland self-employment plays a major role, accounting for approximately 20% of total employment. Self-employment often represents a coping strategy for workers who have lost their wage and salary employment. Self-employment is heavily concentrated in agriculture, especially in countries with a high share of agriculture in employment. The concentration of self-employment in agriculture explains, for example, the high self-employment shares in both Poland and Romania. This is also reflected in those countries' low share of employers among the self-employed, which is only half as much as in Hungary where agricultural self-employment plays only a minor role. In comparison, self-employment accounts for about 14% of total employment in EU15 countries.

Various reasons for the rising share of self-employment in the economies of CEE countries are discussed in the literature (Earle and Sakova, 2000). In the course of privatisation, some entrepreneurs opt for starting their own business because they see the earnings prospects through self-employment as being better than those in traditional employment. Other formerly employed people are forced into self-employment because the restructuring process has left them with few other work opportunities. A further practice, whereby the employer replaces the employee's normal employment contract with a 'self-employment' contract, allows employers to reduce their social security contributions and lower hiring and firing costs and has also contributed to the

49

increase of rate in the self-employment in CEE countries (Rutkowski, 2006). Overall, there is evidence that push factors dominate pull factors, meaning that the increasing share of self-employed reflects the evolution of entrepreneurship to a lesser extent than it does a coping strategy in response to depressed labour markets.

Unemployment dynamics

Unemployment was an unknown phenomenon during the communist era with the exception of the former Yugoslavia. The transition to a market economy led to an increase in unemployment in all countries, especially after the initial drop in output at the beginning of the 1990s. This was an unavoidable phenomenon since some unemployment is a characteristic of all market economies (Rutkowksi, 2006). However, the unemployment rate increased substantially in all CEE countries, reflecting some structural mismatches due to enormous labour reallocation processes. After the initial increase, unemployment figures evolved along different paths yielding a large variation in unemployment rates between CEE countries in 2006.[5] At one extreme, Lithuania, Estonia and Latvia had low unemployment rates of approximately 7% in 2006, whereas countries like Poland and Slovakia are at the other extreme with high rates of between 13% and 14% (Table 2.5). The degree of variation among countries and the overall level in CEE is now similar to Western Europe.

Table 2.5: Unemployment rates in 2006

	Unemployment rate (ages 15-64)	Youth unemploy-ment (ages 15-24)	Long-term unemployment
BG	9.0	19.5	55.7
CZ	7.2	17.5	54.2
EE	6.0	12.0	48.2
HU	7.5	19.1	45.1
LV	7.0	12.2	36.3
LT	5.7	9.8	44.2
PL	14.0	29.8	56.2
RO	7.6	21.4	57.8
SK	13.4	26.6	76.3
SI	6.1	13.9	49.3
EU15	7.8	15.9	42.5

Source: Eurostat (2008)

However, the stabilised unemployment figures mask unresolved structural problems in some countries because labour force participation rates declined during the same period. In several countries these effects of increasing unemployment and decreasing labour force participation rates have occurred in different proportions. For example, although Romania has one of the lowest unemployment rates, labour force participation rates declined drastically during the transition period and are rather low compared to other CEE countries. Hence, there are indications that some Eastern European labour markets have not provided sufficient job opportunities resulting in either in low participation rates (e.g. Romania), or high unemployment rates (e.g. Slovakia) or both (e.g. Poland).

Regarding long-term (12+ months) unemployment, there is little variation between the CEE countries, with the exception of Latvia and Slovakia in which 36.3% and, respectively, 76.3% of unemployment was long term in 2006. Long-term unemployment in all other CEE countries in 2006 averaged approximately 44%-55%, slightly higher than the EU15 average. Long-term unemployment can create a vicious circle as it often leads to individuals loosing employability and income. At the societal level, this translates into both reduced tax payments and increased welfare expenditure for the state.

There are several risk groups for whom integration into the Eastern European labour market is complicated for various reasons. These groups include young people, those with a low level of education and non-nationals (immigrants).[6] For example, as is also the case in Western European countries, the transition of youth from school to active life and labour integration remains an important labour market problem (Nesporova, 2002). First-time labour market entrants, approximated as the youngest age cohort of 15- to 24-year-olds, face an unemployment rate that is at least twice as high as the national average. The situation is especially acute in Poland and Slovakia where nearly every third active youth is unemployed. On average, the youth unemployment problem is more severe in Eastern than in Western Europe, with the exception of Southern Europe (O'Higgins, 2004). High youth unemployment cannot be fully attributed to normal job shopping for appropriate work because yong people also suffer from long-term unemployment. Apart from the labour demand restrictions related to working experience discussed earlier, difficulties in the professional integration of youth are also caused by the insufficient matching between labour demand and qualifications offered by the education system.

Another population at high risk of unemployment are those with a low level of education. The education-specific unemployment rates in Table 2.6 show a high concentration of unemployment in the lowest educational category (International Standart Classification of Education, ISCED 0-2). However, there is again a large variation between countries that can partly be attributed to different overall unemployment rates. Despite this explanation, the variation between 48.6% in Slovakia and 8.4% in Slovenia shows that CEE countries differ in their success in integrating lower-educated citizens into the labour market. Unemployment rates are significantly lower, but still high, for workers with a medium educational level (ISCED 3-4). The unemployment rate drops dramatically to 3%-7% for workers with higher education (ISCED 5-6). In general, the probability of unemployment declines with the increasing level of education. Those with a high degree of education have especially good labour market chances in Lithuania, Hungary and the Czech Republic. Unemployment rates among the highly educated are also low in countries with high overall unemployment rates, suggesting that the fall in labour demand has hit less skilled workers particularly hard (Rutkowski, 2006). Again, detailed analyses suggest that lower education is also connected with a higher risk of long-term unemployment (Schneider and Burger, 2005).

Table 2.6: Unemployment rates by education level in 2006

	ISCED 0-2	ISCED 3-4	ISCED 5-6
BG	20.5	7.7	4.0
CZ	24.8	6.4	2.5
EE	13.5	6.3	3.3
HU	16.7	6.9	2.8
LV	14.9	6.3	3.8
LT	10.6	6.5	2.6
PL	23.7	15.0	6.0
RO	9.0	7.9	3.8
SK	48.6	11.8	3.3
SI	8.4	6.6	3.3
EU15	11.1	7.5	4.6

Notes: Education level is understood to be the highest level achieved by an individual. Figures are for individuals aged 15-64.
Source: Eurostat (2008)

Labour market institutions

This final section discusses the nature of labour market institutions the CEE countries adopted after the transition. In CEE countries, the legal setting of industrial relations is as varied as their differing historical backgrounds (Bronstein, 2003). Whereas Soviet labour policies were law in the Baltic countries, countries like Hungary, Poland and the former Czechoslovakia had undertaken reforms even before the downfall of communism. The same can be said of Slovenia, as administrative and management decentralisation was an important feature of the former Yugoslavia. Despite these differences, labour laws in centrally planned Eastern European economies shared a number of common features (Bronstein, 2003). First, permanent full-time employees as well as large state-owned production units were considered the key labour market characteristics. Second, there were strict rules and procedures for issues such as recruitment and termination of employment. Third, labour allocation and wage setting were highly centralised. During the transition, efforts were undertaken to adjust the labour laws to market system requirements. Hence, an interesting research question is whether CEE countries got rid of their strict labour law regulations and centralised planning structures. This section examines the central dimensions of employment protection regulation and industrial relations. The central dimensions are described, but the aim is not to judge their effects on labour market performance. [7]

Employment protection legislation

Employment protection legislation (EPL) is a central aspect of the general concept of labour market flexibility. It refers to hiring and firing rules that restrict the employer's freedom to dismiss workers. Although the objective of EPL is to protect employment relationships by reducing their exposure to unfair actions and to the risk of fluctuating incomes, these regulations may increase the costs of employing workers. Under the centrally planned economic system, workers enjoyed a fairly high degree of employment protection in their jobs. Unless an employee committed a criminal offence or a serious breach of labour rules, the employer could not end the employment contract other than by agreement with the worker (Cazes and Nesporova, 2003). This high degree of employment protection, combined with high wage compression, induced labour market rigidity and inefficient labour allocation. In the 1990s, structural transformations and market-oriented economic and social reforms led to a substantial reduction of workers' protection. The objective was to facilitate workforce adjustment for firms in order to make enterprises more flexible while at the same time guaranteeing employment protection for workers. During the transition to market economies, reducing employment protection became an important issue for employers because it induces termination costs that make it difficult to fire workers, and therefore also raises the costs of new hires. Furthermore, during the period of accession to the EU, CEE countries were required to harmonise their laws and regulations with the European acquis communautaire, raising the question of where the new member states stand in terms of labour market rigidity.

There are different attempts to measure the degree of regulations that restrict the employer's freedom to dismiss workers. The Organisation for Economic Co-operation and Development (OECD) (1999) constructed one

EPL index that is commonly used in labour law analysis. It is often interpreted as a main indicator of the strictness of labour market policies and institutions. The EPL index considers with 22 quantitative and qualitative indicators the legislation on three dimensions: permanent employment, temporary employment and collective dismissals. Regular employment legislation includes the rules for hiring and firing procedures of permanent workers, notification requirements and severance payments. Temporary employment legislation regulates the use of temporary contracts, their renewal and maximum duration, as well as the functioning of temporary work agencies. Collective dismissal legislation defines the term 'collective', as opposed to 'individual', and stipulates notification requirements and payments associated with such dismissals (Micevska, 2004). The overall EPL index is a weighted average of these indicators taking values from 0 to 6. The higher the value of the EPL index, the stricter the employment protection legislation. Table 2.7 reports the results for CEE countries and the EU15 using the OECD methodology (OECD, 2004; Micevska, 2004; Tonin, 2005). It depicts the three different dimensions of the strictness of EPL and the overall EPL index.

Regulation concerning regular employment varies strongly across CEE countries with some countries below the EU15 average and some above. The most rigid legislation can be found in the Czech Republic and Slovakia, and far fewer restrictions on regular dismissals in Romania and Hungary. In less regulated countries 'unsatisfactory performance' and 'job redundancy' are sufficient reasons for dismissal, but in more regulated CEE countries employers are required to take into account social considerations, to look for retraining or even to ensure the worker's transfer to another suitable position (Riboud et al, 2002). Furthermore, in less regulated countries like Hungary and Poland, notice periods are shorter and severance payment lower.

A different picture emerges with regard to regulation on temporary work. Here, legislation is much weaker in most CEE countries than in Western Europe with the exception of Romania, Lithuania and Slovenia. This is somewhat surprising because the flexible employment analysis has shown that temporary contracts are less common in most CEE countries than in Western Europe. Furthermore, the strict regulation of regular employment in most CEE countries induces high firing costs that are seen as the main reason for using contracts of limited duration. Two hypotheses may explain this contradiction between weak legislative restrictions and the low prevalence of temporary contracts. First, although firms suffer from high potential firing costs and have the possibility of using temporary employees, they do not make use of these work arrangements because they have found different ways of flexibilisation. Second, governments might not see reasons for stricter temporary work legislation because temporary work contracts are of only minor importance in CEE countries.

Table 2.7: Employment protection legislation

	Regular employment	Temporary employment	Collective dismissal	Summary index
BG	2.1	0.9	4.1	2.0
CZ	3.3	0.5	2.1	1.9
EE	2.7	1.3	4.0	2.3
HU	1.9	1.1	2.9	1.7
LV	2.3	2.1	4.0	2.5
LT	2.9	2.4	3.6	2.8
PL	2.2	1.3	4.1	2.1
RO	1.7	3.0	4.8	2.8
SK	3.5	0.4	2.5	2.0
SI	2.7	2.3	3.3	2.6
EU15	2.3	2.0	3.4	2.3

Source: Figures for EU15 (average without Luxemburg), Poland, Czech Republic, Slovakia and Hungary from OECD (2004: Table 2 A2.4; measures situation in 2003); for Estonia, Slovenia, Lithuania and Bulgaria from Tonin (2005: Table 1; measures situation in 2001-04); for Latvia from Eamets and Masso (2005: Table 1; measures situation in 2002); for Romania from Micevska (2004: Table A1.2; measures situation in 2003)

Compared to the EU15, CEE countries tend to be most restrictive concerning collective dismissals. Strict EPL for collective dismissals was maintained from former socialist times in order to prevent mass layoffs during economic restructuring. However, there are also some exceptions, like the Czech Republic and Slovakia, with weaker restrictions on mass dismissals, mirroring their outlier position with low protection of temporary employment.

The overall variation between CEE countries for all EPL indicators reveals the important fact that transition countries do not constitute a homogeneous group. While Hungary, the Czech Republic and Bulgaria have the most flexible regulations, dismissals are strongly regulated in Lithuania and Romania. However, differences in EPL exist not only among CEE countries, but also, and to an even greater extent, among EU members (OECD, 2004). Compared with the EU15 average, CEE countries tend to be more restrictive concerning collective dismissals and less restrictive concerning temporary employment.

Furthermore, there are reasons to believe that employment protection is even weaker in CEE countries because of differences between the written law and actual law enforcement. For example, strict labour laws may have little influence on the economy if economic agents can easily violate them, if law enforcement agencies are weak or if these laws cover only a small proportion of the total workforce. In addition, one has to take into account the role of jurisprudence in interpreting the laws (Bertola et al, 2000). The chief problem of legal regulation of the labour market is that employers do not always enact regulations; in the private sector and in small firms, violations are particularly common (Eamets and Masso, 2005). For example, the data on the violations discovered by national labour inspections in Baltic countries presented by Eamets and Masso (2005) revealed that a very high proportion of enterprises violate labour laws. In these cases, workers' representatives and the government are not able to protect workers sufficiently and/or employees do not initiate individual claims against employers for fear of losing their jobs. The authors conclude that for transition countries, the strictness or flexibility of the labour market cannot be determined solely by formal legislation, but that factors such as enforcement and frequency of violations must also be taken to account. This means that although flexibility can be achieved through flexible employment contracts in Western Europe, transition country employers often attain flexibility by simply not following the regulations.

Industrial relations

Unions and employers' organisations are central institutions that represent collective interests in labour markets. They bargain over the level of wages and other working conditions and thus have an influence on the labour market dynamics. Rights on collective bargaining between unions and employers are usually formalised in labour law and constitutions. Prior to 1990, industrial relations systems in CEE countries were characterised by central political and managerial control exercised by the state (Thirkell et al, 1998). There was, in general, one single union in which membership was quasi-compulsory, and unions were primarily meant to act as a transmission belt for the implementation of policies and decisions taken by the state-party structure (Bronstein, 2003). Although collective bargaining formally existed, its major purpose was to set production targets for the management and the workforce within the centralised planning system. During the transition, efforts were made to develop industrial relations typical of a market economy. CEE countries moved away from a centralised wage-setting system towards a collective bargaining system in the enterprise sector. Relevant features of industrial relations are, among others, rate of unionisation, the proportion of workforce covered by collective agreements, the level of centralisation and the degree of coordination (Table 2.8).

Membership in trade unions, usually measured as union membership as a percentage of all employment, plays a crucial role in most wage bargaining systems. After the abolition of mandatory membership, union membership sharply declined during the 1990s from the 100% coverage of the workforce registered at the beginning of transition.

Table 2.8: Key figures of industrial relations in CEE countries

	Union density[a]	Collective bargaining coverage[b]	Centralisation of wage bargaining	Coordination of wage bargaining
BG	22.2	25.0-30.0	–	–
CZ	25.1	35.0	0.27	1.0
EE	16.6	22.0	0.25	1.0
HU	19.9	42.0	0.26	2.0
LV	20.0	20.0	0.30	1.5
LT	16.0	15.0	0.23	1.0
PL	14.7	35.0	0.20	1.0
RO	31.4	–	–	–
SK	35.4	50.0	0.33	2.0
SI	41.0	100.0	0.43	4.0
EU15	27.3	75.9	0.45	3.1

Notes: [a] Rates are standardised and measure the percentage of salaried workers that belong to a trade union, i.e., without the unemployed, self-employed, retired employees and student members. [b] Measures the percentage of all salaried workers unionised and not unionised who are covered by collective agreements. The degree of centralisation combines a measure of trade union concentration with a measure of the common level of bargaining and ranges from 0 (no centralisation) to 1 (full centralisation). The degree of coordination is an average index measure for both coordination among workers and employers. The index ranks from 1 (no coordination at national or sectoral level) to 5 (high coordination at national and sectoral level). Data refer to the late 1990s/2000.
Source: Union density from Visser (2004: Table 1.3; data refer to 2002, for Poland and Estonia to 2001); for Bulgaria and Romania from Crowley (2004: Figure 2; survey data from the late 1990s); collective bargaining coverage from Van Gyes et al (2007: Figure 4; data refer to 2002); for Bulgaria from Schulten (2005: Table 4; latest available data); centralisation of wage bargaining from Visser (2004: Table 1.9; data refer to 2003); coordination of wage bargaining from Visser (2004: Table 1.10; data refer to 2003)

Table 2.8 shows that union density varies considerably, which is also the case in Western European countries (Crowley, 2004; Visser, 2004; Van Gyes et al, 2007). The figures range from between 14.7% in Poland and 41% in Slovenia. There are clusters at both ends; at the lower end are Poland, Lithuania and Estonia, and at the top are Slovenia, Slovakia and Bulgaria. A generally different picture emerges in the public sector, where trade unions have a markedly stronger position in most CEE countries (Feldmann, 2006). This high degree of unionism in the public sector also reflects the difficulties of unions in recruiting members from the private sector (Visser, 2004).

Even more important than the number of unionised workers is the coverage by collective agreements and their degree of centralisation. Table 2.8 presents estimates of the percentage of employees covered by collective agreements, i.e., the proportion of workers that have their pay and conditions set, at least to some extent, by collective agreements. Again, there is a wide variation between CEE countries ranging from total coverage in Slovenia to only 15% coverage in Lithuania. Most countries have a low coverage rate of less than 25%. In most CEE countries, low coverage rates coincide with a low degree of centralisation of between 0.2 and 0.3 (Table 2.8). Collective agreements concluded at enterprise or plant level and individual employment contracts are predominant in Eastern Europe with the exception of Slovakia and Slovenia (for a detailed overview, see Van Gyes et al, 2007: Table 4). Sectoral bargaining plays the dominant role only in Slovakia and Slovenia and has a relatively significant bargaining level in Hungary. Sectoral bargaining exists in the Czech Republic, Estonia, Latvia and Poland, but is of very limited significance. The numerous newly created private enterprises are particularly opposed to any union activities at their enterprises and refuse to enter into national or sectoral collective agreements with the unions (Feldmann, 2006). Instead, they prefer to conclude agreements at the enterprise or plant level or they prefer individual employment contracts. Therefore, unlike in many countries in Western Europe, collective agreements are rarely universally binding in transition countries, with the exception of Hungary, Romania and Slovenia (Feldmann, 2006). With the exception of Estonia, collective agreements also always apply to non-union employees of companies bound by collective agreements.

In general, collective bargaining coverage in most transition countries is relatively weak. This mirrors the trend toward a decentralised level of bargaining and lower levels of trade union membership after the transition. In view of low and declining union density rates, this is another indicator of weak union power in CEE countries.

Patterns of bargaining levels in CEE countries are unlike those found in Western Europe. The 'classic' Western continental European pattern of dominant sectoral bargaining, as found for example in Austria or Germany, can only be found in Slovakia. Furthermore, the highly centralised Slovenian system has similarities to the situation in Belgium, but the dominance of company bargaining in most CEE countries is only found in the West in the UK.

Another indicator of industrial relations is the degree of union and employer coordination. Unions' negotiating power depends very much on their ability to coordinate with employers. Coordination should be distinguished from centralisation, which refers to the level of bargaining, because highly coordinated bargaining is not necessarily centralised. Table 2.8 displays the coordination index for most CEE countries, where coordination is measured as the unweighted average of union and employer coordination. The index ranks from 1 (no coordination) to 5 (high coordination). Again, one can identify a broad variation between CEE countries with a low degree of coordination in the Czech Republic, Estonia, Lithuania and Poland and a high degree of coordination in Slovenia. This distribution matches the fact that in particular Slovenia is characterised by high union density, high collective bargaining coverage and high centralisation.

Overall, union strength and collective bargaining coverage generally in the new member states remain rather weak, although there are some exceptions (Crowley, 2004). There is not a large difference between Eastern and Western Europe in union power as both regions exhibit wide intra-group variation (Armingeon, 2006). The decrease of union power in CEE countries is generally attributed to the shift towards free choice of union membership status. In addition to this fact, the steep decline in membership rates in some countries, such as the Baltic states, Poland and Hungary, can be explained by falling living standards over the 1990s, high levels of unemployment, privatisation, growing numbers of small businesses and sectoral shifts (Visser, 2004). Furthermore, comparative analyses of labour relations show that trade unions in ex-communist countries are not very effective in reaching their goals (Crowley, 2004; Kubicek, 2004). The unions' weakness is attributed to the contradictory position in which they have to support the establishment of capitalist market relations while at the same time defending employees against the realities of capitalism (Armingeon, 2006). Moreover, workers often oppose trade unions because they are still considered as legacies of the former state-socialist systems.

Conclusion

This chapter sought to identify key labour market patterns that emerged in CEE countries during the transition from state socialism to a market economy and the integration into the EU. We conclude that labour market developments can be interpreted as the outcome of interactions between general economic developments and the evolution of specific labour market institutions.

Based on several quantitative indicators and the qualitative judgement, we found significant differences in initial conditions at the onset of the transition and country-specific pathways during the restructuring process. General patterns in the economic context of transformation, such as the diversity of pathways of privatisation and other institutional economic reforms, emerged.

In some countries employment losses due to increased competition, privatisation and free markets translated predominantly into high open unemployment, while in other countries it led to high economic inactivity or informal sector activity. It became clear that young people, as labour market outsiders, were most heavily affected by increasing unemployment rates and decreasing labour force participation, although differing degrees of success in youth integration produced a wide variation in youth employment among countries. Furthermore, special attention was paid to gender-specific aspects of labour market trends and differentiation across education groups in order to better understand the link between education and labour market outcomes. Detailed analyses have shown that some CEE countries have made substantial labour market flexibilisation efforts that are reflected in increasing shares of atypical work arrangements. Although the level of flexibilisation is still below Western European standards, we consider flexibilisation steps as a crucial labour market trend that affect young labour market entrants in particular.

Specific labour market institutions were evaluated from a qualitative and quantitative perspective, focusing on the central dimensions of employment protection regulations and industrial relations in conjunction with earlier research on CEE countries. The analysis again found some degree of variation, but also common patterns between CEE countries. For example, Hungary and Estonia have weak unions and low levels of collective bargaining coverage and coordination, whereas Bulgaria and especially Slovenia still have strong unions and high levels of coordination.

Notes

[1] In contrast, many transition countries from former republics of the Soviet Union typically displayed L-shaped patterns of real GDP development (Boeri and Terrell, 2002).

[2] The labour force is the total number of people employed and unemployed.

[3] This and other aspects of the gender labour market differences in transition economies are explored in more detail in Paci (2002).

[4] There are direct survey methods as well as indirect indicators where the latter use several macroeconomic indicators that contain information about the shadow economy, e.g. the currency demand or the electricity demand, among others (Schneider, 2002).

[5] For a detailed discussion of the temporal evolution path of unemployment figures, see country chapters (chapters five to fourteen).

[6] Analyses of the unemployment risks of specific minorities can be found in some of the country chapters 5-14.

[7] Whether these institutions facilitated greater labour market adjustment or imposed rigidities in the labour market, leading to adverse labour market outcomes for particular workers, is still an open research question for CEE countries (Feldmann, 2006).

References

Armingeon, K. (2006) 'Trade unions and industrial relations in post-communist nations. A comparison with established democracies', Paper for the Conference of Europeanists, Chicago.

Baranowska, A. and Gebel, M. (2008) *Temporary employment in Central and Eastern Europe: individual risk patterns and institutional context*, Working Paper No 106, Mannheim: Mannheim Centre for European Social Research.

Bertola, G., Boeri, T. and Cazes, S. (2000) 'Employment protection in industrialized countries: the case for new indicators', *International Labour Review*, vol 139, no 1, pp 57-72.

Blanchard, O. (1997) *The economics of post-communist transition*, Oxford: Clarendon Press.

Boeri, T. and Terrell, K. (2002) 'Institutional determinants of labor reallocation in transition', *The Journal of Economic Perspectives*, vol 16, no 1, pp 51-76.

Bronstein, A. (2003) *Labour law reform in EU candidate countries: achievements and challenges*, Working Paper in Focus Programme on Social Dialogue, Labour Law and Labour Administration, Geneva: International Labour Organization.

Cazes, S. and Nesporova, A. (2003) *Labour markets in transition: balancing flexibility and security in Central and Eastern Europe*, Geneva: International Labour Organization.

Cazes, S. and Nesporova, A. (2007) 'Labour markets in Central and South-Eastern Europe: from transition to stabilization', in S. Cazes and A. Nesporova (eds) *Flexicurity: a relevant approach for Central and Eastern Europe*, Geneva: International Labour Organization, pp 9-56.

Crowley, S. (2004) 'Explaining labor weakness in post-communist Europe: historical legacies and comparative perspective', *East European Politics and Societies*, vol 18, no 1, pp 394-429.

Eamets, R. and Masso, J. (2005) 'The paradox of the Baltic States: labour market flexibility but protected workers', *European Journal of Industrial Relations*, vol 11, no 1, pp 71-90.

Earle, J. and Sakova, Z. (2000) 'Business start-ups or disguised unemployment? Evidence on the character of self-employment from transition economies', *Labour Economics*, vol 7, no 5, pp 575-601.

EBRD (European Bank for Reconstruction and Development) (2008) *Transition report 2007*, London: EBRD.

European Commission (2002) *Employment performance in candidate countries*, Luxembourg: Office for Official Publications of the European Communities.

Eurostat (2008) *Data: labour market*, Luxembourg: Eurostat (http://epp.eurostat.ec.europa.eu).

Feldmann, H. (2006) 'Labour market institutions and labour market performance in transition countries', *Post-Communist Economies*, vol 17, no 1, pp 47-82.

ILO (International Labour Organization) (2008) *Key indicators of the labour market programme*, Fifth Edition, Geneva: ILO.

Jackman, R. and Pauna, C. (1997) 'Labor market policy and the re-allocation of labor across sectors', in S. Zechhinni (ed) *Lessons from the economic transition: Central and Eastern Europe in the 1990s*, Boston: Kluwer Academic Publishers, pp 373-92.

Kubicek, P. (2004) *Organized labor in post-communist states: from solidarity to infirmity*, Pittsburgh, PA: University of Pittsburgh Press.

Micevska, M. (2004) *Unemployment and labour market rigidities in Southeast Europe*, Working Paper GDN-SEE, Vienna: Global Development Network Southeast Europe.

Nesporova, A. (2002) *Why unemployment remains so high in Central and Eastern Europe*, Employment Paper No 43, Geneva: International Labour Organization.

OECD (Organisation for Economic Co-operation and Development) (1999, 2004) *Employment outlook*, Paris: OECD.

O'Higgins, N. (2004) *Recent trends in youth labour markets and youth employment policy in Europe and Central Asia*, CELPE Discussion Paper No 85, University of Salerno: Centre for Studies in Economics and Finance.

Paci, P. (2002) *Gender in transition*, Washington DC: World Bank.

Rashid, M., Rutkowski, J. and Fretwell, D. (2005) 'Labor markets', in N. Barr (ed) *Labor markets and social policy in Central and Eastern Europe: the accession and beyond*, Washington DC: World Bank, pp 59-87.

Riboud, M., Sánchez-Páramo, D. and Silva-Jauregui, C. (2002) 'Does eurosclerosis matter? Institutional reform and labour market performance in Central and Eastern Europe countries', in B. Funck and L. Pizzati (eds) *Labour, employment, and social policies in the EU enlargement process*, Washington DC: World Bank, pp 243-311.

Ringold, L. (2005) 'The course of transition: growth, inequality, and poverty', in N. Barr (ed) *Labor markets and social policy in Central and Eastern Europe: the accession and beyond*, Washington DC: World Bank, pp 31-57.

Rutkowski, J. (2006) *Labor market developments during economic transition*, Policy Research Working Paper No 3894, Washington DC: World Bank.

Schneider, F. (2002) *The size and development of the shadow economies of 22 transition and 21 OECD countries*, IZA Discussion Paper No 514, Bonn: Institute for the Study of Labor.

Schneider, F. and Burger, C. (2005) 'Formal and informal labour markets: challenges and policy in the Central and Eastern European new EU members and candidate countries', *CESifo Economic Studies*, vol 51, no 1, pp 77-115.

Schulten, T. (2005) *Changes in national collective bargaining systems since 1990*, Dublin: European Foundation for the Improvement of Living and Working Conditions (www.eurofound.europa.eu/eiro/2005/03/study/tn0503102s.htm).

Svejnar, J. (1999) 'Labor markets in the transitional Central and Eastern European Economies', in O. Ashenfelter and D. Card (eds) *Handbook of labor economics*, vol 3, chapter 42, Amsterdam: Elsevier, pp 2809-57.

Svejnar, J. (2002) 'Transition economies: performance and challenges', *The Journal of Economic Perspectives*, vol 16, no 1, pp 3-28.

Thirkell, J., Petkov, K. and Vickerstaff, S. (1998) *The transformation of labour relations: restructuring and privatization in Eastern Europe and Russia*, Oxford: Oxford University Press.

Tonin, M. (2005) *Updated employment protection legislation indicators for Central and Eastern European countries*, Working Paper, Institute for International Economic Studies, Stockholm: Stockholm University.

UNICEF (United Nations International Children's Emergency Fund) (2007) *TransMONEE 2007 database*, Florence: UNICEF Innocenti Research Centre.

Van Gyes, G., Vandenbrande, T., Lehndorff, S., Schilling, G., Schief, S. and Kohl, H. (2007) *Industrial relations in EU member states 2000-2004*, Dublin: European Foundation for the Improvement of Living and Working Conditions.

Vaughan-Whitehead, D. (2004) 'Employment and working conditions in the new member states', in European Commission (ed) *Industrial relations in Europe*, Luxembourg: Office for the Official Publications of the European Communities, pp 151-72.

Visser, J. (2004) 'Patterns and variations in European industrial relations', in European Commission (ed) *Industrial relations in Europe*, Luxembourg: Office for the Official Publications of the European Communities, pp 11-57.

World Bank (2007) *World Development Indicators*, Washington DC: World Bank.

THREE

Social protection, inequality and labour market risks in Central and Eastern Europe

Clemens Noelke

Following the collapse of socialism, the countries of Central and Eastern Europe (CEE) have undergone substantial changes (Elster et al, 1998; Kornai, 2006). They have adopted the institutions of capitalist democracies, while simultaneously developing the socio-political infrastructure to render capitalism and democracy functional. Additionally, they have had to come to terms with massive economic and demographic crises. Improving individual welfare has always been a central concern in this process for individuals as well as politicians, not least to mitigate the political costs of the transition crisis in the newly founded democracies. Nevertheless, initial hopes of rapid convergence to Western standards have been largely disappointed. The early 1990s were marked by a decline in aggregate output, employment levels and real incomes. Unemployment, poverty and income inequality rose, while fertility levels and individual health deteriorated, and suicide and crime rates climbed. With economic growth returning and living standards rising, some of the initial symptoms of the transition crisis have passed. However, inherent risks of capitalism like unemployment and other forms of social exclusion have become persistent threats to individual welfare and social cohesion.

This chapter assumes that, with the move towards a market economy, individual labour market position becomes a central determinant of individual life chances. Smooth labour market integration and protection against labour market risks are therefore central for individual welfare, particularly in times of rapid change. The chapter therefore focuses on the emerging labour market risks and inequalities after the breakdown of socialism, most notably the risks of unemployment and poverty as well as income inequality. Furthermore, it provides a more general overview of the development of social protection and the welfare state, with a particular focus on active and passive labour market policies. Compared to Western and Southern European Union (EU) member states, the chapter seeks to draw attention to salient problem constellations in the CEE countries as well as the policy responses that have emerged.

The rest of the chapter is structured as follows. It begins with a brief overview of the system of social protection inherited from socialism in view of the main challenges facing social policy makers with the transition to a market economy. The subsequent sections provide an overview of where the CEE countries stand today relative to old EU member states in terms of levels and distribution of material welfare and labour market risks. Next, main reform trends in the area of social policy are discussed. The remainder of the chapter will address main trends and cross-country differences in active labour market policy and unemployment benefit provision.

Social policy under communism

The post-communist accession countries inherited an extensive system of social protection shaped after the Soviet model, in which a paternalist state assumed responsibility for taking care of all the basic needs of the population (Kornai, 1992a; Elster et al, 1998). The main pillars of social policy were a system of cash benefits paid directly by the state (mainly pensions and child allowances), extensive subsidies for basic consumer goods, a large variety of social services provided by enterprises, short-term income replacement benefits contingent on employment (in case of sickness or child birth), and free public healthcare and education. Any needs left unattended were regarded either as principally remediable failures of the planning mechanism or attributed to pathological or anti-social behaviour of individuals. With the state assuming an overarching role, third sector welfare provision was seen as redundant or even subversive, and was therefore discouraged (Sipos and Ringold, 2005).

With the imposition of the Soviet model, formerly independent social insurance systems were absorbed into the state. Social policy was subsequently financed from the state budget. Theoretically, the only source of revenue was direct social insurance contributions paid by employers, but it was left to the discretion of central planning agencies as to how much of the state budget to allocate to social security. No administrative routine existed to record individual contribution history and keep individual accounts (Voirin, 1993). Trade unions played a central role in administering benefits and services to workers (Aidukaite, 2003).

The central objectives of social policy dovetailed with the central economic objective of rapid growth, which required full utilisation of the human capital stock and high fertility rates (Kornai, 1992a). Employment was therefore construed as a civic obligation. Social policy also served an ideological function: it allowed the state to assume the role of a caretaker for

the people and guarantor of economic security. Rather than a right that individuals could claim, social security was interpreted as a gift provided by the state (Offe, 1993; Elster et al, 1998).

Regarding economic objectives, family policy was a central instrument in raising both employment and fertility rates. Traditionally feminised household tasks like care for older people and children were institutionalised in care homes, nurseries and kindergartens, so that more women could take up full-time employment. Maternity and parental leave benefits provided insurance against temporary loss of income due to child birth (Sipos and Ringold, 2005). Furthermore, by Western standards, socialist states provided relatively generous child or family allowances (at least in nominal terms), as an incentive for fertility and to smooth consumption and protect families against poverty. As a percentage of average earnings, the family allowance paid for having two children was substantially higher in Hungary, Czechoslovakia, Poland, Romania and Bulgaria, compared to Sweden, France or West Germany (Atkinson and Micklewright, 1992: Figure 8.1).

Atkinson and Micklewright (1992: 218) conclude in their study on Hungary, Czechoslovakia, Poland and the former USSR that, despite their apparent generosity, the effectiveness of family benefits to reduce poverty was effectively reduced by means testing and other eligibility restrictions. However, regarding raising female employment, the planners achieved their goals: female activity rates were strikingly high. In 1985, the activity rate among women aged 40-44 ranged from 84.7% in Hungary and Poland to 92.4% in Czechoslovakia and 93.3% in Bulgaria (Kornai, 1992a: Table 10.1).

Since planners pursued rapid growth, full employment, and high fertility rates, and sought to provide social security of universal coverage, it appears logical that employment and the workplace were to become central for access to social benefits. Short-term income replacement benefits (sickness, maternity, parental leave) were contingent on employment. Furthermore, employers provided a variety of services, including nurseries and kindergartens, health clinics for general health services, subsidised food, housing and vacation homes (Rein et al, 1997). As employment rates remained high, a large share of the population had access to these benefits and services.[1]

With employment practically and also often constitutionally guaranteed, open unemployment was virtually unknown before the transition. In the former German Democratic Republic (GDR), unemployment insurance legislation was even officially repealed in 1977 as being against the constitutionally guaranteed right to employment. Slovenia, as a former part of Yugoslavia, constitutes an exception where self-managing economic units could not guarantee job security, necessitating protection against unemployment. Furthermore, a limited unemployment insurance system also existed in Hungary before the transition (Voirin, 1993).

Since each individual of working age was normally obliged to be working, there was no perceived need for a universal system of social protection outside the world of work (Atkinson and Micklewright, 1993; Voirin, 1993; Sipos and Ringold, 2005). Most importantly, a comprehensive system of social assistance or poverty relief was lacking because, at least officially, poverty did not exist. If it occurred, poverty was stigmatising for individuals affected by it and dealt with in a discretionary manner by local authorities. Studies reported by Atkinson and Micklewright (1992) indicate that, in the 1980s, poverty according to national poverty lines was relatively low in Czechoslovakia. Around 7.5% of the Czech population was in poverty, while the corresponding figure for Poland ranged between 10%-25% of the population. Within the Soviet Union, poverty rates were lowest in the Baltic states.

While a universal, non-contributory social assistance scheme did not exist, special mention needs to be made of the extensive system of price subsidies lowering the prices of many basic consumer goods, especially food and housing. A World Bank study (quoted in Atkinson and Micklewright, 1992: 160) reveals their enormous fiscal importance for the case of Poland, where they represented around 11% of total gross domestic product (GDP) in 1987.[2] Subsidies were also paid to producers or were implemented as tax concessions. The price subsidies for consumer goods were intended to serve as incentives for workers and to appease their discontent about the increasingly visible shortcomings of the system (for the GDR, see Steiner, 2004).

Altogether, social protection measures were extensive and granted basic economic security to a large share of the population, albeit at a relatively low standard of living (Kornai 1992a, b; Elster et al, 1998). In terms of social expenditure, CEE countries had attained levels comparable to Southern European countries by 1986 (Voirin, 1993: Table 3).[3] The expenditure data do not take into account the extensive system of price subsidies and the in-kind services provided. Altogether, many commentators concluded that social protection under socialism was increased to standards that were fiscally unsustainable given the level of economic development. Citizens had become accustomed to a 'premature welfare state' (Kornai, 1992b), in which benefits and services were provided by a paternalistic state and had no relation to financial contributions made by individuals. While this is likely to have affected people's preferences to rely on the state for individual welfare and social equality (Alesina and Fuchs-Schündeln, 2007), liberal political reformers rejected the overbearing, paternalistic and dictatorial welfare regime of the past in favour of a more liberal ideology of self-reliance (Elster et al, 1998; Aidukaite, 2003).

Reform challenges

With the transition to capitalism, the communist social policy model became incompatible in predictable ways with the new economic order (Offe, 1993; Barr, 2001). It was now confronted with surges of open unemployment and poverty, both inherent risks of capitalism, which in the eyes of communist officials did not exist under the old system. To address these risks, systematic and extensive reforms were necessary. Furthermore, liberalisation of prices brought the system of consumer subsidies to an end. With privatisation of enterprises, it was left to the discretion of the new owners whether to continue to provide extensive 'fringe benefits' like childcare, subsidised housing or healthcare facilities (Offe, 1993).

Privatisation of enterprises and liberalisation of prices set off a predictable chain of events, exposing many individuals to new social risks typical of capitalism and causing the number of claimants of newly introduced benefits to rise rapidly. As product and labour markets began to operate, and government increasingly refrained from bailing out loss-making businesses, efficient, market-oriented production became a matter of economic survival (Kornai, 1992a, b). Hence, employers began to dismiss workers from the over-staffed, formerly state-owned enterprises. Open unemployment emerged in all countries (see Chapter Two, this volume). Simultaneously, as wages began to respond to the forces of supply and demand, wage inequality began to rise. This alone would have increased relative poverty rates, but with declining output, rising unemployment and declining state capacity, both absolute and relative poverty rates were rising (Barr, 2001).

Given official denial of these problems in the past, post-communist governments were facing an 'institutional no-man's land' (Elster et al, 1998: 208). At the same time, the state budget was strained by economic recession, patchy tax compliance and rising informal sector activity, while the number of people in need was rising quickly. The ensuing transformational crisis turned out to be deeper and the resulting unemployment and poverty more persistent than expected (Sipos and Ringold, 2005).

One of the first responses of governments across the CEE countries was to begin paying unemployment benefits as early as 1989 or 1990. Benefits were initially rather high and achieved high coverage rates, but their generosity was reduced rapidly (to be discussed later). Furthermore, they were confronted with the challenge of introducing a means-tested income support system of the last resort to alleviate poverty, particularly among the rising

67

number of long-term unemployed, whose claim to unemployment benefits had expired (Vodopivec et al, 2005). This initially resulted in a 'hodge-podge of subsidies and benefits' (Sipos and Ringold, 2005: 99). As the underlying structural problems persisted, countries had to develop a more coordinated approach. Today, all CEE countries have implemented a tax-financed, means-tested guaranteed minimum income (GMI) scheme, providing income or increasing household income up to a defined poverty line. Furthermore, family benefits play an important role in poverty reduction (Sipos and Ringold, 2005; World Bank, 2007a).

A central element in the successful development of social assistance and unemployment benefits was the strengthening of administrative capacity. in particular, providing earnings-related unemployment benefits or means-tested social assistance is administratively demanding. It requires detailed information on claimants, and complications often arise, for example due to claimants' activities in the shadow economy. Social assistance was one of the first public programmes to be decentralised, in part because local governments can more effectively target benefits to those in need (Barr, 2001). While these administrative difficulties created distortions when the systems were introduced, by the time of EU accession, most of these problems appear to have been overcome (Sipos and Ringold, 2005; World Bank, 2007a).

One of the idiosyncratic features of socialist welfare states was the extensive provision of in-kind services by enterprises. One might have expected that, upon privatisation, firms would find it unprofitable to continue to provide these services. However, Rein et al (1997) argue that such expectations have not been met. For example, a panel study on Polish firms between 1991 and 1993 finds only modest declines in both state-owned and privatised firms, while newly founded business tended to increasingly offer in-kind services. For example, in late 1993, 34% of firms provided childcare, 63% healthcare, 29% housing or housing subsidies and 74% holiday subsidies/resorts (Estrin et al, 1997: 31). While firms tended to divest themselves of services that required extensive infrastructure, like hospitals or kindergartens, other services were likely to remain attractive to managers under capitalism as motivational devices for employees.

Rising wealth, inequality and poverty

How far have living standards developed in the CEE countries since the transition, and to what extent have governments been able to protect their citizens from labour market risks inherent in capitalism? We begin with an overview of the level of economic development as a determinant of living standards, as well as the distribution of income, labour market and poverty risks. The subsequent sections will then address main institutional reform trends, specifically in regard to protection against labour market risks.[4]

Throughout the decline of socialism, the transition to a market economy, and the path towards EU accession, raising individual living standards and catching up with the West have been central concerns in CEE countries (Elster et al, 1998; Heyns, 2005; Kornai, 2006). However, initial hopes of rapid convergence have been disappointed. While GDP per capita grew beyond pre-transition levels in all countries by 2005, only a minority of countries could actually catch up with the EU14 average. In the majority of CEE countries, GDP per capita declined relative to the EU14. Estonia and Poland, initially relatively poor countries, have made significant gains, while the poorest countries at the outset of transition, Bulgaria and Romania, have lost, both relative to the EU14 as well as to the CEE10 average.

During the period from 2000-05, all CEE countries were growing at an average rate significantly above the EU14. In particular, the poorer countries have had impressive growth rates. Growth projections indicate that convergence with Western Europe may be achieved within the next two decades by the Czech Republic and Slovenia (Wagner and Hlouskova, 2005). Furthermore, while economic growth had only inadequately translated into higher employment rates throughout the 1990s and early 2000s (Cazes and Nesporova, 2007), there is preliminary evidence that the association between economic and employment growth has recently been strengthening. In the Baltic countries, employment grew on average by 1% each year between 2002 and 2006, compared to 0.4% growth in the EU14. Estonia was the first CEE country to achieve an employment rate above the EU14 average in 2006 (Eurostat, 2008a). There are similar indications of rising labour demand across the region, and mounting signs of a shortage of skilled workers (Rutkowski, 2007).

An important characteristic of the CEE countries' economies is production in the shadow economy,[5] which provides a source of income for a sizeable portion of the population not captured by official GDP statistics (Table 3.1). The shadow economy is strikingly large in those CEE countries with relatively low GDP, i.e., the Baltic and South-Eastern countries (Schneider, 2006).[6] This pattern may be due to the relatively high payroll contributions for employers that constituted more than 50% of labour costs in some countries in the 1990s (to be discussed later). While providing income for many, the large shadow economy also has negative aggregate welfare consequences, for example because a smaller tax base reduces the quality and quantity of publicly provided goods and services (Schneider and Burger, 2005).

By the time of EU accession, CEE countries have embarked on growth paths leading to higher living standards for the population. However, this rising wealth is also increasingly unequally distributed among the population, which may imply that only certain segments of the population profit from economic growth, while others have stagnated or lost out. As the following paragraphs show, income and regional inequality have been rising substantially in some countries in the 1990s and the first half of the 2000s. In particular the least skilled individuals are occupying increasingly precarious positions in the labour market.

Table 3.1: Levels and trends of material welfare

	GDP per capita		GDP per capita relative to EU14 average		Average growth rate of real GDP, %		Shadow economy, % of GDP
	1990	2005	1990	2005	1991-99	2000-05	2002-03
EE	8,897	13,770	0.44	0.51	0.13	8.03	40.1
LV	9,418	12,141	0.46	0.45	−1.93	8.85	41.3
LT	11,585	12,895	0.57	0.47	−3.08	7.61	32.6
PL	7,338	12,319	0.36	0.45	3.67	3.43	28.9
CZ	14,712	18,272	0.72	0.67	0.08	3.73	20.1
SK	10,981	14,120	0.54	0.52	0.15	4.43	20.2
HU	11,591	15,913	0.57	0.58	0.57	4.74	26.2
SI	13,975	19,815	0.69	0.73	1.77	3.42	29.4
RO	6,764	8,060	0.33	0.30	−1.56	5.76	37.4
BG	6,673	8,036	0.33	0.30	−1.71	6.05	38.3
CEE10	*10,193*	*13,534*	*0.50*	*0.50*	*−0.19*	*5.60*	*31.5*
EU14	*20,372*	*27,213*	*1.00*	*1.00*	*2.09*	*1.84*	*18.2*
ES	17,554	24,171	0.86	0.89	2.25	2.04	22.0
GR	14,541	20,801	0.71	0.76	1.35	4.06	28.2
IT	21,701	25,381	1.07	0.93	1.33	0.64	25.7
PT	14,105	18,158	0.69	0.67	2.48	0.58	21.9
DE	21,303	26,210	1.05	0.96	1.62	1.07	16.8
SE	22,526	28,936	1.11	1.06	1.33	2.27	18.3
UK	21,605	29,571	1.06	1.09	2.08	2.19	12.2

Note: GDP per capita, purchasing power parity (PPP) in constant 2000 international US $.
Source: World Bank (2007b); Schneider (2006: Table 6.5); own calculations

Under socialism, wages were centrally planned in accordance with wage norms that privileged arduous, physical labour but that also rewarded gradations by seniority, managerial authority and levels of education. According to Flemming and Micklewright (1999), earnings inequality in the CEE countries approached levels found in OECD (Organisation for Economic Co-operation and Development) countries in 1989. For the individual distribution of per capita household income in 1989, they report the lowest Gini coefficient for Czechoslovakia (20), and the highest for Estonia (28). The average for the OECD countries at the time was 30 (Flemming and Micklewright, 1999: 869).[7]

In the course of transition, income inequality grew substantially, which was in part a 'healthy' sign of a functioning market mechanism rewarding scarce skills (Barr, 2001), but which also meant polarisation of individual living chances (Milanovic, 1999). The withdrawal of consumer subsidies particularly affected the real incomes of the poorer segments of the population. Unfortunately, data on inequality of wealth are not available, and the reliability of common sources for aggregate statistics on income inequality is disputed, as are the causal factors explaining the rise in monetary inequality (e.g. Flemming and Micklewright, 1999; Heyns, 2005).

Income inequality continued to increase in most CEE countries in the 2000s. Between 2000 and 2006, Hungary and Latvia have witnessed particularly strong increases, followed by Lithuania, Romania and Poland. In contrast to the other two Baltic states, income inequality has declined in Estonia. Considering two measures of income inequality and two time points in the 2000s,[8] there appears to be on average little difference in income inequality between the old and new member states, indicating that convergence has taken place in this regard. Slovenia emerges as the country with the most equal income distribution. Inequality is similarly low in the Czech Republic, Slovakia, Bulgaria, Germany and Sweden. In contrast, income inequality appears to be highest in the Baltic countries, as well as in Greece and Portugal.

To explain rising wage inequality, it has been suggested for the Polish case that technological change has induced a demand shift away from unskilled, manual workers towards workers with tertiary education. Evidence consistent with this explanation are rapidly increasing wages of tertiary-educated workers, while wages for workers with primary education are declining (Newell and Socha, 2007). A similar argument has been made to explain increasing earnings inequality in Hungary (Kezdi, 2002). Table 3.2 shows that, on average, tertiary-educated workers in CEE countries earn 95% more than individuals with lower-secondary or less education, while the corresponding figure is only 58% in Western Europe. Hence, education seems to be an important factor explaining income inequalities in CEE countries.

Table 3.2: Distribution of income and unemployment risks

	Quintile ratio		Gini coefficient		ISCED 5-6/ ISCED 0-2 income ratio	ISCED 5-6 / ISCED 0-2 unemployment rate ratio		Dispersion of regional GDP	
	2000	2006	2000	2006	2006	~2001	~2006	~1995	2004
EE	6.3	5.5	36	33	0.67	2.6	3.3	31.5	43.5
LV	5.5	7.9	34	39	1.34	3.7	4.9	35.5	52.9
LT	5.0	6.3	31	35	1.17	4.0	3.2	11.1	22.2
PL	4.7	5.6	30	33	1.35	4.1	3.9	30.2	29.7
CZ	3.4	3.5	25	25	0.71	8.1	11.9	16.6	24.9
SK	–	4.0	–	28	0.52	7.5	15.3	28.3	29.1
HU	3.3	5.5	26	33	1.04	11.7	5.6	31.4	37.6
SI	3.2	3.4	22	24	0.77	4.9	2.5	19.0	21.6
RO	4.5	5.3	29	33	–	1.9	2.4	22.3	27.4
BG	3.7	3.5	25	24	–	4.5	5.8	24.5	29.4
CEE10	*4.3*	*4.8*	*29*	*31*	*0.95*	*5.3*	*5.9*	*24.7*	*32.7*
EU14	*4.4*	*4.6*	*28*	*29*	*0.58*	*3.2*	*3.3*	*21.5*	*23.3*
ES	5.4	5.3	32	31	0.61	1.5	1.7	20.0	19.2
GR	5.8	6.1	33	34	0.90	1.2	1.1	24.2	26.9
IT	4.8	5.5	29	32	0.74	1.5	1.3	25.5	25.1
PT	6.4	6.8	36	38	1.52	1.4	1.1	26.6	27.3
DE	3.5	4.1	25	27	0.44	3.4	6.3	28.8	29.1
SE	3.4	3.5	24	24	0.17	4.6	4.6	11.7	15.7
UK	5.2	5.4	32	32	0.65	4.5	4.3	19.8	27.3

Notes: See footnotes 7 and 8 at the end of the chapter. Ratio of unemployment rates: values from ~2006 are from 2004 for Estonia and 2005 for Latvia and Lithuania, sample of 18- to 64-year-olds. Dispersion of regional GDP: values in ~1995 are from 2000 for Poland, Greece and 1998 for Romania; averages exclude Romania, Poland, Greece. Dispersion of regional GDP at NUTS (Nomenclature of Territorial Units for Statistics) level 3 is measured by the sum of the absolute differences between regional and national GDP per inhabitant, weighted with the share of population and expressed in percentage of the national GDP per inhabitant.
Source: Eurostat (2008a); own calculations

Individual differences in education are also central determinants of differences in individual unemployment risks. Table 3.2 indicates that, in the majority of CEE countries, the distribution of unemployment risks by levels of education has also become more unequal in the 2000s. In 2006, individuals with low levels of educational attainment (ISCED 2 or less) were over 15 times more likely to be unemployed than individuals with tertiary (ISCED 5-6) degrees in a sample of individuals aged 15-39 in Slovakia. Similar levels of inequality are found in the Czech Republic. In both countries, there has also been a significant upward trend from levels which had already been among the highest in the countries studied here in 2001. Interestingly, while we observed a stark increase in income inequality in Hungary, inequality of unemployment risk was simultaneously declining. Also Estonia and Romania, which are characterised by relatively high income inequality, have rather low inequality in terms of unemployment risks.

Communist planners' attempts to reduce inequalities not only resulted in lower wage inequality, but also, by moving jobs to people, in lower regional inequality (Heyns, 2005). With the closure of large enterprises in 'one-company towns' and declines in agriculture in the course of transition (Schneider and Burger, 2005), regional inequality in CEE countries has grown substantially beyond average levels found in Western European countries (Table 3.2, see also Heidenreich and Wunder, 2007). The dispersion of regional GDP has increased remarkably in Estonia and Latvia, where regional inequality is highest among the European countries considered here. In the group of Central European countries, regional inequality has increased in the Czech Republic and Hungary. Bornhorst and Commander (2006), as well as Fidrmuc (2004), find that cross-regional migration has remained very low and hardly played a role in equilibrating regional unemployment and wage differentials in the Central European countries and Romania. Hence, in the course of restructuring, regional differences have grown and become highly persistent over time. For individuals from disadvantaged regions, lack of information about labour market opportunities as well as affordable housing for rent seems to impair mobility (Bornhorst and Commander, 2006).

In the course of transition, falling output, rising wage inequality and deteriorating state capacity contributed to rising poverty risks for the population. The increase in poverty was larger and more persistent than expected, and it affected individuals, who were educated and accustomed to stable employment and economic security prior to transition. In general, low levels of education, (long-term) unemployment, large household size and rural location emerged as central predictors of poverty. Furthermore, the Roma population, which is sizeable in the Czech Republic, Slovakia, Hungary, Romania and Bulgaria, faces extremely high poverty risks (Sipos and Ringold, 2005; World Bank, 2007a).

Table 3.3 compares different measures of economic deprivation. The World Bank estimates of absolute poverty in transition countries, i.e., the share of the population that lives under PPP $2.15 a day, are meant to capture the share of the population deprived of even their most basic needs. The higher threshold (PPP $4.30 a day) indicates the share of the population that is vulnerable to poverty in case of economic downturn (World Bank, 2005).

Table 3.3: Poverty rates and long-term unemployment

	Absolute poverty (%)		Relative poverty (%) (2006)		Relative poverty after transfers (%) (2006)		Long-term unemployed (%)	
	$2.15/ day	$4.30/ day	Before transfers	After transfers	ISCED 0-2	ISCED 5-6	2000	2006
EE	4	27	25	18	16	6	44	39
LV	3	18	28	23	26	4	52	30
LT	4	30	27	20	18	2	48	38
PL	3	27	29	19	16	2	41	51
CZ	0	1	22	10	9	1	46	49
SK	3	9	20	12	11	3	52	72
HU	0	2	30	16	16	2	45	42
SI	0	1	24	12	13	2	54	43
RO	4	33	24	19	–	–	48	55
BG	12	58	17	14	–	–	58	51
CEE10	*3*	*21*	*25*	*16*	*16*	*3*	*49*	*47*
EU14	*–*	*–*	*26*	*16*	*11*	*4*	*33*	*29*
ES	–	–	24	20	18	4	39	15
GR	–	–	23	21	16	5	56	53
IT	–	–	24	20	15	4	61	48
PT	–	–	25	18	11	2	36	41
DE	–	–	26	13	10	5	40	45
SE	–	–	29	12	6	7	22	11
UK	–	–	30	19	17	6	23	18

Notes: Absolute poverty rates in US $ PPP, data for Estonia, Latvia, Lithuania, Poland and Romania from 2002, Bulgaria from 2003 (World Bank, 2005). Absolute poverty rates for Czech Rebulic and Slovakia from 1997, Slovenia from 1998 (World Bank, 2000). Relative poverty rates indicate the share of individuals with an equivalised disposable income, before/after social transfers, below 60% of the national median equivalised disposable income after social transfers. Pensions are counted as income before transfers and not as social transfers. Long-term unemployed are the share of unemployed who have been unemployed 12 months or more (individuals aged 15-39).
Source: Absolute poverty rates from World Bank (2000, 2005); other indicators from Eurostat (2008a); own calculations

Absolute poverty is highest in those countries with the lowest GDP, Romania and Bulgaria, and virtually absent in the most developed CEE countries. Absolute poverty correlates highly with the level of economic development. The transformational recession and subsequent growth have been central in first increasing and then reducing this form of poverty across CEE countries. However, the coinciding rise of income inequality implied that in some countries the income for richer segments of the population was growing, while there were income declines among the poor. This appears to have been the case in Poland, where absolute poverty actually increased between 1998 and 2002, and possibly Lithuania, where no clear trend was visible, despite rising GDP per capita observed in both countries. In contrast, in Romania, absolute poverty declined over the same period, as income rose for rich and poor alike (World Bank, 2000, 2005).

Relative income poverty measures reflect the share of the population that is below a given income threshold, here 60% of the median income (Eurostat, 2008a). By construction, they are a measure of income inequality in the bottom half of the income distribution focusing on the share of the population unable to afford the living standard of the majority of the society. Comparing pre- and post-transfer changes in relative poverty rates provides an indicator about the extent to which social and tax policy succeeds in reducing the share of people with relatively low incomes.

For example, Poland and Hungary have the highest pre-transfer poverty rates, but they achieve a reduction by more than 10 percentage points through taxes and social transfers. In contrast, Latvia and Lithuania achieve a lower reduction of poverty risks from initially similarly high levels, which results in relatively higher poverty rates after transfers compared to Poland and Hungary. The Czech Republic, Slovakia and Slovenia emerge as the CEE countries with lowest post-transfer poverty rates. Regarding the distribution of poverty risks after transfers by level of education, the less educated are about 5.7 times as likely to be poor than the tertiary educated in CEE countries, while in the old member states the less educated are only 2.7 times as likely to be poor compared to the tertiary educated. This mirrors the finding for education-dependent unemployment rate and income differences.

Finally, long-term unemployment is an important poverty risk factor that is prevalent in several CEE countries. While in 2006, 47% of the unemployed were looking for a job for more than a year in the CEE countries, the corresponding figure for the EU14 is only 29%. Slovakia experienced an almost 20-percentage point increase in the share of long-term unemployed among total unemployment between 2000 and 2006, reaching 72%. Long-term unemployment has also become more prevalent in Poland and Romania. It is worrying that these rises in the shares of long-term unemployed occurred in Poland and Slovakia, despite declines in the overall unemployment rate. In contrast, long-term unemployment declined in the Baltic countries, as well as in Slovenia and Bulgaria.

Institutional reform trends and outcomes

Under socialism, there was no need for workers to insure themselves against labour market risks. They could take lifetime employment as well as the provision of workplace benefits and services for granted. The transition to capitalism therefore not only meant new risks for individuals, but also required a profound reorientation in the understanding of economic and social security. Instead of handing out state gifts, governments faced the challenge to build fiscally sustainable institutions addressing the new risks, collectively financed by employers and employees.

Yet at the time of transition, governments were facing a more fundamental set of problems. The entire institutional structure of the polity and the economy had to be reconstructed, a task that has been likened to 'rebuilding the ship at sea' (Elster et al, 1998). Before engaging in fundamental welfare state reforms, governments had to deal with more pressing constitutional, legal and economic reforms. Apart from introducing unemployment benefits and a variety of ad hoc emergency measures to address the rising poverty rates, governments usually attempted to ensure that the existing schemes (e.g. pensions, healthcare) remained somewhat functional (e.g. Offe, 1993; Elster et al, 1998; Aidukaite, 2003).

By the mid-1990s, most CEE countries had taken substantial steps towards privatisation and liberalisation, and had succeeded in reigning inflation rates back in. Political actors became increasingly embedded in a variety of international networks, which exerted in part a contrary influence on the choice of social policy reform path (Manning, 2004). International money-lending institutions like the World Bank or the International Monetary Fund (IMF) preferred liberal policies, advocating fiscal restraint while mainly focusing social policy on targeted poverty relief. These presumably bore greater leverage, if securing loans was crucial and/or indebtedness to the respective institution was high (Offe, 1993; Deacon, 2000). Nevertheless, there was also substantial domestic support for a liberal reform approach: the inherited social policy apparatus was viewed as too heavy a burden for the consolidating economy, especially in the face of pressures on the social budget resulting from problems in collecting taxes and a large shadow economy. Furthermore, liberal reforms were construed as a desirable break with the 'culture of dependency' nurtured by decades under communist state paternalism (Elster et al, 1998; Aidukaite, 2006), as well as the fiscal naiveté regarding the costs of social security (Kornai, 1997).

In contrast, reformers and citizens drawn towards Western European standards favoured an institutionalised welfare state, as found in Scandinavia or Germany, with an emphasis on redistribution. On the one hand, social policy under communism had clearly striven towards universal access and strong redistribution, similar to Scandinavian welfare states, which has shaped preferences of individuals (e.g. Alesina and Fuchs-Schündeln, 2007). On the other hand, several path dependency arguments can be invoked in favour of the Continental European conservative welfare model: for example, benefit provision was linked to employment and occupational status already under communism, aiming to reproduce the socio-economic status of workers on retirement (Sipos and Ringold, 2005). The close link between employment, earnings and benefit receipt under communism could be easily reproduced in insurance-based, earnings-related benefits (Deacon, 2000). Furthermore, before socialism, the Central European countries, notably those formerly part of the Austro-Hungarian Empire, had already developed Bismarckian social insurance institutions (Offe, 1993; Elster et al, 1998). Finally, in keeping with both conservative and Scandinavian models, the practice of financing social security in part by employer contributions already existed under socialism, and could readily be converted into contribution-based financing of social insurance funds under capitalism.

Despite extensive debate, progress was only made slowly (Kornai, 1997). Reform leaders in this area were the Central European countries (Manning, 2004). Romania and Bulgaria lagged behind because political actors, despite declining resources, attempted to conserve the existing system until the mid- to late-1990s (Sotiropoulos et al., 2003).

It is frequently argued that the path towards EU accession provided another stimulus for social policy reform (Guillen and Palier, 2004; Barr, 2005). EU legislation, like the acquis communautaire, the Stability and Growth Pact and Convergence criteria, as well as the Copenhagen criteria clearly impinges on the member governments' freedom and may indirectly constrain their social policy choices. For example, requirements of budgetary balance may act as a restraint on welfare spending (Barr, 2005). Furthermore, through the open method of coordination (OMC) monitoring, benchmarking and policy learning in the area of social inclusion are promoted. Through OMC measures, governments make public their performance in 'touchy' areas such as child poverty and social inequality, and submit themselves to cross-national comparisons and peer review. Nevertheless, cooperation in this process is voluntary, and member states who do not achieve certain standards cannot be sanctioned. EU legislation also does not impose binding requirements regarding core issues of social protection, like the generosity of benefits (Scharpf, 2002). At the same time, however, CEE countries voluntarily adopted many social policy examples from Western European countries. Particularly during the transition phase, there was no time to experiment and political actors were inclined to copy welfare state institutions that appeared to function well in Western European countries (Elster et al, 1998).

While Western examples were clearly influential, the enormous dynamism observed renders any conclusion about the emergent type of welfare capitalism (Esping-Andersen) in Eastern Europe tentative or premature. Extreme collapses in output severely constrained social policy options at the beginning of the transition. Policy makers could often only react to social problems created by the transformational recession. Retrenchment in certain areas was necessary given declining government revenue and to facilitate economic reform. It need not imply the embrace of the liberal welfare model. Different commentators also point to mistakes and trial-and-error reform processes at the time (Offe, 1993; Boeri, 1997; Kornai, 1997). After the economies returned to growth paths, rising wealth has increased reform options, but the scale of problems has also increased. Unemployment and poverty, population ageing and declining fertility have created new demands for reform.

Refering to the late 1990s, Deacon (2000) argues that the CEE countries themselves were undecided as to what welfare model they wanted to realise given their specific domestic problems, constraints and opportunities. A case in point: in Estonia, a major reversal in the area of unemployment insurance occurred in 2001. After more than a decade of granting very low, flat-rate unemployment benefits, typical of liberal welfare states, the Estonian government has implemented a two-tiered unemployment insurance similar to Germany, with a first tier granting contribution-financed, earnings-related benefits and a second tier granting tax-financed, flat-rate unemployment assistance (see Chapter Six for more details). In effect, the Estonian unemployment insurance was transformed from the least generous among the CEE countries in the 1990s to one of the most generous in the 2000s.

To conclude, the following section will summarise main trends in aggregate social protection financing and expenditure. The subsequent section will then address in more detail the institutional outcomes of the reform process in the areas of active and passive labour market policy. In the area of unemployment insurance, the dynamicity of institutional structures in the course of transition will be described.

Social protection expenditure and financing in CEE countries

Countries with a higher level of economic development tend to spend more on social protection (Wilensky, 2002). This well-known relationship holds when comparing the CEE countries to each other, as well as to the EU14. The cross-sectional correlation between GDP per capita in 2005 (Table 3.1) and social expenditure per inhabitant in purchasing power standards (PPS) in 2005 (Table 3.4) is above 0.9, when considering only the CEE countries as well as when considering the full sample of countries.

Table 3.4: Social protection expenditure and financing

	Expenditure on social protection			Receipts of social protection schemes by source (%), 2005			Employer contributions (% of labour costs)	
	2000	2005	Relative to EU14[a]	Em-ployer	Indi-viduals	Gov't.	~2000	~2005
	as % of GDP							
EE	14.0	12.5	0.25	79.0	0.4	20.4	25.5	25.3
LV	15.3	12.4	0.20	47.1	16.9	35.3	22.4	20.7
LT	15.8	13.2	0.23	53.8	6.0	39.6	27.6	28.1
PL	19.7	19.6	0.32	28.0	22.3	39.2	16.2	16.6
CZ	19.5	19.1	0.47	54.3	26.4	18.1	26.6	26.2
SK	19.3	16.9	0.32	62.0	22.4	14.0	26.2	23.7
HU	19.3	21.9	0.45	42.0	15.9	34.8	30.3	27.4
SI	24.6	23.4	0.65	27.4	40.0	31.7	14.1	13.2
RO	13.2	14.2	0.16	49.7	23.5	11.7	29.9	25.0
BG	–	16.1	0.18	42.4	18.3	36.1	25.8	24.0
CEE10	*17.9*	*17.0*	*0.32*	*49.2*	*18.8*	*29.1*	*24.5*	*23.0*
EU14	*25.4*	*27.0*	*1.00*	*36.2*	*19.4*	*39.3*	*22.9*	*23.0*
ES	20.3	20.8	0.69	48.9	15.6	33.3	24.5	24.9
GR	23.5	24.2	0.74	35.5	22.9	30.7	22.9	21.7
IT	24.7	26.4	0.89	41.7	15.3	41.4	29.5	–
PT	21.7	24.7	0.57	31.7	15.7	42.2	19.4	21.2
DE	29.3	29.4	1.08	35.0	27.7	35.6	23.3	23.1
SE	30.7	32.0	1.23	41.0	8.8	48.0	29.6	30.6
UK	26.9	26.8	1.03	32.4	15.5	50.5	15.7	18.4

Notes: [a]Social protection expenditure per inhabitant in PPS as percentage of unweighted EU14 average in 2005. All values for Portugal from 2004. See Eurostat (2008b) for detailed information on accounting of expenditure and revenue items. Receipts of social protection schemes comprise social contributions, general government contributions and other receipts (not shown). Employers social contributions: costs incurred by employers to secure entitlement to social benefits for their employees, former employees and their dependants; values in ~2000 are from 2002 for Bulgaria, from 2001 for Italy; values in ~2005 are from 2004 for Austria, 2003 for Greece; data for Ireland was unavailable.
Source: Eurostat (2008a); own calculations

If the CEE countries follow a similar path of welfare state development as the old EU member states after the Second World War, then it is to be expected that sustained economic growth will also translate into an expansion of the welfare state in the CEE countries.

Nevertheless, in 2005, the CEE countries were clearly less generous than the EU14 in terms of social expenditure per inhabitant. While CEE average per capita GDP amounted to 50% of the EU14 average in 2005, they spent only a third per inhabitant of what the average EU14 country spent. Romania and Bulgaria spent the least, while Slovenia spent the most relative to the EU-14 average. Considering trends, East and West seem to have moved in opposite directions between 2000 and 2005: while average expenditure levels declined by 0.9 percentage points in the CEE countries, they rose by 1.6 percentage points in the EU14.

Considering social protection receipts, employers tend to contribute more in the East than in the West. Except for Poland and Slovenia, the relative share of social protection revenues from employers is close to or substantially exceeds 50%. In particular in Estonia and Lithuania, the contributions of insured individuals comprise a very small portion of overall receipts. In the 1990s, the percentage of total labour costs due to social insurance contributions from employers was extremely high in some CEE countries. In 1993, employers' payroll contributions amounted to 42% of total labour costs in Bulgaria, 49.5% in the Czech Republic, 50% in Slovakia and 63% in Hungary (Elster et al, 1998: Table 6.3). While employer financing of social insurance played a major role in the acute transition crisis, when benefit claims were rapidly rising while tax revenues declined, their contributions have been declining since then. By 2005, average employers' payroll contributions share for CEE countries had converged to average levels also found in Western Europe. However, employer payroll contributions remain relatively high in Lithuania and Hungary. In contrast, Slovenia relies more strongly on financing from insured individuals, thereby keeping payroll contributions for employers relatively low.

Social protection against labour market risks

With the change of political regime and economic transformation, employment security had effectively ended. To remain competitive on capitalist markets, managers of overstaffed, formerly state-owned companies began to dismiss workers. Governments used different strategies to address the looming unemployment crisis (Elster et al, 1998). They reduced the extent of layoffs by slowly and gradually hardening firms' budget constraints or by lowering wages. Furthermore, labour supply was reduced by awarding early retirement or disability pensions. Most importantly, however, governments introduced income support programmes and programmes aimed at the re-employment of unemployed workers.

Introduction of unemployment insurance

The introduction of the unemployment benefit system was often one of the first reform steps taken by the new governments.[9] Initial systems were remarkably similar in several regards. All countries used payroll contributions from employers and employees to finance the system. Furthermore, all countries granted earnings-related benefits. In the initial arrangements, no or very high benefit ceilings as well as rather high minimum benefit levels were fixed. Estonia and Latvia are exceptions in this regard. In Estonia, flat-rate benefits at 60% of the minimum wage were granted. In Latvia, benefits were fixed between minimally 90% and maximally 140% of the minimum wage.[10]

Eligibility criteria were initially rather wide, often also encompassing non-contributing groups, such as school leavers (e.g. in Poland, the Czech Republic, Slovakia, Hungary and Bulgaria). Typically, workers had to have spent 9-12 months in employment over a reference period from 12-36 months. Benefits were paid for initially up to two years in Hungary and Slovenia, but only up to six months in Estonia, Latvia, Romania, and Bulgaria. While Estonia introduced the least generous system, the most generous system was introduced in Poland, where initially no minimum contribution periods were imposed, benefit levels could be up to 100% of the average wage, and they were initially granted for an unlimited duration.[11]

As unemployment rose to double figures in some countries and became more persistent than expected, budgetary pressures resulted in substantial reductions of benefit generosity within one or two years after their introduction. Eligibility requirements were tightened, statutory replacement rates and benefit minima and maxima lowered, and payment duration shortened. In particular in Poland, the system was scaled back substantially in all of the dimensions mentioned. In 1997, earnings-related benefits were abolished and flat-rate benefit payments, similar to the UK, were introduced. The other countries continued offering earnings-related benefits, but relatively low benefit ceilings in some countries (e.g. Latvia, the Czech Republic and Bulgaria) substantially diminished the actual benefit replacement rates for higher wage earners.

The administrative implementation of earnings-related unemployment benefits was a challenge in the early years of transition. Public employment services were severely understaffed compared to Western standards (Boeri,

1997), which for example led to difficulties in monitoring benefit recipients' compliance with job search requirements (Boeri, 1997; Vodopivec et al, 2005).

Different eligibility requirements, payment duration and implementation problems resulted in widely varying shares of registered unemployed actually receiving benefits. In 1994, 93% of the registered unemployed received benefits (including unemployment assistance) in Hungary, while the corresponding figure for Bulgaria and Estonia was only 23% and 30%, respectively (Vodopivec et al, 2005). The early reforms resulted in substantial reductions in coverage rates across most countries. As long-term unemployment was rising across the region, more and more individuals exhausted their entitlement to unemployment benefits and, usually, had to rely on means-tested social assistance benefits.

Evaluation of unemployment benefit programmes

Much of the literature has focused on the disincentive effects of unemployment benefit, i.e., the prolongation of individual unemployment spells. Along these lines, several studies using micro-data find that a longer duration of benefit payments is associated with longer unemployment spells (e.g. Adamchik, 1999 for Poland; Ham et al, 1998 and Terrell and Sorm, 1999 for the Czech Republic; van Ours and Vodopivec, 2006 for Slovenia). For Slovakia, Lubyova and van Ours (1998, 1999) find insignificant effects of benefit receipt on the exit rate from unemployment to employment, consistent with the findings of Ham et al (1999). Furthermore, the restrictions in the generosity of unemployment benefit in the early 1990s did not seem to raise the outflows from unemployment to employment (Micklewright and Nagy, 1996 for Hungary; Puhani, 2000 for Poland; Boeri, 1997 for a review). Furthermore, no consistent effect of benefit levels on the length of unemployment spells could be documented (e.g. Ham et al, 1998 and Terrell and Sorm, 1999 for the Czech Republic).

Van Ours and Vodopivec (2006) exploit changes in unemployment insurance legislation in Slovenia in 1998 (see Chapter Thirteen, this volume) to assess the effect of changes in the generosity of unemployment benefit on the duration of individual unemployment spells and quality of post-unemployment jobs. They find evidence that the reduction in benefit payment duration as well as reductions in benefit levels in Slovenia in 1998 increased outflows to employment among those affected. Furthermore, while this restriction increased job-finding rates among the unemployed, the quality of post-unemployment jobs has not been affected (van Ours and Vodopivec, 2006).

In conclusion, longer benefit payment durations appear to be associated with longer unemployment spells, while, except for the Slovenia case, no consistent effect of benefit levels unemployment duration has been reported (see also Atkinson and Micklewright, 1991 for Western countries). Ham et al (1998) conclude that unemployment benefit systems did not seem to generate major distortions in the labour market, but that labour demand and individual skill levels are more important determinants of unemployment spell (see also Lubyova and van Ours, 1998, 1999; Boeri and Terrell, 2002). Other authors have suggested that because of low outflow rates from unemployment to employment in some CEE countries throughout the 1990s, many individuals quickly exhausted their claims to unemployment benefit and then had to rely on social assistance. Since social assistance benefits have not always been well targeted or were not adjusted to lower costs of living in certain regions, individuals in certain household constellations experienced real income gains, taking into consideration that social assistance status also often involves access to various in-kind benefits (Boeri and Edwards, 1998; Boeri and Terrell, 2002).

Unemployment insurance in 2007

The following section gives a brief overview of the organisation of unemployment insurance as well as the generosity of unemployment benefits in the CEE countries, focusing on the first (and for most countries only) tier of the unemployment insurance system.[12] As of 2007, Estonia is the only CEE country that operates a two-tier scheme similar to that in Germany, with a first tier granting contribution-financed, earnings-related benefits (introduced in 2001) and a second tier granting tax-financed, flat-rate benefits.

All CEE countries operate compulsory unemployment insurance systems, which are mainly financed from employers' and employees' payroll contributions, while the state usually covers deficits and/or pays contributions on behalf of some assimilated groups (e.g. recipients of maternity benefit in Latvia). In Lithuania, employees do not contribute, while in Slovenia the state provides 90% of the financing. In most countries the contributions by employers are larger than the contributions by employees. Except for Poland, all CEE countries provide earnings-related benefits. However, each country imposes ceilings (and sometimes floors) on benefits, either by defining ceilings for the actual benefits or for the assessment base (i.e. the amount of prior earnings) from which they are calculated. In some countries, these ceilings yield actual replacement rates for average wage earners, which are substantially below the statutory (legally fixed) replacement rate. In general, all employees are covered, as long as they fulfil the contribution requirements. The self-employed are also covered, except for in Latvia and Bulgaria, but their treatment differs across countries. Furthermore, in Latvia, Lithuania and Hungary, some non-contributing groups are also covered.

The main determinants of benefit generosity are their level and their accessibility. Both are designed to reflect the diverse living circumstances and employment histories of the insured. To compare benefit systems cross-nationally, we calculate all variable aspects affecting benefit levels for a pre-defined reference individual, which is, following standard OECD (2007) methodology, a 40-year-old single male, with no children, who has been employed and has paid contributions continuously for the past 22 years, and who has earned an average wage prior to unemployment.[13]

Countries enact a variety of constraints to benefit entitlement, such as minimum periods of employment, during which contributions have to be paid, or waiting periods after registering as unemployed until receipt of the first benefit payment. Furthermore, benefits are only paid for a limited duration. The latter particularly affects the long-term unemployed, who exhaust their claim to unemployment benefit and then have to rely on means-tested social assistance. The most restrictive contribution requirements are found in Lithuania and Slovakia, where individuals must have been employed and paying contributions for three out of the past four years (Slovakia) or 18 months in the past three years (Lithuania). The Latvian system is least restrictive, requiring only nine months of employment and contribution payments in the past year. The use of waiting days to restrict entitlement is less prevalent in CEE countries. However, upon registering as unemployed, individuals who were summarily dismissed or who are voluntarily unemployed, have to wait two months in Latvia, three months in Lithuania and 90 days in Hungary to receive benefits.

In terms of benefit levels, statutory replacement rates vary between 10% and 70% of prior earnings. The reference base for calculation is usually gross earnings. In Romania and Lithuania, benefits are comprised of a fixed and a variable amount. In Romania, the fixed amount is set at 75% of the minimum wage plus 10% of prior earnings. In Lithuania, a more complicated formula is used and the replacement rates given here are approximations: roughly, benefits are calculated from a fixed amount, which is defined by the government at around 30% of the minimum wage, to which a variable amount, around 40% of prior earnings, is added. In Bulgaria, special rules apply for individuals, who were summarily dismissed or who are voluntarily unemployed: they receive the minimum benefit, fixed at approximately 50% of the minimum wage in 2006.

Table 3.5: Unemployment insurance benefits for reference individual 2006/07

	Employment (E) and contribution (C) requirements	Waiting period	Replacement rate			Duration of payment	Coverage rate[c] (%)
			Statutory[a]	% of av. wage[b]	% of min. wage[b]		
EE	E + C: 12 months in past 3 years	7 days	50/40	0.46	1.48	360 days	0.44
LV	E + C: 9 months in past year	0/2 months[d]	60/45	0.53	1.76	9 months	0.50
LT	E + C: 18 months in past 3 years	0/3 months[d]	~40e/~20[e]	~0.41	1.11	6 months	0.22
PL	E + C: 12 months in past 18 months	7 days	flat rate	0.24	0.64	6 months[f]	0.13
CZ	E + C: 12 months in past 3 years	0	50/45	0.48	0.97	6 months	0.28
SK	E + C: 36 months in past 4 years	0	50	0.50	1.60	6 months	0.31
HU	E + C: 12 months in past 4 years	0/90 days[d]	60/flat rate	0.28	0.73	270 days	0.23
SI	E + C: 12 months in past 18 months	0	70/60	0.60	1.32	9 months	0.22
RO	E + C: 12 months in past 2 years	0	10[e]	0.32	1.09	12 months	0.41
BG	E + C: 9 months in past 15 months	0	60	0.60	0.75	11/4[d] months	0.20
IT	E + C: 12 months in past 2 years	8 days	50	0.46	n.a.	210 days	–
DE	E + C: 12 months in past 3 years	0	60	0.60	n.a.	12 months	0.25
SE	E: 6 months in past year, C: 12 months	5 days	80	0.60	n.a.	300 days	–
UK	C: fixed minimum amount of contribution payments within past 2 years	3 days	flat-rate	0.10	0.28	182 days	–

Notes: [a]Statutory replacement rate for months 1-3/4-6 of benefit receipt, 100 days/80 days for Estonia; [b]average monthly amount of unemployment benefit for the first six months of benefit receipt for reference individual as percentage of average monthly wage (see footnote 13)/minimum wage; [c]the percentage of registered unemployed receiving unemployment benefit; [d]in case of summary dismissal or voluntary unemployment; [e]plus fixed amount; [f]if local unemployment rate is less than 125% of the national average unemployment rate

Source: European Commission (2008); Eurostat (2008a); National Employment Agencies (coverage rates); own calculations

In several countries, the statutory replacement rate is reduced after three months of receiving benefits. In Hungary, earnings-related benefits are only available for the first three months of benefit receipt, with a minimum defined at 60% and a maximum defined at 120% of the minimum wage. After three months, only the minimum sum, i.e., 60% of the minimum wage is paid, irrespective of prior earnings. Benefit amounts are further reduced by taxation in Estonia and Hungary as well as by deductions of social security contributions (Poland, Hungary and Slovenia). To assess the relative generosity of benefit levels, Table 3.5 expresses the benefits that reference individuals (see above) who had previously earned an average wage would obtain, as a percentage of the average as well as the minimum wage. Relative to the minimum wage, benefits are most generous in Latvia and Slovakia, followed by Estonia and Slovenia. Benefits are least generous in Hungary and Poland.

The duration of benefit payments varies substantially across countries. In Estonia and Slovenia, the unemployed can receive benefits for up to a year, while in Lithuania, Poland, the Czech Republic and Slovakia, the maximum benefit payment duration is only six months. In Bulgaria, special legislation applies to individuals who were summarily dismissed or who are voluntarily unemployed: instead of 11 months, they may only receive benefits for 4 months. As a consequence of entitlement restrictions, the share of registered unemployed actually receiving benefits (coverage rate) varies substantially across countries. Beyond legal restrictions to entitlement, the coverage rate will be lower if long-term unemployment is high, which implies that many unemployed exhaust their claim to unemployment benefit. The coverage rate is highest in Latvia, Estonia and Romania and lowest in Poland, Bulgaria and Slovenia.

Altogether, Estonia and Latvia emerge as the countries with the most generous unemployment benefit system: replacement rates, payment durations and coverage rates are among the highest. In contrast, the Polish and Hungarian systems are among the least generous.

Active labour market policy

While unemployment insurance benefits provide a source of out-of-work income during a period of unemployment, active labour market policies (ALMPs) are comprised of measures intended to help individuals back into work. ALMPs have been used for a long time in Western countries to facilitate the employment of individuals who, for various reasons, have difficulty finding work. Furthermore, they are an important aspect of the European Employment Strategy (Kluve, 2006).

Figure 3.1 indicates that compared to the EU14, CEE countries spend relatively little on both active and passive labour market policies. Except for Bulgaria and Lithuania, the proportion of GDP spent on passive measures is substantially higher than the proportion spent on active measures. In terms of labour market policy expenditure, the CEE countries are similar to the UK and Greece, who also tend to spend relatively little on labour market policies. Expenditure on both active and passive labour market policies is very low in Estonia and Lithuania.

Figure 3.1: Expenditure on passive and active labour market policies as a percentage of GDP, 2005

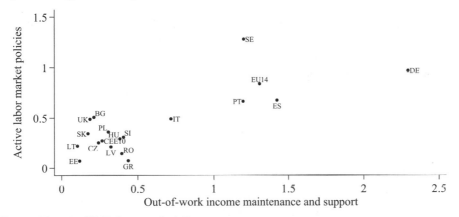

Source: Eurostat (2008a); own calculations

Kluve (2006) distinguishes several types of ALMP: among the most commonly used are training and retraining measures as well as various measures targeted towards increasing the efficiency of the job search process. Training measures are intended to increase the human capital of participants and thereby their employability. Measures for increasing the efficiency of the job search process are typically administered by the public employment service or private agencies. For example, many job seekers receive information on vacancies and some form of counselling. In the case of benefit recipients, public employment service caseworkers also monitor their compliance with job search requirements and may impose sanctions in cases of non-compliance, for example the withdrawal of unemployment benefits. Furthermore, private as well as public sector employment schemes are also used frequently. Private sector employment programmes typically take the form of wage subsidies to private employers. Thereby, the unemployed have a chance to improve their human capital and employers have an opportunity to screen workers' productivity without having to pay full wages. Public sector employment programmes consist of job creation schemes, primarily for the long-term unemployed to maintain their contact with the labour market during spells of unemployment.

Figure 3.2 gives an overview of how the funds for ALMPs are allocated to different types of programmes. In all countries, expenditure on labour market services constitutes an important item of overall expenditure. Furthermore, most countries spend some money on training, employment incentives and job creation schemes. Poland spends most on training, while Hungary spends most on employment incentives. In Bulgaria, a large share of funds goes to public job creation schemes. Some countries also operate start-up incentives, e.g. grants to the unemployed for starting their own businesses.

Figure 3.2: Expenditure on different types of ALMPs as a percentage of GDP, 2005

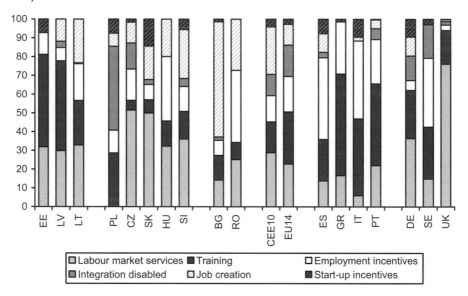

Note: Expenditure data on labour market services is missing for Poland.
Source: Eurostat (2008a); own calculations

Critiques of ALMP measures usually argue that individuals may succeed in finding a job even without programme participation. Furthermore, employers might perceive participation in some programmes, like public employment schemes, as a negative signal. ALMP measures may also lead to substitution of non-subsidised workers by subsidised workers. Fortunately, methods to assess the impact of ALMP measures on participants' subsequent labour market success (relative to non-participants) have been developed. The following paragraphs provide a brief summary of their results focusing on the evaluation of public employment schemes as well as training measures.

Measures aimed at training or retraining of unemployed generally received a positive evaluation. Kluve et al (1999) find significantly higher employment rates for participants in training measures compared to non-participants in Poland for the period from 1992-98. Leetmaa and Võrk (2003) report similar results for Estonia for the period from 2000-02. Rodriguez-Planas and Benus (2006) also find positive effects of training measures on subsequent employment for Romania, similar to the results of Fretwell et al (1999) for Poland, the Czech Republic and Hungary, and Lubyova and van Ours (1998, 1999) for Slovakia.

Public employment schemes often received a negative evaluation (Fretwell et al, 1999; Kluve et al, 1999; Rodriguez-Planas and Benus, 2006). For Poland, Kluve et al (1999) suggest that participants have used these programmes in part to re-qualify for subsequent unemployment benefit receipt. In contrast, Lubyova and van Ours (1998) find positive results for public employment ('community work') programmes, typically aimed at unemployed people with lower skill levels for Slovakia.

Administrative implementation, linkage to unemployment benefit payments and other country-specific context factors influence the success of ALMP schemes. Nevertheless, the results obtained from evaluations of ALMPs from different CEE countries are rather straightforward and compare well with the results obtained from a recent meta-analysis of more than 100 evaluation studies in mainly Western countries (Kluve, 2006; see also Bechterman et al, 2004). For the CEE countries reviewed, training and retraining measures are generally evaluated positively, while public employment schemes, with the exception of Slovakia, have received a negative evaluation. The results of private sector employment incentive schemes are mixed. Despite favourable evaluations, training is only modestly used in most countries, while private and public employment schemes have received the bulk of funding. Given that the least skilled suffer from a substantial disadvantage in CEE countries, the use of training measures, if properly implemented, may be an option to improve their labour market position. At the same time, more efforts should be taken to evaluate the impact of these programmes.

Conclusion

Under socialism, the citizens of CEE countries enjoyed relatively high economic security, albeit with relatively low living standards compared to Western Europe. They had access to a variety of benefits and services through the workplace, provided by a paternalist, dictatorial state. With the transition to capitalism, a fundamental reorientation of social policy and a reform of the welfare state has become necessary. As a first step, governments introduced relatively generous unemployment as well as social assistance schemes. However, as the transformational crisis turned out to be more severe than expected, unemployment benefit systems were scaled back. Poverty rates and income inequality rose across the region.

By 2005, the CEE countries were still lagging behind the West in terms of economic development. The Bulgarian and Romanian economies only achieved one third of the EU14 average GDP per capita. At the same time, the economies in less developed countries grew at rates up to five times above the EU14 average between 2000 and 2005, which has also begun to translate into employment growth. However, these high growth rates have been accompanied by further rises in inequality and labour market risks. Compared to the old EU member states, education appears to play an even stronger role in determining labour market inequalities in the CEE countries. Across the CEE countries, demand for university-educated individuals is high, while the situation of the least educated has become very precarious. Long-term unemployment has emerged in all countries and has become a significant problem in Poland and Slovakia. Furthermore, the high rates of absolute poverty observed in the Baltic countries as well as in Romania and Bulgaria are a cause for concern, as is the precarious situation of the Roma across Central and Southern Europe.

Welfare state reform has been hampered by the severe transformational recession. Retrenchment was necessary given that social expenditure had grown beyond the bounds of fiscal sustainability under socialism. By 2005, CEE countries spent substantially less on social protection than the EU14, which in part reflects their lower level of economic development. If the CEE countries follow a similar path of welfare state development as that of the old EU member states after the Second World War, it is to be expected that sustained economic growth will also translate into an expansion of the welfare state. Nevertheless, the task of establishing a solid tax base to generate the revenue needed for generous welfare services also remains a challenge for the future.

The analysis of labour market policies indicates that CEE countries spend substantially less on both active and passive labour market policies. There is substantial variability in unemployment benefit generosity across countries. The Latvian and Estonian system have emerged as the most generous in 2006/07, while benefits are least generous in Poland and Hungary. ALMPs play a rather marginal role, despite the positive evaluation that some of the implemented schemes receive. Training measures in particular might be a strategy particularly for improving the labour market position of the least skilled, who have emerged as the most vulnerable group in the transition process.

Notes

[1] High employment rates were also a consequence of labour hoarding by employers. Frequent shortages in production inputs caused employers to hoard inputs, including labour, in order to meet or exceed their production goals (Kornai, 1992a).

[2] 3.4% of GDP was allocated food price subsidies, 2.9% for housing subsidies, and 1.6%, 1.3%, and 0.9% were allocated to transport, energy and health/medicine subsidies, respectively (Atkinson and Micklewright, 1993: 161).

[3] Due to their different systems of national accounting, one has to be cautious in comparing aggregate figures from socialist and capitalist countries.

[4] The chapter uses the following conventions for information given in tables. The symbol used for missing data is –, while n.a. indicates not applicable. EU14 is the unweighted average of pre-enlargement EU member states except Luxembourg. CEE10 is the unweighted average of the Central and Eastern European EU accession countries.

[5] Schneider defines the shadow economy as 'all market-based legal production of goods and services that are deliberately concealed from public authorities', to avoid payment of taxes, social security contributions, or to evade other legislative and administrative regulations (Schneider, 2006: 5).

[6] The figures were estimated using a DYMIMIC (dynamic multiple indicator multiple cause) approach and are subject to measurement error (for further discussion see Schneider, 2006).

[7] The Gini coefficient is often used to describe the dispersion of the income distribution. It equals 0 in case of perfect equality and ~100 in case of perfect inequality.

[8] The quintile ratio is the ratio of total income received by the 20% of the population with the highest income (top quintile) to that received by the 20% of the population with the lowest income (lowest quintile). The ISCED 5-6/ISCED 0-2 income ratio is the ratio of the median equivalised net income of tertiary (ISCED 5-6) graduates relative to individuals with lower-secondary educational degrees or less (ISCED 0-2) among individuals aged 18-64.

[9] The regime descriptions for the 1990s are largely taken from Vodopivec et al. (2005), as well as the International Social Seciurity Assoziation (ISSA) (2008) and the individual country chapters in this book.

[10] All CEE countries introduced minimum wages. Irregular adjustment and high inflation rates lowered the real value of benefits considerably in the initial phase.

[11] Boeri (1997, 2000) suggests that such errors resulted in part from a severe underestimation of the rise in unemployment about to occur. The consequence in

Poland was that not only unemployed but also formerly inactive individuals started claiming unemployment benefits.

[12] Unless noted otherwise the information relates to 1 July 2007. The main sources are the European Commission (2008) and Eurostat (2008a).

[13] The section follows OECD (2007) methodology, except for calculation of replacement rates. The average wage is defined as the average gross monthly earnings (wages and salaries) paid directly to the employee, before any deductions for income tax and social security contributions paid by the employee calculated for full-time employees in industry and services (Eurostat, 2008a). Normally, gross earnings are used as the assessment base. If net earnings were defined as the assessment base (e.g. in the Czech Republic), the average net earnings of a single adult earning an average wage (as previously defined) were used. All wage data are taken from Eurostat (2008a). Replacement rates were calculated with data on wages and other reference values (e.g. benefit ceilings) from 2006.

References

Adamchik, V. (1999) 'The effect of unemployment benefits on the probability of re-employment in Poland', *Oxford Bulletin of Economics and Statistics*, vol 61, no 1, pp 95-108.

Aidukaite, J. (2003) 'From universal system of social policy to particularistic? The case of the Baltic States', *Communist and Post-Communist Studies*, vol 36, pp 405-26.

Aidukaite, J. (2006) 'The formation of social insurance institutions of the Baltic States in the post-socialist era', *Journal of European Social Policy*, vol 16, no 3, pp 259-70.

Alesina, A. and Fuchs-Schündeln, N. (2007) 'Good-Bye Lenin (or not?): the effect of communism on people's preferences', *American Economic Review*, vol 97, no 4, pp 1507-28.

Atkinson, A. B. and Micklewright, J. (1991) 'Unemployment compensation and labor market transitions: a critical review', *Journal of Economic Literature,* vol 29, no 4, pp 1679-727.

Atkinson, A. B. and Micklewright, J. (1992) *Economic transformation in eastern Europe and the distribution of income*, Cambridge: Cambridge University Press.

Barr, N. (2001) 'Reforming welfare states in post-communist countries', in L. T. Orlowski (ed) *Transition and growth in post-communist countries*, Cheltenham: Edward Elgar Publishing, pp 169-219.

Barr, N. (2005) 'From transition to accession', in N. Barr (ed) *Labour markets and social policy in central and Eastern Europe*, Washington DC: World Bank Publications, pp 1-29.

Bechterman, G., Olivas K. and Dar, A. (2004) *Impacts of active labor market programs: new evidence from evaluations with particular attention to developing and transition countries*, World Bank Social Protection Discussion Paper No 0402, Washington DC: World Bank.

Boeri, T. (1997) 'Labour-market reforms in transition economies', *Oxford Review of Economic Policy*, vol 13, no 2, pp 126-40.

Boeri, T. (2000) *Structural change, welfare systems, and labour reallocation: lessons from the transition of formerly planned economies*, Oxford: Oxford University Press.

Boeri, T. and Edwards, S. (1998) 'Long-term unemployment and short-term unemployment benefits: the changing nature of non-employment subsidies in Central and Eastern Europe', *Empirical Economics*, vol 23, pp 31-54.

Boeri, T. and Terrell, K. (2002) 'Institutional determinants of labor reallocation in transition', *Journal of Economic Perspectives*, vol 16, no 1, pp 51-76.

Bornhorst, F. and Commander, S. (2006) 'Regional unemployment and its persistence in transition countries', *Economics of Transition*, vol 14, no 2, pp 269-88.

Cazes, S. and Nesporova, A. (2007) *Flexicurity: a relevant approach for Central and Eastern Europe?*, Geneva: International Labour Organization

Deacon, B. (2000) 'Eastern European welfare states: the impact of the politics of globalization', *Journal of European Social Policy*, vol 10, no 2, pp 146-61.

Elster, J., Offe, C. and Preuss, U.K. (1998) *Institutional design in post-communist societies*, Cambridge: Cambridge University Press.

Estrin, S., Schaffer, M.E. and Singh, I.J. (1997) 'The provision of social benefits in state-owned, privatized and private firms in Poland', in M. Rein, B. L. Friedman and A. Wörgötter (eds) *Enterprise and social benefits after communism*, Cambridge: Cambridge University Press, pp 25-48.

European Commission (2008) *Mutual information system on social protection (MISSOC): comparative tables on social protection in the member states and the European Economic Area* (http://ec.europa.eu/employment_social/spsi/missoc_en.html.).

Eurostat (2008a) *Internet database*, Luxembourg: Eurostat (http://epp.eurostat.ec.europa.eu).

Eurostat (2008b) *The European system of integrated social protection statistics (ESSPROS) manual*, Eurostat Methodologies and Working Papers, Luxembourg: Office for Official Publications of the European Communities.

Fidrmuc, J. (2004) 'Migration and regional adjustment to asymmetric shocks in transition economies', *Journal of Comparative Economics*, vol 32, pp 230-47.

Flemming, J. S. and Micklewright, J. (1999) 'Income distribution, economic systems and transition', in A.B. Atkinson and E. Bourguignon (eds) *Handbook of income distribution*, vol 1, pp 843-918.

Fretwell, D.H., Benus, J. and O'Leary, C. (1999) *Evaluating the impact of active labor market programs: results of cross country studies in Europe and Asia*, World Bank Social Protection Discussion Paper No 9915, Washington DC: World Bank.

Guillen, A.M. and Palier, B. (2004) 'Introduction: does Europe matter? Accession to EU and social policy developments in recent and new member states', *Journal of European Social Policy*, vol 14, no 3, pp 203-9.

Ham, J.C., Svejnar, J. and Terell, K. (1998) 'Unemployment and the social safety net during transition to a market economy: evidence from the Czech and Slovak Republics', *American Economic Review*, vol 88, no 5, pp 1117-42.

Heidenreich, M. and Wunder, C. (2007) 'Patterns of regional inequality in the enlarged Europe', *European Sociological Review*, vol 24, no 1, pp 1-18.

Heyns, B. (2005) 'Emerging inequality in central and eastern Europe', *Annual Review Sociology*, vol 31, pp 163–97.

ISSA (International Social Security Assoziation) (2008) *Social security worldwide database* (www-ssw.issa.int/sswlp2/engl/page1.htm).

Kezdi, G. (2002) *Two phases of labor market transition in Hungary: inter-sectoral reallocation and skill-biased technological change*, Budapest Working Papers on the Labour Market No 2002/3, Budapest: Hungarian Academy of Sciences, Institute of Economics.

Kluve, J. (2006) *The effectiveness of European active labor market policy*, IZA Discussion Paper No 2018, Bonn: Institute for the Study of Labor.

Kluve, J., Lehmann, H. and Schmidt, C.M. (1999) 'Active labor market policies in Poland: human capital enhancement, stigmatization, or benefit churning?', *Journal of Comparative Economics*, vol 27, pp 61-89.

Kornai, J. (1992a) *The socialist system: the political economy of communism*, Princeton: Princeton University Press.

Kornai, J. (1992b) 'The postsocialist transition and the state: reflections in the light of Hungarian fiscal problems', *American Economic Review*, vol 82, no 2, pp 1-21.

Kornai, J. (1997) 'The reform of the welfare state and public opinion', *American Economic Review*, vol 87, no 2, pp 339-43.

Kornai, J. (2006) 'The great transformation of Central Eastern Europe: success and disappointment', *Economics of Transition*, vol 14, no 2, pp 207-44.

Leetma, R. and Võrk, A. (2003) *Evaluation of active labour market programmes in Estonia*, Discussion Paper, Tartu: University of Tartu.

Lubyova, M. and van Ours, J. (1998) 'Work incentives and other effects of the transition to social assistance: evidence from the Slovak Republic', *Empirical Economics*, vol 23, pp 121-53.

Lubyova, M. and van Ours, J. (1999) 'Unemployment durations of job losers in a labour market in transition', *Economics of Transition*, vol 7, no 3, pp 665-86.

Manning, N. (2004) 'Diversity and change in pre-accession Central and Eastern Europe since 1989', *Journal of European Social Policy*, vol 14, no 3, pp 211-32.

Micklewright, J. and Nagy, G. (1996) 'Unemployment durations of job losers in a labour market in transition', *European Economic Review*, vol 40, pp 819-28.

Milanovic, B. (1999) 'Explaining the increase in inequality during transition', *Economics of Transition*, vol 7, no 2, pp 299-341.

Newell, A. and Socha, M.W. (2007) *The Polish wage inequality explosion*, IZA Discussion Paper No 2644, Bonn: Institute for the Study of Labor.

OECD (Organisation for Economic Co-operation and Development) (2007) *Benefits and wages 2007*, Paris: OECD.

Offe, C. (1993) 'The politics of social policy in East European transitions: antecedents, agents and agenda of reform', *Social Research*, vol 60, no 4, pp 649-84.

Puhani, P.A. (2000) 'Poland on the dole: the effect of reducing the unemployment benefit entitlement period during transition', *Journal Population Economics*, vol 13, pp 35-44.

Rein, M., Friedmann, B.L. and Wörgötter, A. (1997) *Enterprise and social benefits after communism*, Cambridge: Cambridge University Press.

Rodriguez-Planas, N. and Benus, J. (2006) *Evaluating Active Labor Market Programs in Romania*, IZA Discussion Paper No 2464, Bonn: Institute for the Study of Labor.

Rutkowski, J. (2007) *From the shortage of jobs to the shortage of skilled workers: labor markets in the EU new member states*, IZA Discussion Paper No 3202, Bonn: Institute for the Study of Labor.

Scharpf, F.W. (2002) 'The European social model: coping with the challenges of diversity', *Journal of Common Market Studies*, vol 40, no 4, pp 645-70.

Schneider, F. (2006) *Shadow economies and corruption all over the world: what do we really know?*, IZA Discussion Paper No 2315, Bonn: Institute for the Study of Labor.

Schneider, F. and Burger, C. (2005) 'Formal and informal labour markets: challenges and policy in the Central and Eastern European new EU members and candidate countries', *CESifo Economic Studies*, vol 51, no 1, pp 77-115.

Sipos, S. and Ringold, D. (2005) 'Social safety nets: evolution from inclusion and participation', in N. Barr (ed) *Labour markets and social policy in Central and Eastern Europe*, Washington DC. World Bank Publications, pp 89-134.

Sotiropoulos, D.A., Neamtu, I. and Stoyanova, M. (2003) 'The trajectory of post-communist welfare state development: the cases of Bulgaria and Romania', *Social Policy and Administration*, vol 37, no 6, pp 656-73.

Steiner, A. (2004) *Von Plan zu Plan – Eine Wirtschaftsgeschichte der DDR (From plan to plan: an economic history of the GDR)*, München: Deutsche Verlags-Anstalt.

Terrell, K. and Sorm, V. (1999) 'Labor market policies and unemployment in the Czech Republic', *Journal of Comparative Economics*, vol 27, pp 33-90.

Van Ours, J.C. and Vodopivec, M. (2006) *Shortening the potential duration of unemployment benefits does not affect the quality of post-unemployment jobs: evidence from a natural experiment*, IZA Discussion Paper No 2171, Bonn: Institute for the Study of Labor.

Vodopivec, M., Wörgötter, A. and Raju, D. (2005) 'Unemployment benefit systems in Central and Eastern Europe: a review of the 1990s', *Comparative Economic Studies*, vol 47, pp 615-51.

Voirin, M. (1993) 'Social security in Central and Eastern European countries: continuity and change', *International Social Security Review*, vol 46, no 1, pp 27-65.

Wagner, M. and Hlouskova, J. (2005) 'CEEC growth projections: certainly necessary and necessarily uncertain', *Economics of Transition*, vol 13, no 2, pp 341-72.

Wilensky, H. L. (2002) *Rich democracies: political economy, public policy, and performance*, Berkley and Los Angeles: University of California Press.

World Bank (2000) *Making transition work for everyone*, Washington DC: World Bank.

World Bank (2005) *Growth, poverty and inequality: Eastern Europe and the Former Soviet Union*, Washington DC: World Bank.

World Bank (2007a) *Social assistance in the Central European and the Baltic States*, Washington DC: World Bank.

World Bank (2007b) *World development indicators*, Washington DC: World Bank.

FOUR

Bulgaria

Dobrinka Kostova

During Bulgaria's political and economic transition, changes in its political institutions have been rapid and fundamental. However, Bulgaria's socio-economic systems have changed much more slowly mainly due to the inherited backward structures from pre-socialist and socialist times, the locational disadvantage of the country in terms of its distance to the core markets of Western Europe, general instability in the Balkans and discontinuities in the government's process of privatisation and orientation to a market economy. As a whole, the socio-economic system can be characterised as developing towards diversification. The analyses of the education, labour and welfare systems in Bulgaria illustrate this assumption.

During Bulgaria's period of transformation, its education system passed through substantial reforms from changes in the legal framework and its orientation to the private sector. Two major tendencies developed. First, the phenomenon of students dropping out from school emerged and has resulted in a group of citizens with little or no education. Second, there has been an increased interest in university education.

The labour market of the former centrally planned Bulgarian economy has suffered from quantitative and qualitative imbalance during the transition period. Its unemployment rate increased from 0% to 18%, and decreased to about 7% at the end of 2007. During the 1990s, the crucial problem was unemployment. Currently, the lack of an adequately qualified and educated labour force is the most significant issue in the labour market.

The transition period has negatively affected the welfare system – its resources are very limited and decreased during the period of transformation. Bulgaria's welfare system could not compensate the groups experiencing declining living conditions with the economic difficulties that began in the 1990s. This induced tensions between the state institutions and the economically disadvantaged groups.

Education system

Structure of the Bulgarian education system

Overview of the Bulgarian education system after the Second World War

The problem of illiteracy was tackled quite successfully in Bulgaria long before the Second World War. However, secondary education and in particular higher education lagged behind average European standards. The beginning of the 1950s marked a period of great expansion for higher education, with Bulgaria's education system developing in accordance with socialist ideas. The number of its institutions rose initially from five (in 1939) to 13, then to 20, with 33 faculties and over 100 specialties (Topencharov, 1983: 15). During the socialist era, education served the goals of the centrally planned economy, mainly corresponding to the various economic sectors and branches. It was strongly state controlled in terms of its ideology, curricula and organisational and administrative framework. Of the 30 higher education institutions by 1989, only three – the Universities of Sofia, Plovdiv and Veliko-Tarnovo – were multi-disciplinary institutions. The others followed the specialised professional training institute model favoured by the Soviet approach, e.g. pedagogical, technological, agricultural and medical institutes. The predominant course model was the master's degree, usually following a five-year course structure. Further graduate studies were highly selective, with the government determining the number of students studying for the degree of 'science candidate' (equivalent to doctoral studies). Student teacher ratios were low, at about 7.5:1, while student lecture loads were heavy, at about 30 hours per week.

Education system since 1990[1]

School education is compulsory from the age of six to seven until age 16. It comprises basic education (years 1-8), which is divided into the first stage (years 1-4, International Standard Classification of Education, ISCED 1) and second stage (years 5-8, ISCED 2) (see Figure 4.1). Basic education can be obtained at state, municipal and private schools. These are free of charge with the exception of private schools. There is a single curriculum for primary education, which is compulsory for all pupils from years 1-4. A certificate is issued after successful completion of year 4.

Lower-secondary education (years 5-8) provides the foundations for study of different sciences. A certificate of basic education is issued after the successful completion of year 8. A pupil passes from basic school to secondary school without having to take an entrance examination, instead receiving a basic school certificate. Entrance exams do determine student entry into profile-oriented schools (e.g. a mathematics or language-oriented school) after year 7 or 8. In 2004/05, the net enrolment rate in primary education was 99.7%, 84.2% in lower-secondary education and 77.3% in upper-secondary education (National Statistical Institute, 2005).

Secondary general education (ISCED 3a) covers pupils from years 9-12 (or 13) and is free of charge with the exception of private schools. It is provided by: (1) secondary comprehensive schools, which cover: school grades 1-4; pre-secondary school grades 5-8; secondary school level grades 9-12; (2) specialised secondary schools, i.e., profiled gymnasia,[2] grades 8-12; and (3) secondary schools, i.e., gymnasia, grades 9-12. After students successfully complete the final year of secondary school and pass the compulsory matriculation examinations, they receive a diploma of completed secondary education. Recipients of secondary school leaving qualifications are entitled to continue their education at a higher educational level/university and non-university, without restriction as to the choice of a higher education establishment. The secondary school leaving qualification also gives them access to the labour market.

Secondary vocational education is provided in vocational training schools and/or technical schools, and, since 2003/04, in technical or vocational gymnasia (ISCED 3a), which cover grades 8 or 9 until grade 12. Graduates receive a secondary education diploma and a certificate for second- or third-level vocational qualification (vocational theory and practice exams), which qualifies them for jobs with managerial responsibilities. Estimates are that many of the students from this type of school continue on to higher education.

There are also vocational training schools, which start at grade 6 or 7, offering three-year training programmes, vocational training schools, which start at grade 9, offering two- to four-year training programmes, and vocational training schools offering two-year training programmes after completed secondary education (ISCED 3c). These students receive a diploma for basic education and a certificate for a first-level vocational qualification, which provides access to routine jobs. On completion of secondary vocational education, young people receive a school graduation certificate, a certificate for professional qualification issued on completion of vocational training, and a certificate granting the right to practice a profession issued for licensed professions.

Vocational colleges (ISCED 4c) organise post-secondary vocational training, and last up to two years after completion of secondary education. Graduates receive a certificate for a fourth-level professional qualification, whereas continuation to higher educational levels is possible on the basis of students' secondary diplomas.

Figure 4.1: The contemporary Bulgarian education system, 1998

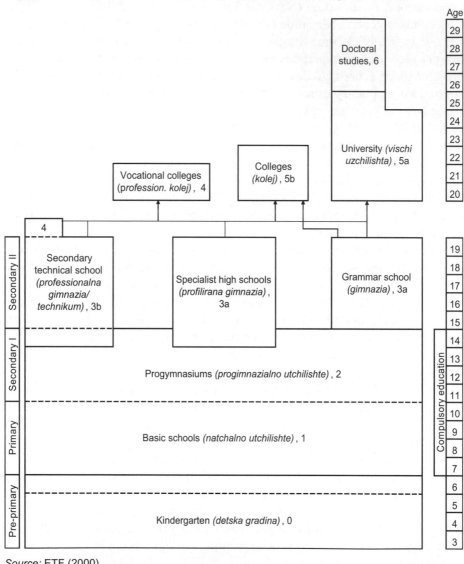

Source: ETF (2000)

Recipients of secondary school qualifications are entitled to continue their education at a higher education level, usually university and non-university, and are not restricted in their choice of higher education establishment. Admission to higher education institutions is based on successful entrance examinations. The type and number of these examinations are determined by the higher education institutions and are closely linked to each institution's respective profile. According to the Higher Education Act, university education institutions in Bulgaria are universities, specialised higher education institutions, institutes or academies. Universities provide a wide range of specialisation in at least three or four basic fields of study (humanities, sciences and technologies), and encompass a considerable number of scientific areas. Specialised higher education schools (academies and institutes) focus on basic fields of humanities, science, arts, sports, and military science. The structure of higher education comprises the following degrees: (1) first degree – at least a four-year programme ending with a bachelor's degree; (2) second degree – between a one to five-year post-bachelor's degree programme ending with a master's degree; and (3) third degree – at least a three-year post-master's degree programme, or a four-year post-bachelor's degree, ending with a doctoral degree. The 1995 Higher Education Act introduced the non-university type of higher education provided by colleges (ISCED 5b). They offer a three-year programme for vocationally oriented education in various fields, and count towards obtaining the specialist degree. They are mainly incorporated within the structure of the universities, and may also be independent, provided they fulfil the required academic and material requirements.

Vertical dimension of the education system

Figure 4.2 charts the trends in the educational enrolment of school-aged citizens in Bulgaria, starting as early as 1960. Obviously, the vast majority of the school-aged population has been enrolled in general schools, but a declining trend is also evident. Enrolment in vocational schools at the lower-secondary education level has diminished starting from the 1980s, and has remained at a very low level since then. Simultaneously, the number of young people enrolled in secondary technical and art schools has remained stable, slightly increasing between the early 1980s and 2004/05, from 6% to 13%. Also, enrolment in secondary vocational technical schools has been stable until the mid-1990s, when its level of 7%-8% declined to about 3% by 2004/05. Enrolment in tertiary education increased both in colleges and in universities, albeit much stronger in the latter, from less than 5% in 1960/61 to 18% in 2004/05. There was a 40% increase in student numbers in tertiary education between 1990/91 and 1999/2000, with the main surge occurring between 1990/91 and 1996/97. Only about 10% of students are enrolled in private institutions.

During 2000-04 the education structure of the population aged 25-64 continued to improve, with an increase both number and population share in higher and secondary education, and with a decrease in the number and the share of people in primary and lower education. The relative share of the population attending higher education (college and university) increased from 18% in 2000 to 22% in 2004, and the share of those enrolled in secondary education remained at 50%. Similarly, the relative portion of individuals with primary and lower education decreased by four points – from 32% to 28%. Therefore, 72% of the most active working-age population (25-64 years of age) attends secondary or higher education, and this is a good prerequisite for faster economic and social prosperity (National Statistical Institute, 2006: 29).

Figure 4.2: Enrolment by type of school in Bulgaria (%)

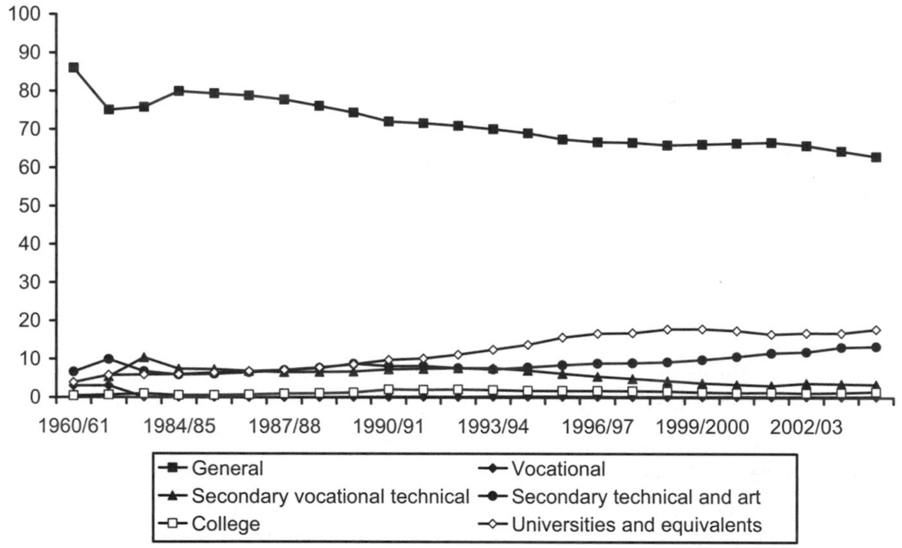

Source: National Statistical Institute (1976-2005)

Figure 4.3 shows that general schools are marked by gender parity. Boys are overrepresented in vocational schools, be it secondary technical and art schools, and even more so in secondary vocational technical schools. Colleges are clearly occupied by more women, whereas increasingly high numbers of young women continue studies at university level. Between 1995 and 1997, approximately 60% of university students were women, but in 2004/05, women represented only 52.09% (National Statistical Institute, 2005: 74).

A meaningful way to explore the vertical dimension of the education system is to study the progression rates of students from primary and lower-secondary education to various types of general and vocational secondary schools, followed by student progression from the secondary to the tertiary level. In 1999/2000, about 40% of all students with compulsory education continue in gymnasia, and about 57% continue in vocational or technical schools. Overall, 67% of students in the 15-19 age group continue their post-compulsory education, 29% continue in gymnasia and 38% continue in vocational or technical schools (OECD, 2003: 178). Thirty-five per cent of the age group 19-24 was enrolled in tertiary education in 1999/2000 (OECD, 2003: 178). The proportion of school graduates going on to tertiary education is even higher, at 60% (OECD, 2003: 248).

Figure 4.3: Proportion of females by type of school in Bulgaria

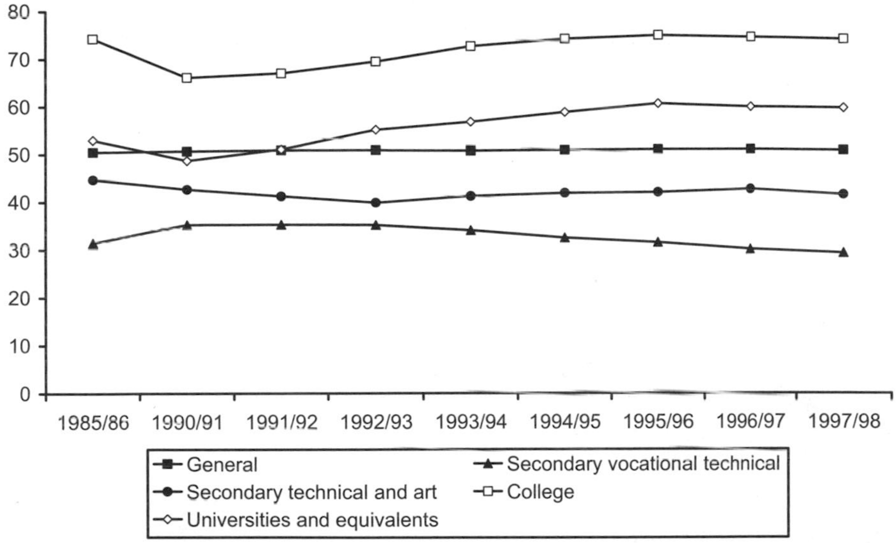

Source: National Statistical Institute (1976-2005)

Secondary level of education

Stratification and track differentiation

Students make their first education decisions at the age of 14, when they can opt for vocational education. At the age of 15, more options are available and they can make decisions to continue in general or to acquire vocational education.

General-track enrolment at the upper-secondary level has been consistently higher than 40% during the 1990s, which is evident in Figure 4.4.

103

Approximately half of secondary education pupils are enrolled in a form of vocational education. There has been a slight shift away from vocational education, although it still accounts for well over half – for example, it accounted for 56% in 2002/03 and 54.9% in 2004/05 (National Statistical Institute, 2005: 41, 57) of all secondary students. Additionally, enrolment in vocational tracks on the upper-secondary level leading to matriculation has been significantly high, at almost 60%.

Figure 4.4: School-aged population by levels of education and type of school on the upper-secondary level (%), 1993-98

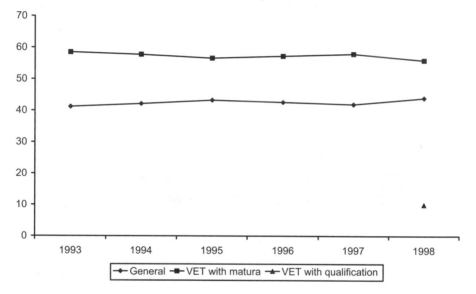

Note:VET = vocational education and training.
Source: ETF (1998-2000)

Organisation of vocational training

Education/training establishments include state and municipal training centres, company training centres, vocational schools and vocational colleges. The management of vocational education and training (VET) is carried out by the National Agency for Vocational Education and Training. State and municipal schools, as well as centres for vocational education, information, vocational orientation and training specialists are financed by the state and municipal budgets, sponsorships, donations, wills, their own budgets and national and international programmes.

Practical training is conducted mainly in school workshops. It does not really exist in companies, and where it does, it concerns companies with foreign investment and consists of one- to two-week training visits. There are two primary reasons for this. The restructuring and instability of the Bulgarian economy, which prevents employers from offering their production facilities and premises for placements in VET schools, is the main one. Another reason is the structure of VET programmes, which do not include obligatory practical training in companies, and which have been further reduced by recent reform.

Standardisation and quality differentiation of secondary education

The Bulgarian school system is characterised by a relatively high degree of standardisation in the organisation of schools and in their academic criteria. As a result of the over-centralisation and prescriptive control proceedings of the education authorities, the existing opportunity for determining the substance of the teaching material is limited. The study content in secondary general and vocational schools is approved by the Ministry of Education and Science, underlying the uniform criteria for evaluating the accomplishment of the students. The acquisition of a secondary education diploma (a precondition for university access) requires a formal examination. The examinations in all secondary schools follow a standardised procedure. The Ministry controls the issuing of diplomas for completed secondary education and professional qualifications.

Tertiary level of education

Horizontal dimension

Figure 4.5 depicts the field-of-study differentiation of tertiary education. Only selected fields of study are plotted. The most popular group of specialties is engineering and technical fields, whose enrolment has been as high as 45% in 1970/71, but decreased to below 20% in 1999/2000.

The attractiveness of economics study has increased from about 15% in the 1960-90s to almost 25% in 2004/05. Similarly, enrolment in law specialties increased from approximately 3% in 1980 to 5% in 2004/05. Other fields of study experiencing substantial decline are health specialties, agriculture and forestry. Arts enrolment has remained stable since the 1960s (National Statistical Institute, 2005).

Figure 4.5: Enrolment in tertiary education by selected fields of study (%)

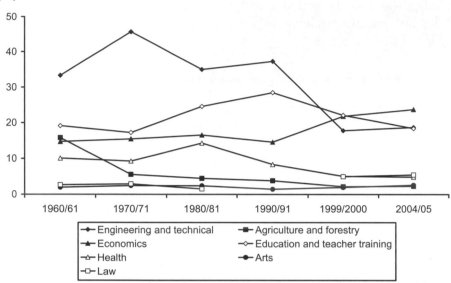

Note: In 1960/61 education and teacher training is called mathematics, natural and humanitarian sciences. In 1990/91 physical culture is grouped together with education and teacher training.
Source: National Statistical Institute (1976-2005)

Figure 4.6 plots the proportion of females in selected fields of tertiary education during the school years 1985/86, 1999/2000, and 2004/05. The information is not directly comparable between these years due to the change in the classification of fields of education. In the mid-1980s, women were overrepresented in education, and were almost at parity with men in other fields. In 1999/2000, women were a minority only in services, agriculture, engineering, manufacturing and construction fields and were overrepresented in all other fields. The fields of education, humanities and arts, health and welfare and social sciences have a particularly large female enrolment level. A further shift in gender distribution is noticeable between school years 1999/2000 and 2004/05. Most obviously, there was a drop in the number of women in sciences and other disciplines (e.g. education, law, social sciences), and an increase in the fields of services, health and welfare and agriculture.

Figure 4.6: Percentage of females in tertiary education by fields of study

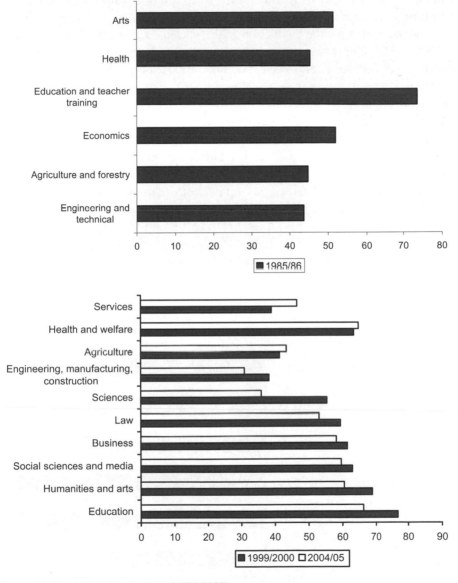

Source: National Statistical Institute (1976-2005)

Standardisation, quality differentiation and openness of tertiary education

According to Bulgaria's education policy universities are allowed autonomy, so that public and private universities may define their own curricula and manage their own budgets. This has led to competition between universities for students, which is reflected in the diversification of programmes and creation of new educational forms as well as courses for instruction. The National Agency for Evaluation and Accreditation of Higher Education Institutions is intended to contribute to the development and application of criteria and norms for the evaluation of the various education establishments.

In 2004/05, there were 53 establishments for higher learning, including private ones (National Statistical Institute, 2005). From those, 36 were state institutions and 10 were independent colleges. Private institutions included seven universities and specialised institutions and nine colleges (National Statistical Institute, 2005: 73) (see also Figure 4.7).

All students in tertiary education pay fees, which vary according to the type of university and acceptance. The public universities are partially funded by the state budget, while the private ones are entirely self-funded, so students in private universities pay higher fees than students in public ones. In public universities, students who pay the lowest fees are those with the highest entrance exam scores. Another student group that pays the lowest fees are those who are accepted within the frame of the state-defined student quotas. The rest of the accepted students pay higher fees. The amount of fees varies according to the field of study.

Figure 4.7: Proportion of public and private institutions in Bulgaria (%), 2004/05

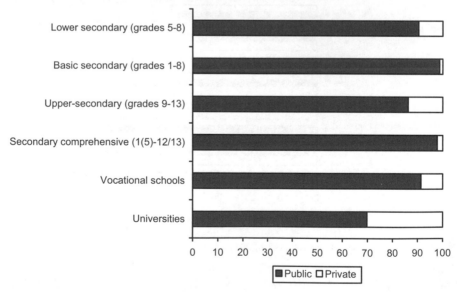

Source: National Statistical Institute (2006: 39, 52, 70)

There are government quotas every year for various subjects in the public universities. Each public university also has a student quota in paid education, and the students there pay higher fees. Following the education aspirations of the Bulgarian youth, the public universities are accepting increasing numbers of paying students, which leads to ungrounded growth of single sectors. The government therefore decided to establish government-set quotas for paid education in public schools, thus aiming to restore the balance between government-set quotas and paid quotas.

Labour market

Economic development

The Bulgarian transition from a centralised economy to a market-oriented one started in 1990, it happened slowly, and resulted in greater economic and social difficulties than in the leading transition economies in Central Europe (Beleva and Tzanov, 2001). On the one hand, the relatively greater transition problems in Bulgaria are explained by its more problematic heritage from socialist times. On the other hand, many problems are also attributable to the comparatively slow pace of reforms after the fall of the Iron Curtain.

Starting in 1989, the gross domestic product (GDP) registered a yearly decline of more than 3% (Figure 4.8). This transitional recession peaked at −9.1% in 1990. The initial economic contraction was followed by growth from 1994 until 1995. However, in 1996 and 1997, Bulgaria found itself on the verge of a severe financial and economic crisis. This crisis brought to the fore the need for speeding up the reforms aimed at stabilising the country's macroeconomic situation. A currency board was introduced, and the fiscal policy was tightened to influence economic efficiency (European Commission, 2002). Economic performance has improved significantly in the new millennium. The growth rates increased from 3.9% in 1998 to 6.1% in 2006. In recent years, Bulgaria has made stable and rapid progress. The new macroeconomic stability resulted in low inflation rates, a balanced state budget and increasing foreign investments, which accelerated job creation and labour demand (Beleva et al, 2007).

Unlike other former communist countries, Bulgaria adopted a more gradual approach towards restructuring and privatising its state-owned sector. Its privatisation process consisted of a large array of different programmes (OECD, 1999). The restitution of urban property promoted the emergence of small private retail businesses in Bulgarian cities. Although the restitution of rural property had already begun in 1991, it had suffered from major complications and delays.

Figure 4.8: GDP growth, 1989-2006

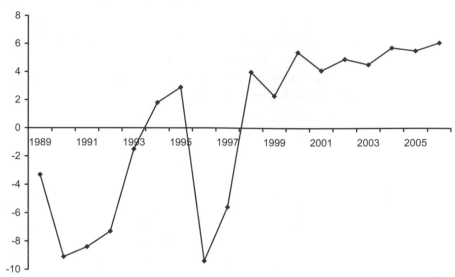

Source: ILO (2008); data for 2006 from Eurostat (2008)

Insufficient property rights and small-scale farms contributed to the particularly poor performance of Bulgarian agriculture throughout the transition period (Giordano and Kostova, 2000). The development of private sector employment in Bulgaria has been rather modest compared to other Central and Eastern European (CEE) countries, rising from a 10% GDP share in 1990 to 75% in 2007 (EBRD, 2008). Relatively high degrees of privatisation have been achieved in agriculture, where the private sector already represented 97.5% of total employment in 2000 (Giordano and Kostova, 2000).

Labour market dynamics

Employment dynamics

At the beginning of the economic transition in 1990, 18.5% of employed individuals worked in agriculture, 44.2% in industry and 37.3% in services (ILO, 2008). This initial pattern reflects the considerable size of agriculture and low share of employment in the services compared to other CEE countries (Beleva et al, 1999). Although the agricultural share of total employment was already high in 1990, it increased to a maximum of 26.2% in 2000. During the transition, agricultural employment represented an important source of secondary income for many workers and pensioners. It was perceived by some land owners as a survival strategy in the course of deindustrialisation. Productivity in the agricultural sector is very low, however, because farmers cultivate with extremely modest technical means. Furthermore, much farming is of the subsistence type.

In contrast, the employment share in industry and construction decreased significantly from 44.2% in 1990 to 27.6% in 2006 (ILO, 2008). Absolute employment in industry declined from 1.8 million individuals in 1990 to 1.0 million individuals in 2006. The agricultural sector absorbed part of the labour force made redundant from industrial employment. Nevertheless, Bulgaria's industry is still very important in a quantitative sense because about one third of employed people are working in this sector. The service sector's share of total employment increased significantly from 37.3% in 1990 to 51.8% in 2006 (ILO, 2008), but it is not yet substantial enough to compensate for the dramatic job destruction in industry (European Commission, 2002). Nevertheless, the service sector seems to be the driving force in the Bulgarian economy. Tourism and communications are among the most dynamic branches of the service sector.

The transition period was characterised by a decrease in employment and an increasing mismatch between labour demand and supply. Employment losses were transformed partly into unemployment, and partly into official economic inactivity (Beleva et al, 2007). Because they were discouraged, many people opted for inactivity because they gave up searching for registered jobs. Figure 4.9 shows that labour force participation rates of the population aged 15-64 declined considerably from 75% in 1990 to 56.9% in 2006.

This was due to the structural economic change that led to large-scale job destruction, which was not fully balanced by new job creation. Figure 4.9 also shows gender-specific time trends in labour force participation. Both rates display similar declining patterns over time, but the gender gap increased from 5.6 percentage points in 1990 to 10.6 percentage points in 2006.

In 2006, the lowest activity rate is registered for the youngest age cohorts (15-24), at 26.4% (Table 4.1). The population aged 15-24 is the cohort most affected by the fall in employment, which fell from 52% to 26.4% between 1990 and 2006. Available studies suggest that this reflects less of an increased participation in education than an important phenomenon of discouraged workers (European Commission, 2002).

A significant contributing factor is the lack of experience among young people. In the employment restructuring environment, young employees were the first to be fired and the least attractive for employers due to lack of experience. Kolev and Saget (2005) show that even if young people find a job, a very large proportion are low-quality jobs without official contracts or social contributions. They estimate that around 18% of employed young people had no contract, and around 42% did not receive social contributions in 2001. Besides young people, other age groups also suffer from a drop in employment rates. Whereas the middle-age cohort (25-55) attained very high activity rates of more than 90% at the beginning of the transition, their rate declined to 75.9% in 2006. the labour force participation rate of the oldest cohort, i.e., those aged over 65, also declined significantly.

Figure 4.9: Labour force participation rate (age group 15-64), 1990-2006

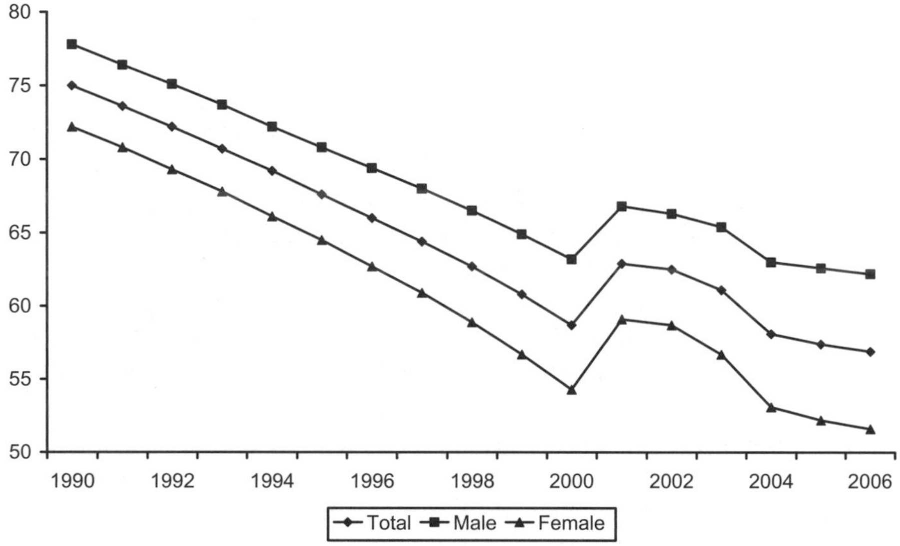

Source: ILO (2008)

Table 4.1: Labour force participation rate by age group, 1990-2006

	1990	1995	2000	2006
15+	63.8	55.7	47.4	45.9
15-24	52.0	40.2	27.5	26.4
25-54	93.7	88.5	78.9	75.9
55-64	41.0	30.4	24.0	26.1
65+	7.3	3.0	1.2	1.9

Source: ILO (2008)

Unemployment dynamics

The transition period is characterised by a sustainable increase in unemployment rates and unequal distribution of unemployment by socio-demographic groups (Beleva et al, 1999; Gallie et al, 2001). Most permanently affected by unemployment are the young, the uneducated, Roma, those with reduced working capacity, women and those older than 50.

Official registered unemployment, measured as a share of the active population (15-64 years old) was quite low at the beginning of the transition period, 1.7% in 1990, as unemployment was an unknown phenomenon during the communist era (Figure 4.10).

Figure 4.10: Unemployment rates, 1990-2006

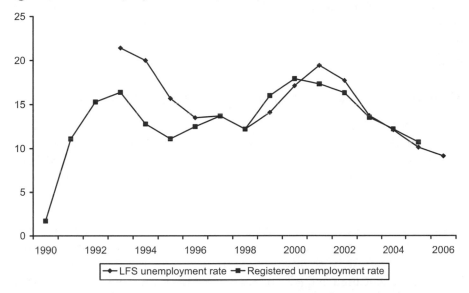

Notes: Labour Force Survey (LFS) unemployment rate for age groups 15-74; registered unemployment rate for age group 16-60.
Source: ILO (2008); LFS unemployment in 2006 from Eurostat (2008)

The transition to a market economy caused a dramatic increase in unemployment figures. Registered unemployment peaked at approximately 16% of the labour force in 1993, after which it fell to an average of slightly under 11%-13% during the mid- and late-1990s. During the economic crisis at the end of the 1990s, it rose again to a global maximum of about 17.9% in 2000. Since 2000, it has been declining sharply in accordance with the economic recovery at the beginning of the new millennium. The LFS-based unemployment rate follows only a slightly different pattern despite different measurement concepts. This is because it is self-assessed and the registered unemployment rate requires official registration at employment offices. Its peak in 1993 was much larger, at 21.4%. Since 1997, both measures have been roughly the same. Thus, both measures show an impressive decline in unemployment rates that in 2006 attain the lowest levels in the transition period.

Bulgarian young adults possess a high unemployment risk (Kolev and Saget, 2005). As in many other countries, the transition of youth from school to active life and labour integration remains an important labour market problem (Nesporova, 2002). Apart from labour demand restrictions related in particular to little working experience, difficulties in the professional integration of young people are also caused by the insufficient match between labour demand and qualifications offered by the education system. However, the unemployment rate of individuals under 25 declined from 33.3% in 2000 to 19.5% in 2006 (Eurostat, 2008). Furthermore, long-term unemployment also decreased substantially, from 9.4% in 2000 to 5% in 2006. Obviously, the strong labour market recovery reached even unemployed youth and the long-term unemployed.

Minority ethnic groups, migration and regional differences

A large percentage of unemployed people belong to minority ethnic groups (Tomova, 1995). Their education levels are significantly lower than for ethnic Bulgarians. It appears that the Roma are significantly disadvantaged in the labour market: unemployment (particularly long-term unemployment) is widespread among the Roma population and Bulgarian Muslims (European Commission, 2002; Kostova, 2005). The unemployment rate of the Roma is difficult to measure because many of them have no ID cards. It should be stressed that the inequality faced by ethnic minority groups in the labour market may not solely be the result of ethnic intolerance, but is also due to a low level of education and job qualifications (Tomova, 1995; Kostova, 2005).

Bulgaria experienced migration, particularly to Turkey. Besides the significant constant and temporary emigration after the first years of the transition period, there are also significant migration patterns within the country. Since the 1990s, the North Central and the Northwestern regions have been most affected by migration to other regions within the country. This led to area depopulation and an unbalancing of age groups within the population. These migration trends are partially caused by variation in strong regional labour market differences. For example, the standard deviation of regional unemployment rates in 2004 (19.9%) is the highest in Eastern Europe (Dietz et al, 2004). The highest level of unemployment is in the Northwestern region (28.3%), which is the region with the lowest level of economic development and the highest agricultural share (ETF, 2003). The lowest level of unemployment is in the Southwestern region (13.1%), which is the most economically developed region in the country, largely because its development and activity is driven by the capital city Sofia. The regional unemployment gap appears to have widened during the last few years (European Commission, 2002).

Labour market institutions

Bulgaria has equipped itself with a new Labour Code in 1986 that is still valid. This replaced the 1951 Labour Code, which had imported the Stalinist model of industrial relations, coinciding with the wave of industrial development and the collectivisation of agrarian production (Beleva and Tzanov, 2001). In 2001, a further important change in labour legislation was made in order to harmonise with European Union (EU) law (Clauwaert et al, 2003). A number of European and international labour market standards were implemented.

Employment protection legislation

While under the centrally planned economic system, workers enjoyed a fairly high degree of employment protection, structural transformations and market-oriented reforms led to substantial moderation of workers' protection in the 1990s. Bulgaria has restrictive laws concerning collective dismissal (see Table 2.7 in Chapter Two of this book). This is in line with Central and Eastern European (CEE) policy, which tends to be most restrictive concerning collective dismissals compared to the EU15 average. However, regulation concerning regular employment is less restrictive in Bulgaria than most EU and CEE countries. Bulgaria's rules regarding termination on temporary employment contracts are also relatively less restrictive. Temporary contracts require a written request as well as strict objective reasons in Bulgaria (Tonin, 2005). Furthermore, temporary contracts are not allowed to last longer than three years (Clauwaert et al, 2003). Regulations of temporary work agencies are very weak, as these employment forms hardly exist in Bulgaria.

Bulgaria has no special system of labour courts, so employment-related cases are dealt with in normal courts. The idea of creating specialised labour courts has been discussed since the beginning of the transition process, and the debate has recently progressed. In recent years, there have been increasing numbers of court cases arising from labour disputes. Numerous recent changes to the Labour Code and Civil Procedures Code have not decreased the amount of time – one to three years – that it takes for labour cases to come to court. This causes serious problems for both employees and employers.

Industrial relations

Before 1990, Bulgaria's industrial relations systems were characterised by central political and managerial control exercised by the state. During the transition, there was a general move from centralised industrial relations determined by the state, to a relatively free, conflict-based industrial relations organisation that is typical for a market economy (Velinov and Mikova, 2003). In 1993, a formalised tripartite dialogue was introduced, where employer and trade union representatives discuss various economic and social issues (Dietz et al, 2004). Bulgaria adopted a combination of centralised and decentralised negotiations. National and enterprise levels of negotiations are most developed, while branch and particularly regional levels have weak representation (Beleva and Tzanov, 2001). There is some degree of subordination between these levels, e.g. minimum wages that are agreed on at lower levels may not be lower than the national minimum wage (Beleva et al, 1999).

Union membership has declined sharply during the 1990s, down from total coverage of the workforce registered at the beginning of transition. According to Crowley (2004: Figure 2), the Bulgarian unionisation rate decreased to 22.2% in the late 1990s. The decrease can generally be attributed to the shift towards free choice of union membership status, falling living standards during the 1990s, high levels of unemployment, privatisation, growing numbers of small and medium-sized enterprises and sector shifts. Trade unions are strong in state-owned and recently privatised enterprises, while their position is weak in the new firms in the private sector. Collective bargaining coverage, measured as a percentage of all salaried workers (both unionised and not unionised) who are covered by collective agreements, lies between 25% and 30% (Schulten, 2005: Table 4).

Welfare regime

Labour market policy

Active labour market policy

Active labour market policies (ALMPs) refer to expenditure on activities for the unemployed that are geared to help them back into work. These comprise preventive and employability-oriented strategies like training measures, subsidies or credits to facilitate (re-)integration into the labour market, job search assistance and special measures for disadvantaged groups such as people with disabilities and youth. Active measures are temporary and are either oriented to increase education (e.g. for minorities) and qualifications or to support temporary jobs.

During the early transition period, labour market policy in Bulgaria was characterised by the tendency to finance passive measures, and by insignificant expenditure on active measures. Training and retraining measures for the unemployed and job creation schemes were the first active measures enacted at the very beginning of the transformation. The diversification of active measures has become more significant despite limited resources. The main types of measures promoted have been recruitment incentives to employers, support for job creation schemes, self-employment promotion, training and retraining schemes, job placement and specialised programmes for problematic groups like labour market entrants (Beleva and Tzanov, 2001). Hence, expenditure on active measures became more significant compared to passive measures, increasing from 7% in 1991 to 31.2% in 1998, but the share of expenditure for active policy decreased again to 23.6% in 2001 (European Commission, 2002). The overall share of ALMPs has increased to 0.35% of GDP in 2001.

The European Commission (2002) gives a detailed analysis of the ALMP budget during 1998-2001: on average, temporary work schemes represented nearly half of the expenditure, recruitment subsidies 36%, support for self-employment 14% and training measures less than 1%. In terms of participants, temporary work schemes and subsidised employment are also the dominant measures, with around 46% and 40% of the total number of participants. Self-employment subsidies accounted for 11% and training accounted for only 3%. In 2001, the total number of participants was estimated at around 16% of the registered unemployed. In general, limited activities and resources have been allocated to evaluating the impact and effectiveness of active employment measures.

Unemployment insurance

Early legislation for the provision of unemployment benefit dates to 1989. Since the economic shifts were assumed to be of a temporary nature, unemployment benefits were rather generous. They were, however, scaled back by reforms in 1990 and 1991. In 1992, the statutory replacement rate was fixed at 60%, and has remained there until today. However, benefits were also subject to minimum and maximum caps, which were defined relative to the minimum wage. The upper cap was set at 140% of the minimum wage, while the lower cap was set at 90% of the minimum wage. Since 2002, the minimum and maximum amounts are no longer linked to the minimum wage but are set annually on the basis of the Social Security Budget Act, while maintaining a close relation to the minimum wage. These caps effectively lower the actual replacement rate for individuals earning an average wage.

A striking characteristic of the Bulgarian system is the dependency of benefit levels on the reason for unemployment. Since the 1990s, in case of summary dismissal or voluntary unemployment, individuals are only entitled to the minimum benefit for four months.

Initially, graduates from higher education and vocational schools could claim benefits, albeit at a rate close to the minimum benefit and for a shorter duration. This right has been revoked, however. As in some other CEE countries, e.g. Latvia, the self-employed are not covered (Shoukens, 2002). The duration of benefit payments has been reduced in the 1990s, especially for individuals with shorter contribution records. For some individuals, e.g. older individuals with long contribution histories, the period of benefit payments even increased. For example, for a 40-year-old person with 22 years of contribution payments, payment duration increased from seven months in 1995 to 11 months in 1999 and remained at that level until 2007.

Table 4.2: Characteristics of the unemployment benefit system in Bulgaria, 1995-2007

	1995	1999	2002	2007
Statutory replacement rate	60	60	60	60
Minimum/maximum benefit as % of minimum wage	90/140	80/150	80/150	50/100
Waiting period	7 days	7 days	0 days	0 days
Duration	6-12 months	4-12 months	4-12 months	4-12 months
Contribution requirement	6 months of past 12 months	9 months in past 15 months	9 months in past 15 months	9 months in past 15 months
Coverage	Employees[a]	Employees[a]	Employees	Employees
Share of registered unemployed receiving benfits	0.30	0.29	0.19	0.20
Unemployment benefit as % of average wage	0.34	0.31	0.35[b]	0.30[c]
Unemployment benefit as % of minimum wage	1.04	0.99	0.91[b]	0.66[c]

Notes: [a]Including graduates from vocational schools and schools of higher education; [b]2001/2003 averages; [c]values from 2006.
Source: Beleva and Tzanov (2001); National Social Security Institute (2007); European Commission (2008); ISSA (2008)

Average benefit levels have remained rather stable at a relatively low level compared to the average wage. They reached their lowest level in 2006, due to a relatively low ceiling in that year. However, by 1 January 2007, the minimum wage was raised by 12%, while the benefit ceiling was raised by 66%, yielding more generous income replacement levels. The share of unemployed actually receiving benefits was 51.7% in 1991, but declined steadily thereafter, reaching a low of 20% in 2007. Unemployed people no longer entitled to unemployment benefit have the right to receive social assistance benefits.

Minimum wage

A legal minimum wage exists and is set at national level. However, minimum wages comprise only a small share of average wages in Bulgaria. The ratio between the minimum and average wage had decreased from 54% in 1991 to 27% in 1997. Since then it increased continuously and was 35% in 2003 (Dietz et al, 2004). Nowadays the minimum wage plays a special role in the policy on income – it not only has economic but social functions too. The increase of the minimum wage in 2006 led to an increase of the income of more than 200,000 people by approximately 6.7%.

Family policy

Cash benefits

For each child they have, a family can receive a monthly allowance to the amount of 18 leva (36 leva if the child has a chronic disease) if total income of the family is less than 180 leva per person. In case family income exceeds this threshold, parents are entitled to a reduction in income taxes. The value of the child allowance has declined slightly over the past few years. It amounted to 7% of the average wage in 1993 and 5% of the average wage in 2006 (National Social Security Institute, 2007).

Beyond child allowance, a mother may receive financial support if she lives permanently in Bulgaria and earned approximately 200 leva when giving birth to a child in 2007. She has the right to remain at home on paid leave 45 days before the birth of the child. After the birth the child, the mother has the right to stay at home for three years. During this time she is socially insured, receives health insurance and the time is added to the employment duration. The financial support during the three years differs. During the first nine months, the mother gets 90% of her salary before the birth. In the next 15 months, the benefit amounts to the minimum income. During the last year, she does not receive any financial support. If the mother was not working or not insured before the birth of the child, she can receive financial support to the amount of 100 leva. The above described rights can be used by the father or grandparents of the child.

Kindergarten

Working hours in kindergartens are from 7.00 am until 19.00 pm from Monday to Friday. The salaries of the staff in the public kindergartens and maintenance of the buildings are paid for by the state budget. Parents must pay for any meals for their children while they are in the kindergartens. A variety of special benefits related to kindergarten and school attendance are also available for children from families in need, e.g. payment of fees for crèches and kindergartens, payment of food at a school canteen, buying and providing of school appliances.

The number of kindergartens declined substantially during the transition period. While in 1990/91 there were still 4,450 kindergartens, their number dropped to 2,470 in 2006/07. At the same time, enrolment of children aged three to six in pre-primary education has grown, despite initial declines until the mid-1990s. Enrolment declined from 66.7% in 1989 to 55.7% in 1993, but grew beyond the 1989 value to 73.7% in 2005 (UNICEF, 2007). Declining fertility rates were probably a factor behind this upward trend, despite declining numbers of kindergartens.

Notes

[1] This section is based on Eurydice (2003), OECD (2003, 2004a) and ETF (2003) publications.

[2] Public opinion considers the profiled gymnasia to be elite, and the education they provide to be of high quality.

References

Beleva, I. and Tzanov, V. (2001) *Labour market flexibility and employment security: Bulgaria*, Employment Paper No 30, Geneva: International Labour Organization.

Beleva, I., Tzanov, V. and Tisheva, G. (2007) 'Bulgaria', in S. Cazes and A. Nesporova (eds) *Flexicurity: a relevant approach in Central and Eastern Europe*, Geneva: International Labour Organization, pp 57-92.

Beleva, I., Tzanov, V., Noncheva, T. and Zarareva, I. (1999) *Background study on employment and labour market in Bulgaria*, Torino: European Training Foundation.

Clauwaert, S., Düvel, W. and Schömann, I. (2003) *The community social acquis in labour law in the CEECS and beyond: fighting deregulation*, Brussels: European Trade Union Institute.

Crowley, S. (2004) 'Explaining labor weakness in post-communist Europe: historical legacies and comparative perspective', *East European Politics and Societies*, vol 18, no 1, pp 394-429.

Dietz, B., Knogler, M. and Vincentz, V. (2004) *Labour market issues in Bulgaria, Romania, and Turkey*, Working Paper No 254, Munich: Osteuropa-Institut.

EBRD (European Bank for Reconstruction and Development) (2008) *Transition report 2007*, London: EBRD.

ETF (European Training Foundation) (1998-2000) *Key indicators: vocational education and training in Central and Eastern Europe*, Luxembourg: Office for Official Publications of the European Communities.

ETF (2003) *Short country report: Bulgaria*, Torino: ETF.

European Commission (2002) *Joint assessment of employment priorities in Bulgaria*, Brussels: European Commission.

European Commission (2008) *Mutual information system on social protection (MISSOC). comparative tables on social protection in the member states and the European Economic Area*, Brussels: European Commission (www.ec.europa.eu/employment_social/spsi/missoc_en.htm).

Eurostat (2008) *Data: labour market*, Luxembourg: Eurostat (http://epp.eurostat.ec.europa.eu).

Eurydice (2003) *Structures of education, vocational training, and adult education systems in Europe: Bulgaria*, Brussels: Eurydice European Unit.

Gallie, D., Kostova, D. and Kuchar, P. (2001) 'Social consequences of unemployment: East-West comparison', *Journal of European Social Policy*, vol 11, no 1, pp 39-54.

Giordano, C. and Kostova, D. (2000) 'Understanding contemporary problems in Bulgarian agricultural transformation', in C. Giordano, D. Kostova and E. Lohmann-Minka (eds) *Bulgaria: social and cultural landscapes*, Fribourg: Universitätsverlag Fribourg Schweiz, pp 159-75.

ILO (International Labour Organization) (2008) *Key indicators of the labour market programme*, Fifth Edition, Geneva: ILO.

ISSA (International Social Security Administration) (2008) *Social security worldwide database*, (www-ssw.issa.int/sswlp2/engl/page1.htm).

Kolev, A. and Saget, C. (2005) 'Understanding youth labour market disadvantage: evidence from South-East Europe', *International Labour Review*, vol 144, no 2, pp 161-87.

Kostova, D. (2005) 'Living on the periphery: Roma in Bulgaria', in F. Ruegg, R. Poledna and C. Rus (eds) *Interculturalism and discrimination in Romania*, Berlin: LIT, pp 135-154.

National Social Security Institute (2007) *Statistical reference book* (www.noi.bg/en/).

National Statistical Institute (1976-2005) *Statistical yearbook*, Sofia: National Statistical Institute.

National Statistical Institute (2005, 2006) *Education in the Republic of Bulgaria* Sofia: National Statistical Institute.

Nesporova, A. (2002) *Why unemployment remains so high in Central and Eastern Europe*, Employment Paper No 43, Geneva: International Labour Organization.

OECD (Organisation for Economic Co-operation and Development) (1999) *OECD Economic surveys 1998-1999: Bulgaria*, Paris: OECD.

OECD (2003) *Reviews of national policies for education: South Eastern Europe*, Paris: OECD.

OECD (2004a) *Reviews of national policies for education: Bulgaria*, Paris: OECD.

OECD (2004b) *Employment outlook*, Paris: OECD.

Schulten, T. (2005) *Changes in national collective bargaining systems since 1990*, Dublin: European Foundation for the Improvement of Living and Working Conditions (www.eurofound.europa.eu/eiro/2005/03/study/tn0503102s.htm).

Shoukens, P. (2002) *The social security systems for self-employed people in the applicant EU countries of Central and Eastern Europe*, Antwerp: Intersentia.

Tomova, I. (1995) *The Roma in the transition period*, Sofia: International Centre for Minority Studies and Intercultural relations.

Tonin, M. (2005) *Updated employment protection legislation indicators for Central and Eastern European countries*, Working Paper, Institute for International Economic Studies, Stockholm: Stockholm University.

Topencharov, V. (1983) *The higher education in Bulgaria*, Bucharest: CEPES.

UNICEF (United Nations International Children's Emergency Fund) (2007) *TransMONEE 2007 Database*, Florence: UNICEF Innocenti Research Centre (www.unicef-icdc.org/resources/transmonee.html).

Velinov, A. and Mikova, V. (2003) 'Social dialogue and labour relations in Bulgaria', in W. Düvel, I. Schömann, S. Clauwaert and G. Gradev (eds) *Labour relations in South East Europe*, Brussels: European Trade Union Institute, pp 45-63.

FIVE

Czech Republic

Jana Straková[1]

Since 1989, several factors have increased the expected length of education in the Czech Republic. The traditional system of public schools was supplemented by private and denominational schools. Additionally, the proportion of students only attending secondary vocational schools decreased significantly, while the proportion of students attending secondary schools with matriculation examinations and then enrolling in tertiary education increased significantly. The education system, however, retained a strong relationship between a student's education attainment and his/her socio-economic background. After 1989, stratification of the education system became even more pronounced. The upper-secondary system retained its structure. However, in compulsory education long academic programmes appeared (six-year and eight-year gymnasia), schools received more autonomy, and in order to attract students, schools offered classrooms with specialised curricula. Nevertheless, curricula and teaching approaches have not undergone any significant changes.

Structural changes in the Czech economy are indicated by the redistribution of employment among economic sectors. Employment shares in industry as well as in agriculture have decreased to shares comparable to the Western European Union (EU). However, the service sector still remained relatively small. Labour force participation rates dropped during the transition period and unemployment rates increased. The decrease in employment was most pronounced for women and young people. Flexible employment forms have evolved, but only minor parts of the labour force are affected. Unemployment exhibits large regional differences. It is especially strong among the Roma minority. Labour market entrants, approximated as the youngest age group of 15-24, comprise the category most exposed to unemployment. This is a source of concern among young people without matriculation diplomas.

During the early transition period, active labour market policies (ALMPs) in the Czech Republic were focused on the subsidisation of private sector job creation and public works, and not towards activation schemes. Only in 2005 were measures enacted to assist working people. This chapter explains in more detail the development of education, the labour market and welfare in the Czech Republic during 1990-2006.

Education system

Structure of the Czech education system

Overview of the Czech education system after the Second World War

Shortly after 1948, basic education was universalised in Czechoslovakia. Formal education began at the age of six and was provided for in basic schools.[2] After graduation from compulsory basic schools, increasingly large proportions of students attended one of three main tracks of secondary education: gymnasia, secondary technical schools and secondary vocational schools. About 15%-20% of the basic school graduates studied in gymnasia, which took three years to complete during 1953-68, and four years from 1969 onwards. Graduation was achieved after passing matriculation examinations (*maturita*). Another 20% attended four-year secondary technical schools, which offered a combination of professional education and general education leading to occupational qualifications. Approximately 60% of basic school graduates entered secondary two-to-four-year vocational schools that combined school with apprenticeship training, offering students practical training in various industrial sectors. These schools were intended to provide an education with an intermediate level of professional qualifications on the assumption that these students would move directly into the labour market. Secondary vocational schools are historically associated with different forms of practice-oriented apprentice training that was accompanied, to a limited extent, by general education.

Although the expansion rate in tertiary education was quite high throughout the socialist period, far fewer places at universities were available to satisfy potential demand (Wong, 1998). Entrance to tertiary education was conditional on having a matriculation diploma in secondary education and passage of the university entrance examination. Theoretically, students from secondary grammar and technical schools should have had similar chances of entering tertiary education, but, in reality, the great majority of university enrolments were recruited from gymnasia (70%) versus only 25% from technical schools (Wong, 1998).

Current status of the Czech education system[3]

Since 1990, school attendance has been compulsory for nine years, usually from the ages of 6-15 (see Table 5.1). All pupils start in a basic school; at the second stage of compulsory education, it is possible to attend a gymnasium. During the first stage of compulsory education, pupils can take entrance examinations for classrooms or schools with extended curricula of certain subjects (foreign languages, mathematics, natural sciences, arts, etc.).[4] At the end of the fifth year, pupils can leave the basic school to attend a gymnasium with an eight- or six-year academic programme (see Figure 5.1). For all gymnasia, pupils must pass the school's entrance examination. A total of 9.75% of pupils in the 6 -15 age group study at a gymnasium.

Table 5.1: Primary and lower-secondary education in the Czech Republic

	Typical age	ISCED level
Basic school (single structure, primary and lower-secondary)	first stage: 6-10 second stage: 11-15	1 + 2
Gymnasium (general lower-secondary)	11 (or 13)-15	2

Note: ISCED = International Standard Classification of Education.
Source: Eurydice (2007)

There are two main prerequisites for attending an upper-secondary school: completing compulsory education and successfully passing the entrance examination.[5] Pupils can apply for one school of their choice (see Table 5.2). Gymnasia provide students with a general academic education and are attended by less than 20% of all secondary students. Gymnasia may offer four-year courses for pupils aged 15 who have completed their compulsory school attendance, six-year courses for pupils aged 13 who have finished 7th grade, or eight-year courses for pupils aged 11 who have finished the 5th grade. These differing age groups may attend the same school. Gymnasia studies end with the matriculation exam, which is comprised of a written and oral section. The matriculation examination consists of two compulsory subjects: the Czech language and literature, as well as a foreign language; and two optional subjects. Each school determines the content of the matriculation examination, since no specific requirements are set externally by the state. Successful completion of the matriculation examination is a prerequisite for admission to a higher education institution or tertiary professional school.

Secondary technical schools combine general and vocational education; the proportion of general subjects to vocational subjects is about 40:60. Secondary technical schools traditionally offer four-year courses completed by matriculation examination. Secondary technical schools are attended by 40% of secondary students. At vocational schools, also attended by 40% of secondary students, the proportion of general subjects to vocational subjects and practical training varies. General education usually constitutes about 30% of classes. Practical training in three-year courses (which are prevalent) constitutes 30%-45% of classes.

Figure 5.1: The Czech education system

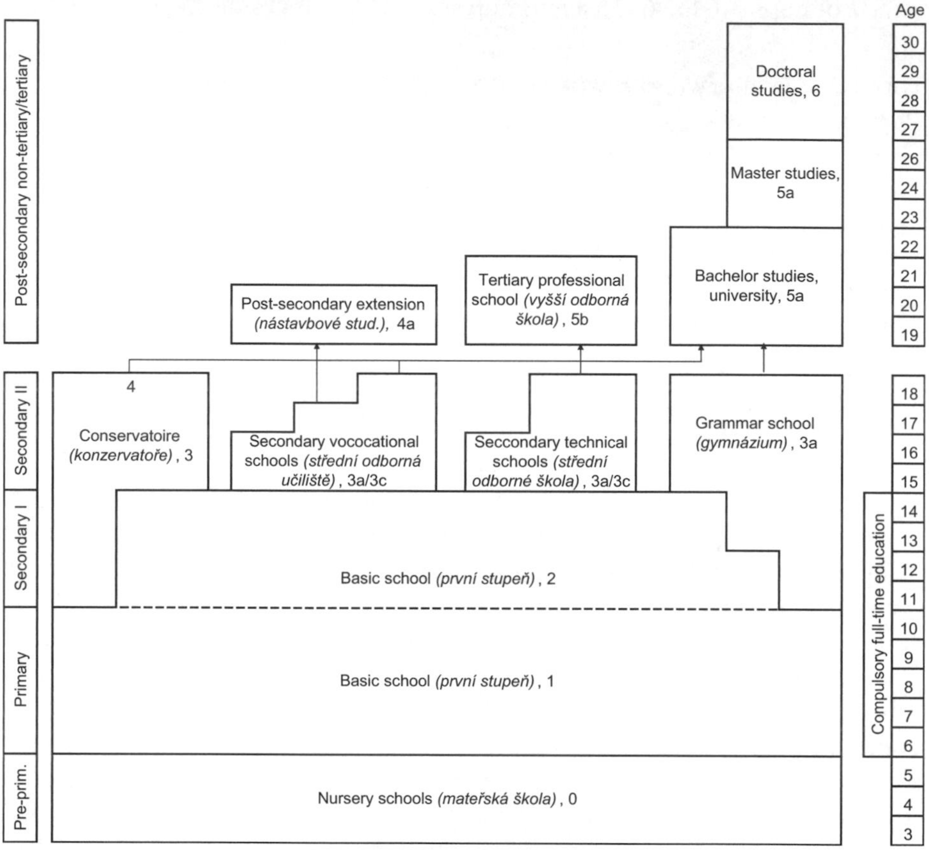

Source: ETF (2002)

Under current legislation, secondary vocational schools are obliged to train pupils for a vocational qualification required in professions where two- or three-year education accomplished by attaining an apprenticeship certificate is prescribed. Training is completed by a final examination, which does not entitle pupils to enter post-secondary education. In addition, secondary vocational schools are also authorised to train pupils in four-year courses leading to the matriculation examination. These secondary vocational schools also offer follow-up courses leading to the matriculation examination. This enables pupils with secondary education completed by attaining apprenticeship certificates to obtain matriculation diplomas and to apply for tertiary education. A maximum of 30%-35% of secondary vocational school pupils complete their studies by matriculation examination (Veselý, 2006). Secondary vocational schools offer a shortened study programme for those having completed their secondary education with a matriculation examination, and these programmes last 12-18 months for students enrolled full time.

Table 5.2: Upper-secondary education in the Czech Republic

	Type of education	Length (years)	ISCED level	Typical age
Gymnasium	General upper secondary	4	3a	15-19
Technical secondary school	Technical upper secondary	4	3a	15-19
Vocational secondary school	Vocational upper secondary	3	3c	15-18
		2	3c	15-17
		3	3c	15-18
		4	3a	15-19
Post-secondary extension	Post-secondary	2	4a	18-20

Source: Eurydice (2007)

Schools at ISCED 1, 2 and 3 levels are public, private and denominational. Public schools provide education free of charge, while private and denominational schools may charge fees.

Traditionally, higher education institutions provide a tertiary education of ISCED 5a and 6 levels; they may be of university and non-university types (see Table 5.3). Study programmes are prepared by individual institutions/faculties and approved by the Accreditation Commission of the Ministry. The matriculation certificate is the minimum entrance qualification for all forms of tertiary education. Each institution defines its own admission criteria and determines the content of its entrance examination.

Tertiary professional schools were introduced during the 1992/93 school year on an experimental basis, and since 1995 they have been included in the education system.[6] Their aim was to cover the gap in qualification needs between secondary and tertiary education. Tertiary professional schools provide students with an advanced technical knowledge. Their curriculum is prepared by the school and accredited by the Ministry of Education. The proportion of general, basic vocational and specific vocational subjects is about 20:40:30. Tertiary professional education ends with an *absolutorium*, and its graduates are referred to as 'specialists with a diploma'.

Table 5.3: Tertiary education in the Czech Republic

	ISCED level	Length (years)	Typical age
Tertiary professional school	5b	2-3.5	19-21 (22)
Higher education institution	5a	3,4,5,6	19-22 (26)
	6	3	–

Source: Eurydice (2007)

By law, higher education institutions are of two types – the university type, providing all levels of study programmes, and the non-university type, usually offering only bachelor's degree programmes. All existing higher education institutions established before the Higher Education Act are university-type institutions. Recently established higher education institutions have been accredited as non-university types.[7] All accredited bachelor's degree study programmes provide an education of ISCED 5a level, i.e. education that enables students to continue in follow-up master's degree study programmes. Private higher education institutions have often developed from private tertiary professional schools, and can only function as legal entities after having obtained the approval of the Ministry of Education, which is provided based on the recommendation of the Accreditation Commission.

Bachelor's study programmes are three- to four-year programmes focused on professional training, and provide a basis for studies in master's study programmes. Bachelor's degree study programmes prevail at private institutions. Master's study programmes are aimed at providing theoretical knowledge based on the latest scientific findings, research and development. They are intended as follow-ups to the bachelor study programmes, and they generally last between one to three years. If the study programme requires it, accreditation can be granted to a master's degree programme (four to six years long), which is not a follow-up of a bachelor's degree programme. A doctoral study programme can follow after the completion of a master's programme. It is offered solely in the university study setting, and lasts between three and four years.

On completion of coursework at higher education institutions, students take a state examination and defend a thesis. Graduates of the first cycle of courses (three to four years) are awarded the title of bachelor (Bc). Graduates of the second cycle of courses continuing after the bachelor level (one to three additional years) or longer courses (five to six years) are mostly awarded the title of master (Mgr); for some branches, there are specific titles: MgA (Master of Art), Ing. (technical and economic branches), Ing.Arch. (architecture); in medicine and veterinary medicine (and after an additional exam), the title doctor – MUDr, MDDr, MVDr. For holders of a master's degree, it is possible to be awarded the title of JUDr, PhDr, RNDr, PharmDr, or ThDr after this exam. On completion of doctoral studies, students take a doctoral examination and are awarded the title PhD (ThD in theology).

Vertical dimension of the education system

Figure 5.2 displays the trends in education enrolment of the school-aged population in the Czech Republic starting as early as 1975. Obviously, the vast majority of this population has been involved in 9-grade basic schools. The proportion of these pupils is decreasing due to an increase in other forms of schooling. The proportion of pupils enrolled in vocational upper-secondary education has been traditionally high in the Czech Republic. Up to the mid-1990s, the majority of those in the upper-secondary education have been enrolled in secondary vocational or apprenticeship schools.

Figure 5.2: Enrolment by type of school in the Czech Republic (%)

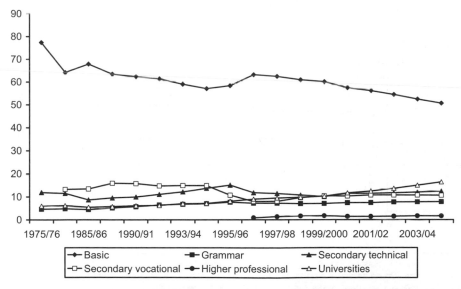

Notes: Higher professional schools are listed in the statistical yearbook of the Czech Republic starting from 1996. Secondary vocational schools are also called secondary trade or apprenticeship schools, whereas secondary technical schools are also named secondary vocational schools in the statistical yearbook of the Czech Republic.
Source: Czech Statistical Office (1980-2005)

From 1975-95, the proportion in secondary technical schools has been lower than in secondary vocational schools, but has been increasing. Since the late-1990s, both types of vocational education have been catering to a similar proportion of upper-secondary school pupils. Concurrently, the proportion of those enrolled in grammar schools has been generally lower than those enrolled in vocational schools, but enrolment has been increasing over the last two decades. Similarly, an increase in the proportion enrolled in tertiary education has also been evident, from 5% in 1975 to 16% in 2005. Additionally, since 1996 a small proportion of young people have been attending post-secondary non-tertiary higher professional schools.

Czech law provides for gender equality in schools. Boys and girls are more or less equally represented at secondary schools, with a slightly higher proportion of girls at secondary general schools (1998/99 enrolment: 21% of girls and 17% of boys in secondary general education, 79% of girls and 83% of boys in secondary technical education) (ETF, 2002).

Another way to evaluate the vertical dimension of the education system is to explore the pathways pupils from primary education choose, and to estimate the proportion of students from various types of general and vocational secondary education who progress to the next tertiary level. From Figure 5.3, it is evident that almost half of all basic education pupils proceed to secondary professional education,[8] whereas a total of 20% enter gymnasia and about 28% proceed to vocational education.[9]

Figure 5.3: Graduates of basic and secondary schools by type of continuing studies, 1998/99

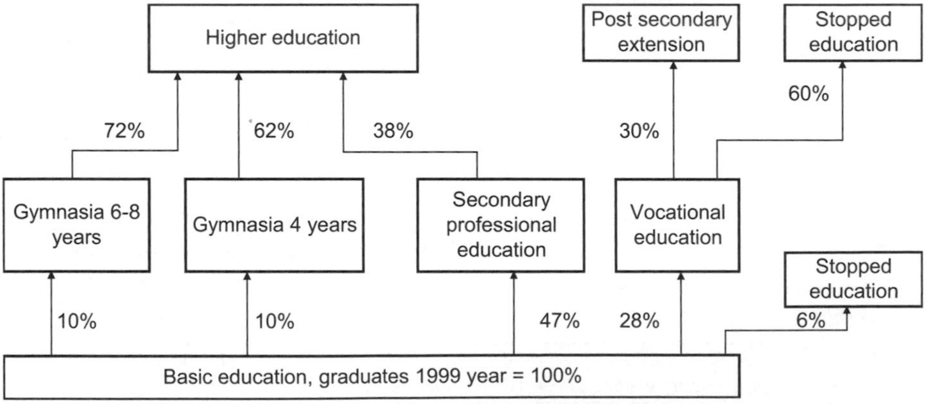

Source: Czech Statistical Office (2000); Matějů and Straková (2006)

While 72% of graduates of six to eight-year gymnasia proceed to universities, 10% fewer leavers of four-year gymnasia do the same. On the other hand, only 38% of leavers from secondary professional schools progress to tertiary education. A total of 30% of vocational education graduates progress to any kind of post-secondary education, while the majority do not continue to pursue further education.

Secondary level of education

Stratification and track differentiation

The first education transition occurs quite early in the Czech Republic. At age 11 while in 5th grade, Czech pupils might choose to stay in basic school or switch to a gymnasium. A similar decision might be made at the age of 13 while in 7th grade. About a quarter of 5th and 7th grade pupils apply for gymnasia, and about 10% are accepted. At the age of 15, pupils decide between the general versus technical versus vocational educational track.

However, students' very first decision occurs in the education system much earlier. Czech students can take their first entrance examinations at the age of eight, and on passing them, they can apply for classes with extended curricula of foreign languages. About 10% of students pursue compulsory education in schools with extended curricula of certain subjects. Due to students' very early first decision and large differences between achievement of students in individual school tracks and their social composition (Straková, 2007), the Czech education system, similar to the Slovak and Hungarian ones, should be characterised as highly stratified. International comparative studies repeatedly show a strong relationship between student achievement and socio-economic background in the Czech education system (OECD, 2001, 2004b, 2007).

The Czech education system has traditionally been characterised by a stronger emphasis on vocational rather than general education. The enrolment in the general tracks on the upper-secondary level has been somewhat below 20% and began slightly increasing in the 1990s, which is evident from Figure 5.4. Simultaneously, the enrolment in vocational tracks on the upper-secondary level has been much higher, particularly with regard to vocational or technical education leading to matriculation. The number of pupils gaining vocational education and matriculation diplomas increased from 37% in 1992 to 48% in 2004. Additionally, a decrease in the vocational programmes without matriculation is also evident, from 46% in 1992 to 30% in 2004.

Figure 5.4: Enrolment in education and training at the (upper) secondary level (%)

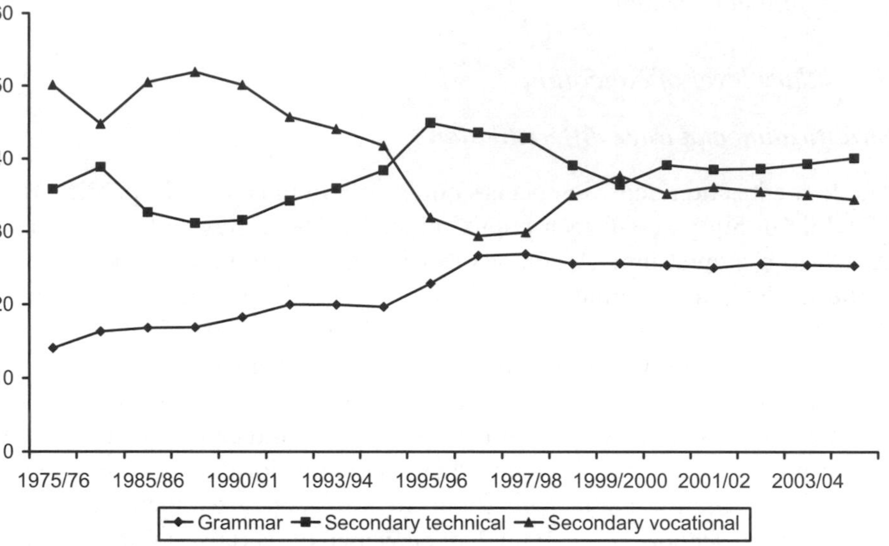

Source: Czech Statistical Office (2006)

Organisation of vocational training

Vocational education and training (VET) plays an important role in the Czech Republic, with 81.5% of basic school graduates entering vocational schools, which is one of the highest rates in Europe (Eurydice, 2003). A total of 37.2% of those attended secondary vocational schools that combine school and work (OECD, 2005). Education in secondary vocational schools is organised as a dual system. Students typically attend one week of school and one week of work. Secondary technical schools do not usually provide any regular work experience. The content of general education in secondary technical schools covers only 40% of the curricula, but otherwise education is organised in the same way as in the general education track.

Standardisation and quality differentiation of secondary education

The degree of standardisation of the Czech education system was traditionally very high. Standardisation was not ensured at the level of outcomes (there were no standardised examinations at any level) but at the level of processes. The content was defined by detailed state curricula and by a uniform set of textbooks. Pre-service training with identical syllabi at all teacher training faculties conveyed an identical notion about the correctly taught lesson to future teachers throughout the country. Czech school inspection regularly monitored whether the curricula were strictly followed and whether teaching procedures corresponded to the requirements (Matějů and Straková, 2005).

After 1989, the degree of process standardisation decreased. Uniform curricula were replaced by less detailed standards, schools and teachers began choosing from a broader range of textbooks, and the pre-service training at individual teacher training colleges began differing. In spite of these changes, the education content and teaching practices in most schools remained the same, whereas evaluation mechanisms changed only slightly. The most important evaluation vehicle at the state level is still represented by the Czech school inspection, which follows similar criteria for school evaluation as it used to in the past.

Traditionally, there are large differences in the achievement of students in various tracks. In Programme for International Student Assessment (PISA) 2003, 75% of students in vocational schools did not attain the minimal level of reading literacy (necessary for functioning in everyday situations), while in secondary technical schools there were 25% of such students, and in gymnasia only 5% of such students (Palečková and Tomášek, 2005).

Tertiary level of education

Horizontal dimension

Figure 5.5 depicts horizontal, or field-of-study, differentiation at the tertiary level. The most popular fields of study are obviously social sciences and services, with enrolment of more than 40% of all students in 1992/93. The attractiveness of these fields has grown further, so that in 1994/95, 47% of all students were enrolled in social sciences and services. The second most popular education specialty is the field of technology. However, the proportion of students enrolled in this field has been decreasing from 1992 to 1994. A similar decline has been observed in the proportions of those students enrolled in the medical and agricultural fields.

Humanities, arts, education, health and welfare are traditionally female fields of study (more than 70% of tertiary qualifications are awarded to females), whereas engineering, mathematics and computer sciences are dominated by male graduates (more than 70% of tertiary qualifications are awarded to males) (OECD, 2004a). Social sciences, business, law, services, life and physical sciences and agriculture are relatively neutral fields of study with respect to the gender composition.

Figure 5.5: Enrolment in tertiary education by field of study (%)

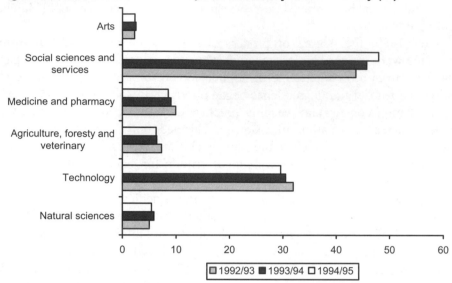

Source: Czech Statistical Office (1993-95)

Standardisation, quality differentiation and openness of tertiary education

Higher education institutions have full autonomy, so that one could conclude that standardisation is not pronounced at the tertiary level. The only vehicle of quality assurance is the accreditation process carried out by the Ministry of Education.

The vast majority of universities in the Czech Republic are public. In 2005, 24 of 28 universities were public, and two were state-run. However, non-university type institutions are all private.[10] Thus, private tertiary professional schools constitute 60% of institutions, and account for 6.1% of all tertiary-educated students in 2004/05.

Public higher education institutions provide education free of charge. In recent years, many institutions introduced so-called 'life long learning programmes' for students who had not succeeded in the entrance procedure. Students attending these programmes pay fees and can usually progress to regular programmes or receive diplomas (Matějů and Straková, 2005).

Labour market

Economic development

The Czech economic transition process is divided into the period before the division of Czechoslovakia in 1993 and the period after. After the breakdown of the communist system in 1989, social and political reforms initiated the rapid progress of the Czech economy, as a part of Czechoslovakian Republic, into a functioning market economy. The basic elements of initial Czechoslovakian reforms after 1989 were price and trade liberalisation, reduced public subsidies to enterprises, institutional changes and a large privatisation programme (European Commission, 2000). A restrictive monetary and fiscal policy had been implemented since the beginning of the transformation process. The building up of the private sector was enforced during the period from 1991-93 within three programmes (Munich et al, 1999). First, restitution returned some property nationalised by the communist regime to the previous owners. Second, small-scale privatisation consisted of public auctions of small businesses, primarily in retail trade, catering and services. Third, large-scale privatisation was the most important part of the programme in terms of the value of assets. The Czech Republic profited from the early economic and social reforms in Czechoslovakia. Furthermore, the Czech Republic was the richer part of Czechoslovakia, significantly ahead of Slovakia, and in a leading position relative to other Central and Eastern European (CEE) countries. Hence, the gross domestic product (GDP) registered only a small-sized decline in real terms compared to other CEE countries during the first years of transition (Figure 5.6). This transitional recession peaked at −11.6% in 1991.

Figure 5.6: GDP growth, 1991-2006

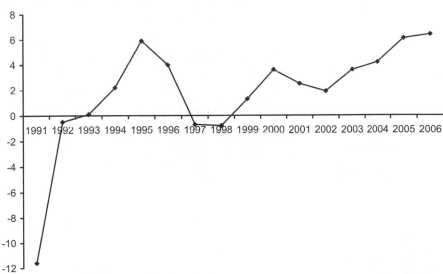

Source: ILO (2008); data for 2006 from Eurostat (2008)

In 1993, when the former Czechoslovakia was dissolved, the Czech Republic had to master both the transition from a socialist to a market economy and from being part of Czechoslovakia to becoming an independent nation. However, the Czech Republic did not suffer much from the economic turmoil arising from the division of the Czechoslovakian Republic in 1993. For example, the initial economic contraction was followed by fast growth from 1994-96 with yearly growth ranging between 2% and 6%. Despite the rapid and early privatisation efforts, ambiguous forms of cross-ownership remained of particular concern: the state remained an important shareholder in large banks, which in turn controlled the most important Investment Privatisation Funds, and through them the firms themselves. The funds had incentives to maximise their allocation of capital but not to put pressure on management or to promote the restructuring of firms.

Weak corporate governance structures created economic difficulties for many firms and even led to their collapse, particularly after banks underwent hard budget constraints and radically limited their credits in 1997. Therefore, the GDP expansion in the mid-1990s was followed by a brief and small decline in real GDP per capita caused by the international crisis at the end of the decade. The lack of micro-level restructuring, as well as the state's lack of concern for corporate transparency and governance, became apparent. The largest firms fell into financial difficulty. In 1997, the Czech government implemented a package of economic measures to redress the structural problems. The privatisation of companies was accelerated. Remaining state shares in banks and mines, Czech Telecom, and other distribution and communication companies were privatised. In parallel, as the role of the Investment Privatisation Funds declined, the ownership structure of the economy was gradually consolidated. Together with increasing foreign direct investment inflows, this contributed to an accelerated pace of enterprise restructuring (Večerník, 2007). Subsequently, the economy returned to a higher growth path in the new millennium. Growth rates increased substantially from 1.9% in 2002 to 6.4% in 2006.

Labour market dynamics[11]

Employment dynamics

The emerging economic structure has been moving towards that of market economies, away from an over-sized manufacturing and an inefficient agriculture sector, and towards services that were underdeveloped before the transition. In 1990, 12.3% of employed individuals worked in agriculture, 45.5% in industry and 42.2% in services (ILO, 2008). The industrial sector was characterised by a predominance of large enterprises, especially in heavy industry and engineering fields that were developed mostly after the Second World War under communist rule. Until 2005, employment shares in industry as well as agriculture decreased to shares comparable to the Western EU. The

136

service sector's share of total employment increased to 56.5% in 2005 (ILO, 2008). Thus, the service sector seems to be the driving force in the Czech economy. Banking and financial services ballooned, but began to decline again in the late 1990s, after the final privatisation of the banking giants. Within the tertiary sector, public administration and services for firms underwent considerable expansion, especially in comparison with the stagnating level of personnel in health services, education and research.

The transition period was characterised by a very strong decrease in employment and an increasing mismatch between labour demand and supply. Figure 5.7 shows that labour force participation rates of the population aged 15-64 sharply declined from 78% in 1990 to 70.7% in 2006. Regarding the development of participation rates, the transitional period can be divided into two sub-periods. Until 1993 there was a relatively sharp decline in participation rates, disproportionately burdening females. After 1993, participation rates remained fairly stable. Figure 5.7 also shows gender-specific time trends in labour force participation. In general, the female activity rate was eight percentage points below that of males in 1990, but the gender gap in labour force participation has widened during the transition.

Figure 5.7: Labour force participation rate (age group 15-64), 1990-2006

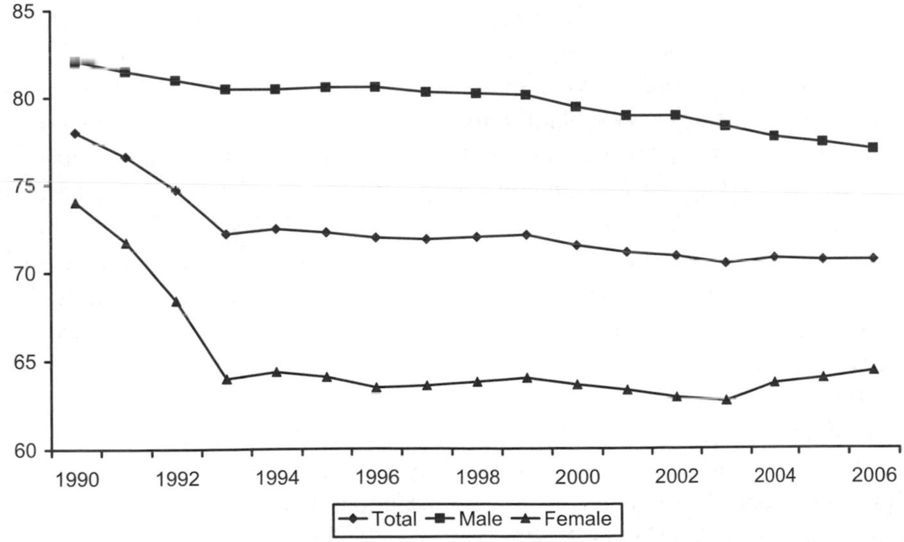

Source: ILO (2008)

In 2006, the lowest activity rate is registered for the youngest age cohorts (15-24) at 35.5% (Table 5.4). The population aged between 15 and 24 is the cohort most affected by the fall in employment: their activity rate fell from

57.7% to 35.5% between 1990 and 2006. The main reason is the increasing enrolment in higher education among the young.

Table 5.4: Labour force participation rate by age group, 1990-2006

	1990	1995	2000	2006
15+	66.9	61.5	60.4	59.4
15-24	57.7	50.6	46.0	35.5
25-54	95.2	89.2	88.4	88.3
55-64	39.3	35.9	38.2	47.0
65+	8.3	5.6	4.1	3.5

Source: ILO (2008)

Labour market flexibilisation

During the period of transition, flexible employment forms emerged. However, they are still less distributed than in most Western European countries. For example, part-time work is significantly less prevalent in the Czech Republic (4.4%) than in the EU15 (20.2%) (Eurostat, 2008). In 2006, fixed-term contracts were used by 8% of workers in the Czech Republic, compared to the 14.4% EU15 average (Eurostat, 2008). Self-employment as an alternative flexible employment form increased slightly from 12.7% in 1993 to 15.3% in 2005 (ILO, 2008). Hence, the Czech Republic has a high self-employment share, especially in non-agricultural sectors, compared to other CEE countries. The share of non-salaried family workers remained very low at around 0.3%-0.7%, and is comparable to the EU15. The share of agriculture among the self-employed was 5.8% in 2000 and 4.4% in 2005.[12] In fact, self-employment is much more used as a part-time rather than full-time activity. In the early 1990s, about one quarter of non-pensioner households declared some income from self-employment based on a business licence. Until the late 1990s, the share of households with a person possessing a business licence increased to 40%. Among those households, those declaring self-employment as their only source of income was about 12%; those declaring self-employment as the main source of income was about 33%; and those declaring self-employment as a complementary source of income was 42% (Večerník, 2007).

Unemployment dynamics

Unemployment was an unknown phenomenon during the communist era. Official registered unemployment of the public employment service, measured as a share of the active population (15-64 years old) remained under 4% until 1996 (Figure 5.8). This is a very low unemployment rate at the beginning of the transition period when most of the other CEE countries suffered from a dramatic increase in unemployment rates. Explanations of this 'Czech miracle' have focused on a number of factors, including the high rates of labour market turnover and the restrictive unemployment insurance system, among others (OECD, 1998). In addition, favourable initial conditions, including a well-educated population and a technologically advanced economy are mentioned. However, in accordance with the second economic recession in 1997, jumps in unemployment rates appear. The highest level was reached in 2003, with approximately 10.3% of the labour force unemployed. In the last few years, unemployment decreased slightly because of the strong economic recovery.

Labour market entrants, approximated as the youngest age cohort of 15-24, is the category most exposed to unemployment. The unemployment rate of people younger than 25 years increased from 8.4% in 1993 to 19.3% in 2005, and the level is about two to three times higher than the average unemployment rate for the entire adult population. Apart from labour demand restrictions related especially to working experience, difficulties in the professional integration of youth are also caused by the insufficient match between labour demand and qualifications offered by the education system.

Figure 5.8: Unemployment rates, 1990-2006

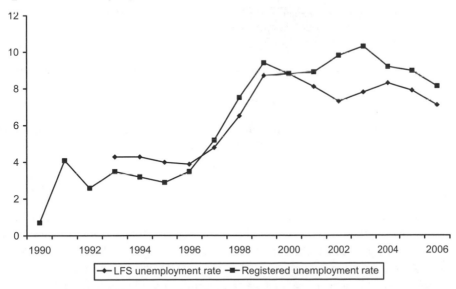

Note: Both unemployment rates refer to individuals aged over 15.
Source: ILO (2008); LFS unemployment for 2006 and registered unemployment rates for 2004-06 from Czech Statistical Office (2008)

Although there is a negative correlation between unemployment and education, this general rule is counterbalanced by the high exposure of school graduates to unemployment, which was increasing. The most at risk are adolescents who drop out of school without a diploma; people who are often also not willing to seek a job, are not motivated due to their disadvantaged family background, and thus preferring social benefits instead of wages. In 2005, 60% of unemployed individuals aged 15-24 did not have matriculation diplomas (Table 5.5).

Table 5.5: Unemployment rate by level of education, 2001-06

	2001	2002	2003	2004	2005	2006
Vocational	18.3	20.3	23.4	23.2	17.9	15.7
Vocational with matura	19.2	21.4	23.5	21.2	16.1	14.0
Technical	17.0	15.2	16.3	15.0	12.2	11.0
Gymnasium	6.6	7.2	6.4	6.1	4.8	4.4
Tertiary 5b	9.6	12.9	13.2	13.6	10.9	9.1
University 5a	6.2	6.8	8.8	7.7	5.5	4.8

Source: NÚOV (2006).

In 2006, unemployment decreased in all age groups, the least among those aged below 18 and over 50, and most among those aged 19-25. This is due to demography (less numerous population years), increasing enrolment in higher education, better labour market conditions and higher adaptability of the young.

Minority ethnic groups, migration and regional differences

Unemployment rates are unevenly distributed among ethnic groups and regions. The ethnic structure of the Czech population is very homogeneous. The only sizeable ethnic group is Roma, who probably represent about 200,000 individuals (Munich et al, 1999). Unemployment rates among Roma are estimated to be above 50% (OECD, 2004a), and some recent studies give an estimate of 70%. In socially excluded localities, the unemployment rate is 90%-100% (Gabal, 2006). Unemployment is particularly severe among the Roma minority because they have on average a very low level of education and suffer from social exclusion. An external factor contributing to Roma unemployment is a welfare system that, especially in the case of numerous families, creates welfare dependency. Roma citizens are also subject to discriminatory practices from employers (People in Need, 2006).

In the Czech Republic, the variation in employment and unemployment rates at the regional level is marked (Table 5.6). Unemployment is lowest and the employment rate is the highest in the capital Prague, where a thriving commercial and urban area with international headquarters and central administration has developed. High unemployment exceeding 10% remains a serious problem in North Bohemia and North Moravia (OECD, 2003). Regions with high unemployment rates are characterised by declining industries, e.g. mining and agriculture. However, these disparities have not encouraged migration (European Commission, 2000). The lack of mobility could reflect problems in the housing market or a low willingness of the Czech labour force to move.

Table 5.6: Unemployment rate by region, 2006

Czech Republic	7.0
Praha	3.0
Středočeský	4.5
Jihočeský	4.6
Plzeňský	4.7
Karlovarský	10.7
Ústecký	12.9
Liberecký	7.8
Královéhradecký	5.8
Pardubický	5.7
Vysočina	5.1
Jihomoravský	8.0
Olomoucký	7.9
Zlínský	7.0
Moravskoslezský	11.3

Source: Czech Statistical Office (2008)

Labour market institutions

The Czech Republic has equipped itself after independence with a regulatory framework for the labour market that is similar to many other countries in Europe. Parts of the labour law dated back to 1965 have remained valid. It has been amended several times to gradually adjust to the needs of a market economy. The governmental influence in labour relations was reduced significantly. Furthermore, collective labour relations changed substantially (Večerník, 2001). Additionally, Czech labour law was harmonised with binding international agreements and EU law.

Employment protection legislation

The Czech Republic tends to be more restrictive concerning regular employment contracts, as the EU average that is lower than the CEE average (see Table 2.7 in Chapter Two of this book). Regulation concerning temporary employment is negligible. Its value is measured at 0.5, which is considerably lower than the EU average (2.0). In contrast to other CEE countries, Czech firing rules concerning collective dismissals are less restrictive than in the EU. In general, the comparison of overall employment protection legislation (EPL) finds that, because of significant liberalisation efforts, the Czech Republic has on average a lower EPL strictness than the EU average.

Industrial relations

Before 1990, the Czech Republic's industrial relations systems were characterised by central political and managerial control exercised by the state. During the transition, the Czech Republic moved away from a centralised wage-setting system towards a collective bargaining system in the enterprise sector, similar to those of many other CEE countries. Wage bargaining in the Czech Republic is multi-level. Wage bargaining usually takes place at the enterprise level, but sectoral agreements also exist (Visser, 2004: Table 1.8). Structures for higher-level collective agreements exist at the national level (OECD, 1998). In the early 1990s, the Czech government played an active role in wage setting and imposed obligatory guidelines, which included maximum and minimum wage increases. During this period, a tripartite central wage bargaining institution also set standards on industrial relations, employment, etc. However, since 1995, the government has played a less active role.

Union membership has declined sharply during the 1990s, down from the 100% coverage of the workforce registered at the beginning of transition. According to Van Gyes et al (2007: Figure 2), the Czech unionisation rate decreased from 41% in 1995 to 22% in 2004. The unionisation degree is, in general, lower in the private than in the public sector.

Van Gyes et al (2007: Figure 4) estimate the percentage of employees covered by collective agreements in the Czech Republic to be 35% in 2002, representing a medium level of union coverage compared to other CEE countries. Furthermore, the degree of coordination in the Czech Republic lies at the lowest level compared to other CEE countries (Visser, 2004: Table 1.10). The degree of centralisation ranges in the middle of CEE countries (Visser, 2004: Table 1.9)

Welfare regime

Labour market policy

Active labour market policy

During the early transition, ALMPs in the Czech Republic were focused on the subsidisation of private sector job creation and public works, and not on activation schemes (OECD, 2004a). Subsidised job creation schemes were the main active measures, in terms of participants and expenditure. Retraining has been used modestly and the rest of the programmes claimed only a negligible share of total expenditures. In 1992, ALMPs amounted to 0.2% of GDP and 54% of total employment expenditures (Večerník, 2001); during the 1990s, the amount of expenditure for ALMPs rapidly decreased to 0.03% of GDP in 1997. Consequently, the ALMPs share of total employment expenditures decreased to 14% in 1997 (Večerník, 2001). Such strong decline affected in particular subsidised employment schemes. When unemployment rose at the end of the 1990s, ALMPs were largely re-activated. Between 1997 and 1999, the share of ALMPs in GDP almost tripled (Večerník, 2001). During the last few years, the expenditure on ALMPs was about 0.2% of GDP (OECD, 2004a). Spending on retraining still accounts for a relatively small share of ALMP expenditure. Limited activities and resources have been allocated to evaluating the impact and effectiveness of active employment measures.

Important changes have been introduced since 2005. School graduates can no longer be registered as unemployed, and if they are not successful in the labour market, they are supposed to take a subsidised job. Young job seekers up to the age of 25 are considered one of the group at risk, and therefore have wide access to youth training and retraining programmes, as well as individual action plans.

Measures have already been enacted that advantage working people over those not working, such as tax credits. The new benefit system introduced in January 2007 is expected to support work motivation by the possibility of reducing or even withdrawing benefits due to lack of work activity or non-cooperative behaviour on the part of recipients. Additionally, those working for the minimum wage will be further entitled to social benefits. For calculating benefits, only 70% of earnings will be counted for consideration of material need.

Regarding education and training, the new Act on Employment (in force since October 2004) expands access to training for all interested people. Labour offices can also finance courses for people other than registered job seekers. However, there is no systematic approach to further education. The relevant legislation deals only with the issue of the verification and recognition of the results of various forms of education (Act on the

Recognition of Professional Qualifications, in force as of May 2004). According to an April 2006 report of the National Training Fund, the Czech Republic ranks 21st among the EU25 in terms of participation in further education programmes (30% of the population participates in such programmes, compared to the 42% EU average). The unemployed and individuals with low qualifications fare the worst in terms of access to further education programmes (Večerník, 2007).

Unemployment insurance

A system of unemployment benefits was established in 1990. Initially, benefit levels were set at 60% of previous net wages, or even 90%, if job loss was due to restructuring, and payment duration of 12 months. This generous arrangement was scaled down with reforms in 1991 and 1992. In 1992, payment duration was fixed at six months and benefits were set at 60% of the previous wage for the first three months and 50% for the remaining months (Večerník, 2004). The system did not undergo major changes thereafter. The required contribution period has remained at 12 months within the last three years and the maximum duration of payments has remained at six months. The conditions used to be favourable for labour market entrants, since the period of study was recognised as a basis for entitlement to unemployment benefit. In order to avoid benefit dependency among young people, the condition to pay social and health insurance for at least one year was included into the new Employment Act (435/2004). Since 2005, the period of study is also no longer recognised as a basis for entitlement to unemployment benefit. This reform was, however, partially attenuated since 1 January 2006 by crediting six months of study/training against the required contribution period, thereby reducing the required period in employment to six months. According to the new arrangement, young people who cannot find a job will be obliged to take a subsidised job.

Table 5.7 indicates that unemployment benefit, after being quite generous in 1990, was kept at a rather low level relative to the average wage, but was at times higher than the minimum wage. Furthermore, social assistance benefits for single people are higher than unemployment benefit as well as the minimum wage. Hence, welfare dependency has emerged as a problem particularly among older people (Večerník, 2004) as well as the Roma population.

As mentioned above, important changes have been introduced since 2005 to strengthen work incentives. The new benefit system introduced in January 2007 is expected to support work motivation by the possibility to reduce or even withdraw benefits in the case of the lack of activity or non-cooperative behaviour. Additionally, those working for the minimum wage will be further entitled to social benefits. For calculating social benefits, only 70% of earnings will be counted for consideration of material need.

The new measures introduced in 2005 and 2007 are rather insufficient to enhance motivation to work instead of remaining dependant on welfare. Moreover, even implementing these measures might be difficult. Benefits are provided separately by labour offices (state social support) and municipalities (social assistance). Labour offices are understaffed and can only formally comply with new measures of activation and the possibility to withdraw the benefits in cases of non-cooperation on the side of job seekers.

Table 5.7: Wage and benefits levels, 1990-2005 (% average wage[a])

	Minimum wage	Average unemployment benefit	Subsistence amounts for single adult	Subsistence amounts for family of four[c]
1990	60.9	59.6	–	–
1992	47.4	39.4	47.7	157.2
1994	31.9	34.4	39.2	119.6
1996[b]	25.8	30.7	35.4	112.5, 121.1
1998	22.7	25.7	33.4	115.2
2000[b]	29.6, 42.6	33.3	36.1	102.0
2002	36.3	26.2	33.9	92.4
2003	36.6	26.0	32	87.1
2004	37.0	25.4	29.2	79.5
2005	37.8	28.5	29.1	83.9

Notes: [a]Only the minimum wage is related to gross average wage, all other items are related to net wage, estimated on family expenditure data by the Ministry of Labour and Social Affairs. [b] In those years, the minimum wage or subsistence amounts were increased twice.[c] Two adults and two children 10-15 years old.
Source: Večerník (2007)

Minimum wage

A legal minimum wage exists and is set at the national level by the government after negotiation with trade unions and employers. It does not vary across regions or education (Munich et al, 1999). The minimum wage was first implemented in 1990 at 60.9% of average wages (see Table 5.7) and subsequently raised gradually in nominal terms, but due to faster growth in prices and average wages, the minimum wage decreased in real terms. Although the minimum wage has been increased in real terms since 1998, it does not appear to create important distortions in the labour market. In 2004, the minimum wage applied to few workers, e.g. Organisation for Economic Co-operation and Development (OECD) (2004a) reports that less than 1% of employees earn the minimum wage. The Czech Republic ranks around the middle of the OECD with a relatively high minimum (OECD, 2004a) at around 37% of the average net wage.

Family policy

Kindergartens have a long tradition in the Czech education system. Pre-school education first appeared in the Education Act in 1869, and in 1948, kindergarten became part of the education system. During communist rule, it was strongly supported by the state, which promoted employment of women and preferred collective education that weakened the role of family. Kindergartens have traditionally provided very good care and education, and have exhibited high enrolment rates. Kindergartens are set up by municipalities who also cover their running costs (with the exception of teacher salaries and teaching aids that are covered by the Ministry of Education). Parents can be asked to pay a maximum of 50% of the running (not education) costs, with the exception of the pre-primary year that must be accessible to all free of charge (parents pay only per day costs).

Kindergartens are attended by children aged three to six. Attendance is optional. Under exceptional circumstances, children younger than age three can be enrolled. Kindergartens are also attended by children older than six. These are mainly children whose primary school enrolment has been deferred either at the request of their parents or by recommendation of the school or guidance centre.

Children usually stay in kindergarten for half a day (arriving between 6.00 am and 8.30 am and leaving between 12.00 pm and 13.00 pm), or a full day (leaving between 15.00 pm and 17.00 pm). In the late 1990s and early 2000s, demand exceeded supply by less than 1%. In 2003, 79% of three-year-olds, 93% of four-year-olds, 94% of five-year-olds, 25% of children younger than three, and 24% of children older than six attended kindergartens. In recent years, we observe again slightly increasing birth rates, with demand for kindergarten placement increasingly exceeding supply.[13]

New legislation endorses kindergarten attendance. According to the 2004 Education Act (561/2004), the last year of kindergarten became free of charge to increase the enrolment of children from socially disadvantaged families and to prepare them for basic school entry. Since the beginning of 2004, parents retain the claim for child-raising allowance[14] if the attendance of a child younger than three years in crèches does not exceed five days a month and attendance of a child older than four years in nursery school does not exceed four hours a day. Parental income is not relevant.[15]

Crechés – institutions intended for children younger than three years – are usually established by municipalities. Relative to kindergartens, crèches are quite rare and their numbers have been declining further. While in 2004/05 the number of kindergartens was 4,776, there were only 46 crèches (compared to 113 crèches in 1997). Enrolment figures are not recorded. Czech mothers usually leave their children with their family members or hire a babysitter when returning to work before their children reach two. Children older than two can usually stay in kindergarten, and only a quarter of children younger than three attend kindergarten.

Social assistance

The Subsistence Act defines the subsistence level that serves as a basis for calculation of the entitlement to social benefits and is updated yearly according to the index of consumer prices in a given period. During the 1990s and early 2000s, the subsistence level was defined by Subsistence Act 463/1991. According to this act, social assistance has two components: 1) amount for meeting personal needs (including nutrition) and 2) amount for covering household costs (according to number of people living in the household). Table 5.7 (see above) indicates that since the mid-1990s, social assistance to both single people and families has been declining relative to the average net wage, as well as to the minimum wage.

From 1990-2000, an individual could have asked for *benefits of state social support* (Social Support Act 117/1995): child benefits, social benefits, housing benefits (depending on income) and child-raising allowance, birth grants, burial allowance (benefits not depending on income); and *benefits of social care* (Social Need Act 482/1991): social care benefits and child nutrition benefits (depending on income).

In 2006, a new Subsistence Act (110/2006) that changed the definition of subsistence level came into operation. Also, the Social Need Act was substituted by the Material Emerency Act (111/2006), which changed the nature of social care benefits. The new benefits system is expected to support work motivation by the possibility of reducing or even withdrawing benefits in the event of a lack of activity or non-cooperative behaviour on the part of recipients. Also, those working for the minimum wage will be further entitled to social benefits. For calculating benefits, only 70% of earnings will be counted for consideration of material need. The benefit entitlements are both income tested and means tested. There is no age limit.

Notes

[1] The preparation of this chapter was made possible thanks to the project 'Unequal access to education: the extent, sources, social and economic consequences, policy strategies' (grant no IJ005/04-DP2 of the Ministry of Labour and Social Affairs of the Czech Republic).

[2] The length of basic education was initially nine years and was reduced to eight years in 1974. Before 1984, compulsory school attendance was nine years, afterwards

until 1990/91 it was extended to 10 years: eight years at basic school and at least two years at one of the upper-secondary schools.
[3] The section is based on Eurydice (2003) and ETF (2002) publications.
[4] A total of 9.5% of pupils receive compulsory education in such classrooms or schools.
[5] The content of the entrance examination (written and oral) is determined by the school.
[6] Tertiary professional schools including those established by the state can charge fees.
[7] This refers to all private institutions, as well as to the first newly established public institution 'College of Polytechnics Jihlava'.
[8] This figure includes students attending programmes leading to a matriculation examination at both secondary technical and secondary vocational schools.
[9] This figure includes students attending programmes leading to the apprenticeship certificate.
[10] Thirty-nine private institutions of higher education were registered by November 2005.
[11] This section is largely based on Večerník (2007).
[12] Data from European Labour Force Survey (EULFS) (Eurostat, 2008).
[13] Source: Annual report of the Ministry of Education, Youth, and Sports about the state of the education system (2000, 2003, 2005).
[14] Child-raising allowance is awarded to a person taking care of a child younger than four (or a disabled child younger than seven).
[15] According to the previous regulation valid during 1990 throughout early 2000, parents lost the allowance if they regularly sent their child to kindergarten and if the income of a person receiving child-rising allowance exceeded the given amount.

References

Czech Statistical Office (various years) *Statistical yearbook for the Czech Republic* (www.czso.cz/eng/redakce.nsf/i/yearbooks).

ETF (European Training Foundation) (2002) *Vocational education and training and employment services in the Czech Republic*, Luxembourg: Office for Official Publications of the European Communities.

European Commission (2000) *Joint assessment of employment priorities in the Czech Republic*, Luxembourg: Office for Official Publications of the European Communities.

Eurostat (2008) *Data: labour market*, Luxembourg: Eurostat (http://epp.eurostat.ec.europa.eu).

Eurydice (2003) *Structure of education, vocational training, and adult education system: Czech Republic*. Brussels: Eurydice European Unit.

Eurydice (2007) *Eurybase Czech Republic*. Brussels: Eurydice European Unit (www.eurydice.org/portal/page/portal/Eurydice/EuryCountry).

Gabal, I. (2006) *Analýza sociálně vyloučených romských lokalit a absorpční kapacity subjektů v jejich okolí* (*Analysis of socially excluded Roma neighborhoods and absorption capacities in their surroundings*), Prague: Ministry of Labour.

ILO (International Labour Organization) (2008) *Key indicators of the labour market programme*, Fifth Edition, Genova: ILO.

Matějů, P. and Straková, J. (2005) *Kde jsme?* (*Where are we?*), Prague: Institute for Social and Economic Analysis.

Matějů, P. and Straková, J. (2006) *(Ne)rovné šance na vzdělání, vzdělanostní nerovnosti v České republice* (*Unequal chances for education, education inequalities in the Czech Republic*), Prague: Academia.

Munich, D., Jurajda, S. and Cihak, M. (1999) *Background study on employment and labour market in Czech Republic*, Torino: European Training Foundation.

NÚOV (National Institute for Vocational Education) (2006) *Přechod absolventů SOU do praxe a jejich uplatnění na trhu práce* (*The transition of graduates of vocational schools to labour market*), Prague: NÚOV.

OECD (Organisation for Economic Co operation and Development) (1998) *OECD economic surveys: Czech Republic*, Paris: OECD.

OECD (2001) *Knowledge and skills for life: first results from PISA 2000*, Paris: OECD.

OECD (2003, 2004a) *Economic surveys – Czech Republic*, Paris: OECD.

OECD (2004b) *Learning for tomorrow's world: first results from PISA 2003*, Paris: OECD.

OECD (2005) *Education at a glance*, Paris: OECD.

OECD (2007) *PISA 2006: science competencies for tomorrow's world*, Paris: OECD.

Palečková, J. and Tomášek, V. (2005) *Učení pro zítřek: výsledky výzkumu OECD PISA 2003* (*Learning for tomorrow: results of OECD PISA 2003*), Prague: ÚIV.

People in Need (2006) *Zpráva o stavu rasismu, xenofobie a antisemitismuv České republice v roce 2006* (*The report on racism, xenophobia and anti-semitism in the Czech Republic in 2006*), Prague: People in Need.

Straková, J.(2007) 'The impact of the structure of the educational system on the development of educational inequalities in the Czech Republic', *Czech Sociological review*, vol 43, no 3, pp 589-609.

Van Gyes, G., Vandenbrande, T., Lehndorff, S., Schilling, G., Schief, S. and Kohl, H. (2007) *Industrial relations in EU member states 2000-2004*, Dublin: European Foundation for the Improvement of Living and Working Conditions.

Večerník, J. (2001) *Labour market flexibility and employment security: Czech Republic*, Employment Paper No 27, Geneva: International Labour Organization.

Večerník, J. (2004) *Structural tensions in the interface between the labour market and social policy in the Czech Republic*, Prague: Institute of Sociology of the Academy of Sciences of the Czech Republic.

Večerník, J. (2007) *The Czech labour market: historical, structural and policy perspectives*, Prague Economic Papers No 2/2007, Prague: University of Economics.

Veselý, A. (2006) 'Who end why does end up in vocational schools?' In P. Matějů and I. Straková (eds) *(Non) equal chances for education*, Prague: Academia, pp 247-81.

Visser, J. (2004) 'Patterns and variations in European industrial relations', in European Commission (ed) *Industrial relations in Europe*, Luxembourg: Office for the Official Publications of the European Communities, pp 11-57.

Wong, R. (1998) 'Multidimensional influences of family environment in education: the case of socialist Czechoslovakia', *Sociology of Education*, vol 71, no 1, pp 1-11.

SIX

Estonia

Ellu Saar and Kristina Lindemann

For 50 years after the 1940 annexation by the former Soviet Union, Estonia was politically and economically integrated into the Communist Bloc. It was not until 1991 that the country regained its independence and returned to democracy and a market economy. In the subsequent decade-and-a-half, Estonia has experienced profound reforms in all areas of politics, economy and society. These reforms included trade liberalisation, large-scale privatisation, the introduction of the *kroon* as national currency and an overhaul of labour market regulations. The economic transition brought about a substantial decline in employment and activity rates, accompanied by a rapid increase in unemployment. Although Estonia (along with the other Baltic states) suffered the longest and deepest recession of all the Eastern European transition countries in the 1990s (World Bank, 2002: 3), since 2000 Estonia has sustained high growth rates and now outperforms the rest of Europe in this respect. The Estonian labour market has proven to be very flexible, capable of large-scale structural changes during the 1990s; for example, changes in employment structure that generally took 15-20 years in most of Western Europe occurred two to three times faster in Estonia.

The dominance of liberal right-wing parties in all governmental coalitions since 1992 has contributed to the shift towards a minimalist state. Where labour market security is concerned, unemployment benefits are low, and unemployment insurance covers only a small share of the unemployed. Furthermore, the minimal expenditure on active labour market policies (ALMPs) reveals that the government is doing little to provide employment security.

The Estonian education system has been undergoing major changes since 1987. As of 2007, Estonia's secondary education system has been characterised by a high level of standardisation and a medium level of stratification. The 1990s saw a period of expansion of higher education in Estonia in which the number of both higher education institutions and students grew constantly.

Education system

Structure of the Estonian education system

Overview of the Estonian education system after the Second World War

During the socialist period, the Estonian education system was an integral part of the Soviet education system with its party-state institutional structure, main principles of centralisation and standardisation, and utilitarian and egalitarian goals. There was a clear link between each level of education and the future job for which it was meant to prepare the student (Helemäe et al, 2000). The attendance rate for eight-year basic education, which became compulsory in 1949, reached nearly 100% among children born after the Second World War. Secondary education, on the other hand, became one of the main channels for intergenerational social mobility; in the 1960s, having graduated from secondary school also meant being a member of the more educated part of the generation.[1]

In the second half of the 1960s, the Estonian government strove toward universal secondary education, and enrolment in secondary education increased steadily in the 1970s. Despite the increase, however, by the mid-1980s only about 80% of young people of the appropriate age were graduating from secondary education institutions (Saar, 1997: 140). In addition, a network of vocational schools was developed in the 1970s and rapidly expanded throughout the following decade. General secondary schools with special streams (e.g. foreign languages or mathematics) were also established in the 1970s. Such schools were situated primarily in bigger towns, had better teachers and received pupils from the more educated strata of society (Kenkmann and Saarniit, 1994).

This transition to universal secondary education thus resulted in a differentiation within the education system. After graduating from basic school, students were tracked into one of three types of secondary education: general secondary schools (the traditional academic track); vocational schools, which trained skilled workers for industrial work and other applied professions; and specialised secondary schools, which combined vocational training with academic subjects and were originally intended to educate semi-professionals. Vocational schools and, to a lesser extent, specialised secondary schools were oriented toward young people of lower social status (Titma and Saar, 1995). Although the three types of secondary schools were officially equal, the general level of teaching was considerably poorer in vocational and specialised secondary schools. Despite various reforms, general secondary schools gave their graduates the best chance of continuing their studies at a university, while vocational schools were educational dead-ends[2] (Saar, 1997). The vocational track was dominated by negative selection in the sense that those who had been denied admission to other education tracks usually went on to vocational schools.

In the Soviet times, post-secondary education consisted of the following forms: vocational school for one year of study; specialised schools, which typically took one to three years of study; and universities and other institutions of higher education, involving four to six years of schooling. Vocational and specialised schools provided a continuation of studies primarily for young people who had graduated from general secondary schools.

Education system since 1990[3]

The Estonian education system has undergone major changes since 1987. According to the Law on Education, compulsory education starts at age of seven and lasts until the student reaches the age of 17 or graduation from basic school is achieved. Individuals who have passed the minimum permitted school-leaving age and have not acquired basic education may acquire education in the form of evening courses or distance learning, eventually graduating as external students. Youth up to 25 years of age who have not completed basic education are provided with vocational training, parallel to which they can acquire basic education.[4] Tuition for basic education in state and municipal schools is free of charge. The Estonian education system does not differentiate between primary and lower-secondary education but forms a single structure (Figure 6.1). To finish basic school and receive a graduation certificate, pupils have to pass three externally set final examinations, after which they have the right to continue to upper-secondary education.

After graduating from basic school, students, typically aged 15-19, have to choose between general secondary schools, vocational schools and vocational secondary schools.[5] General secondary education is acquired in an upper-secondary school, a comprehensive school spreading over grades 10-12. Final examinations consist of at least three national and two school tests.[6] Those who graduate from an upper-secondary school are issued a graduation and a national examination certificate.

Vocational secondary education can be acquired by students who have only completed basic school, in which case at least three years of vocational education are required, and by students who already have some secondary schooling, in which case only one to two-and-a-half more years of vocational education are required. Graduates of vocational secondary education institutions who would like to continue their studies usually need to take certification examinations.

Recently, the two-track vocational system has been replaced by a system with four options: (1) vocational education for people who do not have basic education and who have exceeded the age of compulsory school attendance (International Standard Classification of Education, ISCED 2); (2) vocational education for those with basic education but no secondary schooling (ISCED 3c)[7]; (3) secondary vocational education for those with basic education (ISCED 3a); and (4) vocational training for those with upper secondary education (ISCED 4a). As of school year 2006/07, students completing track (3) can continue for a supplementary year of general education subjects in order to ensure their competitiveness in applying for higher education.

Figure 6.1: The Estonian system of education since the mid-1990s

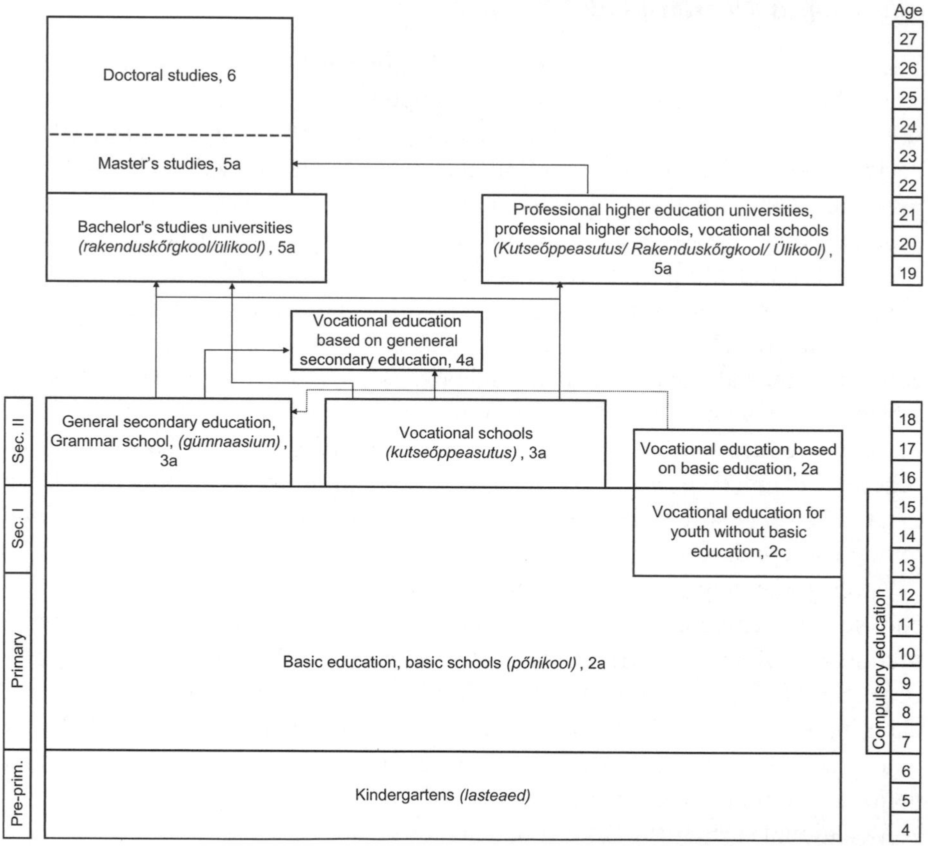

Source: ETF (2000)

Despite the restructuring of the vocational system, general secondary schools still prepare students best for further studies at a university. However, discrepancies among general secondary schools have opened up both in terms of regional differences as well as common schools versus 'elite' schools that select their pupils based on their own (higher) criteria. In general, the tendency among basic school graduates to attend upper-secondary school rather than vocational education has increased.

According to the Law of Education, everyone who has a diploma from an upper-secondary school, a specialised secondary school or a vocational secondary school has the right to compete for admission to universities and institutions of professional higher education. Since 1991, there have been two types of higher education establishments: universities offering academic programmes and institutions of professional higher education offering professional higher education programmes. At the end of the 1990s, the Bologna process was implemented, the '3+2' curriculum was adopted and provisions for professional higher education studies were drafted. Higher education is now divided into:

(1) professional higher education, requiring three years of study based on a professional higher curriculum (ISCED 5b);

(2) academic higher education, for which three years of study are required for a bachelor's degree (ISCED 5a)[8], two years for a master's degree (ISCED 5a), and four years for a doctoral degree (ISCED 6).

At an institution of professional higher education, higher education is acquired following a professional higher curriculum of one level, and starting from 2003, master's study as well as studies according to secondary vocational education curricula conducted on the basis of secondary education may be undertaken. Vocational schools that offer studies according to secondary vocational curricula on the basis of secondary education may also offer professional higher curricula.

The number of state-financed student places at higher educational institutions is limited, and the spots are allocated by the Ministry of Education and Research and its partners. Each higher education institution is also entitled to allocate a number of additional places for which students have to pay fees.

There are six public universities and six private higher education institutions in Estonia, one of which was accredited by the Ministry of Education in 2001. Private higher education institutions provide study programmes in a limited number of fields, primarily social sciences (economics, international relations and law), business administration and theology. Furthermore, there are eight state and five private[9] applied higher education institutions as well as six state vocational education institutions that provide vocational higher education programmes.

Vertical dimension of the educational system

Figure 6.2 reveals the trends in education enrolment of the school-aged population in Estonia from 1980 through 2005. Most school-aged Estonians received basic general education, but enrolment in basic education is declining as the proportion of tertiary education enrolments has increased.[10] Other education tracks exhibit relative stability, with approximately equal proportions being enrolled in secondary general education and any type of vocational training.

Figure 6.2: Enrolment by type of school of school-age population in Estonia (%)

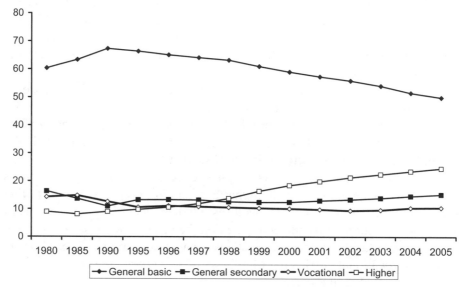

Note: For years 1980-88 the division of grades was: basic education – grades 1-8 and secondary education – grades 9-11; from 1989 basic education – grades 1- 9, secondary education – grades 10-12.
Source: Statistical Office of Estonia (2006)

The Estonian education system is relatively open as most programmes at each education level allow for direct advancement to the next level. However, although there are no legal restrictions, the various programmes are strongly differentiated according to student ability and background. The contrast is especially stark at the secondary level between general and vocational schools. Figure 6.3 indicates that the inflow into higher education institutions is mostly from general secondary schools. The interim report about realisation of the development plan of vocational education in Estonia (Ministry of Education and Research, 2006a: 5) stated that 16% of entrants to the first stage of higher education had graduated from a vocational school in 2005. Seven per cent of graduates from vocational secondary schools based on basic education and 11% of graduates from vocational schools based on secondary education continued their studies in a higher education institution in the same year as they graduated.

Figure 6.3: Transitions in the Estonian education system in 1998

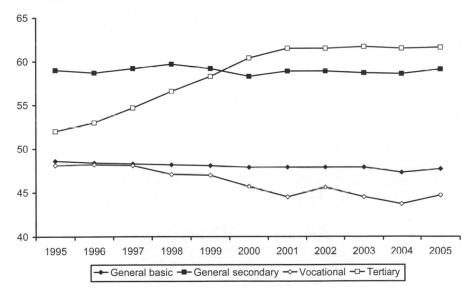

Universities and applied higher education institutions

62.6%   5.2%   1.6%

Vocational schools based on general secondary education

13.0%

10.9%

| Gymnasium | | Vocational secondary schools (based on basic education) |

70.0%   4.6%   24.3%

Basic education

Source: OECD (2001)

Figure 6.4: Proportion of females in various school types in Estonia, 1995-2005

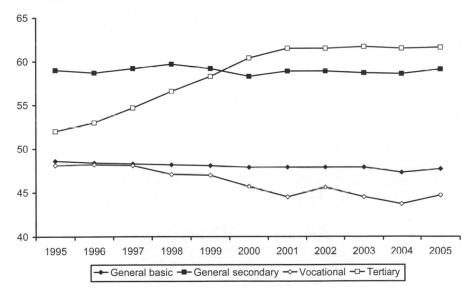

Legend: —♦— General basic —■— General secondary —◇— Vocational —□— Tertiary

Source: Statistical Office of Estonia (2006)

The proportion of vocational school graduates entering tertiary education clearly increased since 1998, when only 1.6% of graduates from basic vocational schools and 5.2% of graduates from secondary vocational schools proceeded to tertiary education (see Figure 6.3).

Figure 6.4 explores gender distribution at various education levels in Estonia. It is immediately visible that men are overrepresented in vocational education and that this trend is increasing. There is less gender differentiation with regard to basic general education. In contrast, secondary general tracks are, in a constant trend since the mid-1990s, over-populated by girls. Women also dominate tertiary education, where an increase from 52% in 1995 to 62% women in 2005 is apparent.

Secondary level of education

Stratification and track differentiation

Even though education in Estonia is compulsory until 16 years of age, at the age of 15 pupils and their parents might make their first decisions about whether to proceed in basic vocational education as opposed to a general track. This is similar to the decision-making age in other Baltic countries and is somewhat later than in Central European countries, Germany and Austria.

General education dominates the secondary education level in Estonia, probably more so than in any other Central and Eastern European (CEE) country. On completion of basic education, three quarters of pupils go on to upper-secondary general and only one quarter to vocational secondary schools. Among those enrolled in vocational education, about 25% are in tracks leading to the *matura* examination, and only a minor proportion (less than 5%) is enrolled in a vocational track certified by a qualification other than *matura* (ETF, 1998, 1999, 2000).

Organisation of vocational training

Vocational training in Estonia is provided in schools. An apprenticeship system does not officially exist, but in some occupations (e.g. smithing) the apprenticeship is used for initial training. There are also some enterprises that train individuals or small groups on their own initiative and at their own cost.

Standardisation and quality differentiation of secondary education

While the high level of standardisation inherited from the socialist period was reduced in the early 1990s, the second half of the 1990s witnessed an increase in standardisation in basic and secondary education, most notably in the form of standardised graduation exams, called 'state exams', at the end of secondary school.

State examination grades at graduation from secondary education fluctuate from 40.2 for vocational school graduates to 71.3 for graduates of secondary schools with specific study branches (Estonian Centre for Examination and Qualification, 2006). Since admission to higher education institutions is mainly based on the results of national examinations, the opportunities to continue studies are unequally distributed by the type of school. Examination results might also provide prospective employers with the information on the quality of graduates from different schools.

Tertiary level of education

Horizontal dimension

Figure 6.5 shows the increase in the number of students by year and their distribution in different types of higher education. The proportion of professional higher education increased until 2001, then started to decrease. In the academic year 2005/06, a third of students were enrolled in applied higher schools.

Figure 6.5: Number of students in different types of higher education, 1993/94-2005/06

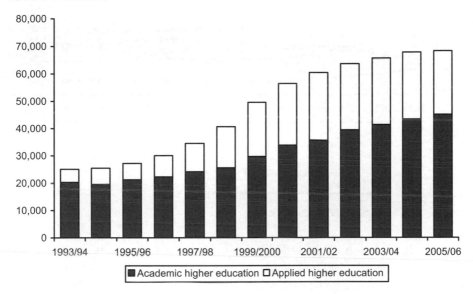

Source: Ministry of Education and Research (2006b)

Another important aspect of the horizontal dimension of tertiary education is a field-of-study differentiation (see Figure 6.6). Similar to the situation in other CEE countries, Estonia experienced a substantial decrease in enrolment in engineering, manufacturing and construction; the proportion of students in these fields fell from 20% in 1994 to less than 15% in 2005. Agricultural fields also declined in popularity from 5% to 2.5% in the same period. Enrolment in humanities and arts, as well as education, also declined, but less substantially. The number of students in business increased dramatically between 1994 and 1999 and then levelled out at about 23%. Enrolment in social sciences and media follows a U-shape, with the higher proportions of students enrolled during the mid-1990s and mid-2000s. An inverted U-shape is evident for law specialties, with almost 10% of all students preferring this field in 1999.

Figure 6.6: Enrolment in tertiary education by field of study (%)

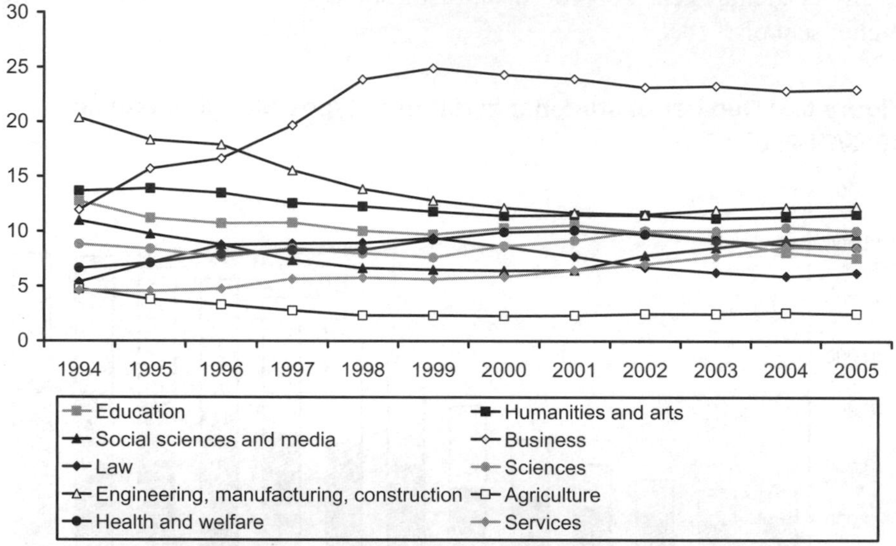

Source: Statistical Office of Estonia (2006)

One of the most notable tendencies in higher education is its increasing feminisation; in the 1993/94 academic year 51% of all students were women, but the proportion grew to 62% by 2005/06. There is also a strong gender differentiation in terms of field of study (see Figure 6.7). Men still prevail in engineering, manufacturing and technology (although the female proportion has been increasing) and in sciences where the male proportion has remained more or less the same over the past 12 years. The proportion of female students is also below average in agriculture and services. The rest of the fields, however, are dominated by women. In recent years the female proportion has been rising especially fast in services and in health and welfare.

Figure 6.7: Percentage of females per field of study

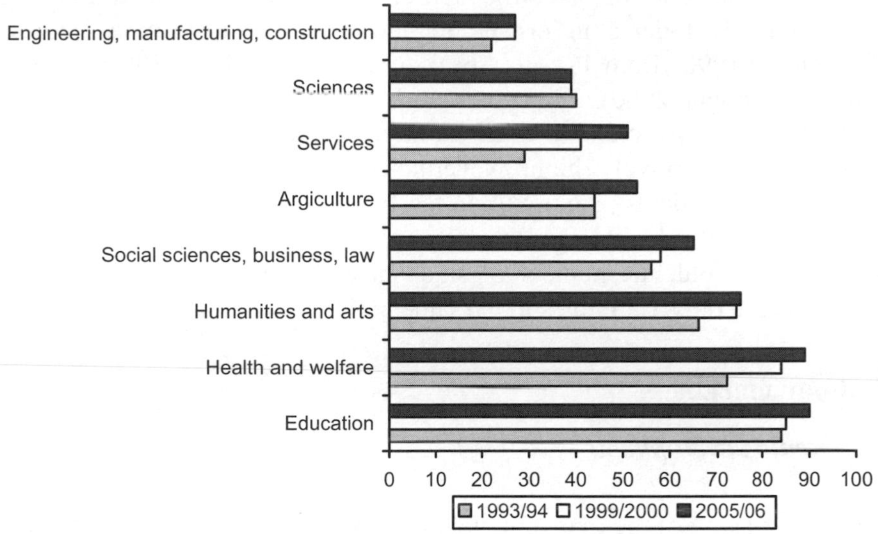

Engineering, manufacturing, construction
Sciences
Services
Argiculture
Social sciences, business, law
Humanities and arts
Health and welfare
Education
0 10 20 30 40 50 60 70 80 90 100
1993/94
1999/2000
2005/06

Source: Statistical Office of Estonia (2006)

Figure 6.8: Proportion and number of students paying tuition fees and receiving state support, 1993/94-2005/06

80,000
70,000
60,000
50,000
40,000
30,000
20,000
10,000
0
7% 12% 17% 19% 28% 35% 43% 45% 47% 50% 52% 53% 54%
93% 88% 83% 81% 72% 65% 57% 55% 53% 50% 48% 47% 46%
1993/94 1995/96 1997/98 1999/2000 2001/02 2003/04 2005/06
State-commissioned places
Non-state commissioned places

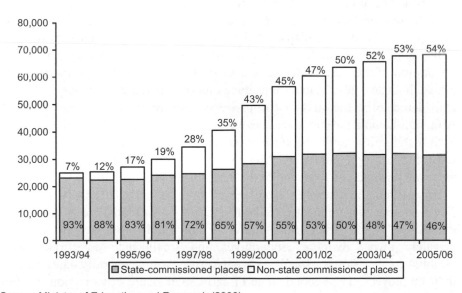

Source: Ministry of Education and Research (2006)

Standardisation, quality differentiation and openness of tertiary education

The standardisation of higher education substantially decreased in the early 1990s, due partly to the diversification of tertiary education institutions. The proportion of students in private higher education institutions increased through the 1990s from 17% to a peak of 25% in 1998 and 1999 (Statistical Office of Estonia, 2000).

At between two and five times average monthly salaries, annual tuition fees are comparatively high. Nevertheless, as Figure 6.8 indicates, the proportion of students paying tuition fees increased from 7% in 1993 to 54% in 2005. Notably, although the number of students paying tuition fees increased 20-fold, the number of students with state-financed scholarships has increased only 1.35 times in the same period.

Labour market

Economic development

At the beginning of the transition, Estonia, like the other Baltic countries, was richer and more linked to the West that the other former Soviet states. (Vodopivec, 2000). Estonia acted also as the Soviet Union's economic laboratory in which several Soviet economic reforms were tested. This 'guinea pig' role brought Soviet Estonia and its business sector slightly closer to a market economy than other Soviet republics (Liuhto, 1996: 121).

Although the first attempts to initiate market-oriented reforms in Estonia took place before the collapse of the Soviet Union, the actual turn towards implementation of market economy principles became possible with the restoration of the independent Estonian state in August 1991 (Rajasalu et al, 2003). In June 1992, Estonia introduced its own currency (kroons), which is considered to be the start of cardinal economic reforms (Arro et al, 2001). Although Estonia suffered from severe economic and social turbulence in the early 1990s, its rapid transformation into a liberal market economy was rewarded by high annual real income gains from 1995 on, except for a temporary setback in 1999 due to the Russian crisis (Figure 6.9).

Privatisation in Estonia took place in three distinct stages (Terk, 2000). The first stage was connected to the former president Gorbachev's reforms in the Soviet Union after 1986. Between 1987 and 1990, several hundred privately owned worker cooperatives and small state enterprises were established in Estonia. Small state enterprises were generally later sold to their employees. The second stage of early small-scale privatisation in 1991 and 1992 favoured employees, but those advantages were removed in 1992. The third stage, the centralised privatisation programme, started with the establishment of the Estonian Privatisation Agency in 1992. Most large enterprise privatisation followed the 'Treuhand' approach of individual sales through evaluated bidding. This meant that groups with access to capital, including foreigners, were in a strong position. An important consideration behind choosing this privatisation model was the government's desire to prevent large-scale managerial buy-outs of the enterprises (Lauristin and Vihalemm, 1997: 107). After the change in privatisation policies, it became very rare for enterprises to be privatised through a sale to employees (Kalmi, 2003).

Figure 6.9: GDP growth in Estonia, 1989-2006

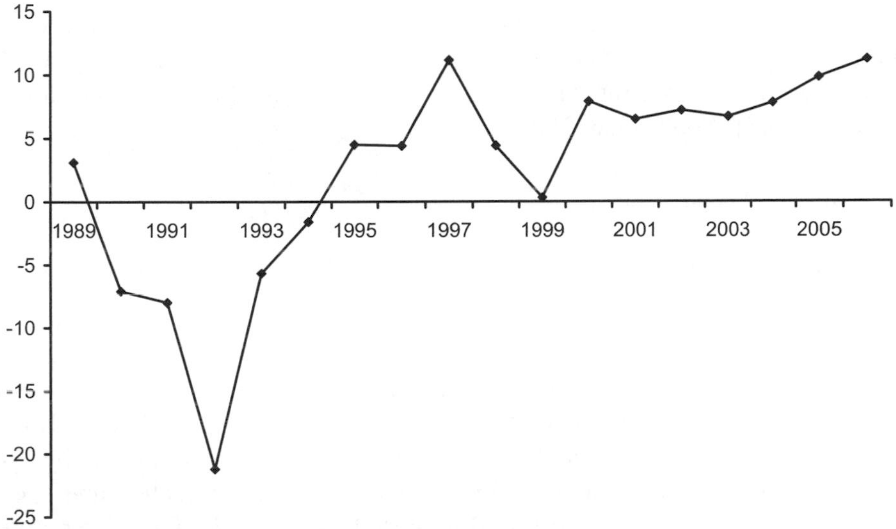

Source: ILO (2008); data for 2006 from Eurostat (2008)

Given the newness of labour market institutions and weakness of social partners, the role of the Estonian state as the main actor of reforms is of great importance for understanding the political context of market reforms (Rajasalu et al, 2003). The domination of liberal right-wing parties in all governmental coalitions since 1992 has contributed to the shift towards a minimalist state, the domination of libertarian faith in the 'invisible hand' of the market and a lack of sufficiently strong political support for developing a proactive social policy (Lauristin, 2003). This right-wing domination has not been total, however. The governments led by Prime Minister Mart Laar in 1992-94 and 1999-2002 also included political parties of social democratic orientation. This resulted in certain tensions and contradictions in government policy. The social democrats, in charge of social policy in these coalitions, succeeded in establishing certain elements of a universal social security scheme.

Another important feature of the political context of Estonian market reforms is related to the role of international institutions in the market reforms. In the 1990s, the main pressure for socio-economic reforms came from international financial institutions such as the World Bank and the International Monetary Fund (IMF). The recommendations of these institutions were both strict and concrete, and they were required for earning positive assessments of transition from the international authorities (Kennedy, 2002).

In the late 1990s, economic reforms became subordinated to European Union (EU) accession aspirations. Since then, the strategic objectives of Estonian economic policy were presented in documents prepared for the EU, and the framework for institutional development came under the influence of the EU (Rajasalu et al, 2003). At the same time, Estonians have perceived EU membership as increasing the pressure for stricter regulation of the labour market (Eamets and Masso, 2005) .

Labour market dynamics

Employment dynamics

Among the Baltic countries, Estonia has seen the fastest changes in the sectoral employment structure and has nearly reached the average indicators of the EU. During the transition period, the sharpest decrease in jobs was in agriculture, where employment fell steadily from 21% in 1990 to 5.3% in 2005 (ILO, 2008). This contraction can be explained primarily by the privatisation policy in agriculture,11 the dismantling of collective and state-owned farms, the entry of subsidised imported food into the Estonian market and the high customs barriers on the Russian market (Arro et al, 2001). In contrast, employment shares in industry and construction remained fairly stable at around 35%. The service sector's share of total employment increased from 41.8% in 1990 to 60.7% in 2005 (ILO, 2008). Dominant activities are in wholesale and retail trade, financial and related services, and in public administration, as is the case in most transition countries (OECD, 2003).

Labour force participation rates of the population aged 15-64 sharply declined from 79.6% in 1990 to 69% in 2006 (Figure 6.10). The female activity rate is below that of men by roughly 10 percentage points. The youngest age group (15-24 years) experienced the sharpest drop in employment, with the group's activity rate falling from 53.4% to 35.1% between 1990 and 2006 (Table 6.1). The decline in youth activity rate is primarily related to increasing enrolment in higher education, but it may also reflect the increasing labour market integration problems of the young age cohort. In contrast, the middle-age cohort had a very high activity of around

84%-95% during the transition period; however, this group's rate also decreased by 10 percentage points over the 15-year period. Participation rates of people aged 65 and over are relatively high at around 12%-16%.

Figure 6.10: Labour force participation rate (age group 15-64), 1990-2006

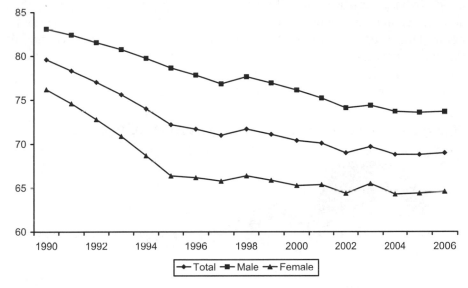

Source: ILO (2008)

Table 6.1: Labour force participation rate (%) by age cohort, 1990-2006

	1990	1995	2000	2006
15+	70.2	62.5	59.8	58.1
15-24	53.4	47.8	41.5	35.1
25-54	95.0	88.6	86.8	84.0
55-64	55.8	45.5	48.3	59.9
65+	16.1	14.9	12.7	13.9

Source: ILO (2008)

Labour market flexibilisation

Among transition economies, Estonia is a leader in labour market flexibility (Cazes and Nesporova, 2001: 40). The early transition period (1990-94) was a period of high mobility in the Estonian labour market. There were many transitions between different labour market statuses (employment, unemployment, inactivity), especially in terms of high rates of job-to-job moves through 1994 (Figure 6.11). Outflows from employment to inactivity significantly exceeded outflows to unemployment as labour market pressures were primarily solved at the expense of vulnerable groups (primarily older workers). Following this period of accelerated restructuring, the labour market gradually stabilised during the period of recovery and economic boom from 1995-97, except for a significant decrease of both rate and number of people who experienced the job-to-job moves. Despite improving economic and labour market conditions during the post-2000 recovery and economic boom, labour turnover has been low, lower even than during the recession of the late 1990s. After the turn of the millennium, there was a significant decrease of outflows from employment (mainly into unemployment), accompanied by a slight increase of inflows into employment.

Figure 6.11: Flows from and into employment (000s), 1992-2005

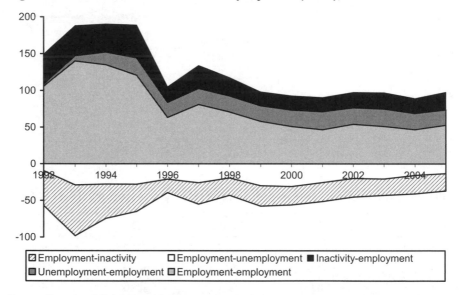

Source: Estonian Labour Force Surveys; own calculations

Temporary employment as a form of external flexibilisation is less pronounced in Estonia than in many Western European countries. According to Labour Force Survey (LFS) data, the share of fixed-term contracts fluctuated in interval from 2.1% to 3.0% during 1998-2004. At the same time, given the very conservative definition of temporary contract in the Estonian LFS (contracts with duration of less than one year), one should not necessarily assume that this corresponds to an extremely high level of standard employment in Estonia.[12]

Unemployment dynamics

The transition to a market economy led to an increase in unemployment figures. A comparison between the LFS-based unemployment rate and the registered unemployment rate reveals that the former increased much more rapidly than the latter (Figure 6.12). Whereas the registered rate captures all unemployed who officially register their unemployment the LFS-based unemployment rate is a self-assessed measure. The difference in the two rates is due to several factors, primarily the inadequacy of social guarantees for unemployment, the poor reputation of state employment offices and the very limited willingness of employers to cooperate with the state job-mediation system (Eamets et al, 1999). In recent years, the gap has started to narrow, especially after the Unemployed Persons Social Protection Act and the Employment Service Act came into force in 2000. These acts extended eligibility for help from the public employment service.

Figure 6.12: Unemployment rates, 1990-2006

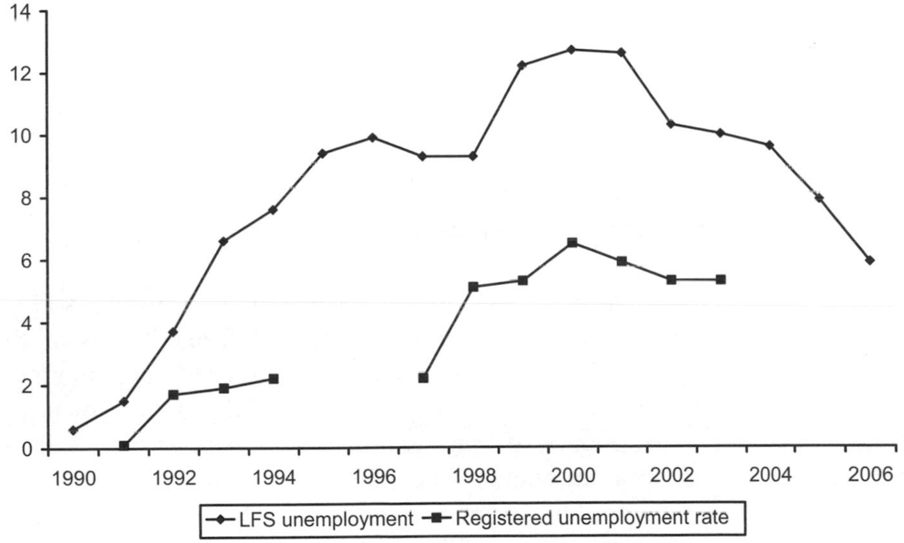

Note: LFS unemployment rate for age groups 15-74; registered unemployment rate for individuals aged over 16.
Source: ILO (2008); LFS unemployment for 2006 from Eurostat (2008)

Figure 6.13 shows that labour market entrants, approximated as the youngest age cohort of 15- to 24-year-olds, is the category most exposed to unemployment. The gap in the unemployment rate of young people and that of the core workforce has been increasing. The unemployment rate of the under-25 age group roughly doubled between 1995 and 2004, and the level was about 2.6 times higher than the average unemployment rate for the whole

167

adult population in 2004. However, a significant decrease from 25.9% in 2000 to 15.9% occurred in 2005. Apart from labour market demands related to working experience, difficulties in the professional integration of youth are also caused by the insufficient matching between labour demand and qualifications offered by the education system.

Figure 6.13: Unemployment rate (%) of different age groups, 1993-2005

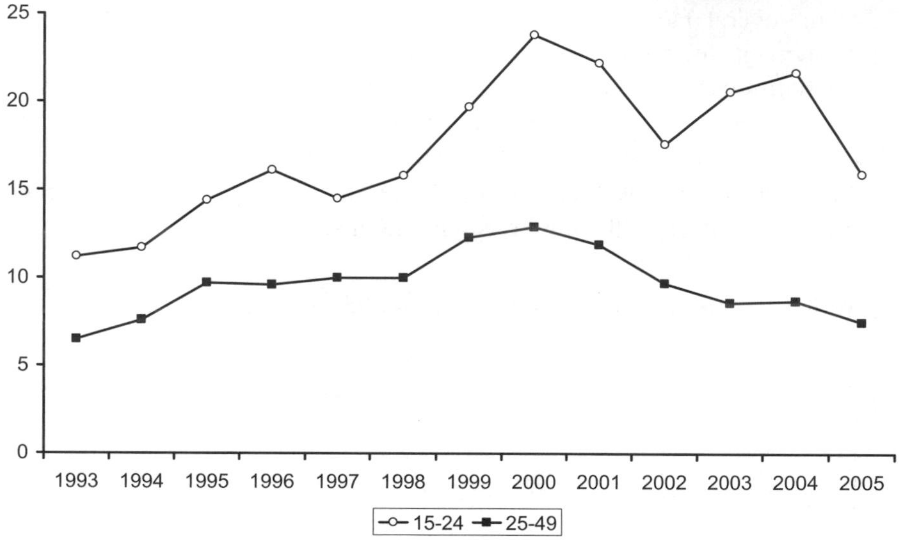

Source: Statistical Office of Estonia (various years)

In addition to youth unemployment, long-term unemployment is a serious problem in Estonia. In 2005, long-term unemployed formed 53% of the unemployed population. The level of extreme long-term unemployment (seeking work for over 24 months) has grown, especially among men and non-Estonians. The persistence of long-term unemployment in rural areas is creating a large number of discouraged people who have lost hope of finding work and given up job seeking. A total 17,700 people fell into this category in 2004 (Ministry of Social Affairs, 2005). The job searching period of young people is shorter than that of older age groups. Long-term unemployed formed a third of unemployed youth in 2005 (Figure 6.14).

Figure 6.14: Number of youth (absolute numbers) by job search time periods, 1997-2005

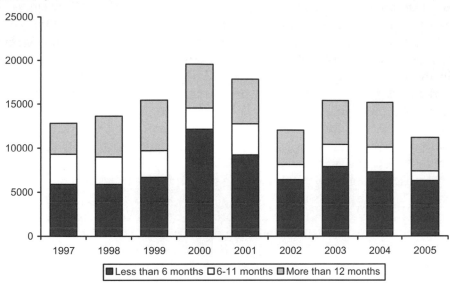

Source: Ministry of Social Affairs (2006b)

Minority ethnic groups

Minority ethnic groups in Estonia are also disadvantaged in the labour market. About one quarter of those living in Estonia are Russian. Due to language problems and an overrepresentation in so-called old industries, this group is more exposed to unemployment. Their unemployment rate (12.9% in 2005) is almost twice as high as the unemployment rate of Estonians (Statistical Office of Estonia, 2006). Ethnic differences in youth unemployment and long-term unemployment are especially significant. In 2004, non-Estonians formed more than a half of the long-term unemployed (64%) and 72% of unemployed females (Ministry of Social Affairs, 2006a).

Labour market institutions

Employment protection legislation

It is often assumed that general legal labour market regulations and hiring and firing rules in Estonia are rather liberal (e.g. OECD, 2003: 11). In the strict legal sense, this is not always the case, but it does become true when considering the application of these regulations. Estonian employment protection legislation (EPL) resembles that common in EU countries. For example, Estonian labour law places the burden of proof of reasons for dismissal on the employer. Yet Estonia is more liberal in the sense that employers are free to dismiss workers if there is not enough work and – with a few exceptions – have the right to select the workers they want to dismiss based on economic criteria. On most indicators, Estonia's EPL strictness is above or close to the EU15 average and the CEE average (Tonin, 2005).

Regarding individual dismissals, according to the 1992 Employment Contract Act, the period of notification of termination varies from two weeks (in the case of long-term incapacity for work) to four months (laying off workers who have continuously worked for the employer for more than 10 years). An employment contract may be terminated at any time if one party presents a written request for termination and the other party gives written consent. Compensation varies from one month's average wage to up to four months' average wage.

The use of temporary employment is significantly less restricted in Estonia than on average in the EU. Altough the law allows the use of fixed-term contracts for short-term temporary work only, a lack of enforcement means that fixed-term contracts in Estonia are often used for non-temporary work as well. Until 2004 there were no restrictions on the maximum number of successive contracts, but maximum cumulated duration was limited to 60 months. EU accession-motivated amendments to the law limited the maximum number of successive contracts to two.

Regulation of collective dismissals is even stricter in Estonia than on average in the EU due to notification requirements and additional delay periods. Some of the 2002 changes in legislation made collective dismissals more costly, increasing the value of the index from 2.6 to 4.0.

From a formal point of view, the labour market is well regulated and Estonian workers can be better protected those than in EU. However, Estonia's strict labour laws appear to have little effect on the economy, perhaps due to frequent violation of the laws, weak law enforcement agencies or due to the fact that the laws cover only a small proportion of the total workforce.

First of all, data from the Estonian LFS 2005 show that over 2% of employees had no written labour agreement, i.e., the conditions had been agreed orally, although according to Employment Contract Act this is allowed only for jobs of less than two weeks' duration. Employers require that employees sign an agreement additional to the employment contract in which the employee waives some of his/her rights. Such agreements significantly reduce formal protection of employees. The use of this additional agreement declined in Estonia from 10% 1998 to 6% in 2002 (Antila and Ylöstalo, 2003).

Violations of labour market regulation are particularly common in the private sector and among small firms. The low coverage rate of trade unions means that violations are often not investigated and workers' representatives cannot protect workers. In addition, in a climate of high unemployment, employees do not initiate individual claims against employers for fear of losing their jobs. Thus, the Estonian labour market is likely to be more flexible than one might conclude if only considering formal regulation.

Industrial relations

During the transition, Estonia moved away from a centralised wage-setting system toward a collective bargaining system as did many other CEE countries. Wage bargaining usually takes place at the company level or to a lesser extent at the sectoral level, whereas the regional or national level bargaining does not exist (Visser, 2004: Table 1.8).

Union membership declined in Estonia from 32% in 1995 to 14% in 2004 (Van Gyes et al., 2007: Figure 2). Even more important than the number of unionised workers is the coverage by collective agreements. Van Gyes et al (2007: Figure 4) estimate that 22% of employees were covered by collective agreements in 2002, representing the third lowest level of union coverage compared to other CEE countries.

Welfare regime

Labour market policy

Active labour market policy

With expenditures of only 0.06% of gross domestic product (GDP) in 2001 (OECD, 2003), ALMP plays a very small role in Estonia compared to Western as well as other CEE countries. However, the expenditure on active labour market measures has increased in recent years due to the implementation of the European Social Fund (see Table 6.2). In 2005, the proportion of state expenditure formed 0.12% of GDP (Ministry of Social Affairs, 2005). Based on the amount of expenditure, the most important active measure is labour market training (72.8%), followed by training allowances (11.3%), subsidies to start a business (10.0%) and employers (5.9%). The share of public sector employment programmes is rather modest. Priority is given to disadvantaged groups such as people with disabilities, youth and the long-term unemployed. There are no specific ALMP programmes for young labour market entrants.

The limited amount of resources spent on active labour market measures is reflected in the small share of unemployed who have access to the measures. In 2003, the involvement of registered unemployed in the active labour market measures was 19.4%. Furthermore, it has been argued that even these few labour market programmes are not appropriately targeted (Leetmaa and Võrk, 2003).

Table 6.2: Expenditure on social protection for the unemployed in Estonia

	1995	2000	2005
Total budget for active labour market measures (millions €)	1.70	3.20	8.20
Expenditure on active measures (% of GDP)	0.07	0.05	0.12
Expenditure on active measures (% of total labour policy budget)	40.50	26.60	49.90

Source: Eamets et al (1999), Ministry of Social Affairs (2004-06) :

Unemployment insurance

Although unemployment appeared as early as 1989, official registration of the unemployed and payment of benefits only began in 1991. In 1995, the Social Protection of the Unemployed Act entered into force, providing legal regulation of unemployment services and payments. A profound reorganisation of unemployment benefits in 2002 established a two-tier system of cash benefits to be paid to the unemployed beginning in 2003 (Püss, 2004). The first tier comprises a contributory earnings-related unemployment insurance benefit, and the second tier is a non-contributory flat-rate unemployment allowance (Ministry of Social Affairs, 2006a, b).

Unemployment insurance (the first tier) is compulsory, i.e., all employees are obliged to pay contributions. In 2007, the employees' contribution rate was 0.6% of gross monthly salary and employers' contribution was 0.3% of payroll. In order to receive unemployment insurance benefit recipients must have been employed and have paid unemployment insurance premiums for at least 12 months during the 24 months prior to unemployment registration. The unemployment insurance benefit consists of 50% of the former wages of the employee for the first 100 days of unemployment, after which time it drops to 40%. The maximum size of the unemployment insurance benefit is between 40% and 50% of the triple average daily income of all insured individuals per calendar day during the previous calendar year.

In 2005, the average gross unemployment insurance payout per person per month was 2,690 EEK, which was six times higher than the unemployment allowance (Aas et al, 2007), but it is also a subject to income tax. The duration of the unemployment insurance benefit depends on the insurance period (calculated from the start of insurance payments) and may last from 180-360 calendar days. The coverage rate of *registered* unemployed is low; only 22% of newly registered unemployed were eligible in 2005, rising to 25% in 2006 (Aas et al, 2007). In 2004, 532 unemployed young people received unemployment insurance (Ministry of Social Affairs, 2005).

The second tier comprises a tax-financed unemployment allowance. Until 2001, the unemployment allowance was the only passive labour market measure used in Estonia.[13] In general, the unemployment allowance is flat-rate (amount subject to government review), means-tested and not taxed. Until 2000, the maximum duration was 180 days, but it was later extended to 270 days. Recipients of the unemployment allowance must be actively seeking a job. Unemployed youth are considered an at-risk group, and their entire 'personal job search plan' is prepared more quickly than for others (Estonian Labour Market Services and Support Act, 2005).

After the reorganisation in 2002, the unemployment allowance became the second tier of the unemployment insurance system and is now paid to the unemployed who do not qualify for unemployment insurance or have exhausted their benefit. Because they have not yet (sufficiently) paid in to the system, labour market entrants are usually not covered by unemployment insurance, but they may register for the unemployment allowance. Although officially recipients of the unemployment allowance must have worked or performed an equivalent activity for at least 180 days of the preceding year in order to be eligible, there are many exceptions. Examples of equivalent activities include having been enrolled in full-time education or caring for a child. Before receiving the allowance, former students must pass a waiting period of 60 days, be actively searching for a job and make a personal job search plan (Estonian Labour Market Services and Support Act, 2005).

Table 6.3 reveals that the unemployment allowance is very low. The replacement rate as a percentage of minimum wage fell from 60% in 1992 to just 11% in 2007. Only a relatively small share of the unemployed actually receives benefits, which is similar to the situation in southern European countries. Until 2007, unemployment allowance was also lower than the subsistence minimum and even lower than the minimum food basket. In 2005, 1.2% of youth aged 16-24 received unemployment benefits.

Table 6.3: Unemployment benefit in Estonia

	1992	1998	2003	2004	2006	2007
Unemployment allowance per month (Euros)	11.5[a]	19.2[b]	25.6	25.6	25.6	64.1
Gross replacement rate (% of average wage)		7.2	5.9/32.5[c]	5.4/4.6	5.0/33.3	4.3/33.2
Coverage rate (% of all registered unemployed)		47.4	51.4	52.7	44.4/6.8	43.7/7.1
Unemployment allowance as a % of minimum wage	60	27.3	18.5	16.1	13.3	11.1
...of poverty line		22.2	24.8	24.1	14.1	
...of subsistence minimum		25.5	28.3	21.8[d]	19.2	
...of minimum food basket		50.1	60.8	52.6[e]	45.1	

Notes: [a]Effective date of unemployment benefit 1 January 1992; [b]effective date of unemployment benefit 1 March 1998; [c]unemployment/unemployment insurance benefit; [d]from 2004 onwards the subsistence minimum is estimated for a one-person household. [e]From 2004 onwards the minimum food basket is estimated for a one-person household.
Source: Arro et al (2001); Eamets and Masso (2005); Ministry of Social Affairs (2004-06); Statistical Office of Estonia (various years)

Minimum wage

A legal minimum wage exists and is set at the national level. However, the Estonian minimum wage is equal to only a small percentage of the average wage in the country (Paas et al, 2003). Over the period 1994-2001, Estonia had the lowest relative minimum wage in the Baltic countries at around 30% of the average wage. Yet in recent years, the minimum wage has steadily increased. In 2001, the Estonian Employers' Confederation and the Confederation of Estonian Trade Unions agreed that the minimum wage should be 41% of the average wage by 2008 (Hinnosaar and Rõõm, 2003). Despite a slow, consistent increase, the minimum wage has not reached the agreed level, mainly due to the rapid increase in average wages. In 2006, the minimum wage formed 32% of the average wage (Statistical Office of Estonia, 2007).

Family policy

Institutional description

The 1992 Law on Education of the Estonian Republic set forth the general principles of the Estonian education system. In 1999, the Law on Pre-school Childcare Institutions established principles for the pre-school education system. Pre-school education is not compulsory in Estonia.

Pre-school institutions are mostly municipally owned and financed from the budget of the local government with contributions from parents. The amount that parents are supposed to contribute is decided by municipalities, but it is not larger than 20% of the minimum wage. As a result, childcare in nurseries and kindergartens is generally the cheapest option for childcare available to parents (the most expensive being a babysitter) (Unt and Krusell, 2004).

The local government determines opening hours in accordance with parental needs. Pre-schools are generally open between 10 and 14 hours per day, but some institutions are open around the clock (about 1% of parents use this). Although the network of kindergartens is well developed and generally considered sufficient, there are long queues for vacancies in pre-schools. In 2004, 52% of municipalities had queues for kindergartens or nurseries (Estonian Ministry of Education and Research, 2004).

The length of the school day in primary school depends on the grade and the school, but compulsory classes are generally in the morning. Many schools organise childcare after-school activities for grades 1-9 in order to support and supervise children in their free time and offer them help in doing homework or developing their hobbies and interests (Estonian Ministry of Education and Research, 2000). Due to insufficient financial resources, some schools do not organise after-school activities, which can limit parents' possibilities for taking on regular employment.

Enrolment

Table 6.4 reveals that enrolment in pre-schools was lower in the first half of the 1990s than in more recent years. From 1992-94, the number of pre-schools decreased due in part to high institutional fees (International Bureau of Education, 2001) and an attempt to restore pre-Second World War values including that women should stay home and care for their children (Narusk, 2000).

Table 6.4: Percentage of children enrolled in pre-school institutions by age

	1990	1992	1994	1996	1998	2000	2002	2004	2005
1	–	4	6	8	10	13	13	12	12
2	–	28	34	40	47	50	52	56	57
3	–	47	54	63	68	74	76	81	81
4	–	54	59	68	74	79	81	84	86
5	–	57	61	71	77	83	83	88	89
6	–	56	60	71	76	82	82	88	87
7	–	–	–	14	16	16	17	18	20
3-6	68	–	–	69	74	79	80	85	86
1-6	–	–	–	60	64	67	67	70	71

Source: Statistical Office of Estonia (2006); UNICEF (2007)

Since the mid-1990s, enrolment has continually risen for most age groups. In 2005, more than 80% of children aged three and older were enrolled in pre-school, an increase of 21% over a decade earlier. One reason for this tendency may be the decreasing birth rate while the number of pre-schools has remained the same. The rate for two-year-olds is considerably lower, indicating that a considerable amount of childcare is conducted within families with possible consequences for parents', especially mothers', labour force participation (Heinlo, 2001).

Social assistance

The 1995 Social Welfare Act regulates social welfare in Estonia, but a subsistence benefit was established for low-income households in 1993. In 1997, the housing allowance and subsistence benefit were combined into one subsistence benefit. All individuals with an income below the established subsistence level may apply for the subsistence benefit. Subsistence benefits are flat-rate and based on minimum consumption expenses. In 2004, subsistence levels were fixed at 500 EEK for the head of household and 400 EEK for dependents, which corresponds to consumption coefficients of one for the head and 0.8 for dependents (Püss, 2004). The amount of the benefit depends on the family's monthly net income, housing expenditures and subsistence level.

Benefits are not taxed and are of unlimited duration, as long as individuals continue to fulfil the eligibility criteria. Local governments administer subsistence benefits, but they may refuse to pay subsistence benefit to individuals who are of working age and capable, but who do not study or work and have repeatedly refused from job offers without an acceptable reason. A large number of Estonian households (12% in 2002) claim these benefits (Püss, 2004). Due to the low level of the unemployment allowance, many recipients of the allowance also apply for the subsistence benefit. The system of subsistence benefits is severely criticised by specialists, politicians and in public opinion because the payout is too low to actually sustain a reasonable standard of living (Kährik et al, 2003).

Intergenerational transfers

In Estonia, often more than one generation of a family live in the same dwelling. In 2003, more than 50% of young people under 25 continued to live with their parents. This age is the breakthrough point when youth generally move out of their parents' house. Women start their independent life earlier than men, but one quarter of the country's youth have not created their own home by the time they are 30 (Kährik et al, 2003). At the same time, approximately one quarter of people over 60 live with their children and their families (Statistical Office of Estonia, 2005). Grandparents and relatives generally participate actively in caring for children, especially if both parents work. About 50% of young parents rely on their own parents or relatives in looking after their children (Unt and Krusell, 2004).

Since the mid-1990s, the share of owner-occupied dwellings has rapidly increased from 40% in 1995 to 90% in 2005. In 2002, only 9% of households rented their dwelling from the private sector, and this percentage has declined in recent years. Private sector rental dwellings are most common in larger cities, especially in Tallinn (14%) (Paats, 2004). The share of dwellings rented from the state has been consistently falling over the past 10 years as the overall number of state-owned dwellings decreased.

Notes

[1] Secondary education was attained by approximately half of the cohort (Helemäe and Saar, 1999: 86).

[2] Officially 10% of graduates from vocational and specialised secondary schools were allowed to go into higher education; in reality never more than 1% of graduates of vocational schools and 5% of graduates of specialised secondary schools did so (Helemäe et al, 2000).

[3] This section is based on Eurydice (2003) and OECD (2001) publications.

[4] Until 2001, basic school drop-outs had no place in the education system. They could not get even minimal vocational training because the previous Vocational

Educational Institutions Act restricted access to such schools to individuals with basic or secondary education.

[5] Up until 1999 they could also opt for secondary specialised education.

[6] National examinations were introduced in 1997. The main aim of the national examinations is to unify marking across all schools, enhance the credibility of graduation certificates and to unify school final examinations and university entrance examinations.

[7] The selection of professions and specialisations for this type of vocational education is narrower than for secondary vocational education, depending on the needs and demands of employers.

[8] The OECD report (2001) also mentions a diploma study as an option in a one-stage applied higher education programme. The graduates who have completed their studies are awarded a diploma (ISCED 5a). Diploma-study can be performed at university or at institutions of professional higher education (rakenduskõrgkool). The study programme may have a common part with bachelor's study.

[9] At which at least one study programme is accredited or conditionally accepted by the Ministry of Education and Research.

[10] It is partially connected with the tremendous decrease of the age group 7-15. Within the last decade, the number of students in general education schools has decreased by 30,000. The number of students may be forecast to decrease by an additional 44,000 students by 2010 (European Commission, 2006).

[11] Two methods dominated the privatisation of collective farms in Estonia. The primary method should have been the restitution of former ownership relations or compensation through vouchers (Tamm, 2001). Although the majority of people wanted to have their old family farm back, only a minority was willing to start farming the restituted land. The land was frequently fragmented as it had to be split up among several beneficiaries. The work-share voucher method was applied to collective assets, which included production complexes as well as the majority of the machinery and livestock.

[12] According to estimations by Eamets and Masso (2005), while the share of standard (unlimited-term) contracts was 76% of employment, the share of temporary work was about 11% of employment in Estonia in 2001 and above the EU average of 10%.

[13] The new State Pension Insurance Act gives the option of retiring two years before statutory retirement age since 2000 and three years before statutory retirement age since 2001. If a person chooses the option of early retirement the amount of pension will be reduced to 0.4% per each month that he or she retired before statutory retirement age.

References

Aas, G., Lühiste, K. and Liimal, P. (2007) *Viis aastat töötuskindlustust Eestis 2002-2006 (Five years of unemployment insurance in Estonia 2002-2006)*, Tallinn: Eesti Töötukassa.

Antila, J. and Ylöstalo, P. (2003) *Working life barometer in the Baltic countries 2002*, Labour Policy Studies No 247, Helsinki: Ministry of Labour.

Arro, R., Eamets, R., Järve, J., Kallaste, E. and Philips, K. (2001) *Labour market flexibility and employment security: Estonia*, Employment Paper No 25, Geneva: International Labour Organization.

Cazes, S. and Nesporova, A. (2001) *Towards excessive job insecurity in transition economies?*, Employment Paper No 23, Geneva: International Labour Organization.

Eamets, R. (2001) *Reallocation of labour during transition disequilibrium and policy issues in the case of Estonia*, Tartu: Tartu University Press.

Eamets, R. and Masso, J. (2005) 'The paradox of the Baltic states: labour market flexibility but protected workers', *European Journal of Industrial Relations*, vol 11, no 1, pp 71-90.

Eamets, R., Philips, K. and Annus, T. (1999) *Background study on employment and labour market in Estonia*, Tartu: European Training Foundation.

Estonian Centre for Examination and Qualification (2006) (http://www.ekk.edu.ee/)

Estonian Labour Market Services and Support Act (2005) *State Gazette* (www2.sm.ee/tta/failid/ServicesandSupportAct.htm).

Estonian Ministry of Education and Research (2000) *Pikapäevarühma töökorralduse alused* (*Bases of arranging childcare after school*), (www.riigiteataja.ee/ert/act.jsp?id=82534).

Estonian Ministry of Education and Research (2004) *Koolieelsed lasteasutused* (*Pre-school children institutions*) (www.vana.hm.ee/uus/hm/client/index.php?0352623012473132).

ETF (European Training Foundation) (1998-2000) *Vocational education and training in Central and Eastern Europe: key indicators,* Luxembourg: Office for Official Publications of the European Communities.

European Commission (2006) *National summary sheets on education systems in Europe and ongoing reforms,* Brussels: European Commission.

Eurostat (2008) *Data: labour market*, Luxembourg: Eurostat (http://epp.eurostat.ec.europa.eu).

Eurydice (2003) *Structure of education, vocational training, and adult education system: Estonia,* Brussels: Eurydice European Unit.

Heinlo, A. (2001) 'Broadening scope of pre-primary education', in R. Vöörmann (ed) *Social Trends 2*, Tallinn: Estonian Statistical Office.

Helemäe, J. and Saar, E. (1999) 'The Estonian education system in the second half of the 20th century: opportunities and choices for the cohorts', in R. Vetik (ed) *Estonian Human Development Report*, Tallinn: UNDP, pp 84-92.

Helemäe, J., Saar, E. and Vöörmann, R. (2000) *Kas haridusse tasus investeerida?* (*Returns to education*), Tallinn: Teaduste Akadeemia Kirjastus.

Hinnosaar, M. and Rõõm, T. (2003) *Labour market impact of the minimum wage in Estonia: An empirical analysis*, Tallinn: Bank of Estonia (www.eestipank.info/pub/en/dokumendid/publikatsioonid/seeriad/konverentsid/_2 0030509/_3.pdf?objId=425479).

ILO (International Labour Organization) (2008) *Key indicators of the labour market programme*, Fifth Edition, Geneva: ILO.

International Bureau of Education (2001) *The development of education: national report of Estonia* (www.ibe.unesco.org/International/Ice/natrap/Estonia.pdf).

Kährik, A., Tiit, E.-M., Kõre, J. and Ruoppila, S. (2003) *Access to housing for vulnerable groups in Estonia*, (www.praxis.ee/data/WP_10_2003.pdf).

Kalmi, P. (2003) 'The rise and fall of employee ownership in Estonia, 1987-2001', *Europe-Asia Studies*, vol 55, no 8, pp 1213-39.

Kenkmann, P. and Saarniit, J. (1994) 'Education and shifts in youths' value orientations in Estonia', in V. Rust, P. Knost and J. Wichmann (eds) *Education and value crisis in Central and Eastern Europe*, Frankfurt: Peter Lang, pp 161-83.

Kennedy, M. (2002) *Cultural formations of post-communism*, Minneapolis: University of Minnesota Press.

Lauristin, M. (2003) 'Social contradictions shadowing Estonias' "Success Story"', *Demokratizatsiya*, vol 11, no 4, pp 601-16.

Lauristin, M. and Vihalemm, P. (1997) 'Recent historical developments in Estonia: three stages of transition (1987-1997)', in M. Lauristin, P. Vihalemm, K. Rosengren and L. Weibull (eds) *Return to the Western world*, Tartu: Tartu University Press, pp 73-125.

Leetmaa, R. and Võrk, A. (2003) *Evaluation of the active labour market policies in Estonia*, Praxis Working Paper No 9/2003, Tallinn: Center for Policy Studies.

Liuhto, K. (1996) 'Entrepreneurial transition in post-soviet republics: the Estonian path', *Europe-Asia Studies*, vol 48, no 1, pp 121-40.

Ministry of Education and Research (2006a) *Interim report about realisation of development plan of vocational education in Estonia*, Tallinn: Ministry of Education and Research.

Ministry of Education and Research (2006b) *Kõrghariduse valdkonna statistilised näitajad (Statistical indicators of higher education)* (www.hm.ee/index.php?048183).

Ministry of Social Affairs (2004-06) *Social sector in figures*, Tallinn: Ministry of Social Affairs. (www.sm.ee/eng/HtmlPages/social_sector_2004/$file/social_sector_2004.pdf)

Ministry of Social Affairs (2006a) *Tööturu riskirühmad: mitte-eestlased (Risk groups of labour market: non-Estonians)*, Tallinn: Ministry of Social Affairs (www.sm.ee/est/pages/index.html).

Ministry of Social Affairs (2006b) *Tööturu riskirühmad: noored töötud (Risk group of labour market: young unemployed)*, Tallinn: Ministry of Social Affairs, (www.sm.ee/est/pages/index.html).

Narusk, A. (2000) *Kutsetöö ja perekonnaelu: tasustatud ja tasustamata töö ühitamine: Teel tasakaalustatud ühiskonda, naised ja mehed Eestis (Work and family life: towards a balanced society, men and women in Estonia)*, Tallinn: Ministry of Social Affairs.

OECD (Organisation for Economic Co-operation and Development) (2001) *Reviews of national education policies: Estonia*, Paris: OECD

OECD (2003) *Labour market and social policies in the Baltic countries*, Paris: OECD.

Paas, T., Eamets, R., Masso, J. and Rõõm, M. (2003) *Labour market flexibility and migration in the Baltic states: macro evidences*, Discussion Paper No 16, Tartu: University of Tartu.

Paats, M. (2004) 'Housing conditions', in A. Purju (ed) *Social Trends 3*, Tallinn: Estonian Statistical Office.

Püss, M. (2004) 'Social security network and its effectiveness', in A. Purju (ed) *Social Trends 3*, Tallinn: Estonian Statistical Office.

Rajasalu, T., Ennuste, Ü., Kiili, J., Kukk, K., Püss, T., Rei, M., Venesaar, U. and Viies, M. (2003) *Understanding Estonian reforms to capitalist market: an economics narrative*, first version of the report prepared for the GDN Global Research Project: understanding reforms. (www.gdnet.org/pdf2/gdn_library/global_research_projects/understanding_reform/Estonia_first_draft.pdf)

Saar, E. (1997) 'Transitions to tertiary education in Belarus and the Baltic Countries', *European Sociological Review,* vol 13, no 2, pp 139-58.

Saar, E. and Unt, M. (2006) 'Self-employment in Estonia: forced move or voluntary engagement?', *Europe-Asia Studies*, vol 58, no 3, pp 415-37.

Statistical Office of Estonia (various years) *Statistical yearbook of Estonia*, Tallinn: Statistical Office of Estonia.

Tamm, M. (2001) 'Appendix: agricultural reform in Estonia' in I. Alanen, J. Nikula, H. Põder and R. Ruutsoo (eds) *Decollectivisation, destruction and disillusionment. A community study in southern Estonia*, Aldershot: Ashgate, pp 407-38.

Terk, E. (2000) *Privatisation in Estonia: ideas, processes, results*, Tallinn: Estonian Institute for Future Studies.

Titma, M. and Saar, E. (1995) 'Regional differences in Soviet secondary education', *European Sociological Review,* vol 11, no 1, pp 37-58.

Tonin, M. (2005) *Updated employment protection legislation indicators for Central and Eastern European countries*, Working Paper, Institute for International Economic Studies, Stockholm: Stockholm University.

UNICEF (United Nations International Children's Emergency Fund) (2007) *TransMONEE 2007 Database*, Florence: UNICEF Innocenti Research Centre (www.unicef-icdc.org/resources/transmonee.html).

Unt, M. and Kruscll, S. (2004) *Lastehoid Eesti peredes* (*Childcare in Estonian families*), Tallinn: Minister of Population Affairs.

Van Gyes, G., Vandenbrande, T., Lehndorff, S., Schilling, G., Schief, S. and Kohl, H. (2007) *Industrial relations in EU member states 2000-2004*, Dublin: European Foundation for the Improvement of Living and Working Conditions.

Visser, J. (2004) 'Patterns and variations in European industrial relations', in European Commission (2004) *Industrial relations in Europe*, Luxembourg: Office for the Official Publications of the European Communities, pp 11-57.

Vodopiveč, M. (2000) *Worker reallocation during Estonia's transition to market: how efficient and how equitable?*, Social Protection Discussion Paper No 0018, Washington DC: World Bank.

World Bank (2002) *Transition, the first ten years: analysis and lessons for Eastern Europe and the former Soviet Union*, Washington DC: World Bank.

SEVEN

Hungary

Erzsébet Bukodi and Péter Róbert[1]

Over a relatively short period of time, Hungary has undergone substantial structural changes concerning its education system, labour market and welfare institutions. During the socialist era, Hungarian society was meritocratic in the sense that the qualification prerequisites for different jobs were well determined, and there was a strong link between education and occupational status. Since the regime transformation, the curriculum of the country's education institutions has become more general and academically oriented. On the one hand, this could make the school-to-work transition more flexible, on the other hand, entrants to the labour market could face an increasing risk of a qualification/occupational mismatch. One of the principal changes in the labour market during the transition was undoubtfully a sizeable increase in the return to skills and a marked decrease in return to employment experience. The transition to a market economy therefore resulted in strong discrimination against older, unskilled workers who lost employment disproportionately in comparison to their well-trained, younger counterparts.

Education system

Structure of the Hungarian education system

Overview of the Hungarian education system after the Second World War[2]

The socialist education system in Hungary was organised into three distinct levels. Comprehensive primary education (ages 6-14) was followed by secondary education for which students had three options (see Table 7.1). The most popular secondary education institutions were apprentice schools where the curriculum covered two to three years and combined three days per week in school with two days per week of work experience.[3] At apprentice schools pupils did not receive 'maturity' (the secondary school diploma), so they were not eligible to continue their studies at tertiary level, but apprentice schools provided direct access to the labour market.[4] The second most common type of school was the technical secondary school, which had four grades, after which pupils sat a 'maturity' exam.

Table 7.1: Description of the education system

Under socialism, until age of 14		After mid-1990s, until age of 16	
Education system	Participation by age	Education system	Participation by age
Compulsory full-time education			
Pre-primary (óvoda) – one preparatory year is compulsory	Age 5-6/7	Pre-primary óvoda – one preparatory year is compulsory (ISCED 0-1)	Age 5-6/7
Primary school (általános iskola)	Age 6/7-14	Primary school (általános iskola) (ISCED 1+2)	Age 6/7-14 (cycle 1: age 6-10; cycle 2: age 10-14)
Secondary grammar school (gimnázium)	Age 14/15-18/19	Secondary grammar schools (gimnázium) (upper-secondary academic track but sometimes also lower secondary education) (ISCED 2+3)	Age 10/12/14-18/19
Vocational secondary school (szakközépiskola)	Age 14/15-18/19	Vocational secondary school (szakközépiskola) (ISCED 3)	Age 14-18/19 (generally 4 years)
Apprentice school (szakmunkásképző iskola)	Age 14/15-17	Vocational training school (szakiskola)[a] – (ISCED 3)	Age 14-18 years (2+2 years)
–	–	Post secondary vocational course (szakiskola)[b] – (ISCED 4)	Age 18-19/20 (1-2 years)
Post compulsory education; upper-, post-secondary and tertiary education			
College (főiskola)	Age 18-21	College (főiskola) (ISCED 5a,b)	Age 18/19-21
University (egyetem)	Age 18/19-23	University (egyetem) (ISCED 5a)	Age 18 or 19 (generally 5 years)
PhD, DLA	Age 23-	PhD, DLA (ISCED 6)	Age 23- (generally 3-6 years)

Notes: [a]Vocational training school (*Szakiskola*) replaced the apprentice school (*Szakmunkásképző*) in the 1990s. It consists of two years of general courses and two years of vocational courses. [b]Supplementary, post-secondary vocational course lasting one or two years organised by vocational training school.

The curriculum of this type of school was practical rather than theoretical, preparing students to enter the labour market as skilled workers (e.g. mechanics or printers) or as skilled white-collar workers (e.g. in administration and commerce). The third possibility was the gymnasium or academic secondary school. These schools had a four-year programme of a more general kind and also ended with a 'maturity' exam. Students finishing this kind of school more frequently went on to higher education. Enrolment rates in tertiary education were relatively low under socialism. Young adults entering tertiary education had two options. The more popular and more vocational-oriented option was college, which took three years. The other option was university with a curriculum that lasted four to six years (see Table 7.1). With regard to recruitment, the universities took most of their students from the gymnasia, while the students at colleges usually came from technical secondary schools.[5] Those who wanted to enrol at university had to pass an entrance examination, which was a combined written and oral examination, and results gained in the maturity examination were also taken into account. This procedure was used to facilitate the selection of students under the guidelines laid down in the admission quotas set by the government and to facilitate positive discrimination in favour of children from the families of manual workers.[6]

An additional feature of the Hungarian education system was the existence of evening and correspondence courses, as an alternative way of completing secondary and tertiary education. The original goal of these courses (in the 1950s and 1960s) was to increase social mobility and to assist the children of manual workers. In the 1970s and 1980s evening and correspondence courses, especially at tertiary level, represented an opportunity for less bright children from families who were not manual workers to secure a degree.

The most dramatic result in education expansion during the four decades of socialism was observable among people with primary and lower-secondary education. A dramatic increase in numbers was visible in secondary education but there was much less impact on tertiary education. Another important feature was the sharp increase in female participation rates in education institutions and the diminishing education difference between larger cities and smaller towns. Completion rates also increased at every level of schooling, while gender differences declined (see also Andorka and Harcsa, 1992; Halász and Lannert, 1995).

Education system since 1990[7]

In the 1990s, significant structural changes took place at both the primary and the secondary level of schooling (see Figure 7.1). The former strict boundaries between eight years of primary and four years of secondary education disappeared. As a consequence of these structural changes three different concepts now need to be considered: the type of school, the education level and the specific education or training programme. Within any institution there can be a variety of education programmes followed, which lead to different education qualifications. Secondary education institutions differ in two respects: first, whether they offer general or vocational education and second, whether they issue the upper-secondary school leaving certificates. The typical institutions at the secondary level are: (1) eight-year single structure schools, (2) upper-secondary general schools (gymnasia), (3) short-term secondary vocational training schools, and (4) four-year secondary vocational training schools.

Pupils who wish to obtain the secondary school leaving certificate will generally choose a gymnasium. There are three main types, which cover different age groups (see Figure 7.1). For those who attend the eight- or six-grade types, the former transition age of 14 from primary to secondary level has gone down to the age of 10 or 12. This means that the lower-secondary level (grades 5-8) of schooling has become much more heterogeneous than before, depending on the education institution and the school programme the student attends. These six- or eight-grade secondary schools are considered by both parents and students as the best preparation for tertiary (mainly university) education.

Secondary vocational school is an institution offering four or five years of full-time education. To gain entry, pupils may have to pass an entrance examination. These institutions provide general upper-secondary education and vocational training; exclusively the latter after the completion of the second year. There are two or three training cycles, at the end of which pupils receive a certificate of completion.

A further important change which occurred at the upper-secondary level of education is that schools started to offer both general and vocational education programmes, in many cases within the same institution. In addition, more secondary schools started to offer a variety of post-secondary programmes for those students who could not enter tertiary education.

Short-term vocational training schools are institutions offering one to two years of full- and part-time vocational education in a single cycle to pupils aged 14-16. Several programmes exist within this type of education institution. At the end of the education/training programme pupils can take a final examination focusing on a particular profession/trade. Those who are successful receive a certificate of completion, which enables the holder to enter the labour market as a skilled worker. In vocational schools where the course is specified in the National Register of Qualifications a dual system operates. The theoretical part is taught at school, and training is offered in school workshops rather than in factories.

Figure 7.1: The Hungarian system of education

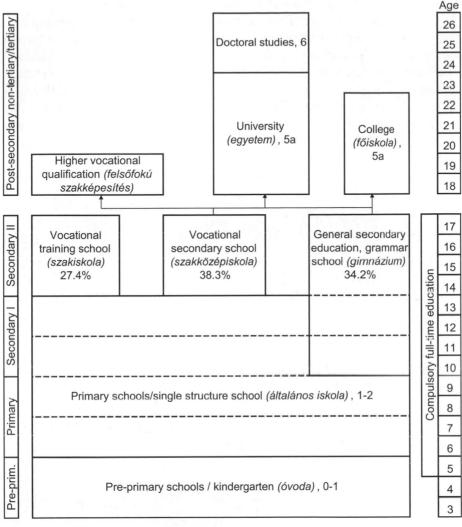

Source: ETF (2000)

Applications to standard programmes at Hungarian higher education institutions can be submitted by anyone with a valid secondary school leaving final examination or equivalent secondary school leaving certificate. In order to be able to compare applicants' suitability for higher education, a standard, centrally approved entrance examination schema is used. By 1 September 2006 a two-cycle degree system was supposed to be introduced in all European countries that had agreed to the general Bologna process. Under this system, students who successfully complete university education courses over six semesters are awarded Bachelor of Art degrees. Universities and other university-level institutions can award a master's degree to students who successfully complete a further course over four semesters.

A higher vocational qualification is awarded at the end of the second year of non-tertiary higher vocational programmes to students who have passed the professional examination (Halász et al, 2001). In order to facilitate international comparison, higher education law in Hungary allows graduate students of Hungarian higher education institutions to use the title Bachelor of Arts if they have completed a college graduate education, and the title Master of Arts if they have completed a university graduate education, with an indication of the area of study. The Hungarian doctoral degree (PhD) and, in the case of arts universities, the Doctor of Liberal Arts degree (DLA) correspond in every respect to what is known and recognised internationally as the PhD degree.

Education expansion

The trends in the number of students entering different levels of the school system are shown in Figure 7.2. First, an increase in upper-secondary education enrolment since the mid-1990s is clearly visible. At the same time, the number of students entering the basic vocational schools (short-term training schools) declined steadily between 1989 and 1999.

Figure 7.2: Number of students entering the school system by level of education, 1989-2004

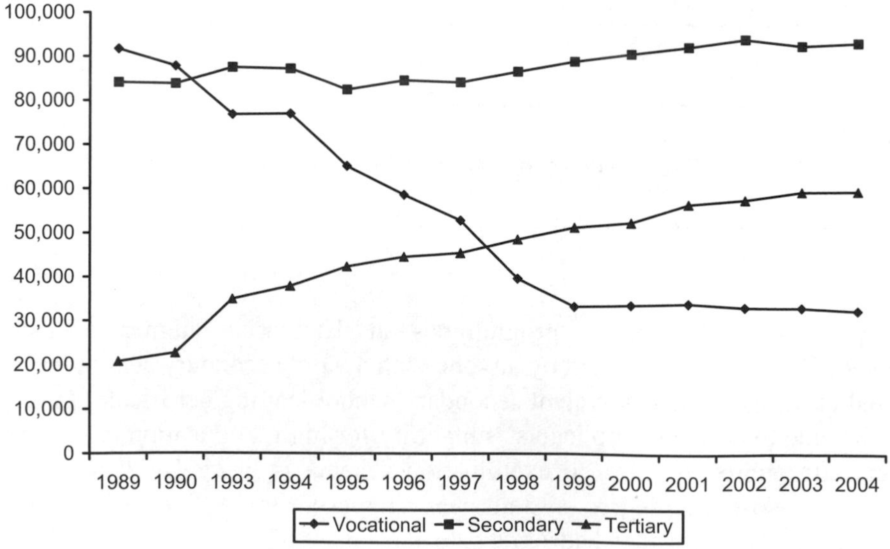

Source: Fazekas and Varga (2005)

The rate of expansion in higher education was even greater than that at upper-secondary level. It should be emphasised that education expansion was accompanied by growing differences between the best and the least effective groups of secondary schools in terms of admission rates to higher education. Since the mid-1990s the proportion of those admitted to higher education from the so-called structure-changing gymnasiums (gymnasiums with 6 or 8 grades) has increased considerably while technical secondary schools and even the traditional (four-grade) gymnasiums seem to have dropped behind (Lannert, 2005).

Accordingly, the number of full-time students from the appropriate (18-22) age cohort increased considerably. In 1990, full-time higher education students made up 8.5% of the 18-22 age cohort, while the corresponding figure in 2002 was 25%.

Girls make up the majority of students at upper-secondary level, although there is an increasing trend towards equal numbers of girls and boys in this type of school (see Figure 7.3). On the other hand, the proportion of women in tertiary education has been increasing since 1990, and in 2004 women outnumbered men in university-level education. Vocational training is mainly male-dominated with women making up less than 40% of those enrolled. A trend towards the feminisation of vocational education is, however, visible.

Figure 7.3: Proportion of women among full-time students at secondary and tertiary level, 1990-2004

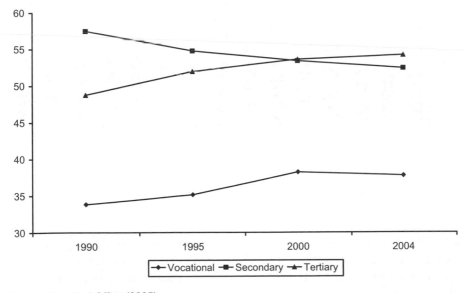

Source: Statistical Office (2005)

Secondary level of education

Stratification and track differentiation

The first education decisions in Hungary are made at the age of 10 or 12, when pupils can opt for a six- or eight-grade gymnasium. Although only about 8%-10% of each cohort continue their study in these kinds of institution, the best pupils – who usually come from advantaged social backgrounds – are selected at this stage. In this respect Hungary is similar to Germany, where first schooling decisions with far-reaching consequences to future education chances are also made at a similarly early age, much earlier than in other Central and Eastern European (CEE) countries. For the majority of pupils in Hungary, however, the first schooling decision takes place at the age of 14, when more options are open to them and they decide whether to continue in general education or to take up vocational training.

Figure 7.4: Enrolment in education and training at the (upper)-secondary level (%), 1990-2004

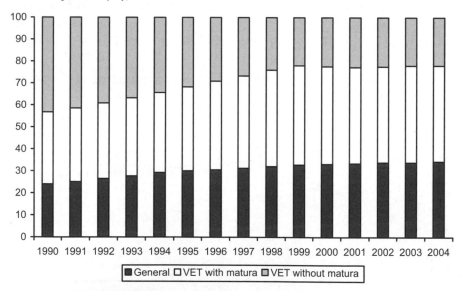

Note: VET = Vocational education and training.
Source: Ministry of Education (2005)

Although the Hungarian education system has traditionally been oriented towards vocational training rather than general education, since 1990 there has been a substantial shift away from basic vocational school programmes towards upper-secondary general education and secondary vocational education, which now account for more than three quarters of all secondary school students (see Figure 7.4). As one would expect, the proportion of those leaving vocational education and training (VET) without maturity decreased from about 35% to 20%.

Organisation of vocational training

In Hungary VET is organised in a dual system. The practical training can be conducted either in school-based form or by working for an employer. The present practice is that vocational training schools and training companies receive an annual fixed amount of money per student from the state for practical and theoretical vocational training. The main sources for financing vocational training are the state budget and compulsory employers' contributions to the Vocational Training Fund (1.5% of their wage cost).

Standardisation and quality differentiation of secondary education

The reorganisation of the education system in the 1990s increased the variation in the value of the upper-secondary school degree ('maturity'). Furthermore, since 1997 there has been a move towards stronger standardisation of secondary education, although the tests for the maturity examination had always been developed centrally and standardised. This means that pupils receive exactly the same tests and tasks in the schools nation-wide. Another recent change in the system has affected the content of the maturity exam; students can now choose between a lower or higher level 'maturity' and the tests now require less lexical ability but more practical-oriented knowledge.

There are clear differences in the academic achievement levels of students attending the various kinds of school. According to the PISA (Programme for International Student Assessment) 2003 survey, students in academic secondary education apparently perform better in reading (their mean score is 543.59 points) than those enrolling in vocational secondary schools (where the mean score is 482.37) and especially in basic vocational schools (where the mean score is 396.20).

Tertiary level of education

Horizontal dimension

First of all, it should be noted that at tertiary level enrolment increased more quickly at vocational-type institutions (colleges) than at traditional universities. Some market-oriented colleges – offering economics and business studies – became especially popular as students anticipated good future career opportunities.

Figure 7.5 shows one of the most important aspects of the horizontal dimension at tertiary level, a field-of-study differentiation. It allows us to compare the distribution of students across different fields in 1990/91 and 2003/04. The most popular field in 1990/91 was teacher training and education science with more than 35% of students enrolled in this field. In 2003/04 the corresponding figure was only 14%. The most popular field in 2003/04 was quite clearly business and administration with almost 24% of students, as compared to only 9% in 1990/91. Engineering, manufacturing and construction proved to be the second most popular fields in both 1990/91 and 2003/04, despite a decrease in the total enrolment from 20% to 14%. An increase can also be observed in the number of students in humanities, social sciences, services and computing. Enrolments in health and welfare and agriculture, on the other hand, declined. Hardly any change can be observed in the numbers of students in science disciplines and the arts.

Figure 7.5: Enrolment in tertiary education by field of study (%)

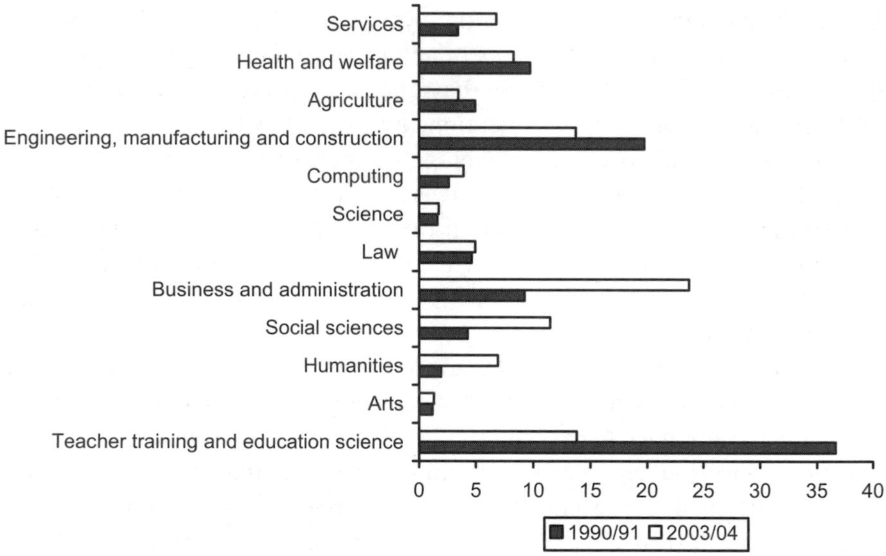

Source: Hungarian Central Statistical Office (2003)

With regard to the proportion of women in various fields of education at tertiary level, results are as one might expect. In 2003/04 health and welfare, teacher training and education science, humanities, business administration, social sciences and law were typically female-dominated fields with more than 60% of those enrolled being female. Typical male-dominated fields with less than 30% of those enrolled being female include engineering, manufacturing and construction, as well as computing. Sciences, agriculture and arts could be considered rather mixed in gender composition, with slightly more women enrolled in arts subjects, and slightly fewer women in science and agriculture.

Standardisation, quality differentiation and openness of tertiary education

A system of accreditation has been in place in Hungary since 1993. Accreditation is carried out by an independent body of experts called the Hungarian Accreditation Committee who are responsible for the general quality (and the minimum level of standardisation) of higher education. Accreditation is compulsory for both new and existing institutions, faculties and programmes, public and non-public alike. The accreditation of existing institutions, faculties and programmes is implemented in the framework of institutional accreditation with a cycle of eight years. The method used for the accreditation of institutions includes an evaluation by external experts and concludes with an evaluation report or an accreditation decision.

Table 7.2 displays the numbers of institutions at tertiary level by its type (public, ecclesiastical or private) as compared to that of secondary education. It can be seen that at tertiary level fewer public education institutions operate. At other levels state-run schools dominate.

Table 7.2: Number of education institutions by type of schools

	Public	Ecclesiastical	Other, foundation, private person
Vocational			
2001/02	385	49	65
2004/05	376	60	81
Secondary general (gymnasium)			
2001/02	429	88	60
2004/05	435	95	195
Secondary vocational			
2001/02	634	23	141
2004/05	601	23	170
Tertiary			
2001/02	30	26	9
2004/05	31	26	12

Source: Ministry of Education (2005)

Faced with budget cuts, even public institutions at tertiary level started to charge tuition fees in the second half of the 1990s. This change in the 'tuition policy' basically involved two things. First, there was a huge expansion in part-time programmes beginning in the early 1990s (in fact, now around 50% of students enrolling in tertiary education are studying part time) and these programmes are more likely to charge tuition fees. Second, a growing number of students have to pay fees even for full-time programmes due to 'quality reasons', i.e., because they have not met the academic requirements for studying free of charge. As a result, the proportion of students paying fees has increased steadily; in 2004 this share made up 25%.

Labour market

Economic development

Important economic transformations took place in Hungary in the 1980s. The Németh government made the first efforts to tighten fiscal and monetary policy, and to liberalise prices. Furthermore, the government introduced a market-oriented tax system in 1988 (Horváth et al, 1999). After the fall of the Iron Curtain, Hungary profited from the early economic and social reforms. In 1990, when the first free elections were held after almost 50 years under communist rule, there was already a private sector of considerable size. However, Hungary had to master the transition from a socialist economy to a market economy and it had to compensate for the loss of the larger part of the internal market of Council for Mutual Economic Assistence (COMECON). Hence, there was a decline in gross domestic product (GDP) in real terms during the early years of transition (Figure 7.6). This transitional recession peaked at –11.9% in 1991, making it a small recession compared to those which occurred in other CEE countries.

Since the fall of the communist regime, a fundamental process of transition from a centrally planned economy to a market economy has taken place in Hungary. The key policy objectives were price liberalisation, liberal foreign trade, macroeconomic stabilisation and the privatisation of state enterprises. Privatisation was completed relatively fast and was accomplished by the sale of state-owned companies at market rates. During the transition a legislative base was established to promote the development of the private sector. First, the more prosperous enterprises were sold to foreign investors in 1991 and 1992. These foreign investors were often attracted by the low labour costs and by the goal of establishing themselves in Hungary and other CEE markets. Second, smaller state-owned companies were sold to domestic investors during the period 1992-94. Workers' share ownership was also supported by the government by means of preferential loans. Third, from 1994 onwards, public utility companies that were often former state monopolies were sold to large foreign firms. Due to these processes, the private sector has increased considerably. These restructuring efforts were rewarded by fast growth in GDP, with an annual growth rate of 2.9 in 1994. The expansion was followed by a short and small decline in real GDP per capita before the economy returned to a higher growth path. Since 1997, economic performance has remained stable with high annual growth rates of

4%-6% because of successful structural reforms and careful macroeconomic management (European Commission, 2001).

Figure 7.6: GDP growth, 1989-2006

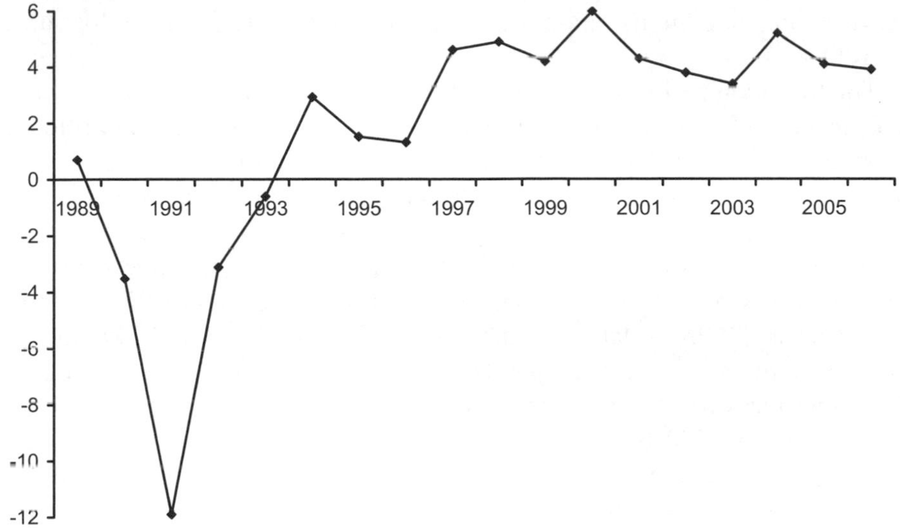

Source: ILO (2008); data for 2006 from Eurostat (2008)

Labour market dynamics

Employment dynamics

Compared to other CEE countries, employment in the service sector was already high at the beginning of the transition period in Hungary. In 1990, 11.3% of employed people worked in agriculture, 35.1% in industry and 53.4% in service industries (ILO, 2008). During the transition, employment in agriculture decreased significantly to 5% in 2005, a value that coincides with the Western European average. Problems in agriculture had already started during the 1980s: many of the cooperatives and state farms were maintained by direct or indirect subsidies. After 1990 the situation deteriorated. The general decline in agricultural employment can be explained by the liberalisation of prices, cuts in agricultural subsidies, the restitution of land and the privatisation of state farms (Horváth et al, 1999).

As a result, employment in industry and construction decreased slowly throughout the whole transition period to 32.4% in 2005 (ILO, 2008). The industrial sector was dominated by large enterprises, especially in heavy industry and engineering, which were developed substantially under Communist rule. The industrial sectors that were most affected by employment slowdown were the iron and steel, engineering, chemical and textile industries. In contrast, growth was stimulated by investments from multinational companies, especially in the automotive industry. The service sector's share of total employment increased steadily to 62.6% in 2005 (ILO, 2008). Growth in services focused on banking and insurance, business services, public administration, education and personal services (Horváth et al, 1999).

The transition period was characterised by a sharp decrease in employment and an increasing mismatch between labour demand and supply. Structural economic change led to job destruction. In fact, as Kézdi (2002) emphasises, the rate of job creation and job destruction varied in extent over different phases of the transition. The major loss of low-skilled jobs – partly towards skill-intensive industries – occurred during the transitional crises, and since 1996 a pervasive skill upgrade has been seen in all sectors of the economy. As Fazekas (2005) calculates, the number of unskilled and skilled jobs decreased by 35 percentage points between 1989 and 1993. During the economic recovery, the number of skilled jobs began to rise, exceeding the initial level of 1990 by 2000. Simultaneously, the destruction of unskilled jobs continued, although with less intensity. As Kézdi (2002) emphasises, the introduction of new (foreign) capital seems to be a major factor behind increasing demand for skill. In fact, foreign direct investment into Hungary was by far the largest among the transition countries until the late 1990s.

Figure 7.7 shows that the labour force participation rate of those aged 15-64 declined from 65.7% in 1990 to 60% in 2006. Regarding the development of participation rates, the transitional period can be divided into two sub-periods. Until 1997 there was a relatively sharp decline in the participation rate, disproportionately burdening females. After 1997, participation rates increased slightly again. The gender-specific time trends in labour force participation are similar, although the female activity rate is roughly 13-17 percentage points below that of men. Compared with other CEE countries, the differences between male and female employment rates are more pronounced, and Hungary performs especially badly in terms of female employment.

Regarding age-specific labour force participation rates, middle-aged people had reached very high activity rates of around 77-84% during the transition period but this also decreased by 7 percentage points (Table 7.3). The participation rate of people aged 65 fluctuates around the 1% mark, representing a relatively low value that is comparable to participation rates in the EU15. The youngest age group is the cohort that has been most affected by the fall in employment where the activity rate fell from 51.4% to 28.2% between 1990 and 2006. This is partly related to increased enrolment in higher education but it may also reflect the increasing labour market integration problems for young people (e.g. an increasing risk of education/occupation mismatch and longer search periods for first jobs, especially for those without any 'marketable' qualification).

Figure 7.7: Labour force participation rate (age group 15-64), 1990-2006

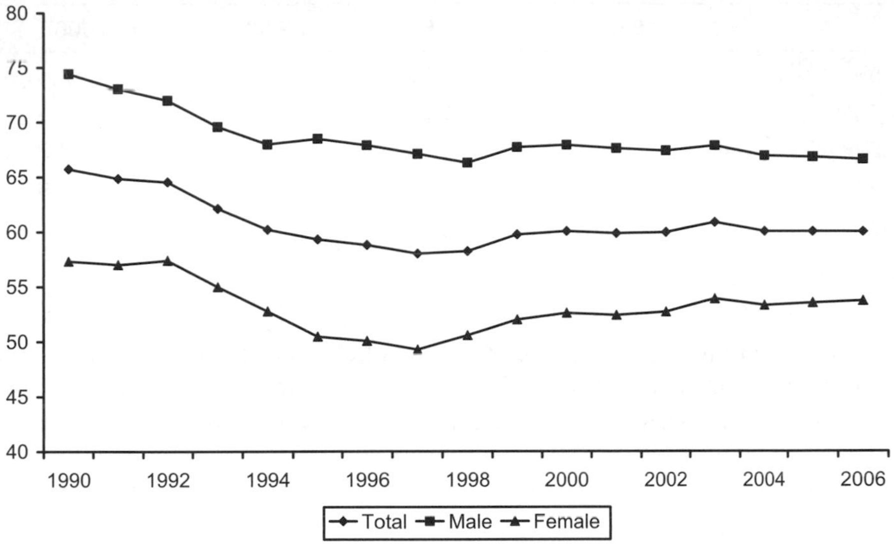

Source: ILO (2008)

Among others, Kertesi and Köllő (2002) emphasise that one of the principal changes in labour market relations during transition was a sizeable increase in the return to skills, but a marked decrease in the return to age and employment experience, as labour market experience which had been accumulated throughout the years of the old regime devaluated after 1990. The transition therefore resulted in marked discrimination against (older) unskilled workers who disproportionately lost employment in comparison to their skilled (younger) counterparts. Furthermore, as noted above, job creation in new firms tended to be biased against employees with low education attainments. It is hence not surprising that the move into inactivity appears to have been most typical for the unskilled, older workers, and those living in economically depressed regions (Fazekas, 2004). Furthermore, low retirement ages are of central importance in explaining the high inactivity ratio. The employment rate of senior workers decreased very quickly during the transition crisis, fostered by various incentives for early exit: in the case of mass dismissals, Hungarian firms made use of early retirement and disability pension schemes as the least painful means of workforce reduction. At the same time, the government explicitly encouraged early retirement in the early transition years. Even though eligibility conditions were gradually tightened recently, only a small minority of the population over 55 years old is currently participating in the labour market due to the use of mass early retirement schemes in former years.

Table 7.3: Labour force participation rate by age groups, 1990-2006

	1990	1995	2000	2006
15+	54.8	49.5	49.8	49.4
15-24	51.4	39.9	37.9	28.2
25-54	84.3	77.5	77.4	77.9
55-64	17.0	18.2	22.4	28.9
65+	0.7	2.5	2.6	1.5

Source: ILO (2008)

Due to structural changes in the labour market, there have been substantial alterations in the occupational class distribution of labour market entrants over the last two decades. A relative majority of young men started to work in manual jobs in both the 1980s and the 1990s, but there was a decline from 43% to 32% over time (Róbert, 2005). While the overall proportion of manual workers declined across the 1980s and the 1990s, it is worth noting that an increasing number of men were entering the labour market as unskilled workers – in spite of the fact that the recent generations of school leavers are more educated than previous ones. Also, the proportion of those who have started to work in routine service jobs has doubled for men over the last two decades, and almost one in five young women started a career in a service industry in the 1990s.

Furthermore, there was a remarkable increase in the degree of job-to-job mobility and a significant decrease in job stability in the first half of the 1990s for all age groups (Bukodi and Róbert, 2006). After the mid-1990s, in the recovery period, employment mobility was stabilised. However, since the early 2000s – due, among other reasons, to the increasing flexibilisation of the Hungarian labour market and the less generous employment-sustaining policies – the rate of job mobility has risen slightly, especially among young people.

Labour market flexibilisation

Although compared with some other countries the incidence of temporary employment is still relatively low in Hungary (around 7%), the proportion of young employees in fixed-term and other types of flexible job is gradually increasing. Moreover, the risk of temporary employment is determined by human capital endowments and occupation (Róbert and Bukodi, 2005). Fixed-term contracts and occasional work are highly overrepresented on the one hand among the poorly educated, and on the other among those working in routine service and in other unskilled jobs.

Unemployment dynamics

Official registered unemployment was already high at the beginning of the transition period with 8.5% in 1991 (Figure 7.8). Both Labour Force Survey (LFS)-based and the registered unemployment rate measured roughly identical levels of unemployment despite their different measurement methods. In general, Hungary suffered from an increase in unemployment that peaked at approximately 12.1% of the labour force in 1992; after that it fell to 5.8% in 2002. This decline in unemployment started in accordance with the economic recovery during the second half of the 1990s. In the last few years, a slight increase can be observed.

Figure 7.8: Unemployment rates, 1990-2006

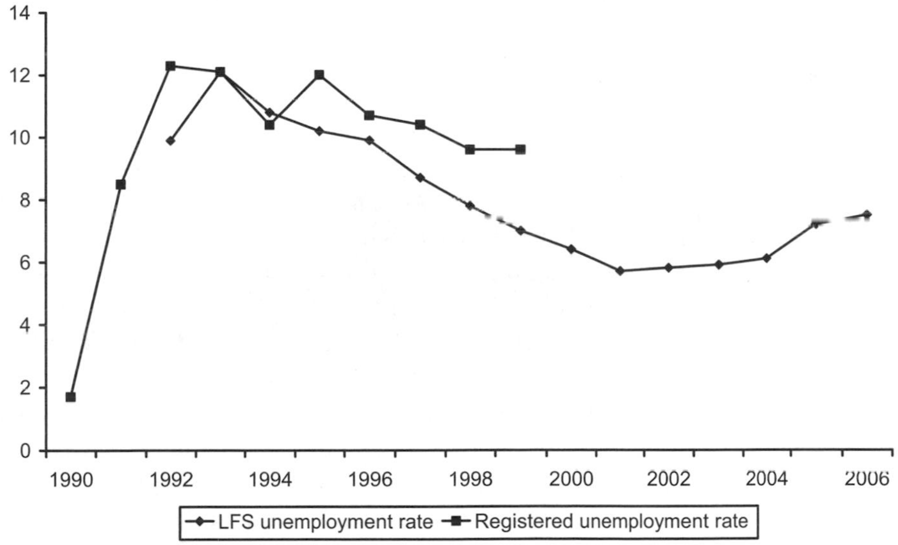

Note: LFS unemployment rate for individuals aged over 15.
Source: ILO (2008); data for 2006 from Eurostat (2008)

Young people are the most vulnerable to unemployment. The unemployment rate for people younger than 25 decreased from 18.8% in 1992 to 11.2% in 2001 and increased again to 19.4% in 2005 (ILO, 2008). In addition to young people, another disadvantaged category in the labour market is that of the long-term unemployed. According to Eurostat (2008) data, the share of long-term unemployed, i.e., people unemployed for over 12 months, decreased from 54.8% in 1996 to 45.1% in 2006. In general, one can find a well-established relationship between the level of education and the risk of being unemployed. The higher the education, the lower the level of unemployment (Table 7.4).

Table 7.4: Unemployment rates by education level, 1993-2004

	Primary	Vocational	Secondary	Tertiary	Total
Males					
1993	20.3	15.0	9.7	2.9	13.5
1999	14.3	8.2	5.0	1.5	7.5
2004	14.3	6.4	4.1	1.7	6.1
Females					
1993	14.6	12.8	8.1	3.2	10.4
1999	10.5	8.0	5.2	1.3	6.3
2004	10.3	8.0	5.3	2.9	6.1

Source: Fazekas and Koltay (2006)

Minority ethnic groups, migration and regional differences

Unemployment also varies between ethnic groups and regions. In Hungary, the largest minority ethnic group is the Roma, who probably represent about 450,000-600,000 individuals (ETF, 2003). The figures vary, because many Roma deny their origin for fear of discrimination. The unemployment rate of the Roma population might be three to four times as high as that of the non-Roma population (European Commission, 2001). Unemployment is particularly severe among the Roma minority because they typically have a very low level of education and they are subject to discriminatory practices.

The variation in employment and unemployment rates at the regional level is also marked in Hungary (see Table 7.5). Unemployment is lowest and the employment rate is highest in the capital Budapest where a thriving commercial and urban area with international headquarters and central administration has developed. Other advantaged Hungarian regions can also be found along the Austrian border. High unemployment rates prevail in the Northern Great Plain and Southern Transdanubian regions (OECD, 2000). In general, regions with high unemployment rates are characterised by declining industries, e.g. mining and agriculture. For example, agriculture is concentrated in the Great Plain region and Southern Transdanubia. However, these disparities have not encouraged inner migration (Horváth et al, 1999). The lack of mobility mostly reflects problems in the housing market and a low willingness among the Hungarian labour force to move.

Table 7.5: Labour force participation rates and LFS unemployment rates by NUTS-2[a] level of region, 1993 and 2004

	Labour force participation rate		Unemployment rate	
	1993	2004	1993	2004
Central Hungary	58.4	62.9	9.9	4.5
Central Transdanubia	55.2	60.3	12.6	5.6
Western Transdanubia	60.5	61.4	9.0	4.6
Southern Transdanubia	52.9	52.3	12.8	7.3
Northern Hungary	49.3	50.6	16.1	9.7
Northern Great Plain	48.4	50.4	14.8	7.2
Southern Great Plain	53.4	53.6	12.4	6.3
Total	54.5	56.8	12.1	6.1

Note: [a] Nomenclature of Territorial Units for Statistics (NUTS) of the European Union.
Source: Fazekas and Koltay (2006)

Labour market institutions

After the collapse of socialism, Hungary created a regulatory framework for labour markets – the so-called Labour Code – that exists in many other countries in Europe, protecting the jobs of workers in large firms and limiting the opportunity for flexible employment. The Act on Labour Code was introduced in 1992 and modified in 2001, as well as in 2003. This law includes the most important rules on employer–employee relationships and the legal bases of labour contracts and collective agreements.

Employment protection legislation

As regards the employment protection legislation (EPL), Hungary tends to be less restrictive than the European Union (EU) and the CEE average concerning regular employment contracts (OECD, 2004; Eamets and Masso, 2005). Regulation concerning temporary employment is negligible in Hungary, despite a slight increase in its strictness in 2003. In contrast to other CEE countries and to the EU, firing rules concerning collective dismissals are less restrictive. In general, Hungary has on average a weaker EPL than most CEE countries. Moreover, in reality, the Hungarian labour market is even more flexible than it seems, due to the fact that some employers, particularly in the private sector, appear to be unwilling to follow the legal employment regulations (Köllő and Nacsa, 2005).

Industrial relations

Before 1990, Hungary's industrial relations systems were characterised by central political and managerial control exercised by the state. During the transition, the country moved away from a centralised wage-setting system towards a collective bargaining system in the enterprise sector. Wage bargaining usually takes place at the level of the firm, but sectoral and national agreements also exist (Visser, 2004: Table 1.8). To some extent collective bargaining is also conducted at a national level. Hence, wage bargaining in Hungary continues to exhibit elements of both the centralised and decentralised systems and it remains unclear which, if either, method will dominate as traditions develop (OECD, 2000).

Union membership declined sharply during the 1990s from full registration of the workforce at the beginning of transition. According to Van Gyes et al (2007: Figure 2), the Hungarian unionisation rate decreased from 46% in 1995 to 17% in 2004. The decrease might be attributed to, first, the fact that union membership was no longer compulsory, second, falling living standards over the 1990s, and third, high levels of unemployment and the growing number of small businesses as well as huge sectoral shifts. The degree of unionisation is, in general, lower in the private sector than in the public sector.

As regards coverage by collective agreements, as Van Gyes et al (2007: Figure 4) estimate, the percentage of employees covered was more than 42% in 2002. As far as the private sector is concerned, collective agreements usually operate only in large enterprises, while the small and medium-sized enterprise (SME) sector is scarcely regulated by them.

Welfare regime

Labour market policy

Active labour market policy

During the early transition period, labour market policy in Hungary involved financing passive measures, with insignificant expenditure on active measures. Active measures were given less emphasis because of financial constraints and scepticism about their impact (European Commission, 2001). However, in recent years, there has been a shift towards active measures (Table 7.6). However, active labour market policy (ALMP) plays a rather small role in Hungary even now, with expenditure of about 0.5% of GDP in 2003 (Ministry of Employment and Labour, 2004).

In 2006, several new ALMP measures were introduced. Among them, the following are of particular relevance. The *job search incentive* can be provided to people without jobs who have exceeded their unemployment benefit entitlement period and have cooperated with the employment office. Another scheme, the *job finding incentive*, is a benefit for those who find employment before their job search period ends. There are several initiatives to promote job seekers' participation in adult training. A *training subsidy* can be given to those who are less than 25 years old (or less than 30, if they are university/college graduates) or who take part in public work or receive child-raising benefits. The *make a step forward* scheme makes it possible for individuals to return to the training system – in order to achieve higher education or obtain a vocational certificate – without high costs. In the framework of the *IDEA programme* young people aged 18-26, who do not enrol in school and are not employed, are entitled to work at different non-governmental organisations on a voluntary basis for up to 10 months in order to gain work experience. In the *work experience accumulation* scheme employers can be provided with wage subsidies if they employ school leavers for at least 360 days. The so-called *START programme* also provides incentives for employers to hire school leavers (they are allowed to pay a reduced amount of the mandatory social security contributions).

Table 7.6: Two indicators on temporal change of the role of ALMP in employment policy, 1999-2003

	1992	1994	1996	1998	2000	2002	2003
Participants in ALMP measures (% of participants in active and passive labour market programmes)	0.13	0.27	0.29	0.39	0.37	0.32	0.32
Expenditure on ALMP (% of total labour market policy expenditure)	0.21	0.34	0.34	0.39	0.46	0.58	0.57

Source: Ministry of Employment and Labour of Hungary (2004); Fazekas and Koltay (2006)

Unemployment insurance

The unemployment benefit system was introduced in 1991 but has undergone significant changes since then. According to the original 1991 Act unemployment benefit was granted to anyone who (1) was unemployed, (2) had spent at least 360 days in employment over the four years prior to becoming unemployed, (3) was not eligible for old-age or disability pensions, and (4) wished to find a job. The amount was calculated on the basis of the person's average earnings during the four-year period prior to becoming unemployed. In the first period of payment, the benefit was 65% of the earlier average net earnings of the person; in the second phase it was 50%. The minimum amount of the benefit had to reach the amount of the mandatory minimum wage; the maximum amount was three times that. The duration of payments was dependent on the period spent in employment over the four years preceding unemployment.

The system was reformed successively (see Table 7.7 below). As regards the most substantial changes in the system, in 2000 the minimum duration of payment was cut to between 40 days and a maximum of nine months. The minimum was made to be conditional on 200 days of prior employment, and the maximum required was 45 months. Mean durations of benefit payments declined for almost all, except those with the least prior employment (see Galasi and Nagy, 2002).

In 2003 another type of benefit was introduced, *the support to the job search incentive*, in order to promote closer and longer cooperation between the unemployed and the local job centre. To be eligible, individuals had to have been engaged in active job search, had cooperated with the job centre, and had received unemployment benefit for at least 180 days but their entitlement had expired. The amount they received was 85% of the minimum old-age pension, the duration of the payment was 180 days, although this could be extended by another 90 days for those over 45 years of age.

Table 7.7: Description of unemployment insurance since the mid-1990s

	2nd half of the 1990s	1st half of the 2000s	After 1 November, 2005
Replacement rate for 1st six months	65% of monthly net wage prior to becoming unemployed		1st phase: 60% of monthly net wage prior to unemployment; 2nd phase: 60% of minimum wage
Waiting period	0	0	0
Duration of payment	45-360 days	40-270 days	73-270 days
Minimum contribution period	200 days	200 days	365 days
	over the four years prior to becoming unemployed		
Other qualifying conditions	Active job search, compliance with job centre required Military and civil service, sick leave, prenatal allowance, childcare fee, childcare allowance extend the four years		

In 2005, new types of benefit were introduced. The so-called *job seeker benefit* is practically equal to the former unemployment benefit, and is awarded to job seekers who were employed for at least 365 days over the four years preceding unemployment. The statutory replacement rate amounts to 60% of the earlier average gross wage of the person. The *job search allowance* was introduced to replace the job search incentive and is granted to those who have exhausted their eligibility for the job search benefit and are close to the statutory retirement age or, due to the change in eligibility conditions, are not entitled for job search benefit. It is a fixed sum equal to 40% of the statutory minimum wage.

In 1991 the Employment Act also introduced the *career beginners assistance* (or unemployment benefit for school-leavers) for those who (1) had completed secondary school (at least two years of vocational training), (2) were 25 or younger, (3) did not have an employment record entitling them to unemployment benefits, or (4) were unable to find a job for three months after registering at the job centre (Lázár, 2002). They were entitled to the benefit for six months and until 1995 the payment was 75% of the prevailing minimum old-age pension from 1995 this went up to 80%. It was suspended during military service or during the receipt of childcare allowance. Since poorly qualified first-time job seekers were not entitled to assistance, only very few registered, so they received no help at all. In 1996 new active labour market measures for job seekers were introduced and the career beginners assistance was abolished.

In sum, over the last decade, unemployment benefit systems have increasingly become less generous. This tendency can be seen in the reduction of the level of benefit payments in real terms and in their duration, as well as the tightening of eligibility conditions (see also Cazes and Nesporova, 2003).

Family policy

The total expenditure on family policies in Hungary has not varied much in recent years, chiefly due to the fact that major changes occurred between 1990 and 1997. From 1990-94, there were only minor changes in institutionalised family support. The most important elements of the system developed in the socialist period were preserved with the main aim of ensuring the reproduction of the population. However, the socio-liberal government of the mid-1990s had a totally different ideology. In order to promote economic stabilisation and to use public resources in a more efficient way as well as to establish a fair socio-political system, the government put more emphasis on helping those with lower incomes instead of the population at large. But in 1998 a new conservative government again made radical changes to the family support system. Most measures which were in effect before 1995 were restored as well as new ones introduced.

Kindergartens and nurseries

In principle, children are eligible for *nursery care*[8] if they have reached 20 weeks of age and are less than three years old – in the case of children with a disability, if they are younger than six. In reality, however, because there are fewer nurseries in Hungary than needed, only about 9%-10% of children under the age of three can attend (see Table 7.8). Altogether, there are around 500 such institutions in the country – every settlement with more than 10,000 inhabitants is obliged to operate at least one nursery. Out of the 3,200 settlements in Hungary 3,000 have less than 10,000 inhabitants, so 60% of Hungarian settlements do not have a nursery at all.

There are two types of nurseries in Hungary: (1) daily nurseries, which are usually open between 6am and 6pm, and (2) weekly nurseries, which provide both day and night care and are open for at least 120 hours per week. The latter type can be attended by those children whose normal physical and mental development cannot be ensured given their family situation.

Table 7.8: Proportion of children younger than two enrolled in nurseries, 1995-2004

	1995	1996	1997	1998	1999	2000	2001	2002	2003	2004
1-11 months	1.1	1.2	1.5	1.4	1.1	1.1	0.9	0.7	0.7	0.5
12-23 months	14.5	15.5	15.5	16.2	15.8	15.6	14.8	14.2	13.4	12.8

Source: Hungarian Central Statistical Office (2004)

The *kindergartens*[9] – which are part of the public education system – deal with the daily care of children aged between age three and seven. Their aim is to help develop the physical and mental health of children in this age range. Since 1999, when the 'National Core Programme of Pre-primary Education' was introduced, kindergartens have had standard guidelines to design their own pedagogic programme. According to a survey carried out in 2001 (Vágó, 2002) on behalf of the Ministry of Educational Affairs, the vast majority of these institutions (94%) are maintained by the local or regional governments and only a minority are run by churches, non-profit organisations or private individuals. In principle, kindergarten attendance is free of charge, parents only have to pay for food, but in reality, parents are frequently asked to contribute to the everyday operation of the institution in one way or another.

As the number of children in the respective age range is decreasing year by year, some kindergartens have had to be closed or merged with others. The number of autonomous institutions is gradually decreasing – now fewer than half of them can be regarded being legally autonomous. In small villages the general practice is that the kindergarten is merged with the local school; in larger settlements five or six kindergartens might belong to one central institution.

Although the number of applicants is steadily decreasing, around 5,000 children are not accepted each year. The total number of places in the country is sufficient but the regional distribution is skewed. Half of the kindergartens are located in cities and only 6% of them can be found in villages with less than 500 inhabitants. While parents in cities can choose between two and four institutions, those who live in small villages have no choice at all as the local kindergarten is usually full and only able to accept children for whom kindergarten provision is compulsory, i.e., those over five. In these cases the most common practice is to refuse children under five if their mother stays at home with a younger brother or sister, and/or those whose parents do not have a job. As a result, unemployed parents in small settlements – who are very often Romas – have even less chance to enter the labour market as they have to take care of their small children.

The kindergarten enrolment rate over the last 20 years has been constantly high; today 92% of childrenaged three to six attend kindergarten (UNICEF, 2007). This trend can be traced back to the 1980s (the 'great decade' of kindergarten enrolment) when pre-school education became available for everybody – or at least almost everybody in the relevant age range. The most important reasons for this high enrolment rate are the as follows.[10]

The most obvious reason is that in 1986 a compulsory year of pre-school education was introduced for five-year-old children, and this regulation is still in effect. The financial stress on families should be mentioned as another reason, as the earnings of one parent is usually not enough to ensure a normal standard of living in Hungary, therefore the majority of mothers are eager to return to employment as soon as possible. In fact, the Hungarian childcare benefit system seems to prefer supporting the *families* when the child is under the age of three, but prefer supporting the *institutions* after the child's third birthday. The ideology behind this is that the best place for infants' primary socialisation is the family, while after the age of three, children have to be socialised in a larger community. A third possible reason for the increase in the enrolment rate is people's changing attitudes towards education endowments as assets in individuals' lives. After the regime transformation it became obvious for the members of the middle classes and the lower middle classes that unless they provided their children with appropriate education they would have no chance of being successful in the market economy. Parents believe that a good educational career starts in a good primary school. And as the Hungarian education system has become more selective, primary schools have gained the right to have their own entrance exams; to pass these exams it is clearly important for the child to get a good pre-school education. More precisely, the longer a child stays in kindergarten the better their chances of gaining admission to a good primary school – at least this is what parents believe today.

Social assistance

Between 1993 and 2000 unemployed people received unemployment assistance in the form of income supplements in cases where their eligibility for unemployment benefit had been exhausted and where per capita household income was below 80% of the minimum old-age pension. The assistance was of unlimited duration until 1995, when a two-year limit was introduced. In 2000 unemployment assistance was abolished and replaced by regular social assistance. This regular social assistance was introduced in 1997, so there was a three-year period when both types of subsidies co-existed. Social assistance was originally offered to those who were: (1) living in bad sanitary conditions (had lost 67% of their capacity to work, were blind etc), and (2) unemployed people who had exhausted their eligibility for unemployment benefit and who, before applying for assistance, had cooperated with the employment centre for at least two years over the preceding three years. Since 2002, the unemployed have only been eligible for assistance if they accept public utility work offered by the local government. By 2006, the conditions for eligibility were restricted further. The monthly amount of assistance cannot exceed the mandatory minimum wage. The major change brought by 2007 is that those unemployed who get job-seeking benefit or job-seeking aid are also eligible for regular social assistance, but they receive a reduced amount of the payment. To sum up, those who are currently eligible for social assistance are those who: (1) live in bad sanitary conditions, (2) are unemployed or (3) receive job-seeking benefit or job-seeking aid. The most important indicators on the social assistance scheme are shown in Table 7.9.

Table 7.9: Regular social assistance, average number and ratio of recipients, average monthly amount per capita (in HUF), 2000-04

	Average number of benefit recipients	Recipients per 10,000 inhabitants	Average monthly amount per capita
2000	47,154	46.2	11,056
2001	94,779	93.0	13,019
2002	125,894	123.9	14,650
2003	138,127	136.4	15,010
2004	144,853	143.5	15,864

Source: Hungarian Central Statistical Office (2004)

Intergenerational transfers, housing and informal welfare provision

Hungarian housing provision can be approximated as follows: 88% owner-occupied, 3% private rental, 4% social rental and 5% other (Hungarian Central Statistical Office, 2001). As can be seen, private rentals represent a very small part of the whole housing stock, but it is presumably slightly higher as renting out privately owned flats is a part of the hidden (or informal) economy, mainly for taxation reasons. The lack of flats to rent probably limits opportunities for young adults to move out of the parental home. Conversely, among other factors such as postponing the school leaving age or people getting married later, this leads to a high proportion of young adults still living with their parents, which in turn facilitates access to familial networks and welfare support. In fact, according to the last Microcensus in 2005 33% of individuals aged 25-29 still lived with their parents, while the corresponding figure in 1990 was only 17%.

In Hungary under communism, the role of inter-household exchanges as the basic units of the informal economy was strong (Sik, 1988), and it remained important in preserving households' living standards after the transition. The general conclusion of studies in this field is that the overall inter-household exchange is a supplement to other sources of inter-family support rather than a replacement of them. In addition, the common incidence of non-monetary exchanges among Hungarian households is motivated by reciprocal norms, of which the objective is to maintain and strengthen local social networks (Brown, 2001).

After the transition – as during the communist era – the Hungarian household economy needed female labour because two salaries were required to ensure a certain living standard. Due to this, to conciliate work and family, Hungarians need an extensive family network, despite the fairly well-developed family support system. The majority of women in fact claim that it was their grandparents' help that made it possible for them to reintegrate into the labour market (Lakatos, 2001). Although several generations living together is now less frequent in Hungary than before, help from the family, primarily from grandparents, remains very important for households with children.

Notes

[1] The authors thank Janka Salát for her assistance in collecting statistical material.
[2] This section is largely based on Róbert (1991).
[3] Indeed, the 1945 reform was directed at eliminating the dual system at the primary level and raising the level of mass education, so that only at the level of secondary education elements of the dual system were preserved (Simkus and Andorka, 1982).

[4] Theoretically it was possible to continue studies in secondary school and to obtain the maturity examination for an additional two years after the completion of vocational training, but this was not common practice (Róbert, 1991).
[5] Hanley and McKeever (1997) show that 70%-75% of the graduates of academic high schools entered colleges and universities during the state-socialist period compared to only 25%-30% of the graduates of technical high schools.
[6] Quotas were instituted stipulating that a minimum proportion of all students admitted to universities and gymnasia (approximately 50%) must be from working-class and peasant backgrounds, but this practice was later abandoned (Simkus and Andorka, 1982; Róbert, 1991).
[7] This section is based on Eurydice (2003), ETF (2004) and Halász and Lannert (2000, 2003).
[8] Source: Vágó (2002, 2005) and Török (2005).
[9] Source: Vágó (2002, 2005) and Török (2005).
[10] Source: Vágó (2002, 2005) and Török (2005).

References

Andorka, R. and Harcsa, I. (1992) 'Education', in R. Andorka, T. Kolosi and G. Vukovich (eds) *Social report*, Budapest: TÁRKI.

Brown, D. (2001) 'Household economic behaviour in post-socialist rural Hungary', *Rural Sociology*, vol 66, pp 157-80.

Bukodi, E. and Róbert, P. (2006) 'Men's career mobility in Hungary during the 1990s', in M. Mills, H.-P. Blossfeld and F. Bernardi (eds) *Globalization, uncertainty and men's career: an international comparison*, Northampton, MA: Edward Elgar, pp 203-38.

Cazes, S. and Nesporova, A. (2003) *Labour markets in transition: balancing flexibility and security in Central and Eastern Europe*, Geneva: International Labour Organization.

Eamets, R. and Masso, J. (2005) 'The paradox of the Baltic States: labour market flexibility but protected workers', *European Journal of Industrial Relations*, vol 11, no 1, pp 71-90.

ETF (European Training Foundation) (2000) *Key indicators: vocational education and training in Central and Eastern Europe*, Luxembourg: Office for Official Publications of the European Communities.

ETF (2003) *Short country report: Hungary*, Torino: ETF.

ETF (2004) *Vocational education and training and employment services in Hungary*, Luxembourg: Office for Official Publications of the European Communities.

European Commission (2001) *Joint assessment of employment priorities in Hungary*, Luxembourg: Office for Official Publications of the European Communities.

Eurostat (2008) *Data: labour market*, Luxembourg: Eurostat (http://epp.eurostat.ec.europa.eu).

Eurydice (2003) *Structures of education, vocational training, and adult education systems in Europe: Hungary*, Brussels: Eurydice European Unit.

Fazekas, K. (2004) 'The current situation on the labour market and labour market policy in Hungary', in K. Fazekas and J. Koltay (eds) *The Hungarian labour market 2004: review and analysis*, Budapest: Institute of Economics, Hungarian Academy of Science.

Fazekas, K. (2005) 'Transition of the Hungarian labour market – age, skill and regional differences', Paper prepared for the Project on Intergenerational Equity, Tokyo: Economic Research Institute of the Hitotsubashi University.

Fazekas, K. and Koltay, J. (2006) *The Hungarian labour market 2006: review and analysis*, Budapest: Institute of Economics, Hungarian Academy of Science.

Fazekas, K. and Varga, J. (2005) *The Hungarian labour market 2005: review and analysis*, Budapest: Institute of Economics, Hungarian Academy of Science.

Galasi, P. and Nagy, G. (2002) 'Criteria for benefit entitlement and chances of re-employment', in K. Fazekas and J. Koltay (eds) *The Hungarian labour market 2002: review and analysis*, Budapest: Institute of Economics, Hungarian Academy of Science.

Halász, G. and Lannert, J. (1995) *Jelentés a magyar közoktatásról* (*Report on the public education of Hungary*), Budapest: National Institute of Public Education.

Halász, G., Garami, E., Havas, P. and Vágó, I. (2001) *The development of the Hungarian educational system*, Budapest: National Institute for Public Education (www.oki.hu/printerFriendly.php?tipus=cikk&kod=english-art-bie).

Hanley, E. and McKeever, M. (1997) 'The persistence of educatonal inequalities in state-socialist Hungary: trajectory-maintenance versus counterselection', *Sociology of Education*, vol 70, no 1, pp 1-18.

Horváth, R., Ábrahám, Á., Horváth, T. and Köpeczi-Bócz, T. (1999) *Background study on employment and labour market in Hungary*, Tornio: European Training Foundation.

Hungarian Central Statistical Office (2001) *Population Census 2001*, Budapest: Hungarian Central Statistical Office.

Hungarian Central Statistical Office (2003) *Statistical yearbook of Hungary*, Budapest: Hungarian Central Statistical Office.

Hungarian Central Statistical Office (2004) *Yearbook of social statistics*, Budapest: Hungarian Central Statistical Office.

ILO (International Labour Organization) (2008) *Key indicators of the labour market programme*, Fifth Edition, Geneva: ILO.

Kertesi, G. and Köllő, J. (2002) *Labour demand with heterogeneous labour inputs after the transition in Hungary 1992-1999*, Budapest Working Papers on the Labour Market No 5, Budapest: Institute of Economics, Hungarian Academy of Science.

Kézdi, G. (2002) *Two phases of labour market transition in Hungary: intersectorial reallocation and skill-biased technological change*, Budapest Working Papers on the Labour Market No 3, Budapest: Institute of Economics, Hungarian Academy of Science.

Köllő, J. and Nacsa, B. (2005) *Flexibility and security in the labor market: Hungary's experience*, Budapest: International Labour Organization.

Lakatos, J. (2001) *Család változóban* (*Family in change*), Budapest: Hungarian Academy of Science.

Lannert, J. (2005) 'Facts on expansion of education', in K. Fazekas and J. Varga (eds) *The Hungarian labour market 2005: review and anlaysis*, Budapest: Institute of Economics, Hungarian Academy of Science, pp 50-5.

Lázár, G. (2002) 'The career beginners assistance', in K. Fazekas and J. Koltay (eds) *The Hungarian labour market 2002: review and analysis*, Budapest: Institute of Economics.

Ministry of Education (2005) *Statistical yearbook of education 2004/2005*, Budapest: Ministry of Education (www.om.hu/doc/upload/200506/oe050531.pdf).

Ministry of Employment and Labour (2004) *National employment action plan*, Budapest: Hungarian Ministry of Employment and Labour.

OECD (Organisation for Economic Co-operation and Development) (2000) *Economic Surveys: Hungary*, Paris: OECD.

OECD (2004) *Employment outlook*, Paris: OECD.

Róbert, P. (1991) 'Educational transition in Hungary from the post-war period to the end of the 1980s', *European Sociological Review*, vol 7, pp 213-36.

Róbert, P. (2005) 'Changes in the chances of labour market entry and in the structure of entry occupations', in K. Fazekas and J. Varga (eds) *The Hungarian labour market 2005: review and analysis*, Budapest: Institute of Economics, Hungarian Academy of Science, pp 85-8.

Róbert, P. and Bukodi, E. (2005) 'The effects of the globalization process on the transition to adulthood in Hungary', in H.-P. Blossfeld, M. Mills, E. Klijzing and K. Kurz (eds) *Globalization, uncertainty and youth in society*, London: Routledge, pp 177-214.

Sik, E. (1988) 'The eternity of an institution for survival', *Innovation*, vol 1, pp 589-624.

Simkus, A. and Andorka, R. (1982) 'Inequalities in educational attainment in Hungary, 1923-1973', *American Sociological Review*, vol 47, pp 740-51.

Statistical Office Hungary (2005) *Statistical Yearbook on Women and Men*, Budapest: Statistical Office Hungary.

Török, B. (2005) 'Óvodák és szülők – vonzások és választások' ('Kindergartens and parents – attractions and choices'), *Educatio*, vol 14, no 4, pp 787-804.

UNICEF (United Nations International Children's Emergency Fund) (2007) *TransMONEE 2007 Database*, Florence: UNICEF Innocenti Research Centre. (www.unicef-icdc.org/resources/transmonee.html).

Vágó, I. (2002) 'Óvodai intézményrendszer, óvodai nevelés az ezredfordulón' ('Institutions, kindergarten education at the millennium'), *Új Pedagógiai Szemle*, vol 12, no 12, pp 52-74.

Vágó, I. (2005) 'Felfelé terjeszkedő óvodáztatás – stagnáló hozzáférés' ('Upwards in kindergarten education – no change in access'), *Educatio*, vol 14, no 4, pp 742-61.

Van Gyes, G., Vandenbrande, T., Lehndorff, S., Schilling, G., Schief, S. and Kohl, H. (2007) *Industrial relations in EU member states 2000-2004*, Dublin: European Foundation for the Improvement of Living and Working Conditions.

Visser, J. (2004) 'Patterns and variations in European industrial relations', in European Commission (2004) *Industrial relations in Europe*, Luxembourg: Office for the Official Publications of the European Communities, pp 11-57.

EIGHT

Latvia

Ilze Trapenciere

After regaining independence in 1991, Latvia has undergone essential changes in its education system, labour market and welfare state development. Its political system has been relatively effective in providing comparatively stable government and the benefits of the democratisation process. However, Latvia's existing ethnic, linguistic and regional diversity shows inequitable access to opportunities, as well as social, economic and political differentiation among its population. To some extent, these problems can be attributed to Latvia's economic transition and the development process of its new political and economic system.

The first section begins with a brief overview of the education system during socialism. It focuses on the changes and developments in the Latvian education system after Latvia regained independence, and examines the main components of Latvia's education system (mainly at secondary and tertiary levels). It provides an overview of the vertical and horizontal dimensions of the education system, showing gender disproportion in tertiary education.

There is then a review of the trends of the Latvian labour market. It begins with a short introduction on Latvia's economic development. Employment dynamics in Latvia include labour force activity rates and hidden employment and unemployment dynamics. This section addresses the issue of existing ethnic, linguistic and regional diversity that has resulted in a growing divide between rich and poor, and between urban and rural areas. Finally, the section considers the developments of the labour market institutions.

The final section addresses the Latvian welfare system, which has been central to the political debate in Latvia. It focuses on the issues of active labour market policy (ALMP) and developments of unemployment insurance, guaranteed minimum income (GMI) and family policy. Additionally, it analyses the problems, prospects and achievements of the Latvian welfare system. In the field of employment policy, the main task is to reduce the unemployment rate and to ensure maximum effectiveness in employing citizens, including young people. The Latvian social security reform can be considered successful from the standpoint of consolidating of market and democratic principles. With regard to Latvian family policy the need for more effective policy measures aimed at reconciliation of work and family life is stressed.

Education system

Structure of the Latvian education system

Overview of the Latvian education system after the Second World War

The differentiation in Soviet education began after basic or 'incomplete' secondary education, which lasts eight years, age 7-14. A child could receive this incomplete secondary education either in a general secondary school or in an eight-grade school. At secondary level, schools were divided into three main types: general secondary, specialised secondary, and vocational schools. The majority of students attended general secondary schools, which provided the best quality of education and the most favourable chances of continued tertiary education. Young people recruited into specialised schools (tehnikums) received training for semi-professions, either in the humanities, medicine or engineering fields. One could enter a specialised secondary school either after finishing the 8th grade or after a secondary education.

Vocational schools were designed to produce workers for industry and agriculture, and were therefore closely tied to large industrial enterprises and collectivised agriculture. Vocational schools were intentionally designed to take the less academically gifted and attempted to provide them with both professional training and a generalised upper-secondary education. These schools also performed important social functions for young people who did not gain entry into selective general secondary or secondary professional education. Overall, however, vocational schools were strongly stereotyped as those providing low-quality education. Thus, entering a vocational school substantially reduced a student's chances for entering and attaining tertiary education.

Although during the Soviet era higher education was free of charge, the available openings were strictly planned and limited. The main field of study was engineering (50% in the former USSR), while the proportion of students in the social sciences was less than 10%.

Education system since 1990 [1]

Basic education begins at the age of seven and lasts a total of nine years: four years of primary (International Standard Classification of Education, ISCED 1), followed by five years of basic (lower-secondary) school (ISCED 2). [2] Some schools only provide for grades 1-6, incorporating the entire primary stage but with the following stage incomplete (see Figure 8.1).

Figure 8.1: The Latvian educational system

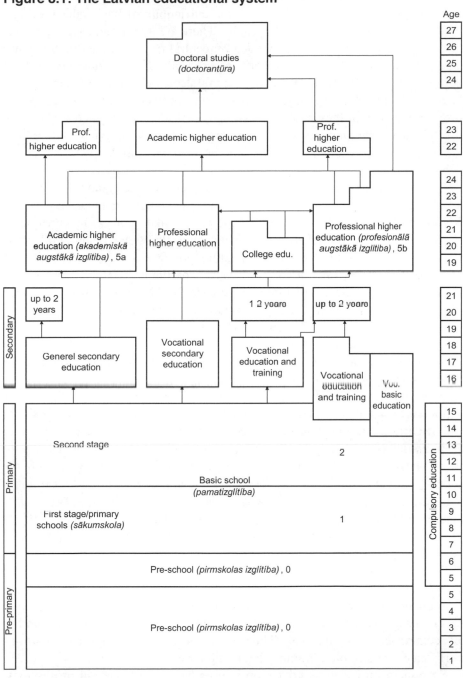

Source: ETF (2000)

Other schools may offer the full nine-year curriculum covering the full basic education of nine years. Furthermore, the curriculum of basic education can be also acquired at evening shift schools. There are no entrance examinations to basic schools, and in those founded by central or local governments there are no tuition fees. Graduates receive a certificate of basic nine-year school completion, which marks the end of compulsory schooling. Students who have not completed the requirements must continue until they finish the programme or until they reach the age of 18. At the end of grade 9, there are formal state examinations – in mathematics, history, Latvian, and a first language for students in minority schools – and compulsory tests in four subjects.

Comprehensive schools are schools that encompass grades 1-12, thus combining primary, low-secondary, and secondary general education. Reflecting the increased demand for general secondary education, enrolments in grades 10-12 increased by 32.4% between 1995/96 and 1999/2000. Part-time and private school enrolments, although only a small proportion of overall enrolments, increased the fastest, particularly in grades 10-12. Between 1995/96 and 1999/2000, the increase for the former constituted 45% and 82% for the latter. The proportion of children whose language of instruction is Latvian is 72% and Russian is 27%. In Riga, Latvian was the language of instruction in only 51% of the schools and for 39% of the enrolments; in rural areas, except in the southeast, the percentage of children whose language of instruction is Latvian is significantly higher.

After leaving basic education, students have a range of options for further schooling: general secondary, vocational education or secondary professional (all ISCED 3). (Upper)-secondary education in Latvia concerns schooling from grades 10-12 (ages 16-18). In order to be admitted to secondary school, pupils have to hold the basic education certificate, although some schools impose further requirements. There are comprehensive day secondary schools, evening shift secondary schools, gymnasia and state gymnasia. There are three types of education programmes in general secondary education: general, humanitarian and social sciences and natural and exact sciences.

To be awarded a certificate of general secondary education, students have to pass final core examinations and reach a satisfactory level in seven non-examination subjects. Examinations at the end of grade 12 are set at two levels: basic and profile (advanced). Students have to pass a certain number of centralised examinations. The recipients of centralised examinations certificates are eligible for admission to higher education.

Secondary professional education is oriented towards certain professions. The current system of vocational education in Latvia is based on the pre-1991 network of institutions adapted in accordance with the 1991 Education Act. Most of these institutions are directly run by the central government, although the creation of private and local authority vocational education institutions has increased. Vocational education is geared to some 330 professions and areas of specialisation, a decrease from over 1,000 in Soviet times. Programmes and enrolments have shifted away from those linked to the former economy toward those in demand in the restructured labour market, including business and commerce, services, transport, and communications. There are several types of schools providing vocational training. Basic vocational education provides instruction and training geared to simple occupations for those who have not completed basic education by the age of 15. Courses in secondary vocational education vary from two to four years of education and training, each of which includes at least some elements of general secondary education. Only students in a four-year programme complete a full course of secondary education and their graduates are eligible for university studies. There are also post-secondary vocational schools for holders of general secondary education certificates, and schools for craftspeople. Secondary professional education institutions, until recently named as 'secondary specialised education institutions', provided education and training in various programmes, such as business, nursing, art, music and technical and technological subjects. The curricula developed from basic education entail four to five years of study and include a full course of general secondary education.

Since 2000, Latvia has introduced college education, which is based on secondary education and lasts two to three years. The curriculum is mainly concentrated on theoretical knowledge and professional training in fields such as nursing and pharmacy, but there are college programmes also in the fields of culture, law and technologies. College education is defined as the first level of higher professional education with ISCED 4 qualification. Some colleges provide two types of programmes – vocational programmes after basic education and college programmes after secondary education.

Latvian institutions of higher education are divided into universities and non-universities. Universities offer three levels of degrees (bachelor, master, and doctor). Non-university type higher education institutions (ISCED 5b) offer applied professionally oriented study programmes, and undertake applied academic research. Their aim is to provide opportunities for acquiring extensive, professional and applied academically based higher education. Some institutions of higher professional education provide doctoral studies, and carry out research in separate branches of science, national economy and arts. The study programmes at these institutions lead to the award of degrees, and correspond to university-type professional education at ISCED 5a and 6.

The academic degree of bachelor is conferred on successful completion of three- to four-year higher education programmes.[3] The academic degree of master is conferred after the second stage of academic education, which takes one-and-a-half to two years. This degree is required for admission to doctoral studies that lead to a doctoral degree (comparable to a PhD).

Vertical dimension of the education system

Figure 8.2 depicts the trends in education enrolment of the school-aged population in Latvia starting from the early 1980s. Obviously, the vast majority of this population has been enrolled in full-time comprehensive schools. However, during the early 1980s, a meaningful proportion of pupils in comprehensive schools were enrolled part time, either in evening schools or via correspondence courses. These types of schools are no longer significant in the 1990s.

Figure 8.2: Enrolment by type of school (%)

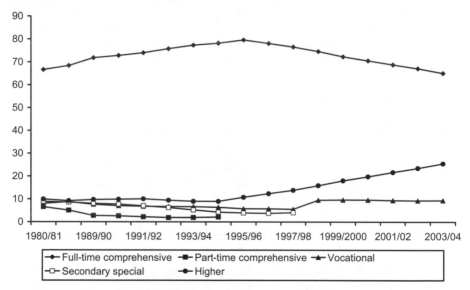

Notes: Starting from 1995/96, no differentiation is made between full and part-time comprehensive schools. Starting from 1998/99, no differentiation is made between vocational and secondary special education.
Source: Latvian Central Statistical Bureau (1990-2004)

The enrolment in any type of vocational education has been decreasing since the 1980s, whereas an equal proportion of young have been enrolled in vocational and secondary special education. Unfortunately since the late 1990s, statistics do not differentiate between these various types of vocational education. Overall, vocational education pupils constitute only a minor part of all those enrolled in schooling in Latvia.

Finally, a substantial increase in enrolment in tertiary education is visible, starting in particular from the mid-1990s. The share of those enrolled in universities grew from 10% of all young people in the mid-1990s to about 25% in 2003/04.

Enrolment in vocational education shows that traditionally more males (60%) than females (40%) prefer vocational education and training than the general education track. Females chose the general secondary track more often (57%) and consequently, the higher education track is much more popular among females (63% from the total enrolment) (Statistical Data Collection, 2006: 15 and 47).

Since 1991, student enrolment has been shifting strongly toward general secondary education, and within secondary education toward selective programmes that lead to higher education. A total of 63% of those who complete grade 9 in 1998 progressed to general secondary education, compared to 20% for vocational schools and 12% for secondary professional schools (see Figure 3). Drop-out rates for 1998 were approximately 13.9% for vocational education schools and 13.8% for secondary vocational education, compared to 3.0% for general education.

Figure 8.3: Graduates of basic and secondary schools of 1998 by type of continuing studies

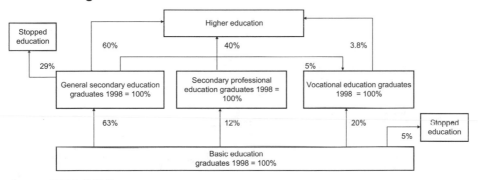

Source: OECD (2001)

Secondary level of education

Stratification and track differentiation

Major decisions concerning education track are made at the age of 15 and 16, when pupils decide whether to continue on a general secondary or professional secondary education track. In some cases, pupils at the age 14 and their parents might make their first decisions, choosing to proceed in basic vocational education rather than on a general track.

The Latvian education system, similar to the education systems of other Baltic countries, has been traditionally characterised by a stronger focus on general rather than on vocational education. Enrolment in the general tracks on the upper-secondary level has even further increased during the 1990s, which is visible in Figure 8.4. Simultaneously, enrolment in the vocational tracks on the upper-secondary level declined (from about 35% to 20%), particularly for programmes not leading to a matriculation diploma. A decrease in the vocational programmes with matriculation is also evident, but of a lesser magnitude. Overall, from 1990/91 through to 2005/06, the number of vocational schools and secondary professional schools has decreased by 33% (from 143 to 96). These changes have resulted mainly from the merging of small, single profile schools and the emergence of private schools.

Vocational education enrolments, especially in vocational schools, remain heavily concentrated in service and engineering programmes. If the new entrants are an indication of demand, 55.6% of school students are entering engineering programmes. The proportion of vocational school students enrolling in social sciences and service professions has also been growing (OECD, 2001).

Figure 8.4: School-age population by levels of education and type of school on the upper-secondary level (%)

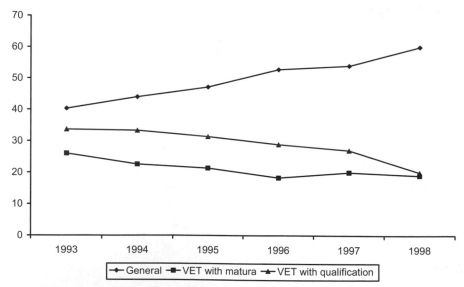

Note: VET = vocational education and training.
Source: ETF (2000)

Organisation of vocational training

Vocational education in Latvia is mainly school-based. The majority of schools are state schools, and a few are municipal schools. Vocational school graduates often lack practical skills, either because they receive no practical training or because what they do receive is of poor quality, partially due to their schools' obsolete technical equipment and their teachers' insufficient knowledge of what the labour market requires.

The Law on Professional Education (1999) has brought several important changes to vocational education. The main principles introduced by this law ensure that the results of training are labour-market accepted, and that the Latvian education system allows involvement of social partners in formulating occupational standards, drawing up education programmes and assessing students' skills.

Standardisation and quality differentiation of secondary education

According to the Organisation for Economic Co-operation and Development (OECD 2001), nation-wide standards exist for lower-secondary education, but not for upper-secondary. Indeed, at the end of their secondary education, students have to pass a number of centralised examinations. Subject standards in curriculum content requirements were introduced in Latvia in 1992, but remained little more than a list of knowledge to be covered and assessed at each grade. In 1996, the Ministry of Education and Science began a process of developing the National Compulsory Education Standard for compulsory schooling. It provides a framework within which local units and schools can design localised syllabi without losing nationally accepted standards. Moreover, it includes explicit learning outcomes in four education spheres for students completing grades 3, 6 and 9: language, self and society, arts and natural sciences. No similar national standards exist for upper-secondary schooling and higher education thus far.

Differentiation within secondary education remains quite pronounced. PISA (Programme for International Student Assessment) results show that, on average, students from schools with Latvian as the language of instruction show better results than students from schools with Russian as the language of instruction, and that students who live in bigger cities show higher results than those who live in rural areas (Kangro et al, 2003).

Tertiary level of education

Horizontal dimension

Restructuring of tertiary education resulted in changes in the field of study chosen by students (see Figure 8.5). Another important issue with regard to the horizontal dimension of tertiary education is the representation of women in various fields of studies. Women are significantly overrepresented in health and welfare (85%), teaching, training and education sciences (83%), as well as in humanities and the arts (79%). There is also a slight overrepresentation of female students in social sciences, business and law (64%), as well as in service specialties, although for the latter the proportion of women enrolled decreased from 58% in 2002/03 to 51% 2003/04. However, such fields of study as engineering, technology, natural sciences and mathematics are largely male-dominated, with only 22% and 38% of females being enrolled in them, respectively (Latvian Central Statistical Bureau, 2002-04).

Figure 8.5: Enrolment in tertiary education by field of study (%)

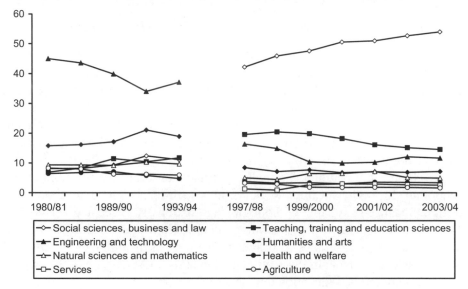

Note: The break in the sequence is due to the change in the classification of the fields of eduction.
Source: Latvian Central Statistical Bureau (1990-2004)

A rapid and dramatic fall from 45% to 12% is observed in the proportion of students choosing engineering. Conversely, an enormous increase in social sciences entrants is observed, with the proportion reaching almost 55% of all students by 2003/04, well above average rates in industrialised countries. The significance of the increase can hardly be overestimated, particularly since in the early 1980s social sciences constituted slightly less than 10% of all specialties studies at the tertiary level. The proportion of students in humanities and arts (15.8% in 1980, 21.1% in 1990, 7.2% in 2003), agriculture (8.3% in 1980, 1.6% in 2003), natural sciences and mathematics (9.4% in 1980, 5.0% in 2003), as well as in health and welfare (6.5% in 1980, 3.4% in 2003) decreased sharply. The already high rate of students in teacher training and education sciences increased further (6.9% in 1980, 11.8% in

1993, 20.5% in 1998, 14.6% in 2003), albeit with a slight decline in the early 2000s.

Another important issue with regard to the horizontal dimension of tertiary education is representation of women in various fields of studies.[4] Women are significantly overrepresented in health and welfare (85%), teaching, training, and education sciences (83%), as well as in humanities and arts (79%). There is also a slight overrepresentation of female students in social sciences, business, and law (64%), as well as in service specialties, though for the latter the proportion of women enrolled decreased from 58% in 2002/03 to 51% 2003/04. However, such fields of study as engineering, technology, natural sciences and mathematics are largely male-dominated, with only 22% and 38% of females being enrolled in them, respectively (Latvian Central Statistical Bureau, 2002-04).

Standardisation, quality differentiation and openness of tertiary education

According to the OECD (2001), nation-wide standards do not exist at the tertiary education level. In 2001, the Cabinet of Ministers adopted standards for 1st and 2nd level higher professional education, which define the compulsory contents of each education level.[5]

Each institution of higher education must register with a Register of Higher Education Establishments, which is a duty of the Ministry of Education and Science, and the data have to be publicly available on request. Higher education institutions must license their programmes before starting them, and must have accreditation at least three years after starting the programme. Accreditation is organised by the Ministry of Education and Science and ensured by the Agency of Assessment of Quality of Higher Education, and has to include both national and international experts. The list of accredited higher education institutions and colleges (i.e., those that may issue diplomas recognised by the state) and accredited programmes have to published in the official newspaper at the end of each academic year.

At the tertiary level in Latvia, there are both public and private education providers. At the beginning of the 2006/07 academic year, there were 17 state colleges, 9 private colleges, 20 state higher education institutions and 14 private higher education institutions. Being a student of a state college or state university does not mean that students do not need to pay tuition fees. In fact, the proportion of students who pay tuition fees increased from 64% in 1999/2000 to 77% in 2005/06 (Latvian Central Statistical Bureau, 2008).

Tuition fees differ in various programmes and various higher education institutions. They might differ from 250 to 8,700 LVL (€356 to €12,379) in state higher education institutions, to 340-4,100 LVL (€484 to €5,834) per academic year in private institutions. There is no real correlation between the real expenses of the programme and the level of the study programme. The tuition fees depend on the number of applicants in the programme and their paying capacity. In general, tuition fees at the higher education institutions in the capital of Riga are higher than in other regions.

In order to assist individuals who want to become students and who have to pay tuition fees, in 1997 a system of study loans was established. Both full-time and part-time students may apply for a study loan. A student (social) loan was also established, which helps students to cover living costs. A student loan is available for full-time students for 10 months a year. It is 120 LVL (€171) per month, starting in February 2006. Loans have to be paid back starting from the 12th month after the graduation or the 3rd month after interruption of studies. Loans have to be paid within five or ten years, depending on the sum. In addition, there are also a number of 'budget student places', which is defined by the Ministry of Education and Sciences.

Labour market

Economic development

Latvia's economic development can be divided into three stages during 1990-2006. Each of these periods is characterised by several important tendencies, which created political and economical changes in Latvia. The first period, from 1990-93, was a period of institutional reform (legal and state administration) in order to develop the infrastructure necessary for the market economy and the reform of prices and market, which started with liberalisation of prices and foreign trade (Trapenciere et al, 1999). This stage ended with the restoration of a national currency. The formerly socialist Latvia started to change from a command economy to a market economy. Deep systematic and structural reforms in the national economy were necessary because the technological level of industry was low in comparison with Western European countries. Privatisation was dominated by two main factors. Instead of mass privatisation, a case-by-case approach was used, with the emphasis on seeking strategic partners and selling controlling interests in enterprises. Additionally, there was a small-scale voucher scheme under which about 15% of company shares were made available in public offerings (OECD, 2000). Primarily, state-owned companies were privatised because privatisation focused on small and medium-sized enterprises (SMEs). However, the large utility companies remained under at least partial state ownership, especially in the fields of telecommunication and energy. When characterising that period, it is important to emphasise the sharp decrease of production and GDP. Beginning in 1990, the gross domestic product (GDP) registered a strong decline in real terms during the first years of transition (Figure 8.6). This transitional recession peaked at 32.1% in 1992, representing one of the strongest recessions in Central and Eastern Europe

(CEE) countries after 1990. Inflation was extremely high because most price controls were removed at the beginning of the 1990s and relative prices adjusted to relative scarcities. This hyperinflation induced a strong decline of the real value of cash benefits and wages. Efforts directed towards macroeconomic stabilisation, such as tight monetary and fiscal policies, were successful and inflation dropped from 951.2% in 1992 to single-digit levels afterwards.

The second period lasted from 1994-99, when the main measures for the stabilisation of Latvia's economy were realised, including reforms of the financial sector and tax reforms. During this period, the private sector started to develop through privatisation and attracting foreign capital. This period was characterised by a policy of economic stabilisation and restructuring. The most characteristic features were increasingly stabilising consumer prices and an annual increase of GDP. The export–import balance of goods and services became negative, but there was a rapid increase in foreign capital and investments, which is related to privatisation. Around 1995, there were crises in the banking sector, which were followed by consolidation and incorporation of banks. In response to these crises, the government accelerated privatisation and other reforms. This positively influenced the national economy, and by 1997, growth in Latvia was among the fastest in transition economies, with a peak of 8.3%. In 1998, a renewed drop in GDP growth took place in Latvia because of the Russian crisis, which, in combination with the Asian crisis, created a serious drying-up of international capital flows to transition countries like Latvia.

The last period that started in 2000 is characterised by dynamic economic development. Structural reforms began in 2000. These reforms were related to Latvia approaching the economic environment of the European Union (EU), and to its preparation to enter the EU and to organise its economy to make it more competitive. The economy returned to its positive growth path in 2000. Economic performance became better and better in the new millennium. GDP growth increased from 3.3% in 1999 to 11.9% in 2006. The increase was concentrated in three dominating branches – the manufacturing industry, commerce and transport. Economic recovery also induced high investment dynamics and increased stability of the financial environment. National debts remained rather low and the budget deficit became less pronounced. However, this period is also characterised by several problems, such as high levels of unemployment, increasing inflation circa mid-2003, and explicit disproportions of regional and social development, with a concentration of resources in Riga.

Figure 8.6: GDP growth, 1989-2006

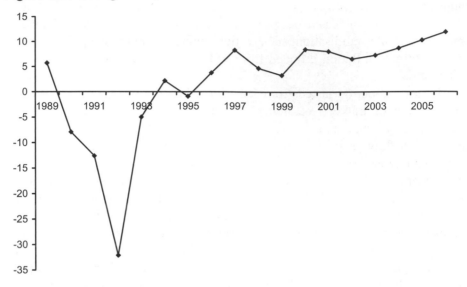

Source: ILO (2008); data for 2006 from Eurostat (2008)

Labour market dynamics

Employment dynamics

In Latvia's economy, structural changes are in progress, which is indicated by the redistribution of employment among economic sectors. In 1990, at the beginning of the economic transition, 17.3% of the employed individuals worked in agriculture, 37.4% in industry and 45.2% in services (Figure 8.7). Although the agricultural share of total employment was already high in 1990, it increased to a maximum of 21.5% in 1997. During the period from 1997-2005, however, the agricultural employment share declined steadily and significantly to 12.1% in 2005. The initial shift toward agricultural employment is the result of the combination of two related policies: the privatisation of agricultural production and agrarian reform. For example, privatisation enabled around 200,000 small businesses in the period between 1992 and 1998 (Trapenciere et al, 1999). These new farms were usually cultivated on small family plots, contributing only marginally to GDP. Agricultural employment was dominated by subsistence farming, and/or as an important source of secondary income. Furthermore, it is often an employment opportunity of last resort for many laid-off workers and pensioners, which might be interpreted as a form of 'hidden unemployment' (OECD, 2003).

In contrast, the employment share in industry and construction decreased permanently during the whole transition period, to 25.8%. The industrial sector is characterised by a predominance of large enterprises, especially in heavy industry and engineering that was developed mostly after the Second World War under Soviet rule. These industries that were formerly deeply integrated in the Soviet economy often had problems avoiding stagnation of output. In contrast, positive trends have largely persisted in the wood and apparel industries (OECD, 2003). The service sector's share of total employment increased to 62% in 2005, and today represents almost as many employees as in most OECD countries. Dominant activities are in wholesale and retail trade, financial and related services and public administration (common in most transition countries) (OECD, 2003). Thus, the service sector seems to be the driving force in the Latvian economy.

Figure 8.7: Sectoral share of employed (%), 1990-2005

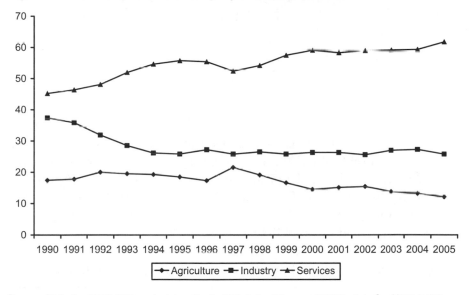

Source: Data for 1990-95 from Latvian Central Statistical Bureau (1996); data for 1996-2005 from ILO (2008)

The transition period was characterised by a very strong decrease in employment and an increasing mismatch between labour demand and supply. Structural economic change has led to large-scale job destruction, which has not been fully balanced by new job creation. Figure 8.8 shows that labour force participation rates of the population aged 15-64 sharply declined from 79.3% in 1990 to 67.4% in 2006.[6] Figure 8.8 also shows gender-specific time trends in labour force participation. Both male and female labour force participation has the same evolution pattern over time, although there is a difference in levels: the female activity rate is roughly 10 percentage points below that of men.

Figure 8.8: Labour force participation rate (age group 15-64), 1990-2006

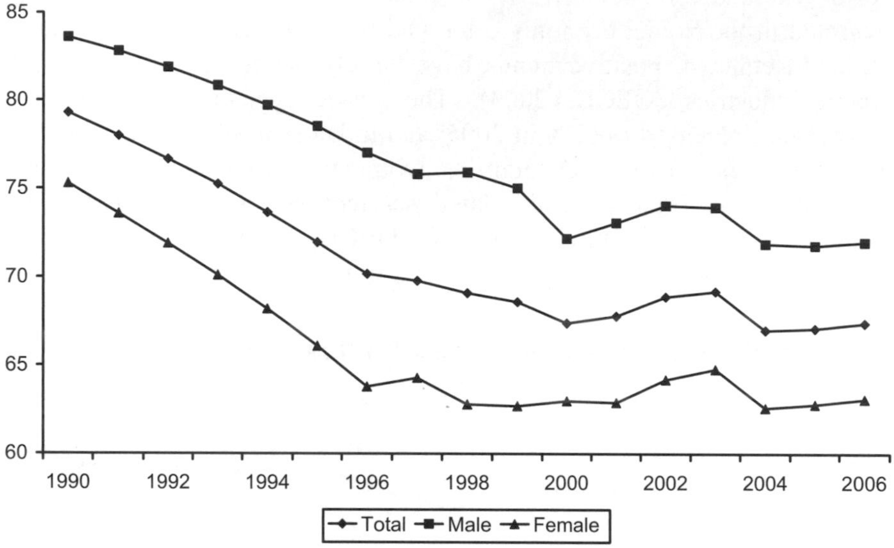

Source: ILO (2008)

In 2006, the lowest activity rate is recorded for the youngest age cohorts (15-24), at 36.4% (Table 8.1). The population aged 15-24 is the cohort most affected by the fall in employment, whose activity rate fell from 56.1% to 36.4% between 1990 and 2006. This fall is partially related to increasing enrolment in higher education, but it may also reflect the increasing labour market integration problems of the young age cohort.

Table 8.1: Labour force participation rate by age cohort, 1990-2006

	1990	1995	2000	2006
15+	69.5	61.2	56.2	56.0
15-24	56.1	50.5	36.9	36.4
25-54	94.2	88.2	85.8	84.5
55-64	54.1	42.2	41.2	46.3
65+	14.6	8.6	7.4	9.3

Source: ILO (2008)

In contrast, the middle- age cohorts reached very high activity rates of between 85%-95% during the transition period, but decreased by 10 percentage points compared to 1990. Participation rates of people aged 65 and over are relatively high, at around 9%-15% compared to the EU15.

Unemployment dynamics

Official registered unemployment in the public employment service, measured as a share of the active population (15-64 years old), was extremely low at the beginning of the transition period, at 2.3% in 1992. This is largely because unemployment was an unknown phenomenon during the communist era (Figure 8.9). The transition to a market economy led to an increase in unemployment figures.

Figure 8.9: Unemployment rates, 1992-2006

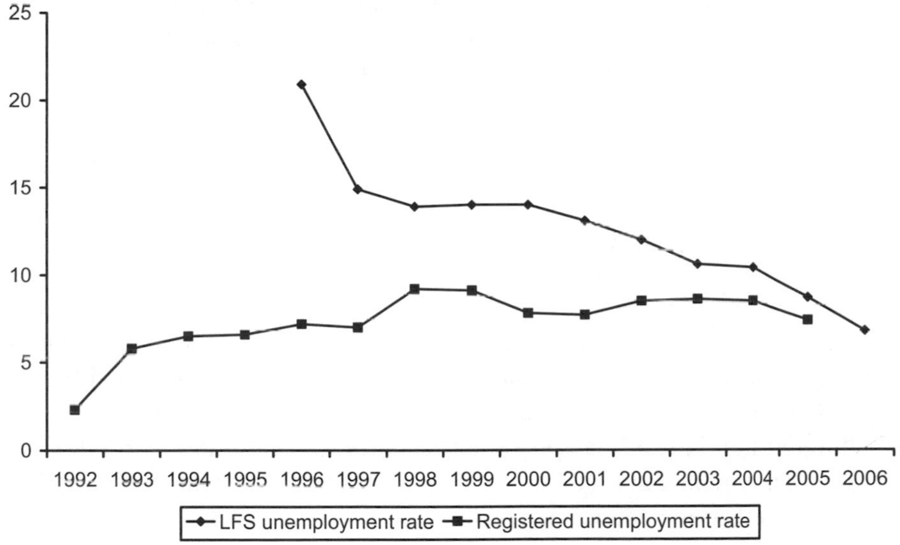

Note: Labour force survey unemployment refers to individuals aged over 15.
Source: ILO (2008); LFS unemployment rate for 2006 from Eurostat (2008).

In accordance with the two economic recessions at the beginning of the 1990s and in 1998, there were increases in the unemployment rates. In general, Latvia suffered from an increase in unemployment rates that peaked at approximately 9.2% of the labour force in 1998, after which it fluctuated at between 7%-9%. A comparison between the LFS unemployment rate and the registered unemployment rate reveals that the LFS unemployment rate is much higher. For example, LFS unemployment was 14.9% compared to 7% registered unemployment in 1997. The differences between registered unemployment and LFS unemployment exist because the former represents all individuals who register officially, whereas the latter is a self-assessed measure. Furthermore, evolution patterns are different between LFS and registered unemployment: LFS unemployment decreased steadily whereas registered unemployment increased. This led to a convergent trend during the last few years, such that the discrepancy between the two measures diminished.

In Latvia, as in many other countries, the transition of youth from school to active life and labour integration remains an important labour market problem. The youngest age cohort of 15- to 24-year-olds is the category most exposed to unemployment. Apart from labour demand restrictions, which are especially related to working experience, difficulties in the professional integration of youth are also caused by the insufficient match between labour demand and the qualifications offered by the education system. However, a significant decrease appeared, falling from 34.1% in 1996 to 13% in 2005 (ILO, 2008). In addition to young people, another disadvantaged category of the labour market is that of the long-term unemployed. According to Eurostat (2008) data, the long-term unemployment rate, i.e., people unemployed for over 12 months, decreased from 9.6% in 1995 to 4.1% in 2005.

Minority ethnic groups, migration and regional differences

In Latvia, unemployment rates also vary between minority ethnic groups and regions. Belonging to a minority ethnic group increased the unemployment risk by 4%-5% in Latvia (OECD, 2003). The minority ethnic group represents a large share of the Latvian society: e.g. Latvians account for 57.7% of the population, Russians for 29.6% and other nationalities for 12.7% (European Commission, 2003).

Although Latvia is a relatively small country, the variation in employment and unemployment rates at the regional level is marked in comparison to other Eastern Europe countries (Antila and Ylöstalo, 2003). There is a sharp distinction between the capital of Riga, a few other large cities, and the remaining towns and countryside. Employment is heavily concentrated in Riga and the Riga region. Low employment and the highest level of unemployment are evident in depressed areas, especially in Latgale in eastern Latvia, which suffers from about 20% unemployment because of the closure of large state enterprises that previously worked for the Soviet market (Trapenciere et al, 1999). Of all the officially registered unemployed, 38.4% live in big cities and 61.6% live in rural areas. Among the long-term unemployed, the distribution is even less balanced: only 29.1% live in cities and 70.9% live in rural areas. These were primarily tractor drivers, dairy maids, cattle-breeders, agricultural workers, truck drivers and construction workers. The figures demonstrate that the enterprises that have dismissed people are primarily located in rural areas.

Labour market institutions

After its independence, Latvia equipped itself with a regulatory framework for labour markets, which is liberal by European standards (OECD, 2003): liberal employment protection regulations, decentralised wage setting and collective bargaining. The old Soviet Labour Law from 1972 was in force during the first transition years but many particular elements of it have been gradually modernised since 1991, especially inspired by the need to conform to EU and International Labour Organization (ILO) standards (Trapenciere et al, 1999).

Employment protection regulation

Whereas under the centrally planned economic system, workers enjoyed a fairly high degree of employment protection in their jobs, a substantial moderation of workers' protection occurred during the transition. The objective was to facilitate workforce adjustment for firms in order to make enterprises more flexible while guaranteeing employment protection for workers. Latvia and other CEE countries tend to be most restrictive concerning collective dismissals compared to the EU (see Table 2.7 in Chapter Two of this book). Latvia's regulation concerning regular employment coincides with the average pattern found in CEE and EU15 countries. Rules for temporary contracts are more restrictive in Latvia than in other CEE countries on average. For example, the use of temporary contracts is restricted to specific objective reasons and cannot last longer than two years, including consecutive temporary contracts (Clauwaert et al, 2003).

Industrial relations

Latvia's industrial relations systems were dominated by the state before the transition. After 1990, the system moved to a free and mostly decentralised bargaining style as in many other CEE countries. Wage bargaining usually takes place at the company level or to a lesser extent at the sectoral level, whereas the regional or national level bargaining does not exist (Visser, 2004: Table 1.8).

Union membership has declined sharply during the 1990s from total coverage of the workforce registered at the beginning of the transition. According to Paas et al (2003), the Latvian unionisation rate decreased to 30% during the mid-1990s to 25% during the late 1990s. Van Gyes et al (2007: Figure 2) report a further decrease from 25% in 1998 to 16% in 2004.

231

This decrease can be explained as in other CEE countries by the abolishment of compulsory membership and economic turbulence. Currently in Latvia there is a new mood of optimism among young people joining the unions (Antila and Ylöstalo, 2003).

Even more important than the number of unionised workers is their coverage by collective agreements. Van Gyes et al (2007: Figure 4) estimate the percentage of employees covered by collective agreements as under 20% for 2002, representing the second lowest level of union coverage compared to other CEE countries. Surprisingly, in contrast to Western European countries, coverage by collective agreements does not usually differ much from union membership in Latvia as well as in the other transition economies (Paas et al, 2003).

Welfare regime

Labour market policy

Active labour market policy

The Law on Employment was implemented in 1992 to define the regulatory role of the state on the labour market. It foresaw the development of the state employment service as an agency to regulate the labour market. Its network was completed in 1993-94. It is also involved in active labour market measures: locating work for the unemployed, educating and retraining them, and involving them in salaried temporary public work. Altogether, during the early transition period, labour market policy was characterised by insignificant expenditure on active measures because of low unemployment rates. Nevertheless, the state tried to take an active role in labour market policy.

The main types of measures promoted have been training and retraining measures for the unemployed, accounting for about 60% of active programme expenditure in 2001 (Paas et al, 2003). A key tool in fighting unemployment was retraining the unemployed, which began in 1992, with around two thirds of the active labour market measures allocated for training. Of the 115,000 newly registered unemployed in 1994, only 8.3% expressed a willingness to change professions. Two thirds of the unemployed willing to study were women. The unemployed were offered more than 30 different study programmes, including computer literacy, accounting, private entrepreneurship, sewing, secretarial skills, welding, brick-laying, tree-felling and carpentry. In order to motivate the unemployed to take up studies, the state granted stipends of 50% of the minimum wage during the courses. As of 1994, the unemployed may receive the grant during their course of studies (for a period not exceeding six months), regardless of whether they are entitled to receive unemployment benefit. This measure has been effective: in 1994 the number of retrained unemployed people from rural areas has increased, particularly in the Latgale region. According to state employment service data, about 35%-50% of such people find employment within half a year after completing their studies.

One of the forms of training was creation of 'job clubs'. Their role is mainly social-psychological rehabilitation, to stimulate the initiative of unemployed people and to encourage the development of a dialogue between employers and the unemployed. Experience showed that the chances of the unemployed successfully completing their studies and adjusting to the labour market demand largely depend on age and education. Furthermore, more than one million LVL was allocated from the state budget for the provision of salaried temporary public works in 1994.

However, data from the late 1990s and early 2000s indicate that, compared to other countries, ALMP plays a small role in Latvia, with expenditure of about 0.14% of GDP during the late 1990s (OECD, 2003). By comparison, such spending in OECD countries ranged from 0.09% of GDP in Japan to about 2% of GDP in Sweden. The total inflow of ALMP participants in 2001 corresponded to 4% of the labour force in Latvia, with public works comprising a large amount of the total. According to the expenditure, the most important active measure is professional training (60%), followed by public works (36%) and job clubs (4%) (Paas et al, 2003: Table 6). Priority of involvement is given to people from disadvantaged groups, such as people with a disability, young people, long-term unemployed and non-Latvian speakers. In contrast, Latvia's volume of expenditure on passive measures, most importantly unemployment benefit, has been remarkable (0.42%-0.86% of the GDP) due to their relatively high average unemployment benefit (Eamets, 2004).

Unemployment insurance

The Law on Employment (1992) fixed the total duration of unemployment benefit receipts to six months within a 12-month period, although this period could be prolonged for up to 12 months by local governments. Unemployment benefit amounted to 90% of the minimum wage for those who lost employment through no fault of their own, and 70% of the minimum wage for those who have never been employed. The latter category included graduates of education institutions, people released from correctional institutions, etc. After expiration of the six-month period during which they were entitled to receive unemployment benefit, many inhabitants who reside far from state employment service departments and offices in rural areas did not turn to the service to register as long-term unemployed.

In 1995, the system was reformed. The Law on Compulsory Social Insurance defined that unemployment benefit directly depended on years of insurance and average salary during the last six months. For example, for insurance periods of one to five years, unemployment benefit amounted to 50% of the average salary of the last six months spent in employment. For longer insurance periods, the replacement rate increased: 55% for 5-15 years of insurance, 60% for 15-25 years of insurance and 65% for over 25 years of insurance. The full amount of the benefit was paid for the first three months of benefit receipt. Thereafter, the amount was reduced to 80% of the initial benefit for the third to sixth month, and 60% of the initial benefit for the sixth to ninth month. Unemployment benefit is still paid for nine months. Furthermore, the law states that both employer and employee pay taxes for insurance against unemployment. In the course of the reforms, the number of registered unemployed who received unemployment benefit declined from 82% in mid-1992 to 30% in mid-1996.

Table 8.2: Characteristics of the Latvian unemployment benefit system

	1992	1995	1999	2000	2002	2004	2006
Average monthly unemployment benefit in LVL by insurance period in years							
1-5 (1999), 1-9 (from 2000)	–	–	41.4	44.7	42.6	55.9	81.6
in % of average net wage			0.40	0.41	0.34	0.37	0.38
in % of minimum wage			0.83	0.89	0.71	0.70	0.91
5-15 (1999), 10 - 19 (from 2000)	–	–	46.2	48.4	43.8	60.4	88.0
In % of average net wage			0.45	0.44	0.35	0.40	0.41
In % of minimum wage			0.92	0.97	0.73	0.76	0.98
15-20 (1999), 20 - 29 (from 2000)	–	–	51.4	53.1	48.9	65.0	88.2
In % of average net wage			0.50	0.49	0.39	0.43	0.41
in % of minimum wage			1.03	1.06	0.81	0.81	0.98
>20 (1999), >30 (from 2000)	–	–	59.8	62.9	58.0	83.8	109
in % of average net wage			0.58	0.58	0.47	0.56	0.50
in % of minimum wage			1.20	1.26	0.97	1.05	1.21
Share of registered unemployed receiving benefits	0.80	0.32	0.44	0.43	0.46	0.44	0.50

Source: Ministry of Welfare (1997-2006); Latvian Central Statistical Bureau (2008)

Subsequently, the rule for calculating unemployment benefit changed. From 2000 onwards, contribution periods of one to nine years were required for a replacement rate of 50% (they previously required one to five years), 0-19 years of contribution payments were required for a replacement rate of 55% (they previously required 5-15 years), and 20-29 years of contribution payments were required for a replacement rate of 60% (they previously required 15-25 years). Replacement rates for people with relatively longer contribution histories therefor decreased. Furthermore, for the third to sixth month of benefit receipt, only 75% (instead of the previous 80%) of the initial benefit is paid, and for the sixth to ninth month, only 50% (instead of the previous 60%) of the initial benefit is paid. The latter reform reduced benefit levels for all recipients.

Table 8.2 summarises the central characteristics of the Latvian unemployment system. Individuals having been insured for one year were receiving, on average, 40% of the average net wage and 83% of the minimum wage in unemployment benefits in 1999. Relative to these reference categories, their position has not declined in the following years. In 2006, they even received 91% of the minimum wage as unemployment benefit. For groups with longer insurance periods, benefit levels declined somewhat between 1999 and 2005 relative to the average net wage. To receive unemployment benefit close to the level of the minimum wage, individuals require rather long contribution periods. The share of unemployed receiving benefits was very high at the beginning of the transition (80% in 1992), but declined substantially thereafter as eligibility criteria were tightened, stabilising at around 40%-50% in the early 2000s.

Minimum wage

A legal minimum wage exists and is set by the government following recommendations by the Tripartite Consulting Council. At the beginning of the transition, the minimum wage was rather low. For example, the ratio of the minimum to average wages was set at 35% in 1991, but fell to just over 26% in 1993 (Paas et al, 2003). Thereafter, the minimum wage rose substantially, reaching 53% of the net average wage of employees in 2004 (Table 8.3). It declined again thereafter, but between 2005 and 2008 the level doubled in nominal terms from 80 LVL in 2005 to 160 LVL on 1 January, 2008.

Table 8.3: Minimum wage in Latvia (in LVL), as of 1 January in respective year

	1995	1996	2002	2003	2004	2005	2006	2007	2008
Monthly minimum wage, LVL	28.0	35.5	60.0	70.0	80.0	80.0	90.0	120	160
As a % of net average wage	0.38	0.45	0.48	0.51	0.53	0.45	0.42	n.a.	n.a.

Source: Latvian Central Statistical Bureau (2008)

Family policy

Data from Eurostat indicate that expenditure on family policies amounts to around 20% of total social insurance expenditure (minus expenditure for old-age insurance). Of this, around 80% is spent on cash family benefits, while in-kind benefits constitute only 20% of expenditure on family policies. These relative amounts have remained almost constant between 1997 and 2004.

Kindergartens are under the responsibility of municipalities, who define the working hours, salaries for staff and support to municipal kindergartens. In 2006, the Ministry of Education began paying part of the salaries for municipal kindergarten teachers. Salaries for staff of private kindergartens and childcare centres are not paid by the municipality or state. Family policy did not foresee the construction of kindergartens, as, according to legislation, it is the responsibility of municipalities. This has resulted in very long queues for kindergarten places. The waiting list constitutes 156,122 children as of 1 January, 2006 (Latvian Central Statistical Bureau, 2008). Legislation imposes strong rules for opening a kindergarten; therefore, the number of private kindergartens has remained small.

The number of kindergartens have decreased dramatically – from 1,123 in 1990 to 611 in 1996 and then to 550 in 2003. Accordingly, enrolment has decreased from 53.9% of children aged three to six in 1989 to 40.1% in 1994. Since 1994, enrolment rates grew again. However, declining fertility rates may be a central factor behind this 'recovery': the total fertility rate declined from 2.0 children per woman in 1990 to 1.11 in 1998 (Central statistical bureau data). Starting in 2002, pre-school education ('compulsory preparation for school') for five to six-year-old children became obligatory. Pre-school for five to six-year-olds is provided in kindergartens, schools and centres for child development. Pre-school education for this group means provision for the preparation for school, which might take place twice a week, three hours per day. It does not mean that each child who is five to six years old is included in full-time childcare facilities. There are no other studies on the topic.

Children not attending kindergartens are obliged to receive some 'preparation for school', which may take place in school buildings, child development centres, etc. The pre-school education at schools or hobby education centres is usually organised twice a week, about two to three hours per day. This has increased the enrolment of five to six-year-olds to 90% in 2005. The enrolment was 40% (ages one to six) in 1995 and has reached 63% in 2005 (ages one to six). The data reflect the number of children in any kind of child care, encompassing full-time enrolment and part-time enrolment in any kind of child centres that provide care for a few hours per day.

A study on the reconciliation of work and family life in Latvia found that availability of pre-school education in Latvia is rather limited, and that the majority of pre-school education establishments offer education to children aged three and older. The earliest age when children are accepted at public child care is one to two years. However, the number of places for young children is very limited. According to statistics, in 2006, there were 1,367 places in nurseries in the whole country for children aged one and younger. Private pre-school establishments usually accept children from the age of two.

Table 8.4: Age group specific pre-school enrolment rates (1997-2005)

	1997	1998	1999	2000	2001	2002	2003	2004	2005
1	5.0	7.0	6.6	7.3	8.2	7.0	7.4	7.0	6.0
2	31.0	32.8	35.0	37.7	40.6	39.0	41.0	43.5	42.0
3	46.0	50.6	54.0	56.0	58.7	62.6	63.0	64.9	67.0
4	43.0	54.0	58.5	60.7	63.0	65.0	68.0	71.3	71.0
5	51.0	55.6	70.0	65.0	66.0	88.0	89.0	91.0	97.0
6	53.7	54.7	67.7	62.0	66.4	87.5	88.2	89.4	96.0
7	6.0	5.7	7.8	5.7	6.6	7.8	8.5	7.5	8.0
3-6	50.0	54.0	59.0	61.3	63.8	75.9	76.7	79.0	82.0

Source: Latvian Central Statistical Bureau (various years)

The majority of public childcare establishments work five days a week, 12 hours per day. The most typical working hours are 7.00am (8.00am) - 19.00pm. Municipalities approve the working hours of municipal kindergartens. The majority of municipal kindergartens request that children arrive before 9.00am, but are flexible about the departure time. The price for childcare depends on several conditions. At municipal kindergartens, parents have to pay for food (breakfast, lunch, afternoon snack). The average price is 1 LVL (€1.4) per day. Although the price for kindergarten care is not very high, there are families that cannot afford to pay it. These poor families may apply for municipal support to cover the costs. They need to apply for poor household status (50% from minimum salary per household member). The municipality will then cover the childcare costs for a definite period (usually three months). If the financial situation of the household has not improved during this time, they may apply for assistance again. Single-parent households do not have any priority on the waiting list for kindergarten places. In private childcare centres, the monthly price in 2006/07 was 160 LVL + 30 LVL for food, which means that only better-off households with two breadwinners could afford it. Municipalities do not support private childcare.

Social assistance

To ensure a minimum standard of living for themselves and their families, individuals may apply for GMI benefit. The GMI level was defined by the Cabinet of Ministers in 2003. In 2007, it amounted to 27 LVL per month. Local governments are in charge of administering payments and determining the benefit level for applicants. Benefit levels are means-tested, taking into account the income (including family benefits) of the household. They are calculated as the difference between the income of the household and the statutory minimum, which amounted to 27 LVL per month for a single person, 63.40 LVL for a single-parent family with two children, and 90.40 LVL for a couple with two children. As a reference, the monthly average income for 2006 was 302 LVL gross and 216 LVL net, while the minimum wage was set at 120 LVL. Benefits are not subject to taxation. Local governments may, however, grant a higher minimum income level if funds permit. The GMI benefit is granted for the time period for which the status of needy family or person has been assigned, but cannot exceed three months. After three months, the person is entitled to apply for the GMI benefit again. Maximum duration of receipt of benefit for one person is nine months in the course of one calendar year.

In order to receive the benefit for ensuring the GMI level, the family or person must address the social office of the local government where he or she has registered his or her place of residence, and submit a number of documents. To stimulate beneficiaries to obtain income from paid work and not to become dependent on benefits, a limitation on the maximum amount of benefit has been established. The local government has the authority to pay other benefits after the demand for the GMI benefit has been satisfied, depending on the situation of the local budget.

Notes

[1] This section is based on Eurydice (1999) and OECD (2001) publications.

[2] The 1998 Education Law specified that compulsory education includes the preparation of five- or six-year-old children and included basic education, which might continue until the age of 18. One year of pre-school was established as the first stage of compulsory education in Latvia for five- or six-year-olds.

[3] In some cases (such as that of teacher education), professional training may take place concurrently with bachelor studies, and may last five years.

[4] The total proportion of women in tertiary education during 2002-04 was 62% (Latvian Central Statistical Bureau, 2002-04).

[5] The scope of the 1st level higher professional education is 80-120 credit points (CP), and the scope for the 2nd level higher professional education is at least 160 CP. Each programme has to include theoretical courses, practice, a qualification work for the 1st level, and a state examination, which includes bachelor thesis or diploma work.

[6] The labour force is the total number of people employed and unemployed.

References

Antila, J. and Ylöstalo, P. (2003) *Working life barometer in the Baltic Countries 2002*, Labour Policy Studies No 247, Helsinki: Ministry of Labour.

Clauwaert, S., Düvel, W. and Schömann, I. (2003) *The community social acquis in labour law in the CEECS and beyond: fighting deregulation*, Brussels: European Trade Union Institute.

Eamets, R. (2004) 'Labour market flows and adjustment to macroeconomic shocks in the Baltic States', *Post-Communist Economies*, vol 16, no 1, pp 47-71.

ETF (2000) *Key indicators: vocational education and training in Central and Eastern Europe*, Luxembourg: Office for Official Publications of the European Communities.

European Commission (2003) *Joint assessment of employment priorities in Latvia*, Brussels: European Commission.

Eurostat (2008) *Data: labour market*, Luxembourg: Eurostat (http://epp.eurostat.ec.europa.eu).

Eurydice (1999) *Structures of education, vocational training, and adult education systems in Europe: Latvia*, Brussels: Eurydice European Unit.

ILO (International Labour Organization) (2008) *Key indicators of the labour market programme*, Fifth Edition, Geneva: ILO.

Kangro, A., Geske, A., Grīnsfelds, A. and Kiselova, R. (2003) *Mācīšanās nākotnei. OECD SSNP rezultāti* (*Learning for future. Results of OECD PISA study*), Riga: Ministry of Education and Science of the Republic of Latvi. (www.izm.gov.lv).

Latvian Central Statistical Bureau (various years) Statistical yearbook, Riga: Latvian Central Statistical Bureau.

Latvian Central Statistical Bureau (2008) *Database*, Riga: Latvian Central Statistical Bureau (www.csb.gov.lv/?lng=en).

Ministry of Welfare (1997-2006) *Annual social reports*, Riga: Ministry of Welfare of the Republic of Latvia.

OECD (Organisation for Economic Co-operation and Development) (2000) *Economic surveys 1999-2000: The Baltic states*, Paris: OECD.

OECD (2001) *Reviews of national policies for education: Latvia*, Paris: OECD.

OECD (2003) *Labour market and social policies in the Baltic countries*, Paris: OECD.

Paas, T., Eamets, R., Masso, J. and Rõõm, M. (2003) *Labour market flexibility and migration in the Baltic states: macro evidences*, Discussion Paper No 16, Tartu: University of Tartu.

Statistical Data Collection (2006) *Education institutions in Latvia at the beginning of the school year 2005/2006*, Riga: Statistical Data Collection, Central Statistical Bureau.

Trapenciere, I., Pranka, M., Lace, L., Tentere, G., Ramina, B. and Martuzans, B. (1999) *Background study on employment and labour market in Latvia*, Torino: European Training Foundation.

Van Gyes, G., Vandenbrande, T., Lehndorff, S., Schilling, G., Schief, S. and Kohl, H. (2007) *Industrial relations in EU member states 2000-2004*, Dublin: European Foundation for the Improvement of Living and Working Conditions.

Visser, J. (2004) 'Patterns and variations in European industrial relations', in European Commission (ed) *Industrial relations in Europe*, Luxembourg: Office for the Official Publications of the European Communities, pp 11-57.

NINE

Lithuania

Meilute Taljunaite

The processes of the labour market, such as economic restructuring, the growth of the private sector and the development of market relations, have a direct influence on employment and, consequently, on the education needs and opportunities of inhabitants. Continued privatisation and de-monopolisation processes have bolstered Lithuania's long-term economic development and the expectations of its market participants for a number of years. However, the process of privatisation is slowing down, as the number of large privatisation deals decreases.

The functioning of the education system, as well as the implementation of the principle of accessibility to education and of equal opportunities in education, has been greatly influenced by social changes of recent years, such as the socio-economic re-stratification caused by the changes in the economic status of different sections of the population. 'The significance of the qualified labour force in the current education system in Lithuania is very vague: tremendous amounts of money are allocated for re-qualification of the unemployed at the Labour Exchange, while a lifelong learning system operating under competition is emerging very slowly' (Kuokštis, 2007: 64).

There is some evidence at a European Union (EU) level of a move towards linking welfare benefits to attending vocational training and this element of compulsion introduces a social control dimension to lifelong learning policies. Social security policy is not yet seen as an important driver for lifelong learning measures in Lithuania. It is hoped that this will result in improved provision of lifelong learning for those who are in receipt of social welfare, and will, therefore, combat social exclusion. Many reports and statistical data demonstrate the need to make projections for social support through the education system, to allocate money for preventive programmes and juvenile care, to pursue programmes intended to reduce the idleness of young people, and to develop the system of education support. The education system has been forced to increase its social commitments, although social support is not its direct purpose.

Education system

Structure of the Lithuanian education system

Overview of the Lithuanian education system after the Second World War

Schooling in Lithuania has inherited a Soviet and even partly tsarist Russian structure. Selection and differentiation in the Soviet education system began after an initial period of primary and lower secondary education, lasting eight years from the age of seven to 14. A child could receive this period of education either within a general secondary school or in an 8-grade school.

After this point, schools were divided into three main types: general secondary, specialist secondary and vocational schools. The best students stayed in general secondary schools, which provided the best quality of education and more favourable chances of continuing into tertiary education. Young people recruited into specialised schools received training for particular professions, either in the humanities (such as to be teachers or nurses) or in engineering. One could enter a specialist secondary school either after finishing the 8th grade or after completing general secondary education. Vocational schools were designed to produce workers for industry and agriculture. Lithuania, like all states previously under the control of the former USSR, inherited a highly centralised vocational education system, comprised of vocational schools and *technikumai*, designed to cater for the special needs of a planned economy. Under the socialist system, vocational education was closely linked to major state-owned enterprises and to Lithuania's agricultural sector in particular. It consisted of a widespread network of relatively small institutions offering very narrow professional and specialist training. Its pre-planned intake came from the ranks of the less academically gifted, for some of whom it attempted to provide both professional training and general education. Up to the beginning of 1980s, nearly 38.3% of the Soviet students left school after the 8th grade, 28% moving to technical-vocational facilities within firms and farms, and 10.3% entering a technical college (Meier, 1989). Among those who finished 10 years of schooling, only 37% went on to technical-vocational institutions and 14% to colleges (Filippov, 1980). According to Titma and Saar (1995), about 10% of graduates from vocational and specialised schools were officially allowed to go into higher education. But in reality never more than 1% of vocational school leavers and 5% of specialist secondary school leavers did so. Thus, entering a vocational school substantially reduced one's chances of entering and attaining tertiary education. All in all, in the Soviet Union the age at which young people were first tracked (i.e., put on special courses preparing them for their future roles and offering different life chances) was 14.

During the socialist period, the higher education system was restructured to meet the priorities of the Soviet-controlled economy and military. Vytautas Magnus University (the former Lithuanian University) was closed in 1950, but other specialist institutions were established. Student enrolments, especially in engineering, medicine, agriculture and other applied sciences, were particularly high. Prior to the re-establishment of independence, 12 higher education institutions functioned in Lithuania, the majority of them teaching in the Lithuanian language, with only 15% of students studying in Russian.

Education system since 1990[1]

The Law on Education of the Republic of Lithuania stipulates that education is compulsory for all pupils up to the age of 16 (inclusive). Schooling starts aged either six or seven and involves four years of primary education followed by six years of lower-secondary education, coming to 10 years in all. Compulsory education is provided not only in publicly maintained schools of general education, but also in private schools that get support from the state if they adopt its curriculum.[2]

Primary schools (International Standard Classification of Education, ISCED 1) in Lithuania are often not separated from basic or secondary schools, and even some gymnasiums operate both primary and lower-secondary school classes (see Figure 9.1). Primary education is part of the statutory period of education and free of charge. All primary schools follow a common state-approved core curriculum and teaching plan. National minorities are free to teach their children (7.1% of all pupils overall) their mother tongue and national history.[3]

Having completed their primary education, pupils move on to basic school (ISCED 2) for their lower-secondary education, corresponding to grades 5-10 and ages 10-16. These schools may be autonomous, operate in conjunction with a primary school, or be part of a secondary school that caters for both upper and lower levels. When pupils complete this level of education, they are awarded a basic school leaving certificate, entitling them to go on with their education at a general upper-secondary or vocational school. A test of attainment of lower-secondary education is also governed by criteria set by the Ministry of Education and Science. However, after four years, at the age of 14 or 15, pupils may choose to enter a gymnasium. Gymnasia are usually better equipped than other general secondary schools and tend to benefit from more generous parental support.[4]

Pupils aged 15 who want to get a vocational qualification and find employment may also leave the basic school and go to a vocational school to complete their lower-secondary education. On completion of basic school, pupils may enter upper-secondary education, a vocational school or go to work (provided they are aged 16). Pupils unsuited to mainstream general education (generally because they lack motivation) may, at the age of 12, after just one year of basic school (and until the age of 16), go to youth schools. These separate institutions offer pupils the opportunity to acquire their lower-secondary education over a 10-year period or more. But pupils may also, if appropriate, re-enter the mainstream education system.

Figure 9.1: The Lithuanian education system after 1990

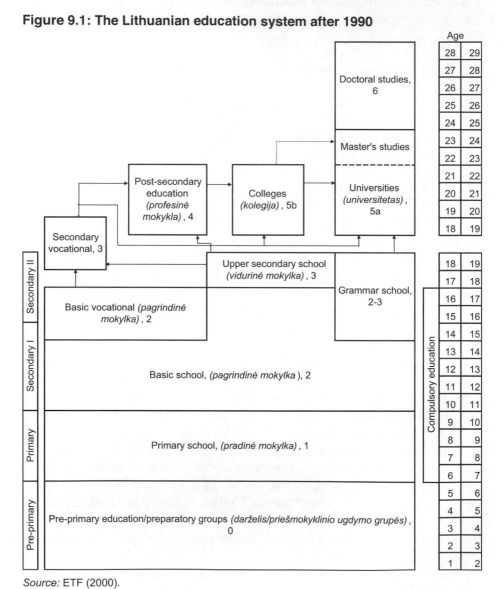

Source: ETF (2000).

On finishing their period of compulsory education, students can continue their studies in upper-secondary schools, gymnasia, vocational schools, boarding or special education schools (ISCED 3). With the transition from a five-year to a six-year period of basic lower-secondary education, upper-secondary education is currently offered in the last two years of schooling (forms 11-12). From the school year 2000/01, all general schools at upper secondary level began offering disciplinary diversification by way of four subject streams: the humanities, mathematics and natural sciences, fine arts and technology. To be awarded the upper-secondary school leaving certificate, pupils have to successfully pass five upper-secondary school leaving examinations, including an obligatory exam on the Lithuanian language (either as a mother tongue or as the state language). Upper secondary school-leaving examinations are carried out and assessed on a centralised basis. The acquired certificate entitles its holders to enter any Lithuanian higher education institution or vocational school.

Four options for vocational school training have existed since 1990/91. The first is aimed at young people who have not finished basic school and who are at least 14 years old. By undergoing this option, they may finish their lower-secondary schooling, and also acquire very simple qualifications (ISCED 2). Within this option there are two types of programmes, one lasting two years (when provision is only offered for vocational education) and the other lasting three years (when provision of both vocational and general lower-secondary education is offered). Those wishing to embark on the second option have to have finished basic school, but are not awarded an upper-secondary school certificate on completion of their studies, which last two years. The third option, lasting three years, is aimed at those who have finished basic school. Through this option, they can acquire both professional qualifications and an upper-secondary school certificate (both the second and third options are classified at ISCED 3). Finally, the fourth vocational education option, which can be classified as post-secondary vocational education (ISCED 4b), is aimed at those who have finished their upper-secondary schooling. Depending on the complexity of the prospective occupation, the duration of study will be between one and two years. Trainees who have completed the first option of initial vocational training and passed the examinations involved are awarded the certificate Kvalifikacijos pažymėjimas. Those who have completed training in the second, third and fourth options, and passed the examinations to be a qualified worker are awarded the diploma Profesinio mokymo diplomas.

Post-secondary non-tertiary education, represented by vocational colleges (ISCED 4b),[5] provides students of any age who have completed upper secondary school, or third- and fourth-option vocational schools, with opportunities for free specialist training (for three years), after which they can acquire the qualification of an associated specialist. In the early 2000s, vocational colleges underwent a period of transitional reform, with those meeting certain eligibility requirements accredited as non-university higher education institutions and those not meeting the requirements accredited as vocational schools. And the first non-university higher education institutions with the name of Kolegija were established on the basis of the former vocational colleges. The college sector (together with the higher education sector as a whole) experienced its highest increase in enrolments – about 40%-45% – between 1994/95 and 1998/99.

All universities can be categorised into three groups: classical, technical and specialised. A secondary school leaving certificate or its equivalent (which includes the International Baccalaureate) is required for admission to higher education institutions. Three levels of university higher education can be distinguished. The first, or basic, level consists of a four-year bachelor's degree, or a professional qualification equivalent to a bachelor's degree, depending on the kind of curriculum followed. This basic level may be followed by a second level, comprising of a one-and-a-half to two-year master's degree or specialised professional qualification. Furthermore, some single-stage programmes may include both basic and specialised professional studies. The third level of higher education is that of doctoral studies.

Vertical dimension of the education system

Figure 9.2 represents trends in the educational enrolment numbers for the school-aged population in Lithuania starting from the mid-1960s. Obviously, the vast majority of the school-aged population has been involved in upper-secondary general education. The trend has an inverted U-shape with the proportion of pupils increasing until the early 1990s and then starting to decrease. A U-shape is also characteristic of lower-secondary education, this time with the proportion of lower-secondary pupils decreasing and then gradually increasing again. An interesting development is a decline in the proportion of evening schools at secondary level, which were quite popular up until the 1980s. Similarly, the proportion of specialised secondary institutions decreased in the time under discussion. At the same time, enrolment in tertiary education amplified substantially, from slightly less than 10%-20% of the education cohort. Furthermore, new educational establishments appeared in the early 2000s – such as gymnasia and colleges – and their proportion grew significantly.

Figure 9.2: Enrolment by type of school in Lithuania (%)

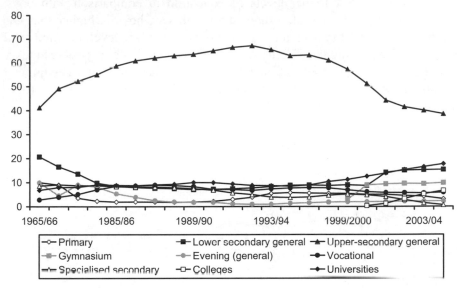

Note: Pre-primary, special and youth schools are excluded.
Source: Statistical Office of Lithuania (various years)

Figure 9.3: Flowcharts for the further education of graduates from different education institutions (%), 1998

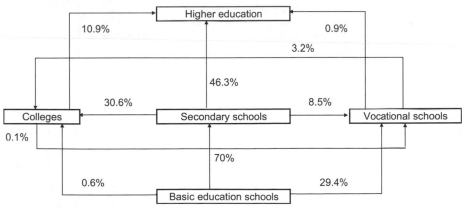

Source: OECD (2002)

The Lithuanian education system appears to be relatively open, with minimal legal restrictions on proceeding to the next education level. Figure 9.3 indicates that in 1999 70% of pupils completing basic school continued their studies in secondary schools, whereas only 30% headed towards vocational education. Figure 9.3 also makes it evident that the flow to tertiary education occurs mainly from secondary education, whereas only 1% of vocational school leavers proceed to the tertiary level.

Girls tend to seek higher levels of education in comparison with boys. While in grades 1-9 of basic school the number of boys is higher than the number of girls, by the beginning of the upper-secondary level the number of girls is noticeably higher. The number of female students in post-secondary non-tertiary and tertiary education exceeds that of male students. The number of girls in vocationally oriented colleges and post-secondary non-tertiary education is declining, however.

Figure 9.4: Proportion of women in various school types, 1996-2006

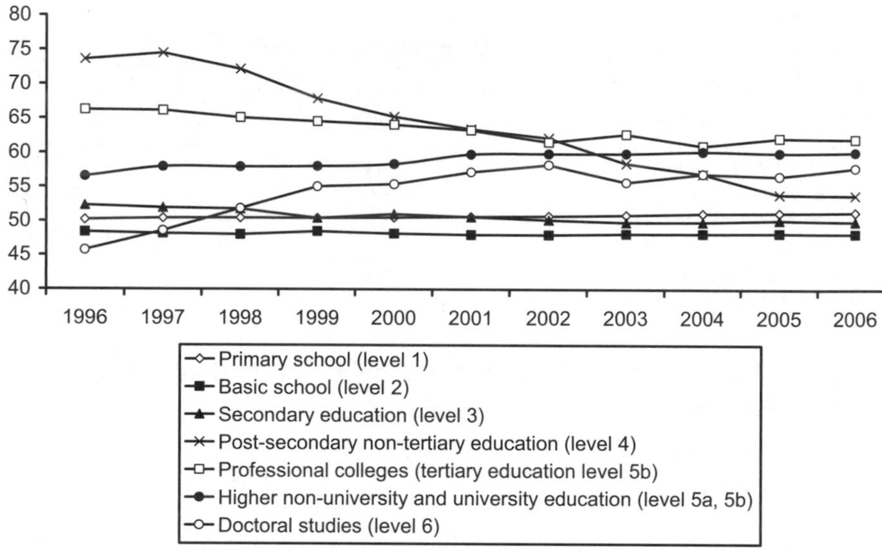

Source: Statistical Office of Lithuania (2008); own calculations

There are clear differences in the proportions of main groups of ethnicity in Lithuania at the highest level of education. The largest proportion of those in higher education is among Ukrainians, followed by Russians and Lithuanians. The lowest proportion is among Poles, who appear to be the least educated minority ethnic group in Lithuania (Statistical Office of Lithuania, 2002: 73).

Secondary level of education

Stratification and track differentiation

Even though compulsory education in Lithuania lasts until the age of 16, at 14 pupils may make their first decisions, in choosing to proceed to a gymnasium or into vocational education. The age at which tracking starts in Lithuania is similar to that in other Baltic countries and is somewhat later than in some Central European countries, such as Hungary, the Czech and Slovak Republics, or Germany and Austria.

The Lithuanian education system has traditionally been characterised by a stronger focus on general rather than vocational education. Thus in 2001, of the 99.7% basic school graduates who continued education, 80.2% of them opted for general upper-secondary education and only 19.5% for vocational upper secondary education. Back in 1996, the figures were 68.2% and 30% respectively (OECD, 2002, 2003). The proportion of pupils in vocational schools without maturation has decreased from 20% to 10% in 1993-98. At the same time the share of vocationally enrolled students graduating with maturation increased during these years (ETF, 1998, 1999, 2000).

Figure 9.5: Students in vocational schools by stage of studies (%)

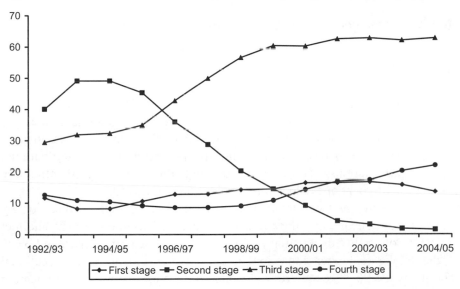

Notes: First stage: students who did not finish 10 classes; second stage: students who finished 10 classes and went on to undergo vocational training; third stage: students who finished 10 classes, and went on to vocational training and simultaneously general education; fourth stage: students who having attained secondary education, underwent vocational training.
Source: Statistical Office of Lithuania (various years)

In Lithuania vocational education can be pursued both after the basic level of education and after secondary education. Figure 9.5 allows one to see the dynamics of utilisation for these various options by Lithuanian students. The proportion of pupils entering vocational education at the age of 14 has traditionally been low in Lithuania, similar to the proportion of secondary school graduates who opt for vocational training after receiving a matriculation certificate. A slight increase in both groups, however, is noticeable between 1992 and 2004. A more pronounced trend is the increase in the number of secondary school leavers opting for a combination of general and vocational studies, whereas the proportion of young people studying only in vocational schools declined substantially.

Organisation of vocational training

Vocational education is mainly *school and training institution-based*. The apprenticeship route to acquiring a qualification is not a part of the education tradition in Lithuania and is presently available in only two schools in only a few professions. The system of work-based vocational training is completely separate from the education system and is represented by the Lithuanian labour market training authority and the territorial labour market training and counselling services.

Standardisation and quality differentiation of secondary education

One can assume that the degree of standardisation is high, as national standards are in place to serve as a basis for the assessment of students' learning. Their fundamental purpose is to ensure that all students receive the same level of education, which they are entitled to by law, to specify what is to be taught and to what extent, to ensure progression from one year to the next and across various schools, etc. In 1996, the National Examination Centre was established to oversee centrally the organisation of the national matura examinations. The certificates and diplomas offered after the completion of vocational education are also state-approved.

Data about entry and enrolment to the institutions of higher education by students from secondary education and vocational training are the indirect indicators of quality differentiation in secondary education: only about 3.6% of the intake to higher education in 2006 were students from vocational schools, while 96.4% came from secondary education (Ministry of Education and Science, 2007).

Tertiary level of education

Horizontal dimension

Figure 9.6 looks at the horizontal dimension, a field-of-study differentiation, at the tertiary level. Fields of study are plotted for various institutions of post-secondary education in Lithuania: professional colleges, colleges and universities (including both Bachelor of Arts and graduate programmes). The most popular field of study in the early 2000s is business administration: 53.5% of all college students graduate with this specialisation and the number of graduates from other institutions of higher education in this field of study is also very high. Pedagogy is another popular specialisation in the newly established colleges. Professional colleges to a large degree cater for students interested in engineering, manufacturing and construction. The proportion of students enrolled in these disciplines is also high in universities. Graduates in medicine come mostly from master's programmes at universities, whereas the number of graduates in the healthcare area more generally are also high in colleges and professional colleges. The humanities, arts, social and behavioral sciences, journalism and, to a large degree, natural sciences remain the domain of the traditional universities in Lithuania, whereas service specialties are largely taught in colleges. Law can be studied both in universities and in more vocationally oriented colleges.

Figure 9.6: Proportion of graduates from post-secondary education by field of study

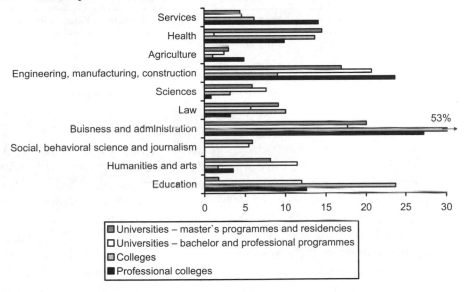

Source: Statistical Office of Lithuania (1999-2004)

Women outnumber men in institutions of higher (tertiary) education (see Figure 9.4), but the distribution of students by gender varies in different fields. Female students make up 78% of those studying social services, 73% of those studying education and 81% of those studying subjects related to healthcare. In transport and security services, however, 88% of students are male, in engineering 82%, and in computing the proportion is 79% (Eurydice, 2003).

Standardisation, quality differentiation and openness of tertiary education

The law in Lithuania stipulates that non-state education institutions may be established, reorganised and liquidated by legal residents registered in the Republic of Lithuania, or individual citizens of the Republic of Lithuania on receipt of written consent from the Ministry of Education and Science. The Centre for Quality Assessment in Higher Education was founded in 1995 with the aim of assessing tertiary education institutions in Lithuania. Table 9.1 shows that non-state institutions have developed slowly in Lithuania, although the number of non-public institutions at the higher education level (especially universities) has been increasing.

Table 9.1: Total number of education establishments and number of non-public schools in Lithuania

	1991-92	1995-96		1998-98		2004	
	Total	Total	Private	Total	Private	Total	Private
Vocational	105	105	1	104	1	73	2
College-type	64	68	15	70	18	27	11
Universities	13	15	-	16	1	21	6

Source: OECD (2002); Ministry of Education and Science (2006)

In 2006, 55,190 students were accepted to state universities at all levels. A total of 38,560 of them were fully or partially funded by the state and 16,630 students were able to pay the full tuition fee. Courses are fully financed for 50% of all non-university students (50% full-time and 50% extramural), for 50% of university students and for 100% of police recruits at university.

The other 50% of the students pay partial or full tuition fees. The partial fee equals 4 minimum living standard (MLS) (520 LTL or €151 per term). The fee varies according to the field of study, mode of studying (full-, part-time or extramural) and its stage (such as bachelor's, master's or doctoral studies).

Students who do not pay for their bachelor's and master's studies at state universities are entitled to receive a student grant based on their academic achievements. It can be up to two-and-a-half times the MLS (2.5*130=325 LTL, €94). There are also social grants for students, which are equal to the minimum standard of living. Doctoral students receive a grant which equals 5.88 MLS during the first year and 6.8 during the second, third and fourth years (Information Source, 2001).

Labour market

Economic development

Different attempts have been made to divide the last 15 years' relative phases of economic development in Lithuania. According to the most general approach, this period can be divided into five relative phases (Rakauskienė, 2006: 690). The first period, from 1990-94, was marked by economic decline, as in all post-communist countries (Figure 9.7). From 1990 until 1992, the key task of the Lithuanian government was to implement statehood by passing new laws and establishing new institutions. A permanent national currency, the Litas (LTL), was introduced in 1993. The second period, from 1995-98 was a period of recovery, characterised by economic stability and rapid growth. The third period, from 1999-2000, was characterised by economic recession due to the Russian crisis that hit Lithuania particularly hard due to its strong ties with the Russian economy. The economy returned to a positive growth path in 2000. Economic performance remained stable with annual growth rates between 6.5% and 10.5% in the period 2001-03, which is known as the fourth period of rapid economy growth. The fifth period from 2004 onwards was dominated by the EU accession process that ended in Lithuania's EU membership.

Rakauskienė (2006: 251) presents a second classification of periods based on Lithuanian's fiscal policy during the transition. The initial period, from 1990-97, was characterised by the establishment of state financial institutions, the creation of a state tax system and the introduction of measures to reduce high fiscal deficits. During the second period, 1998-99, public expenditure increased sharply because of the economic crisis and the fiscal deficit increased significantly up to 7.8 of gross domestic product (GDP). A tight fiscal policy was implemented in the third period, from 2001–2003. In May 2001, Lithuania became a member of the World Trade Organisation. This can be considered as a logical extension of its liberal and open trade policies, and its orientation towards European and world markets. The Memorandum of Economic Policies was signed in 2002 by the government of Lithuania, the World Bank and the International Monetary Fund (IMF). Finally, in the period 2004-05, fiscal policy was coordinated with the EU structural funds and a 20% increase in public revenue and expenditure.

A further classification is possible based on the privatisation process, which may be divided into three major stages (Gruzevskis and Beleckiene, 1999). The first round of privatisation was launched in September 1991 and lasted until 1995. State property was sold for investment vouchers that were distributed free of charge to all Lithuanian citizens. Other naturalised and legal residents could purchase state property for cash. State property was sold through open and closed subscriptions of shares, open and closed auctions, restitution, 'best business plan' tenders and by other methods. A programme of voucher privatisation with some elements of cash sales was implemented, and succeeded relatively rapidly in privatising a substantial part of the agricultural sector, and all small and medium-sized enterprises (SMEs). At the end of 1995, over 95% of construction, agriculture and light industry capital had been moved into private hands. This first phase was a particularly dynamic one compared with other Central and Eastern Europe (CEE) countries. For example, about 97% of the property in the agricultural sector went into private hands (Antila and Ylöstalo, 2003). However, the state kept an important stake in larger industrial enterprises and key sectors.

Figure 9.7: GDP growth, 1991-2006

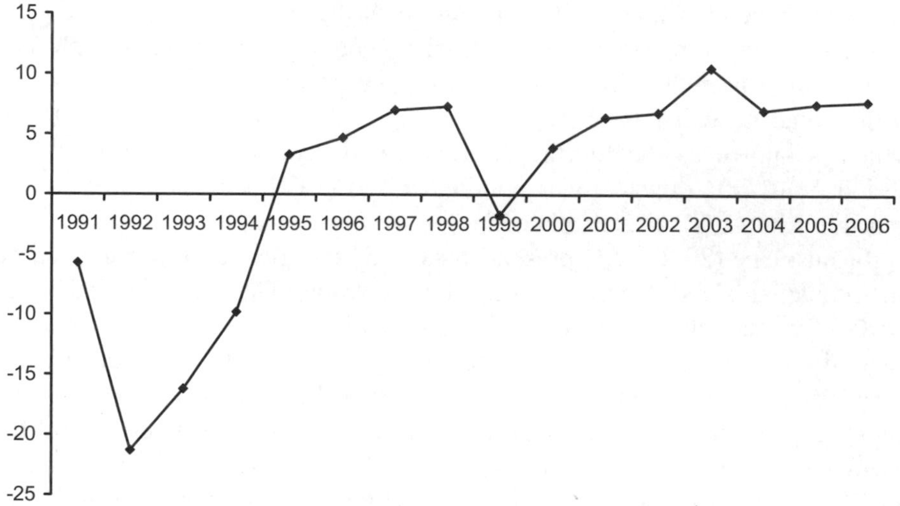

Source: ILO (2008); data for 2006 from Eurostat (2008)

The Privatisation of State and Municipal Property Act was enacted in July 1995 and came into force in September 1995 (EBRD, 2008). This was the beginning of the second stage of privatisation, which lasted until 1999 and had two major differences compared with the first period: all the property had to be sold in cash under market conditions and all the investors had equal rights, whether they were Lithuanian or foreign. The second phase of privatisation started with the cash privatisation of the remaining state property at market prices. However, the small number of remaining public enterprises still accounted for a significant part of the economy's activity.

The third stage of privatisation started in 1997 when the government offered some of the state-owned strategic enterprises in the sectors of transport, energy and telecommunications for privatisation. There were over 3,000 companies available for privatisation with a state-owned value amounting to approximately LTL 5 billion in 2000. The largest companies on the list included two banks, several companies in the transport sector and large enterprises operating in the energy market. Many of the companies were restructured before the final privatisation. In 2001, the major deals were the sales of the Lithuanian Shipping Company (LISCO) and Lithuanian Savings Bank (Lietuvos Tautomasis Bankas, LTB). The last state-owned bank, SC Leituvos Žemės Ūkio Bankas (Lithuanian Agriculture Bank), was privatised in March 2002, which completed the privatisation of the financial sector.

Labour market dynamics

Employment dynamics

At the beginning of the economic transition in 1990, 18.9% of the employed people worked in agriculture, 41.2% in industry and only 39.4% in the service sector (Figure 9.8). This pattern reflects agriculture's considerable initial size. Although the agricultural share of total employment was already high in 1990, it increased to a peak of 24.2% in 1996. The initial shift towards agricultural employment is the result of a combination of two related policies: the privatisation of agricultural production and agrarian reform. Rapid privatisation coupled with the restitution of property rights on land has led to a strongly fragmented ownership structure, resulting in low productivity (European Commission, 2002). Given the economic difficulties from 1991-93, many people chose to be employed in agriculture as an alternative to unemployment, inducing the initial expansion of agricultural employment. These new farms usually cultivate small family plots, contributing only marginally to GDP. During the period from 1997-2005, however, the agricultural employment share declined steadily and significantly to 14%. Despite this drop, this sector still plays a key part in the Lithuanian economy.

In contrast, the employment share of industry and construction decreased permanently during the whole transition period to 29.1%. Employment in industry has been continuously declining since the beginning of the 1990s, from 750,000 individuals in 1990 to 405,000 individuals in 2005 (ILO, 2008). The industrial sector is still characterised by a predominance of large enterprises, especially in heavy industry and engineering, which were developed mostly after the Second World War under Soviet rule. Oil refining and food processing are the main industrial branches (European Commission, 2002). The service sector's share of total employment steadily increased to 56.9% in 2005. Lithuania's service sector was slightly smaller in relative terms than the other two Baltic countries and the EU15 countries. Dominant activities are in wholesale and retail trade, financial and related services, and in public administration, as in most transition countries. More recently, Lithuania alone has continued to increase its employment in public services, notably education (OECD, 2003).

Figure 9.8: Sectoral share of employed, 1990-2005

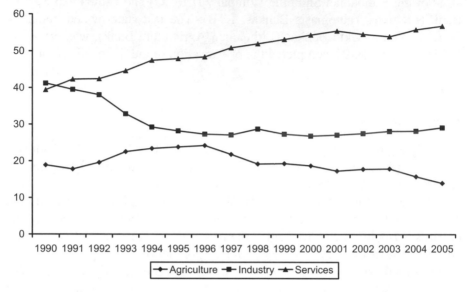

Source: ILO (2008)

The growth of business was especially pronounced in SMEs. At the beginning of 2006, the total number of economic entities operating within the country was 73,344, compared to 69,861 (55,846 of which were SMEs) in 2004 and 72,330 (56,428 SMEs) in 2005 (Statistical Office of Lithuania, 2006). Increasing numbers of economic entities have led to an increasing number of work places. According to the Lithuanian Development Agency for Small and Medium-Sized Enterprises (SMEDA, 2006) and the Department of Statistics to the Government of the Republic of Lithuania, in 2004 the share of the GDP produced by SMEs accounted for 71.3% of the country's GDP, compared to 59.1% in 2001. It can be observed that the share of enterprises with up to nine employees in the total number of operating enterprises decreased from 79.9% in 2001 to 74.6% in 2005, whereas the share of enterprises with up to 49 employees increased from 15.9% in 2001 to 20.1% in 2005, as has the share of enterprises with up to 249 employees (from 3.7% in 2001 to 4.7% in 2005).

During the transition period, the labour force participation rates of the population aged 15-64 sharply declined from 75.8% in 1990 to 69.3% in 2006 (Figure 9.9). This decline is in line with the general pattern found in all other CEE countries. The pace of decline has slowed in recent years and participation rates have stabilised. Variations in the employment rate for different age groups of the population have been diverse. The employment rate dropped visibly among young people (15-24 years), from 49.5% to 28.4% between 1990 and 2006 (Table 9.2). This trend can be explained by prolonged education careers, but it may also reflect increasing labour market integration problems for the young age cohort. Furthermore, the number of young people who moved abroad increased (Ministry of Social Security and Labour, 2004: 14). In contrast, the middle-age cohorts reached very high activity rates of around 90% during the transition period. The participation rates of people aged 65 and over declined from 9.4% in 1990 to 4.1% in 2006.

Figure 9.9: Labour force participation rate (age group 15-64), 1990-2006

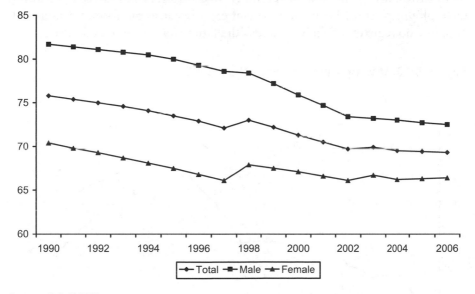

Source: ILO (2008)

Table 9.2: Labour force participation rate (%) by age cohort, 1990-2006

	1990	1995	2000	2006
15+	66.4	63.1	59.8	57.2
15-24	49.5	47.1	36.1	28.4
25-54	93.0	90.8	90.2	88.7
55-64	47.8	43.6	45.2	51.3
65+	9.4	7.5	5.3	4.1

Source: ILO (2008)

Unemployment dynamics

Official registered unemployment was extremely low at the beginning of the transition period, at 0.3% in 1991, due to the fact that unemployment was an unrecognised phenomenon during the communist era (Figure 9.10). The transition to a market economy led to the unemployment figures increasing. In accordance with the two economic recessions at the beginning of the 1990s and in 1998, jumps in unemployment rates appear. In general, Lithuania suffered from an increase in unemployment rates that peaked at approximately 12.9% of the labour force in 2001, after which it declined substantially to 5.4% in 2005. This decline is in accordance with the economic recovery at the beginning of the new millennium. A comparison between the Labour Force Survey (LFS)-based unemployment rate and the registered unemployment rate reveals that the former is much higher, but there is a convergent trend over time. The differences between registered unemployment and LFS unemployment exist because the former captures all people who register officially whereas the latter is a self-assessed measure.

Figure 9.10: Unemployment rates, 1991-2006

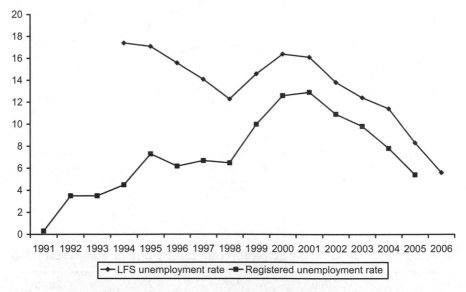

Note: LFS unemployment rate for age groups 16-61; registered unemployment rate for individuals aged over 15.
Source: ILO (2008); LFS unemployment rate for 2006 from Eurostat (2008)

In Lithuania as in many other countries, the transition of young people from school to adult life and employment remains an important labour market problem (Gruzevskis and Blaziene, 2007). Labour market entrants, approximated as the youngest age cohort of 15- to 24-year-olds, are the category most exposed to unemployment. The unemployment rate of those under 25 is about two times higher than the average unemployment rate for the whole adult population (ILO, 2008).

In addition to young people, another disadvantaged category in the labour market is that of the long-term unemployed. According to Eurostat (2008) data, the long-term unemployment rate, i.e., people unemployed for over 12 months, decreased from 7.5% in 1995 to 4.3% in 2005. This coincides with a decline in the absolute number of long-term unemployed from 123,800 to 72,900 from 1998-2005 (Statistical Office of Lithuania, 2006).

The decrease in long-term unemployment can be explained by two factors: the economic growth of the business sector and the emigration of unskilled or semi-skilled workers. The net migration (the difference between the number of immigrants and emigrants) continuously increased, from 2,559 in 2001 to 8,782 in 2005, which means that more people emigrated than arrived in the country. According to the Statistical Office of Lithuania (2006), 83.1% of them were economic emigrants. Although there is no data for emigrants on the duration of their unemployment in their country of origin, negative net migration reflects the general tendency of economic migration to also encompass the long-term unemployed.

Labour market institutions

After independence, Lithuania equipped itself with a Labour Code that is comparable in many respects by European standards (OECD, 2003): including liberal employment protection regulation, decentralised wage setting and collective bargaining. The 1972 Soviet Labour Laws were in force during the first transition years, but many elements of them have been gradually modernised since 1991, inspired especially by the need to conform to EU standards. In 2003 new labour laws were adopted in Lithuania.

Employment protection legislation

Under the centrally planned economic system, workers enjoyed a fairly high degree of employment protection in their jobs. This high degree of employment protection, combined with high wage compression, led to labour rigidity and inefficient labour allocation (Eamets and Masso, 2005). In the 1990s, the need for rapid structural adjustment after the introduction of economic and social reforms was reflected in a substantial moderation of worker protection. The objective was to facilitate workforce adjustment for firms to make enterprises more flexible, while guaranteeing employment protection for workers.

Lithuania and other CEE countries tend to be most restrictive compared to the EU concerning collective dismissals (see Table 2.7 in Chapter Two of this book). Regulations concerning regular and temporary employment are on average somewhat more restrictive in Lithuania than in other CEE countries and the EU. The high value of the temporary employment regulation is related to the strict regulation of fixed-term contract use, whereas temporary work agencies have almost no limitations (Tonin, 2005). Fixed-term contracts can only be applied in certain cases and the maximum number of contracts is strongly limited. There is almost no regulation of temporary agency work as its share is negligible, accounting for approximately 0.4% of those employed (Eamets and Masso, 2005: Table 2). In general, the comparison of overall employment protection legislation (EPL) finds that, despite significant liberalisation efforts, CEE countries and especially Lithuania have on average identical EPL strictness.

Industrial relations

Before 1990, Lithuania's industrial relations systems were characterised by the central political and managerial control exercised by the state. During the transition, Lithuania moved away from a centralised wage-setting system towards a collective bargaining system in the enterprise sector, as did many other CEE countries. Wage bargaining usually takes place at the company level or to a lesser extent at the sectoral level, whereas the regional or national level bargaining does not exist (Visser, 2004: Table 1.8).

Union membership sharply declined during the 1990s, from full coverage of the workforce registered at the beginning of transition. According to Paas et al (2003), the Lithuania unionisation rate decreased to 40% during the mid-1990s and again to 15% during the late 1990s. Van Gyes et al (2007: Figure 2) report a further marginal decrease from 15% in 1998 to 14% in 2004. The decrease is, in general, attributed to the shift towards the free choice of union membership status, falling living standards over the 1990s, high levels of unemployment, privatisation and sectoral shifts.

Even more important than the number of unionised workers is the coverage by collective agreements. Van Gyes et al (2007: Figure 4) estimate the percentage of employees covered by collective agreements as under 15% for 2002, representing the lowest level of union coverage compared to other CEE countries. Correspondingly, Mailand and Due (2004) report that union coverage is 8%-15% at the workplace level. Thus, the organisational degree of the Lithuanian labour force is very low, and comparisons with other Western and Eastern European countries reveal that it stands at the bottom of the rankings regarding its degree of organisation (Gruzevskis and Blaziene, 2007).

Welfare regime

Labour market policy

Active labour market policy

During the early transition period, labour market policy was characterised by insignificant expenditure on active labour market policy (ALMP) measures because of low unemployment rates. ALMP plays a very small role in Lithuania, with expenditures of about 0.09% of GDP in 2001 (OECD, 2003). By comparison, such spending in OECD countries ranged from 0.09% of GDP in Japan to about 2% in Sweden. According to expenditure, the most important active measure is labour market training (42.2%), followed by public works (33.7%) and employment subsidies (18.2%) (Paas et al, 2003: Table 6). Priority of involvement is given to people from disadvantaged groups, such as people with a disability, young people and the long-term unemployed. The total inflow of ALMP participants in 2001 corresponded to 6% of the labour force in Lithuania (OECD, 2003). In general, limited activities and resources have been allocated to evaluating the impact and effectiveness of active employment measures.

Currently, the Lithuanian Labour Exchange at the Ministry of Social Security and Labour is implementing eight European Social Fund programmes, which comprise special measures for integrating risk groups into labour markets and preventing social exclusion. One programme is directly targeted at young labour market entrants. The others, principally also accessible to young people, include preparation for entrepreneurship training programmes and organising entrepreneurship training, the integration of people with a disability into the labour market and organising professional training for people with a disability (state-subsidised work places). ALMPs also include special measures (job search assistance, advice, information, subsidised employment) for prisoners or individuals who have recently served a prison term. The programmes are implemented by the Lithuanian Labour Exchange or its territorial offices.

Unemployment insurance[6]

Unemployment insurance was first introduced in 1991 and reformed in 1996. Compared to later legislation, the early legislation foresaw comparatively generous benefits. The level of unemployment benefit depended on the level of the average monthly wage received at the employee's last place of work (first two months: 70% of average monthly wage; next two months: 60%; next two months: 50%). The required contribution period amounted to 24 months in the last three years. The benefit was paid for no longer than six months in any 12-month period.

From 1996, the unemployment benefit consisted of a fixed and a variable component. The fixed component equalled the state-supported income and the variable component depended on one's social insurance record. In all cases, the unemployment benefit could not be lower than the fixed amount of the state-supported income approved by the government and could not exceed the amount of two minimal subsistence levels, also defined by the government. The duration of payments was a maximum of six months within the past 12 months. Table 9.3 details benefit levels as well the share of the unemployed receiving benefit.

Table 9.3: Characteristics of the unemployment benefit system in Lithuania

	1997	2000	2004	2005	2006
Minimum benefit, LTL	120	135	135	135	155
in % of average net wage	0.21	0.20	0.16	0.15	0.15
in % of minimum wage	0.32	0.31	0.28	0.26	0.29
Average benefit, LTL	n.a.	187	176	328	400
in % of average net wage	n.a.	0.27	0.21	0.36	0.37
in % of minimum wage	n.a.	0.43	0.36	0.62	0.70
Maximum benefit, LTL	220	250	250	693	771
in % of average net wage	0.38	0.36	0.30	0.76	0.71
in % of minimum wage	0.59	0.58	0.52	1.32	1.34
Share of unemployed receiving benefits (%)	41.1	29.9	13.2	17.3	22.4

Source: Ministry of Social Security and Labour (1998-2007); Statistical Office of Lithuania (2008); European Commission (2008); ISSA (2008))

Benefit levels were consistently declining between 1997 and 2004, which is also reflected in a steadily declining share of the unemployed actually claiming benefits; benefit levels have been increasing again since 2005. Within this new system, the minimum unemployment benefit still equals the fixed part of the amount of income supported by the state, but the variable part now depends on the level of income received in someone's former employment during the previous 36 months and the insured income of the current year approved by the government. However, a ceiling is also fixed at 70% of the insured income in a current year.

The duration of payment has also been changed since 2005. Now the duration of payment of unemployment benefit depends on the length of the receiver's insurance record. If their unemployment insurance record is below 25 years, the unemployment insurance benefit is paid for six months; if the record is between 25 and 30 years, for seven months; if it is from 30-35 years, for eight months; if it exceeds 35 years, nine months. Hence, particularly for the long-term employed, the payment duration has increased.

Furthermore, by 2005 the contribution period decreased to 18 months in the last three years. Payment of the unemployment insurance benefit has been extended by two additional months to the unemployed who will reach retirement age in less than five years. It will be paid until retirement age for those unemployed of pre-pension age (less than two years until pension age), for whom the unemployment benefit was prescribed and prolonged due to their age by 1 January 2005. The unemployment insurance benefit is paid every month from the eighth day after registration. In sum, with the 2005 reform, unemployment benefit became more generous, especially for those with higher earnings, who benefit from the substantial increase in the upper ceiling, as well as those with a long employment history.

The qualifying conditions are to be unemployed, to be of working age and not attending a daily education institution, to have a minimum period of insurance, to be registered at the Labour Exchange and to be actively seeking work and ready to accept a job offer or to participate in the ALMP measures. Unemployed people willing to receive or receiving unemployment benefit also have to meet certain behavioural requirements. They are obliged to accept job offers corresponding to their occupational education and health status, as well as proposals for vocational training, and to regularly visit the Labour Exchange Office. Failure to observe these requirements might lead to the refusal to award unemployment benefit, to the reduction of the amount of benefits or to the termination of the disbursement of the benefit in general. The disbursement period of unemployment benefit does not cover periods when an unemployed person was involved in performing public works, Employment Fund-supported works or participating in vocational training programmes.

Unemployment benefit is not awarded or withdrawn if the unemployed person refuses to accept suitable job offers or refuses to participate in ALMP measures. For example, a job offer is still considered suitable if the commuting time to and from the workplace does not exceed three hours, or two hours for people with a disability and individuals with family responsibilities (such as having children under three years of age, sick family members of pension age, or disabled family members in need of nursing and care). The local Labour Exchange has the right to specify the requirements concerning the commuting time to and from the workplace, taking into consideration the individual's actual circumstances and any mitigating circumstances that they may put forth.

Minimum wage

A legal minimum wage exists and is set at the national level. During the period 1994-2001, Lithuania had the highest relative minimum wage among the Baltic states: around 60% of the average wage compared to 30% in Estonia (Paas et al, 2003). Hence, the minimum wage may represent wage rigidity at the bottom of the wage distribution.

Family policy

Since 1996, relative family policy expenditure has increased. Expenditure on in-kind benefits increased relative to cash benefits. Nevertheless, expenditure on cash benefits dominates, representing 36% of expenditure on family policies in 2004 (Eurostat, 2008). In total, family policies comprise 16.9% of the total social protection expenditure, excluding expenditure on old-age insurance.

At the end of 2003, there were 672 kindergartens and nurseries in the country, which is 42 less than in 2000 (Table 9.4). More pre-school education groups are being established in general schools. In 2000, such groups operated in 259 schools and in 296 schools in 2003. The proportion of children attending such establishments is increasing: in 2000 they were attended by 41% of children, in 2003 by 48%, out of which 66% lived in cities and 14% in rural areas. There is a strong difference in enrolment rates between rural and urban regions. While 84.3% of children in urban areas attended some form of pre-school education, in rural areas the figure was only 19.6% (as of 2003).

The fee for attending a nursery or kindergarten is calculated in line with Resolution No 1170 of the Government of the Republic of Lithuania of 31 August 1995 Regarding the Fee for Child Sustenance in Pre-School Establishments. This stipulates that as from 1 September, 1995 the fee for child sustenance in a pre-school establishment (excluding private ones), notwithstanding their jurisdiction, shall make up 60% of the adopted daily norm of child subsistence for every day of attendance. The fee for child sustenance in pre-school establishments (except private ones) is reduced by 50% in the following cases: the child has one only parent; the family raises three or more children; the father is a conscript of the military service; at least one of the child's parents is currently a pupil or student enrolled in the day department of an education establishment. On the basis of Resolution No 1 of the Government of the Republic of Lithuania of 3 January 2003, the fee rate for child sustenance in a pre-school establishment shall be defined by the founder of the establishment (Resolution regarding the Fee for Child Sustenance in Pre-School Establishments).

Table 9.4: Pre-school establishments and enrolment (end of year estimates)

	2000	2001	2002	2003
Number of pre-school establishments				
Nurseries/kindergartens	533	531	531	525
Kindergartens	181	168	155	147
Pre-school education group at general school	259	273	320	296
Pre-school education attendance, by region and age				
Urban				
1-6 years old and older	58	59.3	61.5	66.2
up to 3 years old	19.9	21	24	26.5
aged 3 and older	74.4	75.5	78.6	84.3
Rural				
1-6 years old and older	11.8	13.3	14.1	14.1
up to 3 years old	3.2	3.8	3.5	3.8
aged 3 and older	15.6	17.8	19.5	19.6

Source: Republic of Lithuania (2006)

Notes

[1] This section is based on Eurydice (2003) and OECD (2002) publications.
[2] However, enrolment in private schools is still limited. The number of private institutions is relatively low in Lithuania: in 2001/02 there were only 42 (19 general education schools, one vocational school, 9 vocational colleges, 9 non-university higher education institutions and 4 universities) compared to 2,386 public ones.
[3] In schools in which the instruction is in an ethnic/regional minority language (Russian, Polish, etc), an extensive teaching of the Lithuanian language is offered from the second year.
[4] Vaguely defined criteria for the selection and admission of students allow gymnasiums to accept students from better-off families.
[5] These institutions evolved from the former technicums.
[6] This section is based on the European Commission (2008), ISSA (2008), as well as the Ministry of Social Security and Labour (1998-2007) and Republic of Lithuania (2006).

References

Antila, J. and Ylöstalo, P. (2003) *Working life barometer in the Baltic countries 2002*, Labour Policy Studies No 247, Helsinki: Ministry of Labour.
Eamets, R. and Masso, J. (2005) 'The paradox of the Baltic States: labour market flexibility but protected workers', *European Journal of Industrial Relations*, vol 11, no 1, pp 71-90.
EBRD (European Bank for Reconstruction and Development) (2008) *Transition report 2007*, London: EBRD.

ETF (European Training Foundation) (1998, 1999, 2000) *Vocational education and training in Central and Eastern Europe: key indicators*, Luxembourg: Office for Official Publications of the European Communities.

European Commission (2002) *Joint assessment of employment priorities in Lithuania*, Luxembourg: Office for Official Publications of the European Communities.

European Commission (2008) *Mutual information system on social protection (MISSOC): comparative tables on social protection in the member states and the European Economic Area*, Brussels: European Commission. (www.ec.europa.eu/employment_social/spsi/missoc_en.htm)

Eurostat (2008) *Internet database*, Luxembourg: Eurostat (http://epp.eurostat.ec.europa.eu).

Eurydice (2003) *Structure of education, vocational training and adult education system: Lithuania*, Brussels: Eurydice European Unit

Filippov, F.R. (1980) *Sotsiologia obrazovania* (*Sociology of education*), Moscow: Nauka.

Gruzevskis, B. and Beleckiene, G. (1999) *Background study on employment and labour market in Lithuania*, Torino: European Training Foundation.

Gruzevskis, B. and Blaziene, I. (2007) 'Lithuania', in S. Cazes and A. Nesporova (eds) *Flexicurity: a relevant approach in Central and Eastern Europe*, Geneva: International Labour Organization.

Ministry of Education and Science (2007) 'Ką rodo m. Bendrojo priėmimo į Lietuvos aukštąsias mokyklas duomenys?' ('Data of enrolment in to higher education system in 2006 in Lithuania'), Švietimo problemos analizė (Education problems analyses), *Vasaris*, vol 12, no 1, p 3.

Kuokštis, V. (2007) *A survey of the Lithuanian economy 2007/2008*, Vilnius: Lithuanian Free Market Institute.

ILO (International Labour Organization) (2008) *Key indicators of the labour market programme*, Fifth Edition, Geneva: ILO.

Information source (2001) *The resolution of Lithuanian government No 836, 2001 July 5*, Brussels: Eurydice European Unit.

ISSA (International Social Security Administration) (2008) *Social security worldwide database* (www-ssw.issa.int/sswlp2/engl/page1.htm).

Mailand, M. and Due, J. (2004) 'Social dialogue in Central and Eastern Europe: present state and future development', *European Journal of Industrial Relations*, vol 10, no 2, pp 179-97.

Meier, A. (1989) 'Universals and particularities of socialist educational systems: the transformation from school to work in the German Democratic Republic and the Soviet Union', in M. Kohn (ed) *Cross-national research in sociology*, London: Sage Publications.

Ministry of Education and Science (2006) *Education in Lithuania: facts and figures*, Vilnius: Ministry of Education and Science of the Republic of Lithuania.

Ministry of Social Security and Labour (1998-2007) *Social report*, Vilnius.

OECD (Organisation for Economic Co-operation and Development) (2002) *Reviews of national policies for education: Lithuania*, Paris: OECD

OECD (2003) *Labour market and social policies in the Baltic countries*, Paris: OECD.

OECD (2004) *Employment outlook*, Paris: OECD.

Paas, T., Eamets, R., Masso, J. and Rõõm, M. (2003) *Labour market flexibility and migration in the Baltic states: macro evidences*, Discussion Paper No 16, Tartu: University of Tartu.

Rakauskienė, O. (2006) *Valstybės ekonominė politika* (*State economy policy*), Vilnius: Mykolo Romerio Universitetas.

Republic of Lithuania (2006) *Third report on the implementation of the European Social Charter*, Vilnius: Republic of Lithuania.

SMEDA (Development Agency for Small and Medium-Sized Enterprises) (2006) *Small and medium-sized business in Lithuania*, Vilnius: SMEDA (www.smeda.lt/index.php/en/33712/).

Statistical Office of Lithuania (various years) *Statistical Yearbooks*, Vilnius: Statistical Office of Lithuania.

Statistical Office of Lithuania (2002) *Population by sex, age, ethnicity and religion*, Vilnius: Statistical Office of Lithuania.

Statistical Office of Lithuania (2008) *Internet database*, Vilnius: Statistical Office of Lithuania.

Titma, M. and Saar, E. (1995) 'Regional differences in Soviet secondary-education', *European Sociological Review*, vol 11, pp 37-58.

Tonin, M. (2005) *Updated employment protection legislation indicators for Central and Eastern European Countries*, Working Paper, Institute for International Economic Studies, Stockholm: Stockholm University.

Van Gyes, G., Vandenbrande, T., Lehndorff, S., Schilling, G., Schief, S. and Kohl, H. (2007) *Industrial relations in EU member states 2000-2004*, Dublin: European Foundation for the Improvement of Living and Working Conditions.

Visser, J. (2004) 'Patterns and variations in European industrial relations', in European Commission (ed) *Industrial relations in Europe*, Luxembourg: Office for the Official Publications of the European Communities, pp 11-57.

TEN

Poland

Anna Baranowska

Over the past two decades, Poland has experienced pronounced economic and institutional changes. The transition to a market economy started in 1990 with radical and comprehensive reforms aimed at eliminating detailed state intervention in both labour and product markets (Balcerowicz, 1994). The reform strategy dealt not only with the type of measures, but also with their phasing – they were all launched simultaneously and proceeded at a high rate in what has been referred to as 'shock therapy'. In the literature on typologies of reforms in the Central and Eastern European (CEE) region, Poland was identified as one of the 'reform leaders' (de Melo et al, 1996; Sachs, 1996; Wolf, 1999).

Increasing competition, restructuring and privatisation necessitated massive layoffs. The government set up social security schemes for workers losing their jobs, but due to public finance constraints the generousness of these schemes was soon substantially reduced. Poland's recovery from the transitional recession was spectacular – by 1992 it had already regained its pre-reform gross domestic product (GDP) level, and employment increased throughout the mid-1990s. Still, further growth was brought to a halt by the Russian crisis in 1999, which contributed to dramatic cuts in employment, and the global economic slowdown in 2001 further deepened the country's recession. Nevertheless, after hovering for a while at approximately 20%, the unemployment rate has plummeted since 2004.

The introduction of market rules into the labour market resulted in increasing income inequality, with a growing wage premium for highly skilled workers. Partly as a response to rising returns to skills and partly due to reforms allowing for the establishment of private education institutions, rapid tertiary education expansion has taken place. Higher education enrolment rates increased more than threefold between 1989 and 2004. Still, the challenges connected with the quality of schooling – also at the tertiary level – and the need to reform the system of vocational education remain unresolved.

Education system

Structure of the Polish education system

Overview of the Polish education system after the Second World War[1]

The Polish education system during the socialist period consisted of the three conventional sectors: primary, secondary and post-secondary. Until 1969, primary education included seven years of schooling and was thereafter changed to eight years. The choice of secondary schools after the completion of primary school was the crucial decision that determined the allocation of education to students of different social backgrounds. The secondary sector was composed of three distinct blocks: basic vocational, general secondary at a *lyceum* and vocational secondary at a *technicum.* At the end of both *lyceum* and *technicum*, graduates could take final examinations and obtain matriculation certificate *matura,* which authorised the graduate to apply to a university. In addition, the *technicum* offered a technical diploma, the title of technician (*technik*), and access to various kinds of skilled work. Basic vocational education, which was by far the most frequent and most available sector within secondary education, provided vocational training for skilled workers, technical skills for qualified workers and agricultural training courses for farmers. This sector expanded steadily during the post-war period, and peaked between 1960 and 1965.

The post-secondary sector was broken down into two distinct levels: the non-university level, which normally lasted from one to three years but did not lead to a university degree, and traditional higher education, which granted a university degree after four to six years of study. The non-university route offered training for pre-school and primary school teachers, nurses and a variety of paramedical personnel and thus attracted more than three times as many women as men. In Polish traditional university-level higher education the emphasis used to be on technical and vocational education; humanities and liberal arts grew much more slowly than engineering or other technical field, and polytechnic institutes grew more rapidly than universities. The elite universities, however, remained highly selective in Poland with relatively stable enrolments and with little variation over time.

Education expansion in Poland was a function of state policy, determined by both the availability of resources and numerous political constraints. Enrolment targets for all schools in the secondary and post-secondary sectors were set by the Planning Commission at the Council of Ministers in order to meet the manpower needs defined by economic planning. This accounted for the predetermination of the number of students admitted (*numerus clausus*), and the regulation of access by means of rigid application procedures – including entrance examinations – to virtually all post-primary schools (apart from basic vocational schools, which required only a graduation certificate from primary schools).

The basic education system in Poland changed little in the decades between the Second World War and 1990. The communist regime did institute some reforms intended to increase opportunities for specific groups such as the working class, farmers or children living in isolated or backward regions, but such reforms tended to be sporadic and only moderately successful. The most significant changes occurred in the size and composition of different types of schooling within various levels of the education system, rather than in the organisation of the system as a whole. Major reforms were undertaken in the second half of the 1990s.

Education system since 1990[2]

Beginning in the school year 1999/2000, after the onset of the reform of the education system, full-time education in Poland is compulsory for 10 years and covers education in the 'zero grade', in the six-year primary schools and in the three-year lower-secondary schools (gimnazja). The 'zero grade' is a year of preparation for primary education that is attached to either a kindergarten or a primary school and has been obligatory for all six-year-old children since the 2004/05 school year. At the primary school level, full-time compulsory education starts during the calendar year in which the child reaches seven years of age and normally continues until the completion of the gymnasium, but no further than the age of 18. Part-time compulsory education, however, lasts until 18 years of age (O'Brien and Paczynski, 2006).[3] Compulsory education is free of charge.

Children between the ages of seven and 13 attend primary schools (International Standard Classification of Education, ISCED 1). On completing primary school pupils must take an external standardised test, the results of which appear on the primary school graduation certificate and which is required for admission to a lower secondary general school (gimnazjum, ISCED 2) (see Figure 10.1).

The lower-secondary general school was introduced by shortening primary school education from eight to seven years and cutting education at the secondary level by two years. At the end of *gimnazjum* external standardised exams are conducted, and the results of this exam serve as the basis for the transition to the upper-secondary level.

Upper-secondary education covers the age group 16-18 and 19-20. In the reformed post-gymnasium education the following post-gymnasium schools have been operational since the school year 2002/03. General secondary school – ISCED 3a, 46% of all ISCED 3 students in 2004/05 – a three-year programme of full-time education for students aged 16 to 19. After completion students can take the matura examination, which allows for admission to ISCED 5 type of education institutions.

Figure 10.1 The Polish education system, 2000

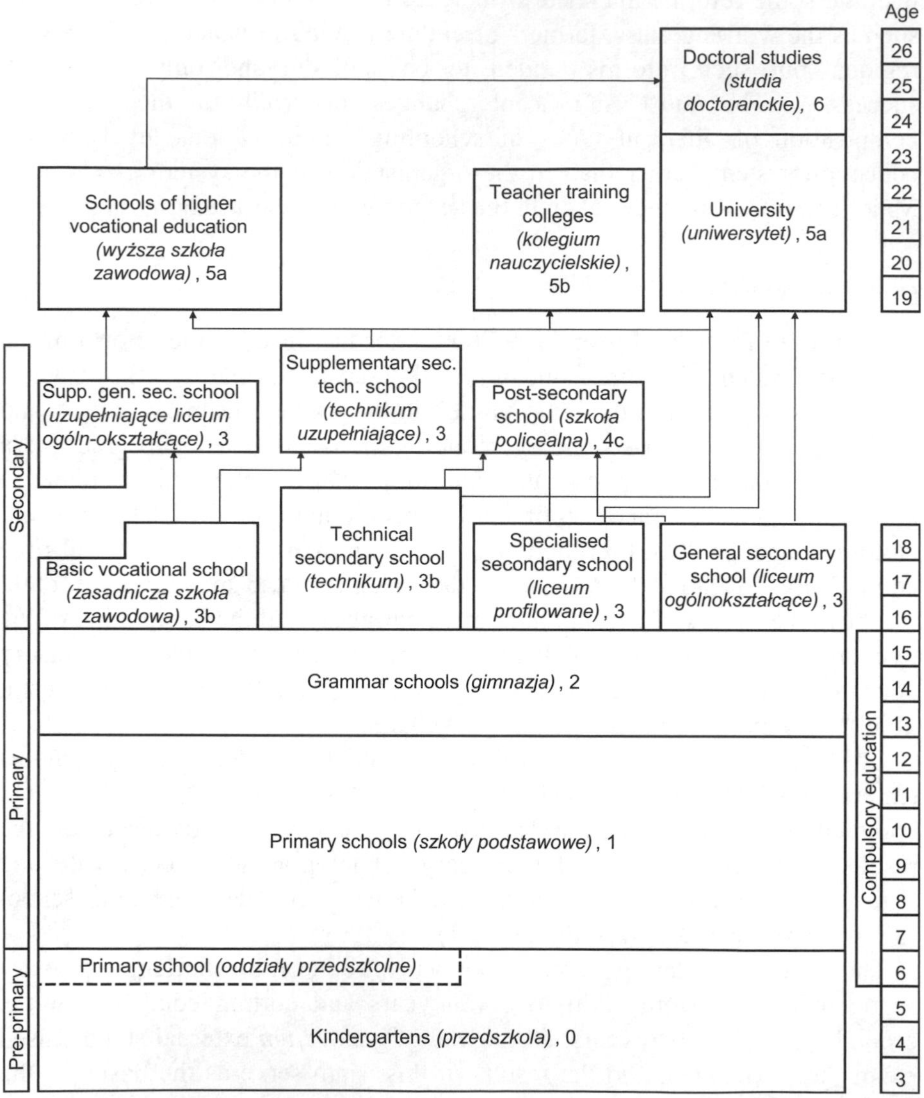

Source: ETF (2000)

Specialised secondary school – ISCED 3a, 15% of all ISCED 3 students in 2004/05 – a new type of school established in 2002/03 offering a three-year, full-time, general programme of upper-secondary education combined with a specialised pre-vocational instruction for students aged 16-19. Students completing this programme can take the matura exam or they can choose to follow specialised vocational training and take vocational exams.

Technical secondary school (technikum) – ISCED 3a, 24% of all ISCED 3 students – a four-year school providing full-time technical and vocational skills needed at the technician level and general education needed for matura examination. Typical students are in the age range of 16-20 years.

Basic vocational school – ISCED 3c, 15% of all ISCED 3 students – a two-to-three-year, part-time programme providing vocational skills needed at the skilled worker level. Students cannot take the matura exam on completion of the basic vocational school, but they can make transition to the supplementary general and technical secondary schools described below.

Supplementary general secondary school – ISCED 3a – a two-year supplementary general secondary school offering full or part-time general upper-secondary education to students graduating from basic vocational schools (ISCED 3c). Students completing supplementary general upper secondary school can take the matura examination.[4]

Supplementary technical secondary school – ISCED 3a – a three-year supplementary technical secondary school offering full or part-time vocational upper-secondary education to students graduating from basic vocational schools (ISCED 3c). Students completing supplementary technical secondary school can take the matura examination.

On completion of the three-year general upper-secondary school, pupils are awarded a graduation certificate based on their grades, without a final examination. The certificate mentions the subjects and the grades obtained at the end of the final year, and gives access to the matura examination or to post-secondary education. At the end of upper-secondary education, pupils may take egzamin dojrzałości (matura), which is non-compulsory and gives access to higher education. Prior to 2005, the matura was arranged by regional education authorities, but the assessment was done by teachers. The new matura was implemented in May 2005 and consists of a written section, prepared and assessed by regional examination commissions, and oral examinations, prepared and assessed by school teachers. The results of the new matura examination currently serve as the basis for admission to higher education institutions, which previously used different selection measures, such as entrance exams, to determine admission.

Because of the type of qualifications they offer, post-secondary schools (ISCED 4c) are actually included as part of secondary education in the Polish classification. Most of them require only a secondary school graduation certificate, not the matura certificate. Post-secondary schools prepare students, mostly women, for work in blue-collar occupations or in occupations and positions that require secondary vocational qualifications.

Graduates from upper-secondary schools in Poland who have obtained the matura certificate have a wide variety of educational possibilities at the level of tertiary education: (1) schools of higher vocational education or three-year teacher training colleges (ISCED 5b) or university-type bachelor's degree studies and (2) university-type master's degree studies (ISCED 5a and 6) of four-and-a-half to six years. The master's and bachelor's degree studies are offered within universities and applied science higher education institutions such as technical universities, schools of economics, medical academies or schools of arts. If graduates of higher vocational schools or from bachelor's degree studies wish to obtain a master's degree or its equivalent, they can undertake supplementary master's degree studies of two to two-and-a-half years. Master's degree holders who wish to obtain a PhD can pursue doctoral studies of three to four years.

Vertical dimension of the education system

Figure 10.2 tracks the trends in educational enrolment of the school-aged population in Poland starting in 1950. The educational participation of baby-boomers from the post-war period and people returning to schooling that was disrupted by the outbreak of Second World War contributed to a high primary education enrolment in 1950s and 1960s. Another baby boom took place in the early 1980s, which led to an increase in primary education later in the decade.

Figure 10.2 The structure of enrolment (%) by type of school in Poland, 1950-2004

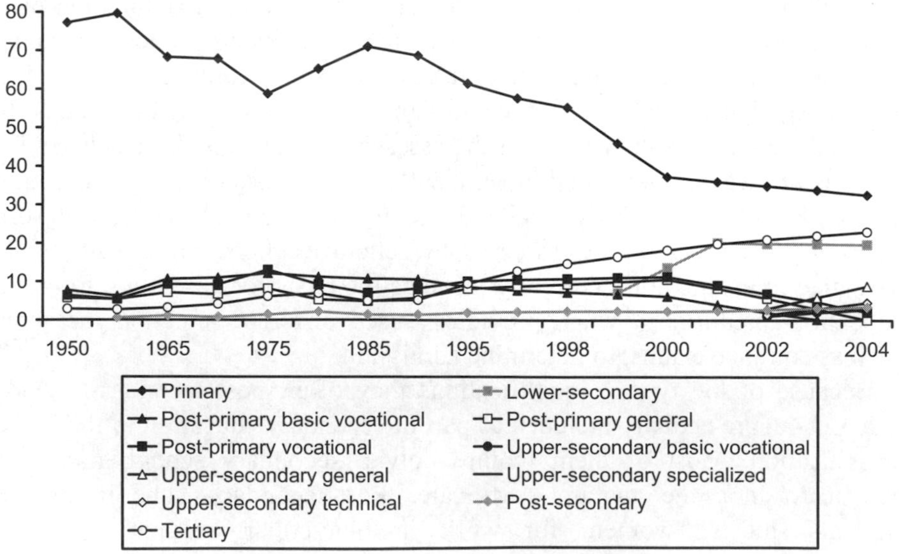

Source: Statistical Office Poland (1966-2006)

In general, however, the proportion of primary school pupils has been on the decline and accounted for only slightly more than 30% of total school enrolment in 2004. Enrolment in post-primary basic vocational education also experienced a spike in the mid-1970s followed by a subsequent decline, recording an overall drop from 7.7% in 1950 to 0.2% in 2003. Some fluctuations are evident for general secondary schooling, as well as vocational programmes. These distortions are not related to the changes in enrolment structure per se, but rather to institutional changes (the reform of primary and secondary schools which shortened primary schooling by two years and introduced lower-secondary schools. At the same time, an increase in enrolment in tertiary education from 2.9% in 1950 to 23% in 2004 is clearly visible. Female participation in tertiary education is higher than for males, and the gap between the two has been growing. According to data provided by Eurostat, the ratio of women graduating from tertiary education (ISCED 5-6) per 100 men grew from 140 in 1998 to nearly 190 in 2004.

Secondary level of education

Stratification and track differentiation

Initial decisions about education in Poland were previously made at the age of 14-15. At this age pupils and their parents faced a choice between continuing general education or selecting vocational options. However, the reforms introduced in 1999-2002 sought to postpone selection of vocational or general tracts, and currently decisions are taken after completion of lower-secondary schools by children aged 15-16. Furthermore, any choice (including specialised secondary schools and, to some extent, basic vocational schools) allows for the pursuit of higher education.

Table 10.1: Secondary enrolment rates by type of school in Poland (%), 1990-2005

	1990	1995	2000	2005
Basic vocational	34.0	27.2	19.5	12.2
Secondary general	18.6	25.9	33.5	54.3
Upper secondary	22.2	27.0	31.0	23.7

Source: Statistical Office of Poland (2005)

Participation in basic vocational education and training (VET) schools decreased considerably in Poland, as is noticeable from Table 10.1. The extreme narrowness of vocational profiles, coupled with the bad image of VET, led to a radical policy reorientation in favour of general education and decreasing the role of vocational education in the second half of the 1990s. There was a significant shift from basic vocational schools to general secondary schools, but the enrolment rates in technical schools remained roughly stable. Specialised secondary schools were also introduced. These changes reflected not only results of the reform, but also the growing aspirations of youth to follow education in the tertiary sector.

Organisation of vocational training

Vocational training previously took place either in school workshops, practical training centres or enterprises. Before the transition, all types of vocational schools, even schools with their own workshops, organised part of their training inside enterprises. Most schools developed relationships with local enterprises. However, the VET system has almost completely collapsed in the course of economic and enterprise restructuring. Most enterprises withdrew from any cooperation with schools, and VET became far more school-based. The infrastructure of school workshops, which had formerly provided practical vocational education, was underinvested in and outdated. In 1996, the concept of practical training centres (CKPs) was launched. These centres provide practical education and training facilities with modern equipment, offering more up-to-date training to young people and adults, as well as specialised training for teachers. The core activities of CKPs are financed by the state budget, and they are authorised to conduct vocational examinations. However, at the beginning of 2002 there were still only 125 CKPs (ETF, 2002).

A specific form of basic VET education is the apprenticeship system managed by the by the Polish Craft Association. Craft organisations belonging to the association run their own schools and cooperate with vocational schools and training centres. Young workers can sign an agreement with an employer on vocational preparation, and on examination they can obtain the title of apprentice or skilled worker. Approximately 60,000 graduates annually obtain vocational qualification in 126 craft occupations in the apprenticeship system managed by the association (ETF, 2002).

Standardisation and quality differentiation of secondary education

Before the transition Polish education was characterised by a high degree of centralised control over finances, staff, curricula and number of students. The structural changes in the labour market, which caused some occupations to vanish and created many new ones, revealed a necessity to provide new vocational standards. Only recently have some actions been taken to establish new standards of vocational qualifications. Furthermore, some shifts towards greater standardisation have been seen in the general secondary schooling, with lower-secondary schools and the new *matura* exam being externally organised. Before the transition, the *matura* was only a basic requirement for taking entrance exams, but now the results of the *matura* serve as a basis for assessment and selection for tertiary education institutions.

Tertiary level of education

Horizontal dimension

Figure 10.3 examines the horizontal differentiation of the education system at the tertiary level. It also allows for the comparison of the distribution of students in various fields in the 1990s and first years of the new millennium.

Figure 10.3: Enrolment in tertiary education (%) by field of study in Poland, 1990-2004

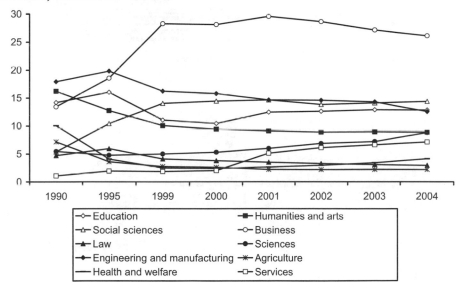

Source: Statistical Office of Poland (1990-2004)

A dramatic increase in the popularity of business specialties is evident, particularly in the late 1990s. While in 1990 slightly less than 15% of all students were enrolled in business, in 2001 the proportion was as high as 30%. An increase is also observed in social sciences (from 5% in 1990 to about 15% in 2004), in services (from 1.1% to 7.1%) and sciences (from 5.5% to 8.8%). In contrast, the following fields of study experienced a decrease in their popularity: humanities and arts, engineering, manufacturing and construction, agriculture and law.

Figure 10.4 sheds further light on female representation in various fields and the trend in this regard in the period 1990-2004. Female-dominated fields are education, humanities and the arts, health and welfare and social sciences. Engineering, manufacturing and construction are male-dominated fields, but there is an increasing trend towards more women entering these fields of education. Similarly, services were dominated by men in the early 1990s, but in 2004 almost half of all students in this field were women. Sciences, on the other hand, have increasingly become a male-dominated field since the turn of the millennium, whereas in the early 1990s females constituted the majority in this field. Finally, law, business and agriculture can be considered mixed fields.

Figure 10.4: Proportion of females in tertiary education by selected fields of study in Poland, 1990-2004

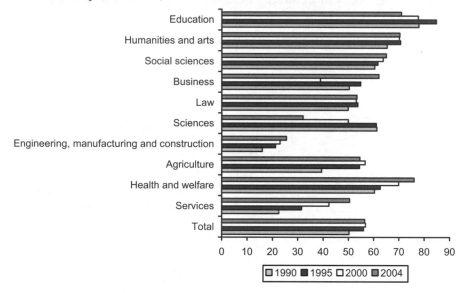

Source: Statistical Office Poland (1990-2004)

Standardisation, quality differentiation and openness of tertiary education

Poland had one of the highest indices of change in tertiary enrolment in the second half of the 1990s. These changes were enabled by reforms in tertiary education introduced in the early 1990s that allowed new education providers to enter the market and to become fully recognised higher education institutions.

The number of non-public higher education institutions grew rapidly between 1990 and 2004. Whereas in 1990 there were no private higher education institutions at all, in 1995/96 there were 45%, in 2000/01 there were 63% and in 2004/05 70% of all higher education institutions were private (Statistical Office Poland, 2005). By 1997 the number of non-public institutions had surpassed for the first time the number of public institutions (World Bank, 2004), and there are now about twice as many private as public higher education institutions in the tertiary sector.

Considering the rapid expansion of the private tertiary sector, some concerns were raised about the quality and standardisation of education services, but the institutional reaction to this challenge came quite late; the State Accreditation Committee was only established in 2002. Its primary objective is to ensure that all new and existing higher education institutions meet quality criteria in teaching particular fields of study. It aims at evaluating all degree programmes, a negative opinion of which could lead to the Minister of Education revoking or suspending the licence for offering higher education courses (O'Brian and Paczynski, 2006).

The Constitution of the Republic of Poland guarantees that higher education is free of charge for full-time day courses in public sector institutions, but there are many exceptions to this rule. The majority of public higher education institutions organise fee-paying extra-mural or part-time evening classes. Although public universities are legally required to limit their intake of fee-paying students to less than 50%, in many cases this requirement is ignored. The result is that the number of paying students, from both public and non-public tertiary education institutions, exceeds the number of non-paying students (Table 10.2). Overall, tuition fees in either state or non-state establishments of higher education vary greatly, and the amount depends not only on the real cost of studies, but also on the demand for different fields of study.

Table 10.2: Proportion of students attending tuition and free of charge courses in Poland, 1995-2002 (column %)

	1995	2002
Students in non-public schools	11	29
Students in public schools paying tuition	35	31
Students studying free of charge	53	39

Source: Sztandar-Sztanderska et al (2004)

Labour market

Economic development

In 1989, Poland regained its independence after almost 50 years under socialist rule. At this time, Poland ranged in the middle of CEE countries in terms of GDP per capita. At the beginning of the transition, Poland was over-industrialised by Western standards and undersupplied with services like many other CEE countries. In particular, Poland was and is still characterised by a large share of agricultural employment reflecting an archaic employment structure. After the fall of the Iron Curtain, Poland profited from the early economic and social reforms. Starting in 1990, Poland's GDP registered only a weak decline in real terms (Figure 10.5). This transitional recession peaked at −7% in 1991, representing one of the weakest recessions in CEE countries after 1990. The relatively mild transition problems in Poland are explained by the country's stronger and earlier orientation towards Western Europe and its implementation of structural reforms aiming at the transformation of the economy and creating macroeconomic stability.

Figure 10.5: GDP growth, 1991-2006

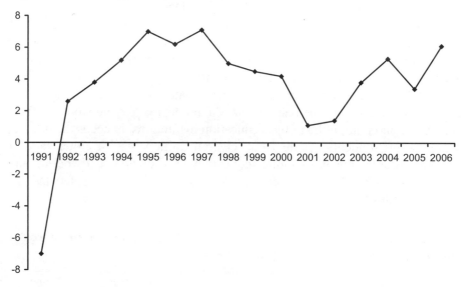

Source: ILO (2008); data for 2006 from Eurostat (2008)

The reforms started with price and trade liberalisation in the early 1990s (Blanchard, 1994). Most price controls were removed at the beginning of the 1990s, resulting in an increase in inflation because relative prices adjusted to relative scarcities. In successive years, inflation steadily decreased to single-digit levels (UNICEF, 2007). During the transition, a legal base was established to promote the development of the private sector. The Polish privatisation process was characterised by a large degree of transparency, which made claims of unfair treatment, typical in other countries, rare in Poland (OECD, 2001).

The Polish economy recovered very quickly from the initial recession and had already regained positive growth rates by 1992. The initial economic contraction was followed by rapid growth of more than five percentage points annually from 1994 until 1997. During the mid-1990s, Poland was one of the most successful transition countries in the field of macroeconomic stabilisation. The expansion was followed by a short decline in real GDP per capita at the end of the decade due to the Russian crisis. A further wave of large-scale privatisation and product market deregulation started in 1998, and the launch of four important structural reforms related to public finances took place in 1999. The growth rates remained high at about 4%. While in most CEE countries economic growth stabilised on a high level within one or two years after the subsidence of the Russian shock, Poland entered another, this time longer, phase of slowed growth that had a cyclical character (Bukowski et al, 2005a). A recovery started to materialise in 2004 and growth rates increased substantially from 1.1% in 2001 to 6.1% in 2006.

Although Poland suffered from a degree of economic and social turbulence in the early 1990s, its rapid transformation into a liberal market economy was rewarded by annual real-income gains from about 1992 on, apart from two temporary setbacks in 1999 and 2001/02. Hence, Poland ranges among the most successful of the formerly centrally planned economies.

Labour market dynamics

Employment dynamics

In 1990, 25.2% of employed individuals worked in agriculture, 37% in industry and only 35.8% in services (ILO, 2008). This initial pattern reflects a share of employment in agriculture five times higher than in the EU15. After the transition, agricultural employment was a source of secondary income and an employment opportunity of last resort for laid-off workers and pensioners. Farmers' lack of additional skills outside agriculture reduced labour mobility out of this sector (Bukowski et al, 2005b). During the transition period, employment in agriculture decreased slightly from 25.2% in 1994 to 17.4% in 2005, a value that is still much larger than the Western European Union (EU) average. The agricultural share of gross value added (GVA) is much lower than the share of agricultural workers (ILO, 2008). This reflects a large degree of economic inefficiency in agriculture and a slow adjustment of agriculture to new economic conditions.

The employment share of industry and construction decreased steadily during the entire transition period from 37% in 1990 to 29.2% in 2005 (ILO, 2008). The industrial sector was characterised by a predominance of large enterprises, especially in heavy industry and engineering. There was a gradual decline of certain industrial sectors, particularly the heavy industry sector, as well as the textile and leather industries (ETF, 2003). The service sector's share of total employment has been steadily increasing from 35.8% in 1990 to 53.4% in 2005. However, it still represents a lower level than in most OECD (Organisation for Economic Co-operation and Development) countries. Employment growth in services can be ascribed to growth in financial services, public administration and hotels and restaurants, among others (Kwiatkowski et al, 2001).

Figure 10.6 reveals that labour force participation rates of the population aged 15-64 sharply declined from 72.1% in 1990 to 63.2% in 2005. In terms of participation rates, the transitional period can be divided into two sub-periods. Until 1995, there was a relatively sharp decline in the participation rate.

Figure 10.6: Labour force participation rate (age group 15-64), 1990-2006

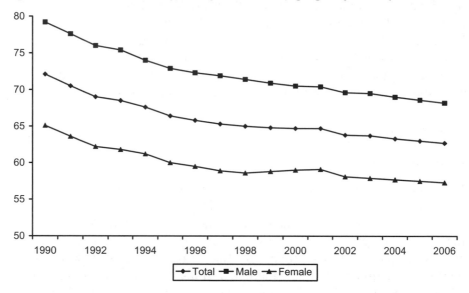

Source: ILO (2008)

A large share of the employment decline was accounted for by early retirements. As time has passed, however, layoffs have become increasingly important, and during the mid-1990s they accounted for more than half of work terminations in state firms. Unemployment rose rapidly partly due to workers being laid-off from state enterprises, but to an even greater extent as a result of remarkably low outflow rates from unemployment to jobs (Góra and Lehmann, 1995; Boeri and Terrell, 2002).

After 1995, participation rates decreased more slowly as a result of rapid economic expansion during the mid-1990s. At the same time, some attempts to limit access to social security benefits, such as reforming the disability system, were made. However, these actions decreased the inflow of new beneficiaries while workers, who already had received entitlement to these benefits, continued to receive the benefits. As a result, labour force participation rates remained extremely low not only compared to the EU15, but also in comparison to the new EU members from Central and Eastern Europe.

Figure 10.6 also shows gender-specific time trends in labour force participation. Both male and female labour force participation reflect the same evolution pattern over time, but female labour force participation rates were roughly 11-14 percentage points below that of men. The lack of participation by females is especially prevalent among women over 50 because of gender and occupation-specific early retirement schemes. The difference between the labour force participation of young women in Poland and in the EU15 is much less pronounced, and women in prime age are even more frequently active in Poland than in Western European countries (Bukowski et al, 2005b).

In 2006, the lowest activity rate was registered for the youngest age cohorts (15-24 years) with 32.7% participation (Table 10.3). The activity rate of the population aged between 15 and 24 fell from 49.4% to 32.7% between 1990 and 2006. To some extent, this development is related to increasing enrolment in education (UNDP, 2004). In contrast, the activity rates of middle-age cohorts declined by four percentage points over the transition period to reach 81% in 2006. Participation rates of people aged 65 and over decreased from 20.2% in 1990 to 5.3% in 2006, representing relatively high values compared to the EU15. The high participation rate in the oldest age group is related to the high agricultural employment share.

Table 10.3: Labour force participation rate by age group, 1990-2006

	1990	1995	2000	2006
15+	65.1	58.5	56.1	53.6
15-24	49.4	38.8	36.5	32.7
25-54	85.9	84.1	82.5	81.1
55-64	47.4	35.8	31.3	31.9
65+	20.2	11.4	7.9	5.3

Source: ILO (2008)

Labour market flexibilisation

Part-time work is significantly less prevalent in Poland than in the EU15 but more pronounced than in other CEE countries; the share of part-time employment hovered around 10% in Poland between 1998 and 2006. Until the late 1990s, fixed-term contracts and temporary work played a minor role, but after the turn of the millennium, the share of temporary employment grew rapidly, reaching a level well above the EU15 average. Self-employment remains stable at relatively high levels, fluctuating at around 21%-23% (ILO, 2008). Self-employment is concentrated in agriculture and is less developed in industry and services. The share of non-salaried family workers remained very high at around 5%-6%, which can also be explained by the high share of agricultural employment.

Unemployment dynamics

Official registered unemployment, measured as a share of the active population, was already high at the beginning of the transition period with 6.5% in 1990, despite the fact that unemployment was an unknown phenomenon during the communist era (Figure 10.7). In general, Poland suffered from an increase in unemployment rates that peaked twice: at 16.4% in 1993, following the transitional recession, and at 18% in 1999-2002, after the Russian crisis.

In Figure 10.7 the evolution of registered unemployed is compared with the evolution of Labour Force Survey (LFS) unemployment. Whereas the former captures all individuals who register officially in order to become eligible for unemployment benefits, the latter is a self-assessed measure. From 1992-96, the rate of registered unemployment was higher than LFS unemployment. Yet when the criteria for awarding unemployment benefits changed, the relative positions of the two measures changed as well. In general, the evolution patterns of both unemployment rates are identical, both displaying two significant increases during the two economic recessions and continuation of a high level in the new millennium. Interestingly, LFS unemployment displays a strong decline in the last few years from 19.9% in 2002 to 13.8% in 2006.

In Poland, as in many other countries, young people constitute the age group at highest risk of unemployment. The unemployment rate of people aged 25 or younger increased from 27.8% in 1992 to 40.8% in 2004; this level is about two to three times higher than the average unemployment rate for the entire adult population (ILO, 2008).

Figure 10.7: Unemployment rates, 1990-2006

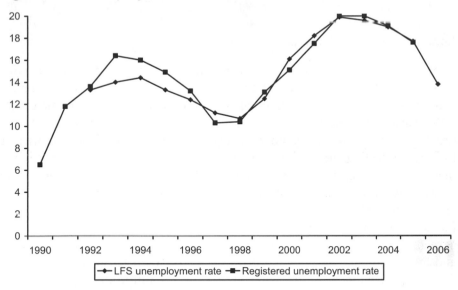

Note: Registered unemployment individuals to individuals aged between 18 and 64 and LFS unemployment refers to individuals aged over 15.
Source: ILO (2008); LFS unemployment rate for 2006 from Eurostat (2008)

Regional differences

There are considerable regional differences in unemployment patterns in Poland. Unemployment rates are highest in the relatively sparsely populated, low-income and low-education agricultural regions in the north and northeast of Poland and lowest in the regions surrounding Warsaw and in the southeast of the country (OECD, 2004b; Bornhorst and Commander, 2006). Regional differences in unemployment rates can be explained by different levels of economic development, sectoral structure and historical differences due to the changes in Polish borders throughout history. Magda and Zawistowski (2006) differentiate several clusters of Polish regions. For example, unproductive agricultural regions are characterised by a low degree of urbanisation, low GDP per capita, low wages and poor labour market performance. There are also regions that 'inherited' poor economic conditions because of the previous dominance of socialist collective agricultural farms and towns in which development seems to be limited due to structural problems. Regions named as 'centres of development' enjoy high employment and high wages. Nearby 'suburban poviats' are created and benefit from the rapid development of the 'centres of development'. The suburban areas attract employees who work in the centres but choose to live in the suburbs and commute because of a crowded housing market in the regions that develop most rapidly.

Labour market institutions

The Labour Code in Poland was gradually adjusted during the transition period in order to better fit the reformed labour market, which no longer consisted of huge state-owned companies that guaranteed employment with little concern for productivity and profitability. As a result, Polish labour regulations are currently similar to legislation in many other countries in Europe, protecting the positions of incumbent workers in large firms but at the same time offering some room for flexible employment. The labour legislation based on the Labour Code of 1975 underwent essential changes in 1989 (before the transformation), in 1994 and again in 1996. Industrial relations were most strongly shaped in 1994 when, for example, collective agreements with respect to wages became widespread at the enterprise level and the government lost most of its influence on the determination of wages. The 1996 amendment to the labour law regulated uniformity of employment in both the public and private sectors. Furthermore, the amendments to the Labour Code introduced at the beginning of the new millennium provided regulations for temporary and fixed-term contracts. The Polish Labour Code has specific rules that apply to youth. Employment of children aged 15 or younger is forbidden, and special regulations limit the number of working hours and the type of work that can be assigned to young workers aged 16-18 – apprenticeships or tasks are allowed that are not connected with a health risk.

Employment protection legislation

Dismissal procedures are relatively uncomplicated; for example, lack of skills or economic factors constitute justified reasons for dismissal, and the definition of the unjustified dismissal covers a very narrow range of reasons (Baranowska et al, 2005). The average notice period is short, and severance payment is low if the termination of employment is caused by the employee.

Poland tends to be as restrictive concerning regular employment contracts as the EU average, which is lower than the CEE average (see Table 2.7 in Chapter Two of this book). Regulation concerning temporary employment is less rigid in Poland than in the EU, but it is on the increase. In contrast, Poland's firing rules concerning collective dismissals are more restrictive than in EU. In general, the comparison of overall employment protection legislation (EPL) reveals that, as a result of significant liberalisation efforts, Poland has a lower average level of EPL strictness than the EU.

Industrial relations

Prior to 1990, Poland's industrial relations systems were characterised by central political and managerial control exercised by the state. During the transition, Poland, along with many other CEE countries, moved away from a centralised wage-setting system towards a collective bargaining system in the enterprise sector. Wage bargaining usually takes place at company level or to a lesser extent at sectoral level whereas the regional or national level bargaining does not exist (Visser, 2004: Table 1.8).

Union membership sharply declined during the 1990s from the 100% coverage of the workforce registered at the beginning of transition. According to Van Gyes et al (2007: Figure 2), the Polish unionisation rate decreased from 33% in 1995 to 17% in 2004. The decrease is, in general, attributed to the shift towards free choice of union membership status, falling living standards over the 1990s, high levels of unemployment, privatisation, growing numbers of small businesses and sectoral shifts. The degree of unionisation is, in general, lower in the private than in the public sector, where trade unions have been conducting centralised negotiations since 1994 within the Tripartite Commission (Baranowska et al, 2005).

Even more important than the number of unionised workers is the coverage by collective agreements. Van Gyes et al (2007: Figure 4) estimate the percentage of employees covered by collective agreements in Poland to be 35% in 2002, representing a medium level of union coverage compared to other CEE countries. Furthermore, the degree of coordination in Poland lies at the lowest level compared to other CEE countries (Visser, 2004: Table 1.10). The same picture appears for the degree of centralisation, which is the lowest in CEE countries (Visser, 2004: Table 1.9).

Welfare regime

Labour market policy

Active labour market policy

Active labour market policies (ALMPs) refer to expenditure on activities for the unemployed that are geared to help them back into work. These comprise preventive and employability-oriented strategies like training measures, subsidies or credits to facilitate (re-)integration into labour market, job search assistance and special measures for disadvantaged groups such as those with disabilities and youth. During the early transition period, labour market policy in Poland was characterised by the tendency to finance passive measures and by low expenditure on active measures.

Public works and subsidised job creation schemes were the main ALMP measures in Poland in terms of participants and expenditures. Public works are aimed mainly at the economic development of a region and provision of employment to long-term unemployed with lower education levels. Subsidised employment schemes aim to reduce the unemployment level by providing temporary employment to the unemployed and a scenario for possible permanent employment (Kwiatkowski et al, 2001). However, expenditure on public works programmes have dropped since the mid-1990s. Training to ensure that unqualified individuals learn skills in line with labour market demand has been used modestly.

Graduate activation programmes encompassing internships for youth without professional experience, vocational training, grants to continue education as well as reimbursement of travel costs have enjoyed growing popularity (Baranowska et al, 2005), and since 2000, their share has been the largest in the total spending on ALMP.

Altogether, ALMP plays a very small role in Poland with expenditure of approximately 0.18% of GDP in 2000 (European Commission, 2001). By comparison, such spending in OECD countries ranged from 0.09% of GDP in Japan to about 2% in Sweden. In 2004, around 40% of ALMP expenditure was devoted to youth measures. Public works still account for 20% of ALMP expenditure, whereas the expenditure share for training measures remains under 10%. Approximately 20% of expenditure is spent on subsidised job creation schemes. Limited activities and resources have been allocated to evaluating the impact and effectiveness of active employment measures.

Unemployment insurance[5]

At the beginning of the transformation, a system of unemployment benefit was created. Initially, it was quite generous and the criteria for receiving benefit were not strict; during the transition period, however, many amendments were introduced, including:

* reducing the duration of the unemployment benefit payment period, from an open-ended scheme with virtually no duration limit to 12 months;
* moving from an earnings-related to a flat-rate scheme;
* differentiating the level and duration of payment of unemployment benefit according to the regional unemployment rate;
* tightening the eligibility criteria;
* altering how particular groups (graduates and workers in pre-retirement age) are treated.

At the beginning of transition, the level of unemployment benefit depended on the recipient's last pay check. The benefit decreased gradually over the period of unemployment, starting at 70% of the level of the last pay check during the first three months of unemployment, then dropping to 50% during the subsequent six months, and finally to 40% thereafter. The benefit could be neither lower than the minimum wage nor higher than the average wage. A 12-month limit for receipt of unemployment benefit was introduced, but the limit could be extended for job seekers with long job tenure. In 1992, the flat-rate benefit amounting to 36% of the national average wage was introduced, but there were several exceptions; for example, in the so-called crisis regions where the unemployment rate was particularly high, the unemployed received higher benefits amounting to 52% of the national average wage. After 1996, the amount of unemployment benefit was defined in cash terms at the level of about one third the average wage at the time, and it was envisaged that this amount would be adjusted according to inflation.

No major changes were introduced to the unemployment system after the turn of the millennium. As in the second half of the 1990s, the waiting period in the new millennium amounted to seven days after registration,[6] and the duration of payment in regular cases remained 12 months (18 months in crisis regions). Eligibility criteria included age (18-59 or 64 years of age) and income. Unemployed people still earning more than half the minimum wage through other means were not entitled to receive benefits. Those eligible for old-age or disability pension or other social security allowances could not receive unemployment benefit. Furthermore, benefit recipients could not own more than two hectares of arable land. Refusing a job offer, training, intervention or public work, as well as not reporting to the labour office, resulted in loss of entitlement to unemployment benefit. In order to receive benefit, an unemployed person must have contributed to the system by earning at least the minimum wage for 365 days during the 18 months prior to applying for unemployment benefit.

It is estimated that the unemployment benefit scheme in Poland covered about 56% of the labour force in the second half of 1990s and about 53% of the labour force in the first half of the first decade of the new millennium. The replacement ratio (measured as the ratio of unemployment benefit to the average wage) decreased slightly (by 2%) over the same period.

Minimum wage

Poland's legal minimum wage is set at the national level and ranks in the middle of the OECD countries with a minimum wage at around 45% of the average wage, but relatively few employees (4% in 2002) work for the minimum wage (Baranowska et al, 2005). Employers have the right to reduce wages to below the minimum wage for labour market entrants, e.g. to 80% of the minimum wage for the first year of employment and 90% in the second year.

Family policy

Institutional description

The burden of childcare in Poland falls to a great extent on families. In the 1990s, the necessity to cut public expenditure contributed to the reduction of institutional family support. Between 1989 and 2003, the number of children admitted to crèches declined by 76% and to nursery schools by 25% (Balcerzak-Paradowska et al, 2003). After institutional childcare administration was decentralised, local authorities were often not provided with the necessary funds, and fees were therefore introduced; in 1994, the fees paid by parents amounted to 20% of crèches' and 40% kindergartens' incomes, rising to 30% in both cases in 2001 (Balcerzak-Paradowska et al, 2003). Childcare fees amount to approximately 8.5%-30% of an average monthly wage (Plomien, 2005).

The minimum working day for kindergartens and pre-school classes in schools is five hours, but most kindergartens are open for approximately nine hours a day, five days a week. Kindergartens and schools are open throughout the school year and remain closed during the two-month summer holidays.

Expenditure

The low level of institutional childcare support is reflected in the level and structure of public expenditure. The in-kind benefits on pre-primary childcare amounted to about 0.4%-0.5% of GDP in 2003. The in-cash benefits amounted to over 0.9% of GDP and approximately 33% of total family policy expenditures (OECD, 2007a). The structure of expenditure indicates that state support is focused more on income maintenance than on facilitating reconciliation of parenthood and paid work. In Poland, the ratio of in-cash to in-kind expenditures is two to one, much lower than in other European countries but higher than in most other CEE countries.

Public childcare enrolment

In 2004, the enrolment rates of three-year-olds in pre-primary education amounted to 26.2%, 35.7% among four-year-olds and 46.2% for five-year-olds (OECD, 2007b). There are regional differences in enrolment rates, with the greatest disparities between eastern and western Poland and between rural and urban areas. To some extent, these disparities reflect not only the accessibility of institutional support for childcare, but also the limited demand for these facilities (O'Brien and Paczynski, 2006). Empirical studies suggest that although low enrolment rates in pre-primary education are partly the result of low quality and availability of childcare facilities, social norms and attitudes may also play a role (Plomien, 2005; Kotowska et al, 2007).

Social assistance[7]

The social assistance system has undergone deep changes over the past two decades; for simplicity, the following description is focused on the availability of benefits in the new millennium with the reference individual defined as a childless person with no income. The decision on whether to grant benefits (or other forms of support) was based not only on documentation of the financial situation of the individual or family, but also on the results of an interview conducted by a social worker. The minimum income threshold for receiving social assistance benefits in 2004 was 461 PLN for a singe person household and 316 PLN per family member in other households. Total benefits received could not exceed 418 PLN. The social security benefits granted to the reference individual were temporary allowances, the level of which was set to the difference in the minimum income threshold and the income received by the given person, meaning that the reference individual would receive 418 PLN (OECD, 2004a).

Other eligibility criteria include the stipulation that only individuals aged 18 or older are entitled to apply for social assistance, as well as the notion of 'dysfunctionality', which refers to conditions such as unemployment, being orphaned, homeless, having physical or mental impairment, chronic disease and alcohol and drug addiction (Pietka, 2003). Individuals who do not claim allowances based on disability must register at the labour office and be ready and willing to take up employment. As is the case with unemployment benefit, refusal of a job offer may lead to suspension or denial of social assistance benefits.

Intergenerational transfers

Intergenerational transfers play an important role in informal welfare provision in Poland. Asking for family support remained the most common strategy when facing financial difficulties; between 1992 and 2005, approximately 35%-43% of Polish households reported requesting assistance from family when unable to make ends meet (Czapiński, 1998; Czapiński and Panek, 2006). On the contrary, receiving social assistance from the state was reported by a mere 6%-7% between 1992-97, and although it increased to 12% from 2000-05, it seems that social networks prevail in providing financial aid.

Private financial transfers in Poland follow a specific pattern, with the households of young people being most likely to be the recipients of such transfers (Cox et al, 1997; Kotowska et al, 2007). Young people are also supported by family through shared living arrangements and services like childcare.

Notes

[1] This section is based on Heyns and Bialecki (1993).

[2] This section is based on Eurydice (2006, 2007) and ETF (2002) publications.

[3] Since 1997 the constitution has required that, up to the age of 18, at least part-time education should continue, either in school or out of school.

[4] Supplementary general secondary schools and supplementary technical secondary schools were introduced in 2004/05.

[5] This section is based on Góra and Schmidt (1998) and OECD country chapters on benefits and wages (various issues).

[6] The unemployed who voluntarily terminated their contract with employers had a longer waiting period – 90 days from the date of registration in the late 1990s and 90-180 days in the first years of the new millennium.

[7] This section is based on Bukowski et al (2006).

References

Balcerowicz, L. (1994) 'Transition to the market economy: Poland, 1989-93 in comparative perspective', *Economic Policy*, vol 9, no 19, Supplement: lessons for Reform, pp 71-97.

Balcerzak-Paradowska, B., Chłoń-Domińczak, A., Kotowska, I., Olejniczuk-Merta, A., Topińska, I. and Woycicka, I. (2003) 'The gender dimension of the social security reform in Poland', in E. Fultz, M. Ruck and S. Steinhilber (eds) *The gender dimensions of social security reform in Europe: case studies of the Czech Republic, Hungary and Poland*, Budapest: ILO.

Baranowska, A., Bukowski, M., Gorski, A., Lewandowski, P., Magda, I. and Zawistowski, J. (2005) 'Labour market institutions', in M. Bukowski (ed) *Employment in Poland 2005*, Warsaw: Ministry of Economy and Labour, pp 95-210.

Blanchard, O. (1994) 'Transition in Poland', *The Economic Journal*, vol 104, no 426, pp 1169-77.

Boeri, T. and Terrell, K. (2002) 'Institutional determinants of labor reallocation in transition', *The Journal of Economic Perspectives*, vol 16, no 1, pp 51-76.

Bornhorst, F. and Commander, S. (2006) 'Regional unemployment and persistence in transition countries', *The Economics of Transition*, vol 14, no 2, pp 269-88.

Bukowski, M., Kowal, P., Lewandowski, P. and Zawistowski, J. (2006) 'Struktura i poziom wydatków i dochodów sektora finansów publicznych a sytuacja na rynku pracy: doświadczenia międzynarodowe i wnioski dla polski' ('The level and structure of expenditures and revenues of the central government and the situation on the labour market'), Warsaw: The National Bank of Poland.

Bukowski, M., Lewandowski, P., Magda, I. and Zawistowski, J. (2005a) 'Employment and growth', in M. Bukowski (ed) *Employment in Poland 2005*, Warsaw: Ministry of Economy and Labour, pp 21-46.

Bukowski, M., Lewandowski, P., Magda, I. and Zawistowski, J. (2005b) 'Structural characteristics of the Polish labour market', in M. Bukowski (ed) *Employment in Poland 2005*, Warsaw: Ministry of Economy and Labour, pp 49-94.

Cox, D., Jimenez E. and Okrasa W. (1997) 'Family safety nets and economic transition: a study of worker households in Poland', *Review of Income and Wealth*, vol 43, no 2, pp 191-209.

Czapiński, J. (1998) *Jakość życia Polaków w czasie zmiany społecznej* (*The quality of life In Poland in the times of social change*), Warsaw: Institute for Social Studies, University of Warsaw.

Czapiński, J. and Panek, T. (2006) *Diagnoza społeczna 2005* (*Social diagnosis 2005*), Warsaw: Social Monitoring Council.

de Melo, M., Denizer, C. and Gelb, A. 'Patterns of transition from plan to market', *The World Bank Economic Review*, vol 10, no 3, pp 397-424.

ETF (European Training Foundation) (2000) *Vocational education and training in Central and Eastern Europe: key indicators,* Luxembourg: Office for Official Publications of the European Communities.

ETF (2002) *Monographs candidate countries: vocational education and training and employment services in Poland*, Torino: ETF.

ETF (2003) *Short country report Poland*, Torino: ETF.

European Commission (2001) *Joint assessment of employment priorities in Poland*, Luxembourg: Office for Official Publications of the European Communities.

Eurostat (2008) *Data: labour market*, Luxembourg: Eurostat (http://epp.eurostat.ec.europa.eu).

Eurydice (2006, 2007) *The database on education systems in Europe. Poland*, Brussels: Eurydice European Unit (www.eurydice.org/portal/page/portal/Eurydice/EuryCountry).

Góra, M. and Lehmann, H. (1995) 'How divergent is regional labour market adjustment in Poland?', in M. Góra and H. Lehmann (eds) *The regional dimension of unemployment in transition countries: a challenge for labour market and social policies*, Paris: OECD.

Góra, M. and Schmid, C.M. (1998) 'Long-term unemployment, unemployment benefits and social assistance: the Polish experience', *Empirical Economics*, vol 23, no 1, pp 55-85.

Heyns, B. and Bialecki, I. (1993) 'Inequality in education in post-war Poland', in H.-P. Blossfield and Y. Shavit (eds) *Persistent inequality: changing educational attainment in thirteen countries*, Boulder, CO: Westview Press.

ILO (International Labour Organization) (2008) *Key indicators of the labour market programme*, Fifth Edition, Geneva: ILO.

Kwiatkowski, E., Socha, M. and Sztanderska, U. (2001) *Labour market flexibility and employment security: Poland*, ILO Employment Papers No 28, Geneva: ILO.

Kotowska, I., Sztanderska, U. and Wóycicka, I. (eds) (2007) *Aktywność zawodowa i edukacyjna a obowiązki rodzinne w Polsce* (*Economic and educational activity and family duties in Poland*), Warsaw: The Gdańsk Institute for Market Economics.

Magda, I. and Zawistowski, J. (2006) 'Regional labour markets', in M. Bukowski (ed) *Employment in Poland 2005*, Warsaw: Ministry of Economy and Labour, pp 73-114.

O'Brien, P. and Paczynski, W. (2006) *Poland's education and training: boosting and adapting human capital*, OECD Economics Department Working Paper No 495, OECD.

OECD (Organisation for Economic Co-operation and Development) (2001) *Economic Surveys: Poland*, Paris: OECD.

OECD (2004a) *Benefits and Wages: Polish country chapter.* (www.oecd.org/document/0/0.3343.en_264934637340532481111.00.html).

OECD (2004b) *Economic surveys: Poland*, Paris: OECD.

OECD (2007a) *Social expenditure database (SOCX)*, Paris: OECD (www.oecd.org/els/social/expenditure).

293

OECD (2007b) *Family database*, Paris: OECD (www.oecd.org/els/social/expenditure).

Pietka, K. (2003) 'Social protection in Poland', Manuscript prepared for the EU8 social inclusion study, Washington DC: World Bank.

Plomien, A. (2005) *Reconciliation of work and private life in Poland*, Luxembourg: Office for Official Publications of the European Communities.

Sachs, J. (1996) 'The transition at mid decade', *The American Economic Review*, vol 86, no 2, pp 128-33.

Statistical Office Poland (2005) *Oświata i wychowanie w roku szkolnym 2005/2006 (Schooling and education in 2005/2006)*, Warsaw: Statistical Office Poland.

Statistical Office Poland (1966-2006) *Statistical yearbook Poland*, Warsaw: Statistical Office Poland.

Sztandar-Sztanderska, U., Minkiewicz, B. and Bąba, M. (2004) *Oferta szkolnictwa wyższego a wymagania rynku pracy (Higher education sector offer and labour market requirements)*, Warsaw: Institute of Knowledge Society.

UNDP (United Nations Development Programme) (2004) *W trosce O pracę: raport o rozwoju społecznym polska (Working out employment: human development report Poland)*, Warsaw: UNDP.

UNICEF (United Nations International Children's Emergency Fund) (2007) *TransMONEE 2007 database*, Florence: UNICEF Innocenti Research Centre (http://www.unicef-icdc.org/resources/transmonee.html).

Van Gyes, G., Vandenbrande, T., Lehndorff, S., Schilling, G., Schief, S. and Kohl, H. (2007) *Industrial relations in EU member states 2000-2004*, Dublin: European Foundation for the Improvement of Living and Working Conditions.

Visser, J. (2004) 'Patterns and variations in European industrial relations', in European Commission (ed) *Industrial relations in Europe*, Luxembourg: Office for the Official Publications of the European Communities, pp 11-57.

Wolf, H.C. (1999) *Transition strategies: choices and outcomes*, Princeton Studies in International Economics No 85, Princeton: International Economics Section, Departement of Economics, Princeton University.

World Bank (2004) *Tertiary Education in Poland*, Warsaw: The World Bank.

ELEVEN

Romania

Cristina Mocanu

After the communist regime collapsed, the education system in Romania had to cope with several problems. The system was designed to provide skilled workers for an industrialised country, and, during the 1990s, the entire industry underwent a difficult and painful restructuring process. Moreover, every government after 1990 had a different vision of how the Romanian education system should be reformed to best cope with the new realities. Hence, a consistent reform approach could not be enforced, despite a growing need for education restructuring.

The Romanian labour market suffered from the economic restructuring process. Unemployment rates were moderate, but participation rates were quite low and a high share of people were engaged in the agricultural sector. These rates reveal that the Romanian labour market did not provide sufficient employment opportunities despite its strong economic growth in the new millennium.

Unlike other Central and Eastern European (CEE) countries, Romania did not embark on retrenchment in the area of social policies until the mid- to late-1990s (Sotiropoulos et al, 2003). Unemployment benefit constituted the central policy measure for dealing with the rising number of unemployed in the course of restructuring. However, despite the introduction of unemployment and social assistance benefits, poverty rates, both in relative and absolute terms, have remained among the highest in Europe.

Education system

Structure of the Romanian education system

Overview of the Romanian education system after the Second World War

Since the 1970s, inspired by models adopted by other communist regimes, Romania reduced the number of enrolments in classical high schools in favour of technical and vocational schools, with the goal of transforming Romania into an industrialised power. By the end of the Ceausescu period, less than 8% of secondary school students were enrolled in theoretical (academic) education, by far the lowest percentage in any post-communist country. The remaining 92% were in different types of vocational programmes (OECD, 2003). The OECD report (2000a) shows that, during the period of 1985/90, the distribution between students enrolled in theoretical and technical high schools and vocational schools was 71% for the former and 20% for the latter, with the remainder primarily enrolled in apprenticeship programmes.

Firms and cooperatives played an important role as 'sponsors' for the vocational education and training (VET) system. The enterprises not only supported the school budget, but also helped to define the number of enrolments and the structure of the programmes. Lessons for practical training sometimes took place in the enterprise itself or in the workshops of the school, with equipment and trainers provided by the enterprises. The relationship between the school and the enterprise was often based on a contract, through which the company had to provide employment after graduation. Enterprises also frequently supplied teachers to teach practical skills, and provided scholarships not far below the future initial salary of a young worker.

During the 1980s, Romania faced a major discrepancy within the education system: high enrolment rates at the pre-tertiary level (98% in primary, 83% in secondary for the 1989), but one of the lowest rates at the tertiary level (11% in 1979). While free and universally accessible in theory, tertiary education development was inhibited by economic constraints during much of the 20th century. By the end of the 1970s, there were 42 higher education institutions, including seven universities.

Another problem that Romania inherited from the communist period was the gap between rural and urban areas with respect to education. Schools in rural areas were poorly endowed in terms of infrastructure and human resources. Teachers in rural areas were those with the lowest job performance or those 'forced' to teach in rural areas before being eligible to apply for jobs in urban areas.

Education system since 1990[1]

The Romanian education structure consists of a vertical system of schooling through the end of compulsory education, which is common for all students. Beyond compulsory education, learning alternatives become more specialised at both secondary and tertiary levels (see Figure 11.1).

Before 1999, all Romanian citizens had to receive education for a period of eight years after pre-primary education (ages 7-15), while the last year of pre-primary education was also compulsory. This eight-year period included primary education (years 1-4) and lower-secondary education at a gymnasium (years 5-8).[2] In 1999, the duration of compulsory education was extended from eight to nine years, but there were numerous obstacles to its implementation. Finally, in 2003, compulsory education was extended to 10 years and the starting age of schooling was reduced to six years.

Figure 11.1: The Romanian education system

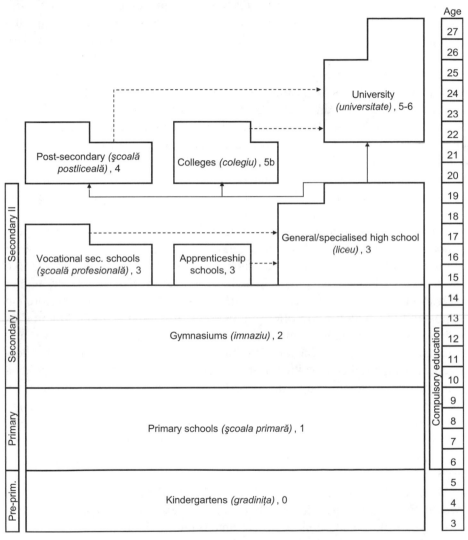

Source: ETF (2000)

Primary education (International Standard Classification of Education, ISCED 1) is provided in three types of school, offering the same structure of education, but covering different levels: (1) schools offering years 1-4; (2) schools offering years 1-8 (institutions covering primary and lower-secondary education); and (3) schools offering years 1-12 (or 13) (institutions covering primary and full secondary education).[3]

Lower-secondary education (ISCED 2) provides general education and covers the last four years of compulsory education (11- to 15-year-old age group). Since 2003/04, lower-secondary education has been extended with two years of general or vocational education. Pupils who have completed primary education are automatically moved to compulsory secondary education without entrance requirements. The lower-secondary studies are completely free of charge. Lower-secondary education can be provided in two types of schools (offering the same structure of education): schools covering years 1-8, and schools covering years 1-12 (or 13). Lower-secondary education ends with a national examination, organised on the basis of the methodology developed by the Ministry of Education and Research. On passing this examination, a graduation certificate is issued, which allows students to attend upper-secondary school. Drop-out rates after the compulsory school are about 17% (1988/89-1995/96). Moreover, about 2%-3% of children (many of them Roma) never attend this school at all.

Post-compulsory secondary education covers general and specialised high schools (or academic and technological tracks), as well as vocational or apprenticeship schools (vocational track), which are normally public and free of charge. All types of upper-secondary education give access to higher education, and most of them also offer a qualification and therefore an opportunity to obtain a job after graduation. Most high schools function as independent institutions. Some function together with lower secondary and primary schools, and some are integrated in combined groups of schools (technical high schools) with vocational schools. High school ends with a final national examination, developed by a commission established by County School Inspectorates. Tests included in this final examination are composed of common tests and differentiated tests, depending on a school's profile, specialisation or pupil's choice. After obtaining their graduation certificate, pupils can apply for the entrance examination to gain admission to higher education.

Vocational secondary schools (ISCED 3c) lead to employment and last two to four years depending on the sector, covering individuals aged 15 to 17-19 years old. In addition to a vocational training school, a combined group of schools can include an apprenticeship school, a sectoral high school, and a sectoral post-secondary school. Every pupil who has completed lower secondary school studies and obtained a graduation certificate can apply for the entrance examination to vocational school. The education programme for vocational schools is comprised of general training, the importance of which is lower and decreasing with each additional year of study, specialisation training and practical training. In the first years of study, which are spent focusing on acquiring the basics of technology, practical training is carried out in school workshops and organised within the school, sometimes with the support of a company with a direct interest. During the final years of study, which are devoted to specialisation and qualification, practical training covers a greater number of hours (over 40%) and is provided through placements in companies during which pupils work together with skilled staff. Vocational studies conclude with a final examination and a certificate of qualification that allows graduates to seek a job. Pupils qualifying from vocational schools and holding a graduation certificate can also apply for the entrance examination to high schools.

Apprenticeship schools offer vocational education and training through sandwich-type courses. The study period in apprenticeship schools is one to two years, depending on student qualifications. Normally, the last year is focused on specialisation and skill development, where pupils are given practical training in companies. Generally, apprenticeship schools are attached to a vocational school or to combined group of schools, and offer full-time and part-time training. The applicants are graduates of compulsory secondary school, even if they do not hold a graduation certificate. Successful completion of the training gives access to the labour market. Apprenticeship studies conclude with a final examination and a certificate of qualification that allows the pupil to seek a job. Pupils qualifying from apprenticeship schools and holding a graduation certificate can apply for the entrance examination to high schools.

Post-secondary education is a form of vocational training for those who complete high school. The duration of study is one to three years, depending on the profile of the school. Every pupil who finishes high school, with or without a graduation certificate, can apply for the entrance examination.[4] The courses normally lead to employment. The practical training in the first years of study is carried out in school workshops, sometimes with the support of a company with a direct interest. In the last year of study, the importance of practical training increases, with students working together with skilled staff within companies. The practical period in companies and institutions has often proved to be a sort of probationary period for people seeking employment. After completion of studies, many of them are hired by the respective company or institution.

Tertiary education is organised in short- and long-term courses. Tertiary education programmes with occupation orientation (ISCED 5b) provide short-term courses (two to three years) geared for entry into the labour market. University colleges are typical institutions for this education level. Pupils who qualify from high schools and have a graduate certificate can apply.[5] Students who pass the graduation examination receive a diploma, leading to employment in their respective area.

Tertiary education programmes with academic orientation (ISCED 5a + ISCED 6) provide long-term courses (four to six years). Typical institutions for this education level are universities, academies, polytechnic universities and institutes. Admission requirements for long-term courses are similar to those for short-term courses. Students who pass the degree examinations receive a bachelor's degree in the respective area. As regards postgraduate studies, the following qualifications are offered: *diploma de studii aprofundate, diploma de master, diploma de studii academice postuniversitare, diploma postuniversitară de specializare.*

Vertical dimension of the educational system

Figure 11.2 charts the trends in educational enrolment of the school-aged population in Romania starting from 1950s. Obviously, the vast majority of the school-aged population has been involved in the primary and low-secondary schooling (since this is the longest educational period in the Romanian education system), but a continuously decreasing trend is also visible.

Figure 11.2: School-aged population by levels of education and type of school (%)

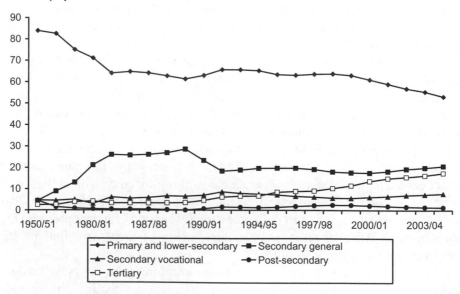

Note: Pre-school children are excluded.
Source: Romanian National Institute for Statistics (1990-2006)

Above all, a decrease in the enrolment in the primary and lower-secondary education occurred between 1950 and 1985, while the participation in the (upper)-secondary general education increased during this period. The participation in the upper-secondary vocational education has also been continuously increasing, starting from the early 1980s, whereas during this period there were practically no people enrolled in post-secondary education. Conversely, participation in the latter increased in the 1990s. Another marked trend is a continuous increase (about 15% between 1950 and 2004) in tertiary enrolment in Romania.

Young men have been overrepresented among those enrolled in vocational and apprenticeship schools, while women have been overrepresented among those in the general education track. Furthermore, beginning in the late 1990s, women overtook men in post-secondary and tertiary education. The share of women/girls in secondary education was 53.8% in 2005/06. Girls are overrepresented in pedagogical high schools (92.2% in 2005/06); economic, administration and services (63.8%); theoretic high schools (60.0%); and the arts (59.8%). Additionally, women are overrepresented in post-secondary education (65.4%) and underrepresented in vocational schools and apprenticeship schools (38.5%) (Romanian National Institute for Statistics, 2005).

Secondary level of education

Stratification and track differentiation

Until 1999, Romanian unified basic schooling lasted until the age of 14. In 1999/2000, basic education was extended to the age of 15. Once this stage ends, students have to decide on their choice of upper-secondary education. Those who passed the national tests and obtained the graduation diploma can apply to theoretical high school and to vocational school, while those who failed can apply to apprenticeship schools.

Figure 11.3 charts educational enrolment on the upper-secondary level, differentiating between *Liceu*, both general and technical,[6] professional (vocational) schools, and apprenticeship schools. It is clear that general and technical high schools have been the main form of upper-secondary education in the 1990s-2000s, followed by professional schools, while less than 10% of students have been enrolled in apprenticeship schools. In 1996, about 85% of all VET institutions offered a final secondary examination (*matura*) (ETF, 1998-2000). Enrolment in vocational education leading to matura examination increased between 1993 and 1998, while vocational tracks offering a qualification decreased in importance. Throughout the 2000s, an increasing trend towards expansion of vocational schools and a decline of apprenticeship schools is further evident.

Figure 11.3: Enrolment in education and training at the (upper)-secondary level (%)

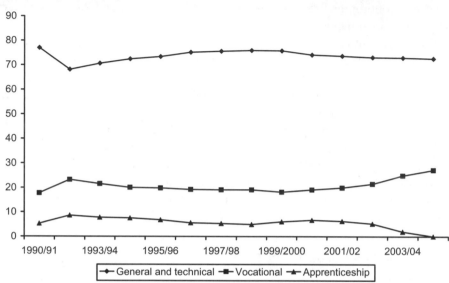

Source: Romanian National Institute for Statistics (1990-2005)

Organisation of vocational training

OECD (2000a, 2003) states that vocational education is organised in the form of a dual system, which is a combination of school-based teaching and an apprenticeship. The problem these reports underscore is the absence of a real partnership between school units and companies. As a result, the majority of education expenses has remained the state's responsibility. Attempts to transfer some education costs to employers have frequently failed because of employer lack of financial resources (OECD, 2003). Currently the apprenticeship schools are locally administered and controlled, and the social partners, together with the local public authority, are responsible for the entire organisation. The OECD report (2003) also highlights the low external efficiency of the VET system. Therefore, matching vocational qualifications to the expectations of the labour market remains a problem.

Standardisation and quality differentiation of secondary education

Starting in the 1990s, education decentralisation has been a major concern of policy makers in the field of education, and the general trend is to continue this process. Nevertheless, the Romanian education system remains rather centralised. According to the 2000 OECD report, it is clear that the education curriculum is standardised in Romania (both for secondary and tertiary education), as it is centrally compiled by the relevant bodies, i.e., the National Council for Curriculum and the national commissions for different subjects.

Lower and upper-secondary education ends with a standardised national examination, organised on the basis of the methodology developed by the Ministry of Education and Research (for lower-secondary schools) and by a commission established by County School Inspectorates (for upper-secondary schools).

In 2006, Romania first participated in the Programme for International Student Assessment (PISA) and the results are far from satisfactory. The Romanian youth's performance is worst in rural areas, where the material and human resources are in shortest supply. As the settlement becomes more urban, their scores usually improve, particularly in reading (see Table 11.1). Similar correlations between the size of the community and the achievement score were also observed for Romanian 8th grade pupils in the sciences (i.e., life science, chemistry, physics and earth science), according to the TIMMS study (Trends in International Mathematics and Science Study) conducted in 2003 (Istrate et al, 2006).

Table 11.1: Pupil achievement in reading, mathematics and science, PISA results for 2006

	Reading	Mathematics	Science
Village school	437	454	467
Small town school	469	474	486
Town school	485	490	500
City school	494	490	496
Large city school	504	489	489

Source: OECD (2008)

Tertiary level of education

Horizontal dimension

An important aspect of the horizontal dimension of the education system at the tertiary level is a field-of-study differentiation. This is presented in Figure 11.4 covering the period between 1980 and 2005 for institutions of tertiary education. The figure indicates that during the 1980s, the vast majority of students were enrolled in technical specialisation fields, while only a negligible proportion were found in artistic and legal fields. The first half of the 1990s is marked by a gradual decline in enrolments in technical fields, so that between 1990 and 1995 it dropped from 70% to 30%, a dramatic decrease in such a short period of time. A slight decrease in the medical fields is also evident. Simultaneously, in the early 1990s, there is an enrolment increase in pedagogical and economic fields and from the mid-1990s, there is a similar enrolment increase in law. Enrolment in pedagogy and economics increased from about 10% in 1989/90 to about 30% in 2004/05.

The share of women enrolled in tertiary education increased from 51.0% in 1998/99 to 55.4% in 2005/06. Women are overrepresented in university – pedagogy (67.5% in 2005/06), medicine and pharmacy (69.0%) and economics (62.2%) – and underrepresented in technical fields (29.4% in 2005/06) and law (49.3%) (Romanian National Institute for Statistics, various years).

Figure 11.4: Tertiary education enrolment by group of specialisation (%)

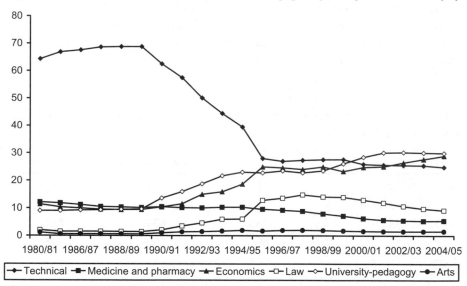

Notes: Technical specialisations include industry (mining, petroleum-geology, electric power and electrotechnics, metallurgy and engineering, chemical technology, wood and building materials industry, light industry, food industry), transport and telecommunications, architecture and construction, agriculture (veterinary medicine included). University-pedagogy includes philology, history-philosophy, geography, biology, chemistry, mathematics-physics, pedagogy, physical education, political and administrative sciences. The arts include fine and decorative arts, drama, cinematography and music.
Source: Romanian National Institute for Statistics (1990-2005)

Standardisation, quality differentiation and openness of tertiary education

A distinctive feature of the transformation of higher education in Romania is the rise of private higher education. The number of private higher education institutions increased from 0 in 1989 to 54 in 1999, with a high concentration in Bucharest (40%) (Nicolescu, 2002). These institutions primarily taught economics (about 36% of students in private higher education institutions) and juridical sciences (38.5%), which were in high demand at the beginning of the 1990s.

Private universities largely relied on the staff of state universities, who totalled between 5%-10% of their staff (Nicolescu, 2002). The rest were professors from state universities who also worked at private universities for extra income. Private universities used to attract students who failed state university examinations and students from low-income families. Overall, public universities seem to be more valued by candidates, parents, teachers and employers. Nicolescu (2002) mentioned the results of research conducted with the Romanian business community showing that private employers have common policies and practices towards graduates of both state and private universities and make no formal differences between the two. Nonetheless, they do consider state university graduates to be more knowledgeable and more responsible than private university graduates.

Places in public university colleges are financed from the state budget and thus public tertiary education is free. Besides the officially approved number of students accepted, the university senates (with the approval of the Ministry of Education and Research) may authorise an additional number of fee-paying students.[7] Candidates who obtained an average mark below the 'admission limit' can apply to be accepted within this additional quota. Students are eligible for scholarships, and grants are also offered to those from low-income families.

Labour market

Economic development

In 1989, Romania was one of the poorest CEE countries. It suffered from an unfavourable set of initial conditions inherited from the social, economic and politic activities of the previous regime. Whereas other communist countries introduced some economic or political liberalisation in the 1980s, the economic policies implemented by the Romanian communist regime were more restrictive, placing additional import restrictions and a forced rural restructuring programme (OECD, 2000b). As a result, the economy had been stagnant for most of the 1980s.

These unfavourable starting conditions translated into a strong gross domestic product (GDP) decline after 1989, widening the gap separating Romania from Central Europe. In 1990, the GDP registered a yearly decline of more than 5% in real terms (Figure 11.5). This transitional recession peaked at −12.9% in 1991. It was mainly triggered by the structural changes in the economic system. The initial economic contraction was followed by growth from 1992 until 1996. However, this partial recovery was not strong enough to push the GDP per capita to its 1990 value. The expansion was followed by renewed decline in real GDP per capita that lasted until the end of the decade. One potential explanation for this substantial output collapse was the Russian crisis that together with the Asian crisis induced a severe decrease of international capital flows to transition countries in particular (World Bank, 2003). This economic decline came to a halt as early as 2000, after three years of consistent recession marked by high inflation and macroeconomic instability. Economic performance has improved significantly in the new millennium. The growth rates increased substantially, from 2.1% in 2000 to 7.9% in 2006. Obviously, economic growth is rather sustainable in the new millennium and has reached very high rates.

Figure 11.5: GDP growth, 1990-2006

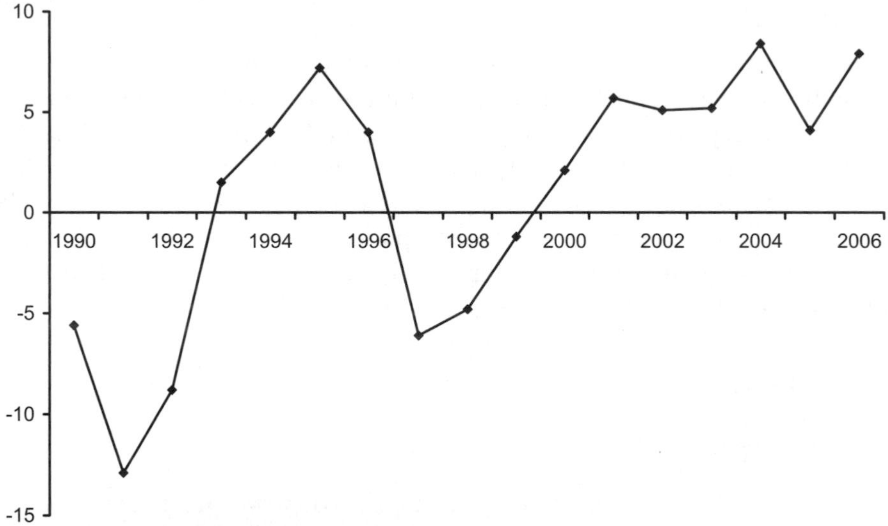

Source: ILO (2008); data for 2006 from Eurostat (2008)

For Romania, the transition from a centralised, state-controlled economy to a market economy occurred more slowly and resulted in greater economic and social difficulties than in the leading transition economies in Central Europe. These relatively greater transition problems in Romania are explained by its more problematic heritage. On the other hand, many problems are also attributable to the comparatively slow pace of Romanian reform (OECD, 2000b). Successive governments adopted a more gradual approach in restructuring and privatising the state-owned sector than other former communist countries. The slow pace of privatisation induced a lack of pressure towards higher economic efficiency (Ciobanu and Parciog, 1999) because inefficient state-owned enterprises were kept alive through large direct and indirect subsidies that heavily burden state funds. Privatisation was only rapid and successful in agriculture, with an overall de-collectivisation and the re-establishment of small and medium-sized private farmers in the early 1990s.

There were two main forms of privatisation in Romania: the transfer of state property to Romanians as a mass privatisation process and the sale of the remaining shares to interested Romanian or foreign investors. The early privatisations frequently took the form of management and employee buyouts, resulting in a strong element of insider control, but auctions and direct sales to outside owners have become more common in recent years (OECD, 2000a). The privatisation of the industrial sector has been lagging behind, but the process accelerated at the end of the 1990s. As a result of the reduction of subsidies provided to some of the industrial sectors, massive layoffs began to take place. Despite the slow privatisation process, the private sector has been constantly growing. Its input to the GDP increased to 70% in 2007, compared to only 10% in 1990 (EBRD, 2008). However, the economic restructuring and privatisation process is far from being finished.

Labour market development

Employment dynamics

The Romanian economy is characterised by a large agricultural sector and an almost equally large industrial sector, whereas the service sector is underdeveloped. At the beginning of the economic transition in 1990, 29.1% of employed individuals worked in agriculture, 43.5% in industry and only 27.4% in services (ILO, 2008). Labour force shifts have differed from other CEE countries, where agricultural employment shares declined. In contrast, Romanian agriculture's share has increased dramatically.

The high employment share of agriculture in Romania represents a rather archaic structure of employment when compared with Europen Union (EU) countries (Ciobanu and Parciog, 1999). Although the agricultural share of total employment was already high in 1990, it increased to a maximum of 42.8% in 2000 (ILO, 2008). During the period from 1997-2002, agriculture became the sector with the highest share in total employment. The increase in farm employment was only slightly reversed after 2000, resulting in a decrease to 32.1% in 2006. The shift toward agricultural employment is the result of two related policies: the privatisation of agricultural production and land restitution (World Bank, 2003). For example, the land restitution policy has placed most arable land into the hands of over 3.5 million households, with holdings averaging about 2 hectares, and dispersed in scattered, fragmented plots. Productivity in the agricultural sector is very low because farmers cultivate with extremely modest technical means (ETF, 2003).

307

Furthermore, much farming is of the subsistence type, i.e., the majority of farmers consume high levels of their own goods (European Commission, 2002).

In contrast, the employment share in industry and construction decreased permanently during the whole period, from 43.5% to 30.3% (ILO, 2008). Employment in industry has been continuously declining since the beginning of the 1990s, from 4.7 million in 1990 to 2.8 million in 2006. The industrial sector is characterised by an extraordinary predominance of large enterprises, especially in heavy industry that was developed mostly after the Second World War, reflecting the political priorities of the time. The service sector's share of total employment is relatively small, at just over 30%, whereas the share lies between 60% and 75% in EU15 countries. It increased slowly from 27.4% in 1990 to 37.5% in 2006, mainly in wholesale and retail trade, financial and related services, and public administration (OECD, 1998).

Figure 11.6 charts the decline in labour force participation rates of the population aged 15-64 from 69.1% in 1990 to 60.1% in 2006, reflecting a relatively low participation rate.[8] Figure 11.6 also shows gender-specific time trends in labour force participation. Both male and female labour force participation shows the same evolution pattern over time. However, there is a difference in levels: the female activity rate is 12-16 percentage points below that of men.

Figure 11.6: Labour force participation rate (age group 15-64), 1990-2006

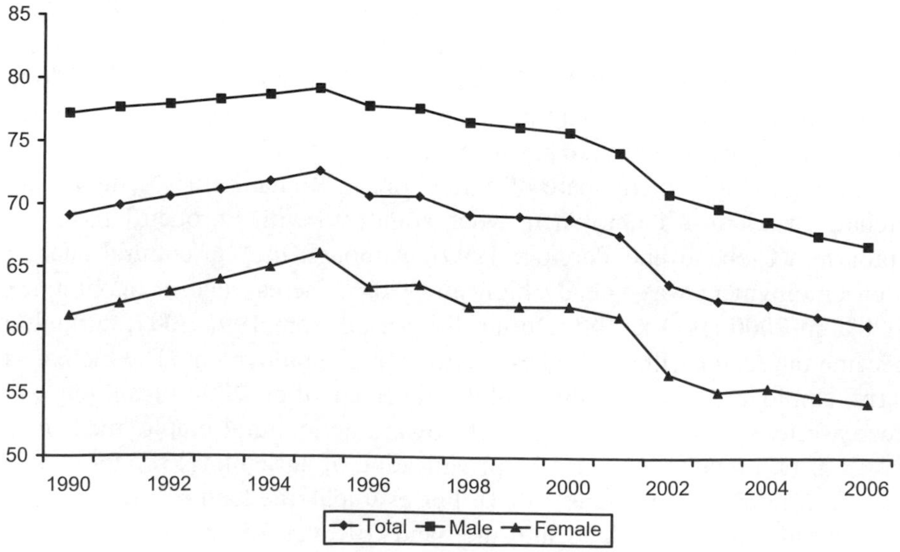

Source: ILO (2008)

In 2006, the lowest activity rate is recorded for the youngest-age cohorts (15-24 years), at 28.2% (Table 11.2). The population aged between 15 and 24 is the cohort most affected by the fall in employment, which fell 30% between 1990 and 2006. In contrast, the middle-age cohorts attain very high activity rates of around 80% during the transition period. A feature of participation in Romania is the high activity rate among those aged 65 and over. Their rate doubled during 1990-2006, from around 15.3% to 31.5%, reaching a level that is much higher than in EU15. The European Commission (2002) concluded that this is very much a Romania-specific effect, where practically all those over 65 are self-employed or family workers in the agricultural sector, and almost one quarter of agricultural workers in Romania are over 65 years of age.

Table 11.2: Labour force participation rate by age cohort, 1990-2006

	1990	1995	2000	2006
15+ years	61.8	67.2	63.4	55.5
15-24 years	58.2	53.4	44.5	28.2
25-54 years	81.2	80.0	82.8	76.3
55-64 years	33.4	53.0	49.9	40.8
65+ years	15.3	36.4	35.7	31.5

Source: ILO (2008)

Unemployment dynamics

Official registered unemployment of the public employment service, measured as a share of the active population (15-64 years old), was quite low at the beginning of the transition period, with 3% in 1991 because unemployment was an unknown phenomenon during the communist era (Figure 11.7). The transition to a market economy caused the unemployment figures to rise significantly: registered unemployment peaked at approximately 11% of the labour force in 1994 and early 1995, after which it fell to an average of slightly under 7% during 1996. During the economic crisis at the end of the 1990s, it rose again to a global maximum of about 12% in 1999. Since 1999, it has been declining in accordance with strong economic recovery at the beginning of the new millennium.

In contrast, the Labour Force Survey (LFS)-based unemployment rate has been accelerating to around 7% during the transition period, as measured on average for the age group of 15 and older. The reason for different unemployment patterns between the official registered unemployment rate and the LFS unemployment rate is deviating measurements. A comparison between the LFS unemployment rate and the registered unemployment rate reveals that from 1994-96, as well as from 2002 onwards, there was little difference between both measurements. A converse picture shows the period from 1996-2002, where the registered unemployment rate increased sharply and ILO unemployment rate remained constant. For example, in 1999, registered unemployment was almost twice as much as International Labour Organization (ILO) unemployment. Interestingly, the LFS unemployment rate shows that unemployment is rather stable despite the substantial economic growth in the last few years. Obviously, the recovery has not yet fully reached the labour market.

Figure 11.7: Unemployment rates, 1991-2006

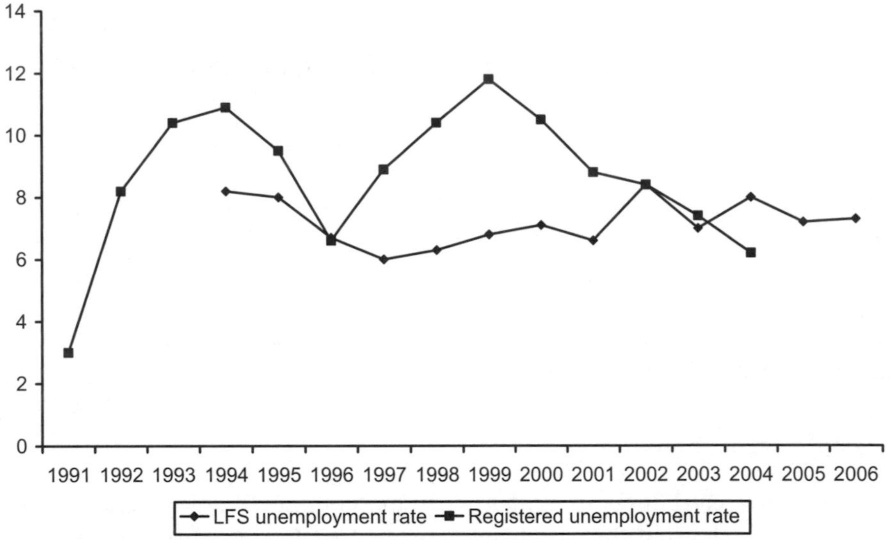

Note: LFS unemployment rate for individuals aged over 15.
Source: ILO (2008); LFS unemployment in 2006 from Eurostat (2008)

In comparison with other European countries, Romania's unemployment figures are relatively low. However, this picture masks unresolved structural problems. This is more a sign of delayed restructuring. There are clear indications that the Romanian labour market has not provided sufficient job opportunities. A decline in industrial employment and low employment in services has been compensated more by an increasing agricultural employment than by decreasing participation and growing unemployment, respectively. Hence, the central labour market problem is not so much unemployment as underemployment, i.e., employment in low-productive activities like agricultural subsistence economy. Furthermore, during the long period of downsizing in the manufacturing sector, job leavers were more likely to leave the labour market than to become unemployed. Many also retired with a pension, or simply quit their jobs voluntarily or in agreement with their employers. Such decisions were often facilitated by the existence of public compensation schemes and alternative income sources in the underground economy (OECD, 2000b).

In Romania, as in many other European countries, the transition of young people from school to adult life and labour integration remains an important labour market problem. Labour market entrants, approximated as the youngest age cohort of 15- to 24-year-olds, is the category most exposed to unemployment. The unemployment rate of individuals under 25 varies at around 20%, i.e. a level that is about 3.5 times higher than the average unemployment rate for the whole adult population (ILO, 2008).

In addition to young people, another disadvantaged category in the labour market is that of the long-term unemployed. According to Eurostat (2008) data, the share of long-term unemployment, i.e., people unemployed for over 12 months, increased from 43.8% in 1998 to 57.8% in 2006. However, these official data do not reveal the true picture of long-term unemployment in Romania. Browne et al (2006) conclude that because discouraged workers have typically been unemployed for a long time and have given up searching the long-term unemployment problem is still much greater than implied by official statistics. These discouraged long-term unemployed are not officially registered.

Minority ethnic groups and regional differences

The minority ethnic Roma group is another disadvantaged group in the labour market. Their number is estimated at between 500,000 and 2.5 million. The figures vary because many Roma deny their origin for fear of discrimination (European Commission, 2002). It appears that the Roma are significantly disadvantaged in the labour market: unemployment and in particular long-term unemployment is widespread among the Roma population. Their overall unemployment rate was estimated to be around 45% (O'Higgins and Ivanov, 2006). This high unemployment rate is mainly explained by their low education level and by ethnic discrimination.

The variation in unemployment and unemployment rates at the regional level is not very marked in comparison to other Eastern European countries (European Commission, 2002). This is mainly due to the previous regime, which aimed to ensure a geographical balance of economic development, primarily by bringing jobs to people by the imposed creation of new industrial units. At the regional level, the highest unemployment rates are registered in the north-east and south-west, the lowest values being in Bucharest and the north-west regions (ETF, 2003). Thus, unemployment is generally highest in the least industrialised regions, especially in northeastern and southwestern Romania.

Labour market institutions

The original Romanian labour law dated back to 1973 and coincided with socialist standards of harmonised state-controlled labour regime (Trif, 2004). There were some changes and amendments applied in the years after the 1989 revolution, making the regulation more liberal in terms of European standards (OECD, 1998). In 2003, a new Labour Code was introduced after lengthy debates and consultation between the social partners. It provided a considerable degree of harmonisation of the Romanian employment law with the aquis communautaire of the EU (Mocanu and Mares, 2005).

Employment protection legislation

Under the centrally planned economic system, workers enjoyed a fairly high degree of employment protection in their jobs. During the 1990s, the need for rapid structural adjustment after the introduction of economic and social reforms was reflected in substantial moderation of workers' protection. The objective was to facilitate workforce adjustment for firms in order to make enterprises more flexible, while guaranteeing employment protection for workers. There were also counteracting labour law amendments: the new 2003 Labour Code increased employees' information and consultation rights in the case of dismissals. For example, collective redundancies may be made only after previous consultations with trade unions or employees' representatives (Micevska, 2004).

Romania and other CEE countries tend to be most restrictive concerning collective dismissals compared to EU15 (see Table 2.7 in Chapter Two of this book). Regulation concerning regular employment is less restrictive in Romania than in EU15 and CEE countries on average. In contrast, in comparison with EU and other CEE countries, Romania's termination rules on temporary employment contracts are more restrictive. The use of temporary contracts is restricted to specific objective reasons, and such contracts are not allowed to last longer than 18 months (Clauwaert et al, 2003). Regulations of temporary work agencies are very weak, as these employment forms hardly exist in Bulgaria. In general, the comparison of overall employment protection legislation EPL finds that, despite significant liberalisation efforts, Romania has stricter regulations than other CEE and EU15 countries on average.

Industrial relations

Before 1990, Romania's industrial relations systems were characterised by central political and managerial control exercised by the state (Vasilescu and Contescu, 2003; Trif, 2004). During the transition, Romania moved away from a centralised wage-setting system towards a collective bargaining system in the enterprise sector, much the same as in many other CEE countries. Wage bargaining usually takes place at the enterprise level, whether private- or state-owned, with a central collective agreement as a framework (Schneider and Burger, 2005). It is not heavily influenced by public policy intervention, apart from general regulations in law and apart from the government's role as employer in the public administration.

As in all other CEE countries, union membership declined during the 1990s, whereas the communist era was dominated by almost full coverage of the industrial labour force (Vasilescu and Contescu, 2003; Trif, 2004). According to Crowley (2004: Figure 2), the Romanian unionisation rate decreased to 31.4% at the turn of the millennium. The decrease is generally attributed to the shift towards free choice of union membership status, falling living standards throughout the 1990s, high levels of unemployment, privatisation, growing numbers of small and medium-sized enterprises (SMEs), and sectoral shifts (European Commission, 2002). Trade unions are often strong in state-owned and recently privatised enterprises, yet often weak in new firms in the private sector (OECD, 2000b).

Welfare regime

Labour market policy

Active labour market policy

Active labour market policies (ALMPs) have been designed and implemented by the Ministry of Labour and Social Protection and funded by the unemployment fund and by international assistance programmes. During the early transition period, labour market policy was characterised by the tendency to finance passive measures, and by insignificant expenditure on active measures. Training and retraining measures for the unemployed were the first active measures put into place at the very beginning of the transition period (European Commission, 2002). In 1995, active measures became more significant, when privatisation and restructuring accelerated and resulted in massive layoffs. The main types of measures promoted have been recruitment incentives to employers, specifically support of job creation in SMEs. Hence, expenditure on active measures became more significant (Schneider and Burger, 2005). Some programmes have been created especially for problematic groups like labour market entrants. For example, a hiring subsidy for unemployed graduates of secondary and higher education was introduced, amounting in most cases to 70% of the initial salary for a period of 9-12 months. About 24,000 youths participated in this programme in 1998 (OECD, 2000b).

The European Commission (2002) provides a detailed analysis of the planned ALMP budget in 2002. The budget for ALMP from the unemployment fund represented 16.3% of the total labour market expenditures and 0.15% of GDP. Recruitment incentives represented 32.3% from the total ALMP expenditure in 2002, support to business start-up represented 31.5%, public works within the community represented 19%, vocational training represented 5.87% and mobility measures represented 11.25%. The ALMP plays a comparatively small role in Romania, with expenditure of about 0.1% of GDP during the late 1990s, which is lower than in most CEE and EU countries (Micevska, 2004: Table 5). Furthermore, limited activities and resources have been allocated for evaluating the impact and effectiveness of active employment measures.

Unemployment insurance

The legal framework regarding unemployment in Romania was designed to respond to the necessities of the transition from planned to market economy. At the beginning of the 1990s, benefits were rather generous in terms of replacement rates and payment duration. The delayed core reforms of economic transition starting in 1996/97 are reflected in modifications of the legal framework governing unemployment benefit: several benefits were paid by the public employment services through the unemployment fund to redundant workers from state-owned enterprises under restructuring and/or privatisation. They were granted without conditions regarding work search or acceptance of job offers. Restrictive conditions in 1999 and 2000 limited the companies and the number of workers entitled to compensatory payments. For example, there were approximately 200,000 beneficiaries in April 2001 compared to 600,000 between 1997 and 1999. Towards the end of the massive restructuring, which mainly affected the industrial sector, entitlement conditions were further restricted.

With the end of core reforms and economic recession, a comprehensive reform of unemployment insurance was implemented with Law 76/2002, amended and completed by Law 107/2004. The three previous financial benefits (unemployment benefit, professional integration allowance and support allowance) have been replaced by a single benefit, i.e., unemployment benefit. Furthermore, the 2002 reform reduced the maximum length of unemployment benefit from 27 months to 12 months and re-introduced the minimum wage as the reference for the calculation of unemployment benefit, which had been suppressed in 1997. The new system maintains a flat-rate unemployment allowance (former vocational integration allowance) for school leavers. The last unemployment benefit reform is presented as one level of a broader activation strategy. Both the amount and the shorter duration of the basic unemployment benefit are expected to provide higher incentives for unemployed people to find work.

Unemployment benefits are administered and paid by the National Agency for Employment from the unemployment insurance fund. Under the new legal framework, unemployment benefit is fixed at 75% of the legal minimum wage and is tax free in order to prevent discouraging effect on the low-paid employees, while assuring a decent living standard. Duration of receipt depends on the length of contribution, the maximum period being 12 months (six months for a length of contribution up to five years, nine months for a length of contribution between five and 10 years, 12 months for a length of contribution 10 years and over). To be eligible, individuals must have been contributing to the insurance, i.e., be employed for at least 12 months within the previous 24 months. Eligibility for unemployment benefit is conditioned by a monthly visit to the public employment services and participation in training or other employment stimulation measures offered by the public employment services. Refusal to participate in training or other employment stimulation measures can result in withdrawal of unemployment benefit. Beneficiaries of unemployment benefit who find a job before their entitlement to it expires continue to receive 30% of their benefit amount for the time remaining until the benefit would have expired.

Other categories of beneficiaries introduced by Law 76/2002 are the following: jobless young graduates and young people returning from military service meeting specific conditions (young graduates eligible for unemployment benefit are those aged 18 and over who are without a job within 60 days after gradation, young people having been jobless before their military service and remaining without a job within 30 days from service completion are also eligible). For these so-called 'assimilated unemployed', the unemployment benefit is a flat amount of 50% of the gross national minimum wage and is paid over a maximum of six months.

The ratio of average unemployment benefits relative to average net wage has remained constant, while benefit take-up declined just prior to the 2002 reform. Thereafter, it returned to the levels achieved in the late 1990s, i.e., around 40% of registered unemployed are receiving benefits.

The unemployed who are or are not entitled to unemployment benefit (i.e., long-term unemployed) have the only source of income support in the social assistance system – guaranteed minimum income (GMI), and there is no clear information with respect to the coverage of the long-term unemployed by social assistance schemes.

Table 11.3: Characteristics of the unemployment benefit system, 1998-2005

	1998	1999	2000	2001	2002	2003	2004	2005
Registered unemployment rate	10.4	11.8	10.5	8.8	8.4	7.4	6.3	5.9
ILO unemployment rate	6.8	7.2	6.8	6.4	8.0	6.7	8.1	6.8
Ratio of registered to ILO unemployment rate	1.5	1.6	1.5	1.4	1.1	1.1	0.8	0.9
Ratio of average unemployment benefit to average net earnings (%)	32.4	32.5	31.8	32.0		34.6	35.4	34.2 31.6
Proportion in the total number of registered unemployed (%)								
Benficiaries of unemployment benefit[a]	39.3	34.2	30.5	38.3	28.1	44.7	40.4	41.1
Beneficiaries of support allowance	38.1	39.5	38.9	34.6	16.2	0.2		

Note: [a]Including vocational integration allowance.
Source: Romanian National Institute for Statistics (2006)

Family policy

Public child-care

During the transformation, responsibility for crèches (taking in children up to the age of two) was transferred from enterprises to the Ministry of Health. Their numbers dropped from 847 institutions in 1989 to 573 in 1995, and declined further thereafter. Correspondingly, child enrolment halved until 1995. However, the small number of institutions even before transition indicates the relatively minor role of this form of childcare, which was even further weakened thereafter (Lokshin and Fong, 2006). Hence, childcare for those below the age of three is therefore mostly conducted in the home environment, usually by mothers taking maternity leave or dropping out of the workforce without pay. Children aged three to seven may attend kindergartens, which are usually open for only part of the day (Fodor et al, 2002).

Kindergartens are under the jurisdiction of the Ministry of Education. Public childcare services have been a low priority among political authorities. No proper mechanism for financing the system of crèches and kindergartens has yet been identified. Due to the restructuring process, as well as to the increasing length of parental leave, public care services progressively diminished in both coverage and quality, while their prices rose continuously.

Pre-school enrolment decreased somewhat after transition, but it began to rise in the mid-1990s. By 2005, nearly three quarters of children were enrolled in pre-school education. However, the number of kindergartens dropped substantially, from 12,772 in 1995 to 3,769 in 2005. The substantial decline in fertility rates, 1.23 live births per woman aged 15-49 in 2001 (2.20 in 1989), probably contributed to rising enrolment rates despite declines in the number of kindergartens (Unicef, 2007).

Table 11.4: Pre-school education in Romania, 1990-2005

	1990	1995	2000	2001	2002	2003	2004	2005
Enrolment rates children aged three to six	54.3	60.9	66.5	67.7	71.1	70.6	72.2	73.8
Number of kindergartens	12,529	12,772	10,080	9,980	9,547	7,616	5,687	3,769

Source: National Institute for Statistics (2006); UNICEF (2007)

While kindergarten fees doubled in relation to the average wage in 1990, they dropped again to pre-transition levels thereafter. Although subsidies are available, kindergarten fees are still presenting a serious obstacle to poorer households. A study by Lokshin and Fong (2006) suggests that the monetary costs of formal childcare indeed have a powerful effect on a household's decision to choose home care over formal care in Romania. Poorer families more often chose to rear their children at home, with mothers reducing their labour force participation, if costs of formal childcare are high. The authors therefore conclude that government subsidies for kindergarten fees are effective in raising kindergarten attendance and female labour force participation (Lokshin and Fong, 2006).

Cash benefits

Three policy measures are particularly targeted at children and family. There are two major types of benefits with a major impact on a household's welfare and parents' behaviour in the labour market: child and family benefits (some of them means-tested), and benefits related to maternity and child rearing until the child's age of two, which have been traditionally been a part of the social insurance system.

Since 1993, child allowance is awarded unconditionally and in the same amount to every child in Romania, regardless of the parent's income or the child's rank, if there is more than one child in the family. The benefit level is adjusted through governmental decisions. However, its level never represented any real support, not even to the poorest families. Due to its universal character, the population coverage rate is very high. Although a controversial measure, the 1997 child allowance was conditioned on school attendance. Overall, the school attendance rate did not rise substantially, but this reform was an important contribution to raise the attendance rate for Roma children.

Table 11.5: The value of child allowance relative to net average wage, 1994-2005

	1994	1996	1998	2000	2002	2004	2005
Child allowance as % of net average wage	2.5	2.8	6.0	3.5	4.4	3.6	3.1

Source: Romanian National Institute of Statistics (2006)

Social assistance

Social assistance includes minimum income support paid by the municipalities – the guaranteed minimum income (GMI). This support is a monthly cash payment granted to the family, and is calculated as the difference between the family's actual income and the relevant GMI. Child allowances[9] are included in the determination of the family's income. The unemployed must be registered at the labour office to be eligible. In addition, they are obliged to participate 72 hours a month in municipal community work programmes.

There is no data on the number of registered unemployed receiving income support from social assistance. The total number of families receiving income support sharply declined from around 600,000 in the mid-1990s to 28,000 at the end of 2001. During the first four months of 2002, 517,000 claims were registered and 375,857 accepted, but then the number of beneficiaries consistently declined. The revision of the system brought by the last reform (Law 416/2001) in January 2002 introduces new financing principles that guarantee that the amount necessary for the income support is earmarked in the town budgets and provide for transfers from the state budget.

The levels of GMI are set by the law but there are no common rules to determine the actual income of the families, and each municipality uses its own methods. The information is collected at the municipal level by some 3,000 municipalities, but is not centralised at national level.

According to the Romanian authorities, there are deficiencies in enforcing the required 72 hours of community programme work. The impact of this obligation on participants' chances to resume a sustainable job or in maintaining their links to the labour market is also a matter of concern, as the impact studies until now revealed the fact that the beneficiaries of GMI who are involved in municipal community work programmes tend to become dependent on social assistance.

Finally, it is necessary to consider the substantial importance of in-kind income, for example food from own agricultural production, which played a more important role until 2000, when the share of in-kind incomes reached a peak, representing approximately 31% of gross total household income. Apace with economic growth, the importance of in-kind incomes decreased constantly. Nonetheless, in-kind incomes and production for self-consumption are still very important for households with farmers and pensioners (i.e., subsistence-type agriculture). For some groups, reliance on alternative sources of income may also promote detachment from the formal economy (OECD, 2000b).

Table 11.6: The share of in-kind income from own agricultural produce as a percentage of gross total household income, 1998-2005

	All households	Households of			
		Employees	Farmers	Pensioners	Unemployed
1998	29.1	17.7	55.1	37.5	33.1
1999	29.0	16.3	56.0	37.3	33.4
2000	31.2	16.1	59.9	39.5	33.5
2001	24.7	12.7	57.5	32.0	29.5
2002	22.7	11.2	53.3	30.3	28.2
2003	23.4	11.2	53.8	31.7	24.6
2004	21.8	11.3	50.8	29.1	25.1
2005	17.3	8.9	42.4	23.6	19.8

Source: Romanian National Institute for Statistics (2006)

Notes

[1] This section is based on Eurydice (2003), OECD (2000a, 2003) and ETF (2004) publications.

[2] According to the law, the obligation to attend school ended when pupils were 16 years old or when they had completed lower-secondary school, whichever occurred first.

[3] Children can obtain a primary education both in Romanian or in the language of one of the national minorities. There are no entrance requirements for primary education and it is free of charge.

[4] A leaving certificate is required for medical post-high school courses.

[5] The institutions themselves organise the entrance examination, based on general criteria established by the Ministry of Education and Research.

[6] Overall, technical liceu have been slightly more numerous in Romania (Romanian National Institute for Statistics, 2006).

[7] The amount of fees is comparable between public and private universities providing the same specialisation.

[8] The labour force is the total number of people employed and unemployed.

[9] Family benefits are part of the social assistance system and are paid for each child until the age of 16 (or until the end of their education).

References

Browne, J., Earle, J., Gimpelson, V., Kapeliushnikov, R., Lehmann, H., Telegdy, A., Vantu, I. and Voicu, A. (2006) *Nonstandard forms and measures of employment and unemployment in transition: a comparative study of Estonia, Romania, and Russia*, Budapest Working Papers on the Labour Market No 0602, Budapest: Institute of Economics, Hungarian Academy of Sciences.

Ciobanu, A. and Parciog, S. (1999) *Background study on employment and labour market in Romania*, Torino: European Training Foundation.

Clauwaert, S., Düvel, W. and Schömann, I. (2003) *The community social acquis in labour law in the CEECS and beyond: fighting deregulation*, Conference report, Brussels: European Trade Union Institute.

EBRD (European Bank for Reconstruction and Development) (2008) *Transition report 2007*, London: EBRD.

ETF (European Training Foundation) (1998-2000) *Vocational education and training in Central and Eastern Europe: key indicators*, Luxembourg: Office for Official Publications of the European Communities.

ETF (2003) *Short country report Romania*, Torino: European Training Foundation.

ETF (2004) *Vocational education and training and employment services in Romania*, Luxembourg: Office for Official Publications of the European Communities.

European Commission (2002) *Joint assessment of employment priorities in Romania*, Brussels: European Commission.

Eurostat (2008) *Data: labour market*, Luxembourg: Eurostat (http://epp.eurostat.ec.europa.eu).

Eurydice (2003) *Structures of education, vocational training and adult education system: Romania*, Brussels: Eurydice European Unit.

Fodor, E., Glass, C., Kawachi, J. and Popescu, L. (2002) 'Family policies and gender in Hungary, Poland, and Romania', *Communist and Post-Communist Studies*, vol 35, pp 475-90.

ILO (International Labour Organization) (2008) *Key indicators of the labour market programme*, Fifth Edition, Geneva: ILO.

Istrate, O., Noveanu, G. and Smith, T. (2006) 'Exploring sources of variation in Romanian science achievement', *Prospects: Quarterly Review of Comparative Education*, vol 36, no 4, pp 475-96.

Lokshin, M. and Fong, M. (2006) 'Women's labour force participation and child care in Romania', *Journal of Development Studies*, vol 42, no 1, pp 90-109.

Micevska, M. (2004) *Unemployment and labour market rigidities in Southeast Europe*, Working Paper, Global Development Network Southeast Europe, Vienna: GDN-SEE.

Mocanu, D. and Mares, N. (2005) 'The Romanian labour market: towards the European labour market?', *South-East Europe Review*, vol 8, no 1, pp 123-36.

Nicolescu, L. (2002) 'Reforming higher education in Romania', *European Journal of Education*, vol 37, no 1, pp 91-100.

OECD (Organisation for Economic Co-operation and Development) (1998) *Economic surveys 1997/98: Romania*, Paris: OECD.

OECD (2000a) *Reviews of national policies for education: Romania*, Paris: OECD.

OECD (2000b) *Labour market and social policies in Romania*, Paris: OECD.

OECD (2003) *Reviews of national policies for education: South Eastern Europe*, vol 2, Paris: OECD

OECD (2008) *Database: PISA 2006*, Paris: OECD (http://pisa2006.acer.edu.au/interactive.php).

O'Higgins, N. and Ivanov, A. (2006) 'Education and employment opportunities for the Roma', *Comparative Economic Studies*, vol 48, pp 6-19.

Romanian National Institute for Statistics (1990-2006) *Statistical yearbook*, Bucharest: Romanian National Institute for Statistics.

Schneider, F. and Burger, C. (2005) *Formal and informal labour markets: challenges and policy in the Central and Eastern European new EU members and candidate countries*, CESifo Economic Studies, vol 51, no 1, pp 77-115.

Sotiropoulos, D., Neamtu, I. and Stoyanova, M. (2003) 'The trajectory of post-communist welfare state development: the cases of Bulgaria and Romania', *Social Policy and Administration*, vol 37, no 6, pp 656-73.

Trif, A. (2004) 'Overview of industrial relations in Romania', *South-East Europe Review*, vol 7, no 2, pp 43-64.

UNICEF (United Nations International Children's Emergency Fund) (2007) *TransMONEE 2007 Database*, Florence: UNICEF Innocenti Research Centre (www.unicef-icdc.org/resources/transmonee.html).

Vasilescu, L. and Contescu, V. (2003) 'Romania: the role of the trade unions in labour relations', in W. Düvel, I. Schömann, S. Clauwaert and G. Gradev (eds) *Labour relations in South-East Europe*, Brussels: European Trade Union Institute.

World Bank (2003) *Romania poverty assessment: main report*, Report No 26169-RO, Washington DC: World Bank.

TWELVE

Slovakia

Ján Košta and Rastislav Bednárik

The political changes that took place in 1989 had far-reaching implications for Slovakian society, for whom the building of democratic institutions started from scratch. The smooth transition to democracy was most visibly confirmed when Slovakia, together with other transition economies, became a member of the European Union (EU). The democratic process in Slovakia also has implications for education, the labour market and the social system. These were all greatly influenced by the overall economic transformation of the country. Institutions and individuals had to adjust to previously unknown problems such as unemployment (Slovakia has the highest long-term unemployment rate in the EU), regional disparity, and external and internal competitive pressures.

When it comes to the transformation of the education system, the most important changes include the degree of autonomy in all levels and types of schools, the decentralisation of governance and financing and the adjustment of the curriculum to the needs of the students, with the ultimate goal of increasing their success in the labour market. The development of the labour market has not been smooth, mainly due to the higher rate of unemployment, which has also caused the loss of young people who have migrated to other countries. The labour code and other institutions have helped to create a more flexible and globally compatible labour market. There has been a gradual reduction in expenditure on unemployment benefit and an endeavour to create more vibrant and active labour market programmes.

Education system

Structure of the Slovak education system

Overview of the Slovak education system after the Second World War[1]

Prior to 1984 compulsory school attendance lasted nine years; between 1984 and 1990/91 it was extended to 10 years: eight years of uniform education at primary school, and at least two years at an upper-secondary school (which could usually be attended for two to four years). Formal education began at age six at the basic or primary school with the length of education being initially nine years and consequently reduced to eight years in 1974. After graduation from compulsory primary school, increasingly large proportions of students attended one of three main streams of secondary education: gymnasia (secondary grammar schools), vocational and secondary vocational schools and apprentice training centres and schools. About 15%-20% of primary school graduates studied at a gymnasium, which took four years to complete (three years between 1953 and 1968), and received school leaving certificates or diplomas (*maturita*). A further 20% attended four-year secondary vocational school, which offered a combination of vocational training and general education leading to occupational qualification and a school leaving certificate. The vast majority of primary school leavers (60%), however, entered apprenticeship training centres and schools in which students received practical training in various industrial sectors for two to four years.

The School Reform Act of 1960 resulted in further expansion of vocational and technical education, and a greater emphasis on polytechnic and technical studies at all levels. Between 1948 and 1961 the number of places in vocational education increased by more than 150% (Wong 1998), but by the mid-1980s they actually declined slightly. Secondary grammar schools expanded in the 1970-80s, but a significant majority of secondary school students continued to choose vocational training.

Although the rates of expansion in tertiary education were quite high throughout the socialist period, far fewer places at universities were available than could satisfy the potential demand (Wong, 1998). Entrance to tertiary education was conditional on having a diploma in secondary education and passing the university entrance examination. Theoretically, students from secondary grammar and secondary vocational schools (with diplomas) should have had similar chances of entering tertiary education, but in reality, the great majority of university students were recruited from the former. According to Wong (1998), close to 70% of the graduates from secondary grammar schools, but only about 25% of the graduates from secondary vocational schools, were admitted to university.

All in all, secondary grammar school and university education typically prepared graduates for non-manual and professional positions; other types of schooling were largely for manual jobs at various skill levels. Consequently, lower-vocational education could have been considered a dead-end in an education career. In Czechoslovakia the choice between lower vocational education on the one hand, and *gymnasium* or *technicum* on the other, was therefore a crucial life decision.

Education system since 1990s[2]

In Slovakia compulsory school attendance starts at the age of six and lasts 10 years until a person is 16 years old. It comprises primary school (nine grades) and the first year of upper secondary school (see Figure 12.1).

Figure 12.1: The Slovak education system

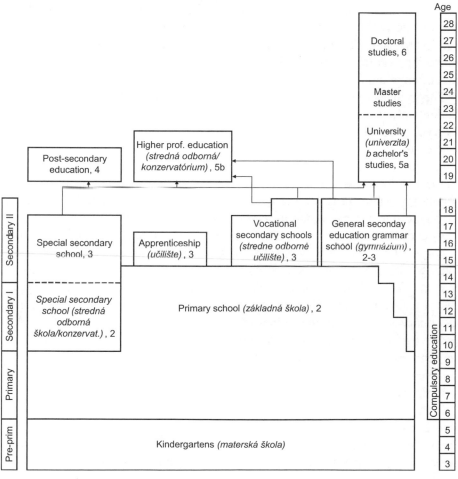

Source: ETF (2000)

Primary schools have two stages: the first stage, years 1-4 (International Standard Classification of Education, ISCED 1), and the second stage, years 5-9 (ISCED 2). Primary education in state schools is free, coeducational and is also offered in some ethnic minoritiy groups' mother tongue (Hungarian, Ukrainian and German). Slovakia has a nation-wide curriculum. After successfully completing primary school, pupils may be admitted to the first year of full-time study in secondary school. On completing the fourth year of primary school, pupils may be admitted to the eight-year gymnasium or on completing the sixth year to the six-year gymnasium.

Secondary schools in Slovakia are divided into the following: *gymnasium* (ISCED 3a) providing general education, vocational secondary school (ISCED 3a or 3c) and specialised secondary school (ISCED 3a) providing vocational education. Admission to secondary school is conditional on the successful completion of primary school. Secondary education lasts from two to five years and ends with a school leaving examination. The drop-out rate from general education in 1999/2000 was 1.4%, from vocational education leading to matriculation certificate 3.4%, and from vocational education without matriculation 4.8%.

The gymnasium is a general, internally differentiated school that prepares students primarily for studies in higher education institutions. Studies last for four years minimum and eight years maximum. The four-year gymnasium is linked to nine years of primary school. Admission to an eight-year gymnasium is subject to the completion of year 4 of primary school and admission to a six-year gymnasium subject to the completion of year 6. Secondary school programmes enabling access to higher education end with the school-leaving examination (*maturita*).

Vocational secondary education in Slovakia is represented by stredná odborná škola, stredné odborné učilište, učilište. Specialised secondary schools (stredná odborná škola) prepare pupils principally for professional activities as well as for higher education studies. The programmes usually take four years and end with a school-leaving examination.[3] Vocational secondary schools (stredné odborné učilište) prepare pupils for: (1) trades and vocational activities corresponding to the particular branch of apprenticeship pursued;[4] and (2) certain more demanding trades and some technical-economic activities of an operational nature.[5] Secondary vocational schools provide theoretical and practical courses to pupils and practical training and education outside classes. They may also provide purely theoretical teaching and out-of-school education or practical training. Finally, apprenticeship centres (*učilište*) provide vocational training for less demanding occupations to pupils who have completed compulsory school attendance at primary school for less than nine years or for pupils who did not succeed in completing the nine years of primary schooling. Training at apprenticeship school ends with a final examination. In all types of vocational school pupils acquire necessary skills through practical exercises, laboratory work, school workshop practice and operational practice.

In Slovakia, non-university higher education was not developed until the beginning of the 1990s. Higher professional studies are now provided at six secondary schools. They are offered in experimental specialised post-secondary fields of study (for example, finance, information processing, tourism, management and business). Higher professional education ends with a graduate examination and successful students receive the graduate diploma certificate.

Higher education institutions are generally state-run institutions which are financed from the state budget and free of charge.[6] In 1999, the first non-state higher education institution was established. Each institution sets its own criteria for admission and decides on student numbers on the basis of financial and staffing conditions. The primary criterion for admission is secondary education with a school leaving qualification (except for some arts-based courses). At each institution, there are also entrance examinations.

Since the Bologna process the degree structure has been organised into two main stages (undergraduate and two levels of postgraduate): (1) undergraduate studies, lasting three to four years and leading to the bachelor degree; (2) postgraduate studies, lasting one to three years and leading to the master's degree or, in artistic fields of study, Master of Arts; and (3) PhD studies, the third level of university education, lasting three to four years full time and five years part time. Graduates from doctoral studies are awarded the scientific-academic appellation *philosophiae doctor* (PhD).

Vertical dimension of the education system

Figure 12.2 shows trends in the education enrolment of the school-aged population in Slovakia beginning in 1980. Obviously, the vast majority of the school-aged population has been enrolled in 9-grade basic schools, but a declining trend is also evident. Similarly, a decrease has been observed in vocational enrolment, more so in vocational secondary schools, whereas the proportion of young people in specialised secondary schools has been more stable over time. Finally, an increase in enrolment in general education streams and tertiary education is also apparent.

In Slovakia, similar to other Central and Eastern European (CEE) countries, girls are overrepresented in grammar schools and specialised secondary schools (or secondary vocational schools), whereas boys are more numerous in vocational secondary schools and apprenticeship training centres The proportion of women in institutions of higher education has been increasing; in 1990 46.5% of all people enrolled in tertiary education were women, in 1995 this rose to 48.5%, in 2000 51.4%, and finally in 2004 55.5% of all students in higher education were women.

In the academic year 2000 23% of the relevant age group entered the general education branch (*gymnázium*), compared to 19% in 1995. In the same year 55% of the age group entered secondary specialised schools leading to *maturita* (51%, 1995). Twenty-two per cent entered the secondary vocational schools leading to a certificate (30%, 1995). In 2005 the proportion of the relevant age group finishing basic school and going on to gymnasia (secondary grammar school) did not change significantly (22.8%), but the proportion of new entrants into vocational secondary schools and apprenticeship decreased (26.3%). Figure 12.3 confirms that the majority of new entrants to university were students from gymnasia, who represented 51.5% of all new entrants to the first year of university.

Figure 12.2: Enrolment by type of school in Slovakia

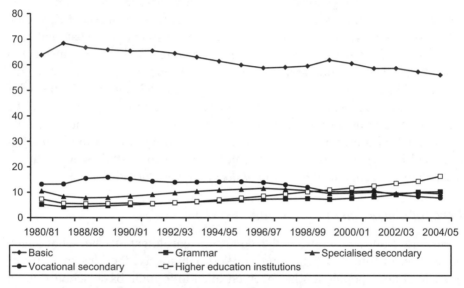

Notes: Associated secondary and special schools are excluded. Specialised secondary schools are also called secondary vocational schools in some yearbooks, while vocational secondary schools are named secondary vocational apprentice training centres.
Source: Statistical Office of the Slovak Republic (1980-2005)

Figure 12.3: Transitions in the Slovak educational system in 2005

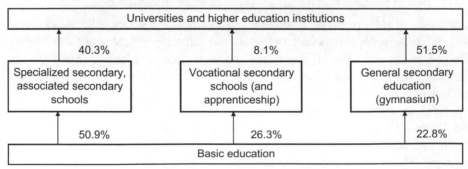

Source: Institute of Information and Prognoses of Education (2005)

Secondary level of education

Stratification and track differentiation

The first education choices are made quite early in life in Slovakia. At the age of 10 Slovakian pupils (and their parents) choose either to stay in the basic school or to switch to a gymnasium. A similar decision might also be taken at the age of 12. Another meaningful decision is then taken at age 15, when pupils are faced with a choice between the general and vocational education paths. Due to this very early first decision, the Slovakian education system, similar to the Czech one, should be characterised as stratified, definitely more stratified than education systems in the majority of other CEE countries.

The system of secondary education is marked by a predominant share of vocational schooling. The trends in enrolment in (upper-)secondary education are shown in Figure 12.4. Although vocational education dominates, a decline in the proportion of vocational secondary pupils is evident. While in 1989 almost 56% of all secondary pupils were attending vocational secondary schools, in 2004 the proportion was 28%.

Figure 12.4: Enrolment in upper-secondary education in Slovakia

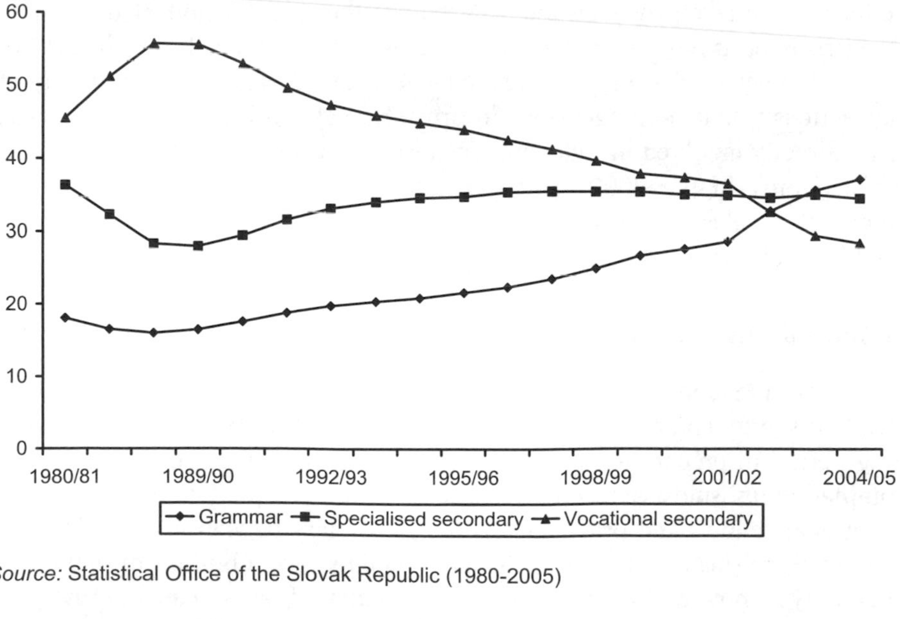

Source: Statistical Office of the Slovak Republic (1980-2005)

Enrolment in specialised secondary education has been more stable, particularly since the mid-1990s. An increase in enrolment in general education is apparent, from about 18% in 1980 to 37% in 2004/05. A continuing shrinking of enrolment in secondary vocational schools, visible

329

from Figure 12.4, contrasts with the substantially increased number of the schools themselves, as suggested by European Training Foundation (ETF, 2002).

Women made up 47.57% of all students in secondary education in 2005. Unsurprisingly, few women enroll in technical sciences (where the proportion of women is 17.12%), but in certain other major fields of study they outnumber men. The proportion of women in medicine is 75%, in social sciences 63.9%, in arts 57.4%. In agriculture and forestry the proportions of men and women are roughly the same, about 47.6% (Statistical office of the Slovak Republic, 2005).

Organisation of vocational training

According to the Organisation for Economic Co-operation and Development (OECD, 2005) in 2003 only 24.6% of all pupils in upper-secondary education were enrolled in the general education stream. On the other hand, 75.4% were enrolled in a vocational stream. About 38.9% of those in vocational education combined school and work.

According to the OECD (2007: 62) study of vocational training in Slovakia, a dual apprenticeship system does not exist in the country. At the beginning of the 1990s all secondary vocational schools (Stredné odborné učilište) were taken over by the state before the privatisation of large state enterprises occurred.[7] Although the state assumed responsibility, it has not invested much in training centres for the past 15 years. The training of apprentices is thus no longer done in firms. Slovakian firms have also ceased to be directly involved in financing vocational education. With the revival of the economy in the 2000s and the number of unfilled vacancies in the automotive industry (Volkswagen, Kia, Peugeot), links are now being re-established between schools and some big firms.

Standardisation and quality differentiation of secondary education

Many examination certificates at the secondary level of education are standardised by comprehensive scale and evaluation criteria. In 2005 after a long period of preparation the Ministry of Education changed the decree on completion of study at secondary schools and completion of training in vocational schools and practical schools (secondary education). The leaving examination (maturita) after which students are eligible to study at university is now divided into external and internal parts. The external part and written section of the internal part of the maturita are uniform across all schools in Slovakia, which ensures a unified level of requirements and a high degree of standardisation.

According to Zelmanova et al (2006) there is a large achievement gap between gymnasium schools and nearly all non-gymnasium schools in mathematics. Students in grade 9 of gymnasia who were selected early scored on average about 113 points higher in the PISA (Programme for International Student Assessment) tests than their non-gymnasium counterparts.

Tertiary level of education

Horizontal dimension

Figure 12.5 looks at one of the most important aspects of the horizontal dimension of tertiary education, field-of-study differentiation. The most popular fields of study are obviously social sciences and services, accounting for 37% of all students enrolled in 1991. The attractiveness of these fields has been increasing; in 2004 47% of all students were enrolled in social sciences and services. The second most popular group is technical sciences. It should be mentioned, however, that the proportion of students enrolled in these fields of study decreased from 40% in 1991 to 31% in 2004. A certain decline has been observed in the proportions of those enrolled in medical fields. The numbers of students enrolled in the fields of agriculture, forestry and veterinary science, as well as the arts, have been steady since 1991.

Figure 12.5: Enrolment in tertiary education by field of study (%)

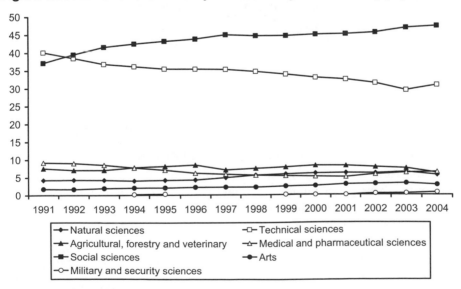

Source: Statistical Office of the Slovak Republic (1980-2005)

331

According to the available data on the gender structure of the students in tertiary education institutions the proportion of women increased between 1995 and 2005, resulting in a higher proportion of women than men being enrolled in tertiary education. The proportion of women has increased in all the main groups of fields of study with the exception of technical sciences (see Figure 12.6). As a result, by 2005 women were overrepresented in natural sciences, medical and pharmaceutical sciences, social sciences and the arts.

Figure 12.6: The proportion of women in tertiary education (excluding PhD students), 1995-2005

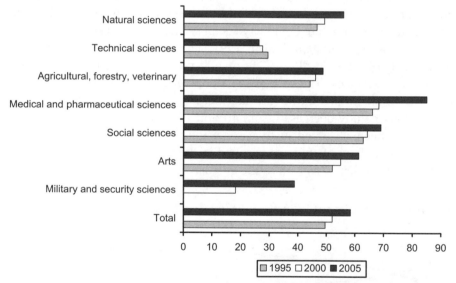

Source: Own calculations based on data from Institute of Information and Prognoses of Education (1995, 2000, 2005)

Standardisation, quality differentiation and openness of tertiary education

Today there are 33 universities in Slovakia (20 public, three state and 10 private), from which as many as 18 have the word 'university' in their name. Currently, there are a number of quality evaluations of university studies being conducted by the accreditation committee, an advisory body of the Slovakian government. The result of comprehensive accreditation could lead to the suspension of some universities. The committee's other goal is the reinforcement of differentiation between universities – focused on research – and other education institutions.

The basis for keeping the status of a university or faculty consists of fulfilling certain formal criteria before the accreditation committee will certify the fields of study in which the faculty can teach students and award a degree. Increasing attention is paid to the quality of professors, who can be guarantees for individual subjects. The relative lack of funds at public universities has caused some university teachers to leave for the private universities.

The proportion of students at private universities increased from 0.4% in 2002 to 7.6% in 2006. Part-time study prevails at private universities. The proportion of students in part-time education increased from 28.7% in 2002 to 37.9% in 2006. The Ministry of Education is not satisfied with the increased proportion of part-time students and the quality of part-time education and it seeks to discourage part-time study.

The Act on Universities allowed public universities to charge tuition fees from 2002. The base rate for the tuition fee was (and after the revision of the law in 2007 continues to be) 10% of the average sum per full-time student from the total running expenses provided for public universities by the Ministry from the state budget. The yearly tuition fee cannot exceed five times the base rate. The dean of the university can lower or waive the tuition fee depending on the study results, health and social situation of the individual student.

The practice of charging tuition fees had not previously been transparent although some universities had charged tuition fees mainly for part-time study through the medium of establishments that had delivered different services to the universities. Payment of tuition fees had not been statistically monitored.

The amendment to the Act on Universities in 2007 defined exactly the maximum level of tuition fee for both full-time and part-time study. For full-time study the maximum level remained five times higher than the base rate, for part-time study the tuition fee cannot be higher than the cost of running the study programmes.

Labour market

Economic development

After the breakdown of the communist system in 1989, social and political reforms initiated a rapid transformation of the Slovakian economy, as a part of Czechoslovakia, into a functioning market economy capable of successfully competing with growing European and global competition (European Commission, 2001). The building up of the private sector started in 1990 and continued in 1991 with the privatisation of smaller-scale state enterprises, together with the establishment of new small businesses (Lubyova et al, 1999). Large-scale privatisation followed in 1992 with the first round of the so-called voucher scheme.

Despite the early market reforms, gross domestic product (GDP) registered a strong decline in real terms during the first years of transition (Figure 12.7). This transitional recession peaked at −14.6% in 1992. Furthermore, the substantial economic turmoil arising from the division of Czechoslovakia in 1993 temporarily halted the initial positive results of the transition process. Privatisation and economic restructuring were gradually slowed down and there was a lack of depth in structural reforms (Lubyova et al, 1999). Besides the transition from a socialist to a market economy, Slovakia also had to master the transition from being part of Czechoslovakia to becoming an independent nation, as well as the transition from a regional to a national economy. In particular, it had to compensate for the loss of the larger part of the internal market of the former Czechoslovakia. The process of large-scale privatisation has come under criticism for lack of transparency. Direct sales to domestic owners were frequently made for a fraction of the market price of the privatised companies. As a result, the growth of the private sector share slowed somewhat because of the cancellation of voucher privatisation and the identification of strategic enterprises to be excluded from the privatisation process.

Figure 12.7: GDP growth, 1989-2006

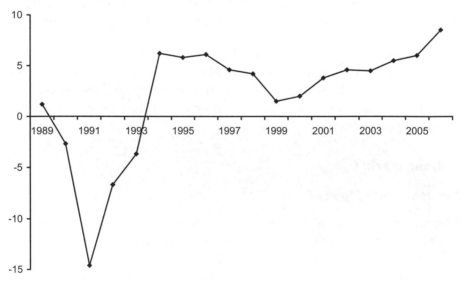

Source: ILO (2008); data for 2006 from Eurostat (2008)

However, in the late 1990s and at the beginning of the new millennium, Slovakia introduced far-reaching macroeconomic and structural reforms. The initial economic contraction was followed by fast growth from 1995 until 1998, with yearly growth of more than 5%. During the mid-1990s, Slovakia was one of the most successful of the transition countries in the field of macroeconomic stabilisation (Lubyova et al, 1999). The expansion was followed by a short and small decline in real GDP per capita at the end of the decade because of the Russian crisis. The economy returned to a higher growth path in 2000 and economic performance improved substantially in the early part of the new millennium. There was a continuous increase in growth rates from 2% in 2000 to 8.5% in 2006. The value for 2006 represents the highest growth rate in the whole Slovakian transition period. Slovakia became a fast growing economy and it is now increasingly recognised as a model case of macroeconomic stabilisation with tight monetary policy, improved fiscal conditions and structural reforms such as product, capital and labour market liberalisation (OECD, 2005). Slovakia also introduced a simple and low flat-rate tax system. This reform process was stimulated by Slovakia's accession to the EU in 2004 among other things.

Labour market dynamics

Employment dynamics

In the first year after Slovakia's independence, in 1994, 10.2% of employed people worked in agriculture, 39.7% in industry and only 50% in services (ILO, 2008). Slovakia was traditionally the more agricultural part of the former Czechoslovakia, but the share of agriculture in the economy was not very large. During the transition period, employment in agriculture decreased significantly to 4.7% in 2005 (ILO, 2008).

In contrast, employment in industry and construction remained fairly stable during the whole transition period fluctuating at around 38%-39% (ILO, 2008). The dominant industrial branches are heavy industry, chemical industry and engineering. The latter sector in particular was in crisis because it suffered from the massive cutbacks in military production (Lubyova et al, 1999). The service sector's share of total employment steadily increased to 56.3% in 2005. Within the services sector, the financial and business services as well as distribution, hotels and restaurants remain particularly underdeveloped in employment terms relative to the EU average (European Commission, 2001).

Figure 12.8 shows that the labour force participation rate of the population aged 15-64 sharply declined from 76.5% in 1990 to 69.3% in 2006. Regarding the development of participation rates, the transitional period can be divided into two sub-periods. Until 1994, there was a relatively sharp decline in the participation rate, disproportionately burdening females. After 1994, participation rates remained fairly stable at around 70%. Figure 12.8 shows additional gender-specific time trends in labour force participation.

Both male and female labour force participation has had the same evolution pattern over time, but the female activity rate is roughly 12-14 percentage points below that of men.

Figure 12.8: Labour force participation rate (age group 15-64), 1990-2006

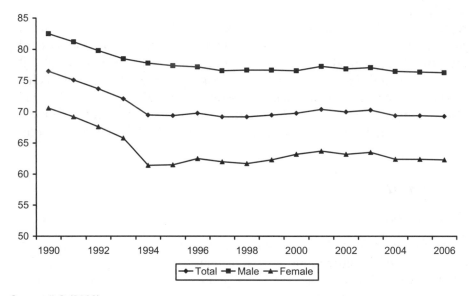

Source: ILO (2008)

As can be seen in Figure 12.8, the most significant decrease of the labour force participation rate in Slovakia occurred during the early 1990s. There were three main factors which influenced the development of the labour force. Two of them are included and quantified in Table 12.1: the higher number of students remaining at school and the decrease in the number of working pensioners (who received both a pension and wages). These factors have contributed, together with withdrawals from the labour market, to a decreasing labour force. The labour force in this period was naturally affected by an increase in the age of the working population.

In 2006, the lowest activity rate was registered for the youngest age cohorts (15-24 years) at 40.8% (Table 12.2). The population aged between 15 and 24 was the cohort most affected by the fall in employment whose activity rate fell from 58.3% to 40.8% between 1990 and 2006. This is partly related to increasing enrolment in higher education but it may also reflect increasing labour market integration problems for the younger age cohort. In contrast, the middle-age cohorts reached very high activity rates of around 87%-93% during the transition period but it also decreased by 5 percentage points. Participation rates of people aged 65 and over decreased from 6.3%

in 1990 to 0.9% in 2006. The very low participation rate in the oldest age group reflects the low statutory retirement age in Slovakia.

Table 12.1: Changes in main groups of population influencing the labour force, 1990-98

	Working-age population	Students	Women on maternity leave	Working pensioners
1990-93	+124.9	−52.9	+42	−101
1994-98	+180.5	−41.5	+28	−10 to −20
1990-98	+305.4	−94.4	+70	−111 to −121

Source: Mikelka (2000: 11)

Table 12.2: Labour force participation rate (%) by age group, 1990-2006

	1990	1995	2000	2006
15+	66.8	59.9	60.1	59.6
15-24	58.3	46.5	46.1	40.8
25-54	93.2	88.4	88.3	87.9
55-64	33.8	23.5	24.3	30.5
65+	6.3	1.7	1.1	0.9

Source: ILO (2008)

Recently the most important factor of employment has become migration into other member states of the EU. Certainly the poor situation in the labour market in Slovakia has sent part of the labour force abroad, primarily the younger workers. In the second quarter of 2007 according to the Labour Force Survey (LFS) 173,900 employees, i.e., 7.44% of the total number of employed people in Slovakia (2,337,700) worked abroad. In some sectors of the economy employers began to signal that they were having problems recruiting sufficient numbers of qualified people.

Unemployment dynamics

Registered unemployment was already high at the beginning of the transition period, at 6.6% in 1991 (Figure 12.9). The transition to a market economy led to an increase in unemployment figures. Due to the two economic recessions at the beginning of the 1990s and in 1999 there were increases in the unemployment rate. In general, Slovakia suffered from an increase in the unemployment rate that peaked at approximately 18.3% of the labour force in 2001, after which it fell substantially to 11.6% in 2005.

Figure 12.9: Unemployment rates, 1991-2006

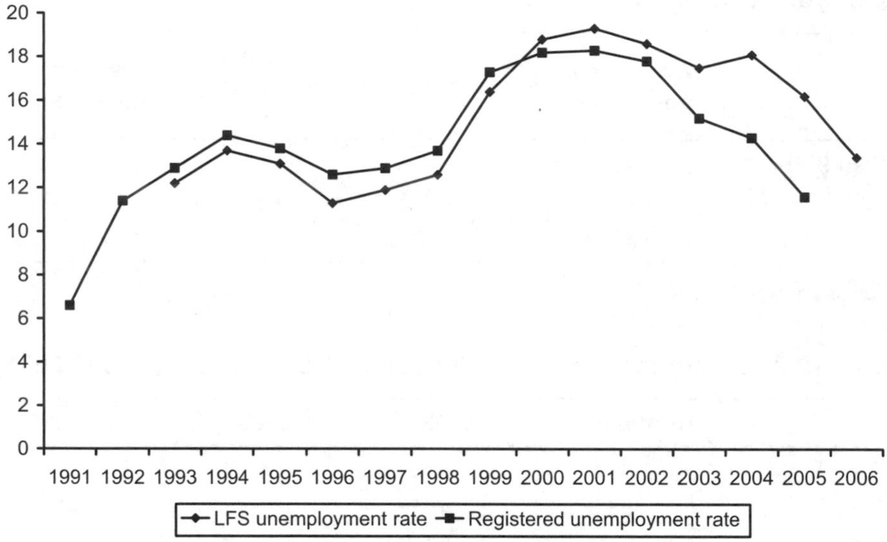

Note: Both LFS and registered unemployment rate for individuals aged over 15.
Source: ILO (2008); registered unemployment in 2006 from Eurostat (2008)

Despite different measurement concepts, the LFS-based unemployment rate shows only slight deviations from registered unemployment. The dramatic decline in both unemployment rates recently is rather impressive. Obviously, continuing economic growth has considerably improved the general labour market situation in terms of unemployment.

In Slovakia, as in many other countries, the transition undergone by young people from school to active life and labour integration remains an important labour market issue (Nesporova, 2002). Labour market entrants, approximated as the youngest age cohort of 15-24, form the category most exposed to unemployment. Their unemployment rate increased from 25.2% in 1993 to 29.9% in 2005 and the level was two to three times higher than the average unemployment rate for the whole adult population (ILO, 2008). Apart from labour demand restrictions related particularly to work experience, difficulties in the professional integration of young people are also caused by the insufficient matching between labour demand and qualifications offered by the educational system. In addition to young people, another disadvantaged category in the labour market is that of the long-term unemployed. According to Eurostat (2008) data, the long-term unemployment rate, i.e., people unemployed for over 12 months, increased from 6.5% in 1998 to 10.2% in 2006. As the overall unemployment rate declined in the last year, this represents an increase in the incidence of long-term unemployment.

Minority ethnic groups, migration and regional differences

The unemployment rate also differs between ethnic groups and regions in Slovakia. There are two large minority ethnic groups in Slovakia: the Hungarian minority representing about 10.6% of the total population and the Roma ethnic group accounting for 6.5% of the total population (Lubyova et al, 1999). The estimated number in the latter group is much higher than the self-reported measure in the Slovakian Census. Hungarians are heavily concentrated in the south-east part of the country, adjacent to the Hungarian and Ukrainian borders. The few existing studies claim that labour market outcomes for Hungarians are broadly similar to those for the population overall (European Commission, 2001). However, systematic data on relative labour market outcomes are not available. The situation of the Roma minority, however, is very different. Unemployment is particularly severe because the Roma population have a very low level of education on average and they are subject to discriminatory practices. A further factor contributing to the poor employment situation of the Roma minority is the concentration of Roma in isolated settlements without good road access, where unemployment can reach 90% (OECD, 2002).

Although Slovakia is a relatively small country, the variation in employment and unemployment rates at the regional level is marked in comparison to other Eastern European countries. There is a sharp distinction between the capital city Bratislava, with the lowest unemployment rate of 7.2% in 2000, and rest of the country, especially the disadvantaged Kosice, Banska Bystrica and Presov regions, which have an unemployment rate of around 21%. Regional unemployment figures tend to be relatively high if the dominant local sector is a troubled one, such as heavy engineering or agriculture. However, these disparities have not encouraged regional migration (OECD, 2002).

Labour market institutions

Employment protection regulation

After independence Slovakia equipped itself with a Labour Code that is similar to that of many other countries in Europe, protecting the positions of incumbent workers in large firms and limiting the room available for flexible employment (OECD, 2005). However, parts of the socialist labour law that dated back to 1964 remained valid. Firing costs were relatively high due to the strict requirements for layoffs. According to the Labour Code which applied during the 1990s, employees can be laid off only for special reasons, such as the closure or major restructuring of a company or serious misconduct (Lubyova et al, 1999). At the same time, the labour market is flexible in terms of the frequency of institutional changes and reforms. The Labour Code has been amended extensively since 1989. In 2002 and 2003, it was thoroughly reformed, making hiring and firing easier. The amendment in 2003 also facilitated temporary and part-time employment and allowed for the indefinite repetition of fixed-term contracts. Furthermore, there was a cut in severance pay and a considerable easing of the conditions under which workers could be dismissed. The new Labour Code also weakened the powers of the trade unions and worker councils. As a result, Slovakia is now considered to have a relatively flexible labour market (OECD, 2005).

Slovakia and other CEE countries tend to be more restrictive concerning regular employment contracts compared to the EU as a whole (see Table 2.7 in Chapter Two of this book). This remained true even after the change in Slovakian labour law in 2003. Regulation concerning temporary employment is less rigid in Slovakia and considerably lower than the EU15 and CEE10 average. In contrast, Slovakia's firing rules concerning collective dismissals were more restrictive. In general, the comparison of overall employment protection legislation (EPL) finds that, because of significant liberalisation efforts, Slovakia has on average a lower EPL strictness than the EU15 average in 2003.

A new Labour Code was approved in June 2007 by the new government, in which the strongest political party is the social democrats (SMER). The main feature of the revision of the Labour Code is the strengthening of the position of employees. The new Labour Code grants workers more generous severance conditions and introduces a definition of dependent work, which, according to the approved text, can only be carried out by employees and not contractors. This amendment came into effect in September 2007. The second most important change in the Labour Code is the restriction on employers in terms of repeating fixed-term contracts. Now employers will be allowed to do this only once within a period of three years, which is generally the maximum time for a fixed-term contract. With respect to termination of employment, there is no specific protection guaranteed by the new Labour Code to young workers. They are subject to the same rules as other workers.

Industrial relations

During the transition, Slovakia moved away from a centralised wage-setting system towards a collective bargaining system in the private sector as did many other CEE countries. Wage bargaining usually takes place at company level or sectoral level as well as, to a lesser extent, at the national level (Visser, 2004: Table 1.8). Bargaining at the national level is conducted in the tripartite Council for Economic and Social Accord consisting of members of the trade unions, the employers' associations and the government. This council sets a minimum nation-wide wage increase by sector.

Union membership declined sharply during the 1990s from full registration of the workforce at the beginning of transition. According to the OECD (2004), the Slovakian unionisation rate decreased from 57% in 1995 to 36% in 2000. Van Gyes et al (2007: Figure 2) reported a further decrease to 30% in 2004. The decrease can be explained, as in other CEE countries, by the abolition of compulsory membership and economic turbulence.

Even more important than the number of unionised workers is the coverage by collective agreements. Van Gyes et al (2007) estimate the percentage of employees covered by collective agreements at 50% in 2004, representing a relatively high level of coverage compared to other CEE countries. The degree of coordination lies in the middle with an index of 2 compared to other CEE countries, where the index varies from 1 to 4 (Visser, 2004: Table 1.10). Slovakia has the second highest degree of centralisation in CEE countries, which is significantly below EU15 average (Visser, 2004: Table 1.9).

Welfare regime

Labour market policy

Active labour market policy

During the early transition period, labour market policy in Slovakia was characterised by the tendency to finance passive measures, and by insignificant expenditures on active measures. Both passive and active labour market policies were financed from contributions paid to the Employment Fund, mainly by employers and employees (Lubyova et al, 1999). The National Labour Office supervised financial flows within the system. Community work and subsidised job creation schemes were the main active measures, in terms of participants and expenditure; these were put into place at the very beginning of the transition period. Retraining has been used modestly and the rest of the programmes claimed only a negligible share of total expenditure.

The tightening of the payment of unemployment benefits in the late 1990s coincided with an increasing emphasis on active labour market policy (ALMP). Due to reform in 1997, ALMP has become more central in Slovakian labour market policy (Lubyova et al, 1999). A wage subsidy was made available to employers who agreed to hire school leavers for 12 months. From 2004 on, this wage subsidy has also been available for the employment of disadvantaged job seekers (which comprises other disadvantaged groups besides young people) and has been administered by the Office of Labour, Social Affairs and Family. The subsidy payable to employers is up to 100% of the monthly total labour costs for a maximum period of 24 months. In part, it is specifically designed for people up to 25 years old in regions with a high unemployment rate. Another form of wage subsidy is given to employers to provide school leavers with work experience. This amounts to SKK 1,500 per month for school leavers up to 25 years of age and SKK 1,000 per month for employers.

Although steps were taken to intensify ALMP programmes, the overall share of expenditure on these programmes is comparatively very low in Slovakia despite its very high unemployment rate. Eurostat data (own calculations) indicate that compared to Slovakia in 2004, the Czech Republic spent four times as much, while Hungary spent 8.6 times as much of their GDP on ALMP measures, while their unemployment was less than half the Slovakian level.

In 2004, a new law on employment services came into force. Counselling of job seekers became more closely adapted to their individual needs, for example, with the introduction of individual action plans and increased resources. A recent evaluation of counselling services has shown that the capacity and staff resources of employment service offices are more limited in eastern regions, where unemployment is particularly high. A new programme ('Graduate Practice') supporting the employment of disadvantaged job applicants was also introduced, partly in response to the difficulties school leavers were facing on entering the labour market. Low-skilled individuals who have been unemployed for more than six months comprise the main target group. Furthermore, unemployed school leavers under the age of 25 as well as unemployed people above the age of 50, regardless of the duration of their unemployment spell, are eligible. The main features of the programme are outlined in Table 12.3.

Table 12.3: Characteristics of graduate practice programme

	2004	2005	2006
Individuals	14,462	24,838	14,503
Total expenditure in millions of SKK	199.9	334.3	138.3
Expenditure/person in SKK	13,821	13,460	9,533

Source: Center for Labour, Social Affairs and Family (2004-06)

Women represent 67.4% of participants of the 'Graduate Practice' programme. Recently financial contributions to employers have been abolished. Nevertheless, employers, particularly in the public sector, remain interested in this programme.

Unemployment insurance

Overall, Slovakian unemployment insurance has been reformed in response to the high unemployment rate from the late 1990s onwards. Older workers in particular benefited from the old system. They received unemployment benefit payments over a longer period (Law No 387/1996 on employment), since contribution requirements were diminished by allowing for periods of invalidity, care for children and people with disabilities. For school leavers, unemployment benefit was given after evidence of six months of unemployment. The amount of benefit was about 42% of the net average wage.

In the early 2000s, entitlement to unemployment benefit became more restricted. From 1 January 2004 (Law No 5/2004 on employment), the period for which it was necessary to pay contributions was prolonged to three years and the credited periods (for childcare etc) were erased. The duration of benefit payment was made uniform for all unemployed people – a maximum of six months without regard for previous economic activity. Under these conditions, the number of young receivers of unemployment benefit was lowered and the amount of benefit was about 35% of the net average wage.

Table 12.4: Number of receivers of unemployment benefit

	1998	2005
Total number of unemployed people (000s)	317.1	427.5
Total number of UB receivers (000s)	120.0	132.6
Percentage of unemployed receiving benefits	37.8	31.0
Number of young unemployed (15 to 24 years old) (000s)	105.9	95.5
Number of young benefit receivers (15 to 24 years old) (000s)	34.0	7.5
Percentage of young unemployed receiving benefits	32.1	7.9

Source: Statistical Office of the Slovak Republic (1999, 2006); Social Insurance Agency (1999, 2006); Ministry of Labour, Social Affairs and Family of the Slovak Republic (1999, 2006)

These reform trends are reflected in the proportion of the unemployed actually receiving benefits. When unemployment insurance was introduced, a high proportion of the unemployed were receiving unemployment benefit. This proportion, however, declined rapidly throughout the 1990s and early 2000s. At the starting point in 1991, 82% of the unemployed were receiving benefits. In 1992, this figure was down to 33% and dropped further to 27% in 1993, where it roughly remained until the late 1990s. New legislation that came into force on 1 January 2000 toughened the conditions for receiving unemployment benefit in reaction to the previous surge in the unemployment rate. At the end of 2000, the share of receivers of unemployment benefit had already declined to 18%. By the end of 2005, it had declined further to only 8.8%. The decline was brought about both by shortening the period of benefit payment,[8] by prolonging the qualifying period (from 12-36 months of paying contributions) and by rising long-term unemployment.

Initially, unemployment benefit was relatively valuable for young people, especially for school leavers. For example, in 1995 47% of unemployed people received unemployment benefit in the 15-19 age group and 23.4% in the 20-24 age group. After 1996 (Law No 387/1996 on employment), the benefit became less accessible to young people. Benefit receipt among 15- to 19-year-olds declined to 29% in 1999. From 1 January 2000 onwards, the marked measures affected the number of young receivers of unemployment benefit more strongly. Since then, only an insignificant number of unemployed young people have received the benefit – about 3% from the 15-19 age group and about 15% from the 20-24 age group. This stark decline is mainly due to a lengthening of the required contribution period, which cannot be fulfilled by young people who are entering the labour market for the first time. The reform also rests on the assumption that young people could be supported by their parents in case of difficulties entering the labour market.

The influence of the unemployment benefit system in relation to the labour market entry of young adults has not been thoroughly analysed. The problem of unemployed young people has not been a popular research topic compared to other unemployed social groups in Slovakia – there were (in the late 1990s as well in the early 2000s) more problems with the employment of Roma people, people with low levels of education, the long-term unemployed and with employment in eastern and southern regions of Slovakia. For young people, there was one solution – participation in a more extensive school system and lengthening periods of vocational training, which is reflected in rising high school and university enrolment rates. Furthermore young people can often extend the period in which they live with their parents and are supported by them during unemployment. One consequence of unemployment among young people was the increase in the average age of first marriage. From 1992 until 2004, the average age of first marriage rose about 3.5 years.[9]

Minimum wage

A legal minimum wage exists and is set at a national level. The minimum wage applies directly to a few workers but is used as reference point. Slovakia ranks around the middle of the OECD with a relatively high minimum wage of around 40% of the average wage (OECD, 2005). This level is appropriate in Bratislava, and other western regions, where productivity levels are generally higher. However, it may be too high in the eastern regions, where both living costs and average productivity levels are much lower. A new law on the minimum wage is currently being prepared by social partners and should be approved by the end of 2007. Table 12.5 indicates that between 1991 and 1997/99, the minimum wage declined relative to both the subsistence minimum (for a single adult) and the average gross wage, but increased again thereafter.

Table 12.5: Development of gross monthly minimum wage, relative to gross average wage

	1991	1993	1995	1997	1999	2001	2003	2005	2006
Gross minimum wage as % of gross average wage	0.53	0.41	0.34	0.29	0.34	0.36	0.39	0.4	0.41

Source: Statistical Office of the Slovak Republic (1992-2006)

Family policy

After 1995, overall expenditure on family policies declined somewhat from 10% to 6% of total social protection expenditure (minus old-age insurance expenditure) in 2003, while it rose again to 8% of GDP in 2004. Comparing the relative importance of in-kind versus in-cash benefit expenditure, hardly any changes are visible. Cash benefits dominate, accounting for over 90% of all family policy expenditure since 1995 (own calculations based on Eurostat data).

Public childcare

Nearly all kindergartens in Slovakia are under public authority (approximately 98%). Some kindergartens are private (0.6%) or run by churches (1.1%). The opening hours are in line with the working times of mothers (usually from 7.00am until 16.00pm). Monthly payments for day care in kindergartens in Slovakia consists of two parts: board costs (fully paid by parent) plus a monthly fee on costs in kindergartens (only partly paid by parent). The monthly fee varies between SKK 50 and 375 per child according to the situation of the individual family.[10] Table 12.6 shows that the enrolment of children aged three to five has decreased by 26% from 1989 to 1995, with enrolment rising again to 72.7% in 2005, which is still below pre-transition levels. The percentage of children below the age of three enrolled in kindergarten is negligible.

The decrease in enrolment until 1995 coincided with the closing down of kindergartens that were run by large employers (e.g. factories). Table 12.7 indicates that between 1989 and 1995 the number of kindergartens dropped significantly (by 18%). After 1995, we can observe rising enrolment, which may be due in part to previous declines in fertility.

Table 12.6: Age-specific enrolment rate: children aged 3-5 (percentages enrolled within age group), 1989-2005

1989	1990	1993	1994	1995	1996	1997	1998	2001	2002	2003	2004	2005
77.9	72.0	63.1	61.2	57.4	60.6	65.1	68.2	68.7	70.7	72.1	73.3	72.7

Source: UNICEF (2007)

As Table 12.7 indicates, enrolment grew despite declining numbers of kindergartens and kindergarten teachers, and while the share of pupils per kindergarten and the pupil – teacher ratio was also steadily declining. This lends further support to the explanation that growing enrolment is in part due to declining fertility, which dropped from 2.08 life births per woman (aged 15-49) in 1989 to 1.52 life births in 1995 and 1.25 life births in 2005. Furthermore, rising GDP, real wages and a stabilisation of the unemployment rate may have contributed to rising enrolment in the latter half of the 1990s.

Table 12.7: Development of kindergartens in Slovakia (absolute figures), 1989-2006

	Schools	Teachers	Pupils	Pupils per school	Pupils per teacher
1989	4052	18729	241458	59.59	12.89
1990	4025	18620	216336	53.75	11.62
1995	3322	14933	161697	48.67	10.83
2000	3263	15229	154232	47.27	10.13
2005	2945	13201	141814	48.15	10.74
2006	2928	13149	140014	47.82	10.65

Source: Ministry of Education of the Slovak Republic (2007)

Cash benefits

The Slovakian government operates an extensive system of cash transfers comprising birth grants, child allowance, childcare benefits and special targeted transfers. Child allowance takes the form of both direct transfer benefits (child benefit) as well as tax bonuses. It is seen as a central instrument in family policy. Parents may receive these benefits for children under the age of 16 (or up to the age of 25 in case of enrolment in full-time education).

In 2006, child benefit amounted to SKK 540 per month per child. Additionally, for parents whose income was six times higher than the minimum wage, a tax deduction of SKK 540 per month per child was available. Among childcare benefits, the most important benefit is parental allowance, which has been raised repeatedly.

Table 12.8: Main cash benefits for children in Slovakia, 2001 and 2005

	Sums of benefits in % of average gross monthly wage		State expenditure on family benefits in % of GDP	
	2001	2005	2001	2005
Child benefit + tax bonus	between 3.4 and 6.8	3.1 + 3.1	0.894	1.212
Parental allowance	22.1	25.7	0.448	0.46

Source: Statistical Office of the Slovak Republic (2002,2006)

By the end of 2006, parental allowance amounted to SKK 4,440 per month, which is about 25% of gross average monthly wage. The claim conditions for parental allowance are: regular care for at least one child up to the age of three (or the age of six if his/her health status is long-term negative); the permanent or temporary residency of both parent and child in Slovakia; and that the child must not attend a kindergarten supported by state. Apart from child allowances and childcare allowances, a variety of other monthly, annual and one-off benefits exist. Furthermore, special benefits exist for families in material need and for young parents still in education or other labour market preparation programmes.

Social assistance

Slovakia has operated a guaranteed minimum income (GMI) scheme since 1988. The so-called 'subsistence minimum' is calculated primarily on the basis of consumption, but also with reference to the minimum wage. Before 2004, the subsistence minimum also served as the official poverty line. It is regularly indexed each year.

The adjustment of the subsistence minimum takes into account increases in net income (or in the costs of living in lower-income households). In the late 1990s, social assistance benefits were calculated as the difference between the subsistence minimum and the actual income of a family. With a reform in 2004, a new calculation method was implemented. Social assistance benefits have been subject to means-testing from the early 1990s onwards. The amount of benefit for the household is calculated by taking into account the number of people living in that household as well as their incomes. Participation in labour market programmes is important for recipients. Non-compliance results in lower benefit payments. There is no age limit.

Table 12.9: Social assistance in Slovakia, 1995-2005

	Maximum amount of social assistance/benefit in material need (from 2004)						
	1995	1997	1999	2001	2003	2004	2005
Single adult, SKK	2,080	2,218	3,115	3,490	2,900	3,704	4,155
as % of gross average wage	0.29	0.24	0.29	0.28	0.2	0.23	0.24
as % of gross minimum wage	0.85	0.82	0.9	0.77	0.51	0.6	0.63
2 adults with 2 children[a], SKK	6,485	6,912	8,105	9,090	9,000	7,638[b]	8,680
as % of gross average wage	0.9	0.75	0.76	0.74	0.63	0.48	0.5
as % of gross minimum wage	2.65	2.56	2.35	2.01	1.58	1.23	1.32
Individuals in 'material need' (000s)	426	389	537	632	543	383	374
% of population	7.6	7.3	10.8	11.7	10.1	7.1	6.9
Expenditure (million),	4,679	4,600	9,537	11,386	9,029	6,302	7,058

SKK

Notes: [a] Children: first child aged 6-10 years + second child aged 10-15 years; [b] the maximum for all members in any household is only SKK 10,500.
Source: Regulation No 378/1991 on social dependence, Regulation No 105/1992 on social dependence, Regulation No 243/1993 on social dependence, Law No 195/1998 on social assistance, Law No 599/2003 on help in material need; Statistical office of the Slovak Republic (1996-2006); Social Insurance Agency (1996-2006); Ministry of Labour, Social Affairs and Family of the Slovak Rebublic (1996-2006)

While the number of recipients rose between 1995 and 2001, there were significant declines thereafter, due both to reforms as well as to economic growth. Hence, the population share receiving social assistance declined from the late 1990s to a low of 6.9% in 2005. Maximum benefit levels for single adults have declined steadily since 1995, relative to both the gross average as well as the gross minimum wage. For families there were pronounced declines in relative benefit rates after 2000, especially in 2004 (Table 12.9).

Intergenerational transfers

In Slovakia, parents frequently help young people and young families in the form of monetary transfers as well as taking care of their grandchildren. Help for young single people usually takes the form of shared accommodation. In the mid-1990s, about 30%-35% of all Slovak families reported receiving some kind of help, either in cash or in-kind, from the wider family. Among families in a precarious situation, the share of help from the wider family was higher, up to 50% (Bednárik et al, 1995).

According to the data from the 1991 and 2001 Censuses, there is substantial support in terms of provision of accommodation to young single people from the side of their parents, which rose throughout the 1990s. Among 20- to 24-year-olds, the percentage of adult children living with their parents rose from 44.7% in 1991 to 52.6% in 2001. At the same time, married couples are much less likely to share accommodation with their parents. Among 20- to 24-year-olds, only 8% (in 1991) and 11% (in 2001) of married men and 4% (in 1991) and 5% (in 2001) of married women were living with their parents.[11]

Note

[1] The section is based on Wong (1998).
[2] The section is based on Eurydice (2003) and ETF (2002) publications.
[3] The exceptions are studies at two-year schools of commerce, specialised schools for girls and five-year hoteliers' schools.
[4] Studies last for two or three years and end with a final examination.

[5] Studies last for four years and end with a school leaving examination (*maturitná skúška*).
[6] There are also grants for students with very good results or those from poor social backgrounds.
[7] Earlier enterprises were involved in preparing apprentices for their needs.
[8] In the early 1990s, duration of payments was 12 months. Subsequently the duration of benefit receipt was shortened for young people, until in the early 2000s, it was cut down to six months for all unemployed people.
[9] It is 27.9 years for men and 25.3 years for women (Pilinska, 2005: 23).
[10] Regulation of Ministry of Education of Slovak Republic No 353/1994, amended by Reg No 540/2004.
[11] Source: Census Slovakia, 1991 and 2001, Statistical Office of the Slovak Republic.

References

Bednárik, R., Valná, S., Daneková, Z., Rybárová, S. and Filipová, J. (1995) *The social consequences of transformation in Slovakia: national report*, Vienna: Institute for Human Sciences.

Center for Labour, Social Affairs and Family (2004-2006) *Realizácia nástrojov aktívnej politiky trhu práce za rok* (*Realization of active labour market policies in 2004, 2005, 2006*), Bratislava: Center for Labour, Social Affairs and Family.

ETF (European Training Foundation) (2000) *Vocational education and training in Central and Eastern Europe: key indicators*, Luxembourg: Office for Official Publications of the European Communities.

ETF (2002) *Vocational education and training and employment services in the Slovak Republic*, Luxembourg: Office for Official Publications of the European Communities.

European Commission (2001) *Joint assessment of employment priorities in Slovakia*, Luxembourg: Office for Official Publications of the European Communities.

Eurostat (2008) *Data: labour market*, Luxembourg: Eurostat (http://epp.eurostat.ec.europa.eu).

Eurydice (2003) *Structure of education, vocational training, and adult education system: Slovakia*, Brussels: Eurydice European Unit.

ILO (International Labour Organization) (2008) *Key indicators of the labour market programme*, Fifth Edition, Geneva: ILO.

Institute of Information and Prognoses of Education (1995, 2000, 2005) *Štatistická ročenka školstva Slovenskej republiky* (*Statistical yearbook of education of the Slovak Republic*), Bratislava: Institute of Information and Prognoses of Education.

Lubyova, M., Ochrankova, D. and Vantuch, J. (1999) *Background study on employment and labour market in Slovakia*, Torino: European Training Foundation.

Mikelka, E. (2000) *Analýza komparatívnych výhod a nevýhod ekonomiky Slovenskej republiky vo vzťahu k vysokej miere nezamestnanosti*, Bratislava: Institute of Slovak and World Economies.

Ministry of Education of the Slovak Republic (2007) *Koncepcia v oblasti predškolskej výchovyv nadväznosti na prípravu detí na vstup do základnej školy* (*Conception in the area of pre-school education in connection with the pupils preparation to enter the primary school*), Bratislava: Ministry of Education.

Ministry of Labour, Social Affairs and Family of the Slovak Republic (1992-2006) *Annual reports on Slovak population social situation*, Bratislava: Ministry of Labour, Social Affairs and Family.

Nesporova, A. (2002) *Why unemployment remains so high in Central and Eastern Europe*, Employment Paper No 43, Geneva: International Labour Organization.

OECD (Organisation for Economic Co-operation and Development) (2002) *Economic surveys: Slovak Republic*, Paris: OECD.

OECD (2004) *Employment outlook*, Paris: OECD.

OECD (2005) *Economic surveys: Slovak Republic*, Paris: OECD.

OECD (2007) *Jobs for youth: Slovak Republic*, Paris: OECD.

Pilinska, V. (2005) *Demographic characterisation of family in Slovakia*, Bratislava: Demographic Research Centre.

Social Insurance Agency (1999, 2006) *Annual report*, Bratislava: Social Insurance Agency.

Statistical Office of the Slovak Republic (1980-2006) *Statistical yearbook*, Bratislava: Statistical Office of the Slovak Republic.

UNICEF (United Nations International Children's Emergency Fund) (2007) *TransMONEE 2007 Database*, Florence: UNICEF Innocenti Research Centre (www.unicef-icdc.org/resources/transmonee.html).

Van Gyes, G., Vandenbrande, T., Lehndorff, S., Schilling, G., Schief, S. and Kohl, H. (2007) *Industrial relations in EU member states 2000-2004*, Dublin: European Foundation for the Improvement of Living and Working Conditions.

Visser, J. (2004) 'Patterns and variations in European industrial relations', in European Commission (ed) *Industrial relations in Europe*, Luxembourg: Office for the Official Publications of the European Communities, pp 11-57.

Wong, R. (1998) 'Multidimensional influences of family environment in education: the case of socialist Czechoslovakia', *Sociology of Education*, vol 71, no 1, pp 1-11.

Zelmanova, O., Korsnakova, P., Tramonte, L. and Willms, J. (2006) 'Education inequality in Slovakia: the effects of early selection', *Prospects*, vol 34, no 4, pp 529-38.

THIRTEEN

Slovenia

Angela Ivančič

At the time of the fall of the Iron Curtain, Slovenia was in a privileged position relative to the other members of the former Socialist Federal Republic of Yugoslavia (SFRY) as well as many other Central and Eastern European (CEE) countries. It was the wealthiest part of the SFRY and had more contact with Western markets (Silva-Jáuregeui, 2004). Slovenia, however, also inherited a large public debt burden and hyperinflation. Real output was already declining even before independence because of a crisis that engulfed the Yugoslav federation at the end of the 1980s. Transitional reforms therefore had already begun at the end of the 1980s, resulting in strong restructuring processes in the Slovenian economy and society. These entailed privatisation processes, the decline of traditional industrial sector, an expansion of the service sector and, as a consequence, a massive loss of jobs for the less qualified industrial labour force. Old institutions of individual social subsystems have been also changed or abolished in line with requirements of the market economy. Economic and social restructuring was accompanied by the loss of the employment security and a reduction of social rights provided by the state. The country's underskilled labour structure and the failure of the education system to provide appropriate skills to labourers prevented the labour force from adjusting rapidly enough to the economic and social changes, resulting in an unemployment explosion. Because of rigidities in the Slovenian labour market and the nature of employment relationships, the heaviest burden from the reduction in employment opportunities was carried by young first-time job seekers, most of them in the middle of the transition from school to work. This phenomenon is reflected by the high youth unemployment rate and youth's high share in the flexible labour force (Kanjuo-Mrčela and Ignjatović, 2004).

In the second half of the 1990s, however, the economy started to recover, and unemployment began to decline. This economic growth, which by 2005 had turned into an economic boom, decreased the unemployment rate among all social groups, increased the activity rate of the population and transformed Slovenia into one of the most successful new members of the European Union (EU). Despite this success, the increasing share of highly educated workers in the population and the persistent lack of stable employment opportunities for young people reveal that Slovenia needs to invest in overcoming structural unemployment.

Education system

Structure of the Slovenian education system

Overview of the Slovenian education system after the Second World War

In Slovenia, the most important turning point in primary education was the 1958 education reform, which implemented a comprehensive eight-year primary school, reduced the number of primary schools and began the formation of full eight-year and subsidiary four-year grammar schools. Secondary technical education experienced a boom from 1945 to 1963 prompted by the need for a rapidly developing industrial sector.

The 1949 Higher Education Act reorganised the previously unified university into a university with four faculties (arts, mathematics and natural sciences, law and economic studies), the technical higher school, the higher school of medicine, the independent faculty of agriculture and forestry and the theological faculty.[1] Higher artistic education was also organised at art academies of music, visual arts and acting. The Secondary Education Act, passed in 1967, regulated the entire secondary education sector. Vocational schools, technical schools and other schools of economic and commerce subjects, social services and public administration, art schools and grammar schools were all defined as secondary schools.

In the 1970s, higher education also experienced important changes. Old, mostly uniform, four-year syllabuses were replaced by new ones that, in many fields of study, introduced a graduated degree system with a shorter two-year and a longer four-year stage (first degree and second degree). In addition to higher and university institutions, two-year professional colleges were founded, mostly in technical fields. In 1981, a reformed type of education – the so called career oriented education – came into force. It introduced a unified system of both youth and adult education. At the secondary level, the reform abolished the differentiation between the vocational and the academic track as well as eliminating the general maturity exam. All education programmes were required to deliver qualifications both enabling students to make the transition to employment and allowing them to continue education at the tertiary level. The process of education was entirely school-based and continuing education was to be delivered with the support of firms and enterprises who would provide occupation/job-specific skills. However, this system was never implemented in practice.

At the higher education level, the following programmes were available: shorter-cycle higher professional education of maximum two-year duration,[2] four-year higher professional education, specialisation and master programmes (two years) and doctoral programmes.

Education system since 1990 [3]

The education reform carried out in the 1990s in independent Slovenia aimed to re-establish an efficient education system that would be responsive to the needs of the economy and society and comparable to educational systems in other European countries. It extended primary education from eight to nine years, starting at the age of six and lasting to the age of 15 (1996 Primary Education Act). The eight-year 'basic' education was divided into two education cycles each lasting four years: the first stage from class one to class four and the second stage from class five to class eight (see Figure 13.1). The nine-year elementary school is divided into three cycles consisting of three grades each.

Secondary education starts at the age of 15 and lasts until 18-19 years of age. The following types of education and training are provided at the secondary level: general secondary education; professionally oriented general education; secondary technical education; vocational/technical education; three-year secondary vocational education; lower-vocational education; maturity course,[4] vocational course; and master craftsman, foreman and managerial examinations (Ignjatović et al, 2003). General education programmes (gymnasia) prepare students for higher education. They last for four years and are completed by passing an external maturity exam.[5] The professionally oriented high school programmes are designed as part of the general education stream and introduce theoretical professional subjects into general education.[6] After passing the maturity exam, students can directly enrol in any higher education studies. In the period 1996-2004, vocational education and training (VET) in Slovenia comprised programmes of short-term vocational education, secondary vocational education, technical education; two-year vocational/technical education, post-secondary non-tertiary vocational courses, maturity course and post-secondary vocational education (two-year post-secondary vocational colleges).

Lower-vocational education programmes last between two to two-and-a-half years. They consist of theoretical and practical parts and they finish with a final exam. Pupils can enrol in short-term vocational programmes if they have completed at least six grades of primary education and thus fulfil the basic legal compulsory education requirement. After completing a short-term vocational programme, students can enter the labour market as assistants of skilled workers or continue education in the first year of any other secondary education programme.

Figure 13.1: The Slovenian education system, 1996-2004

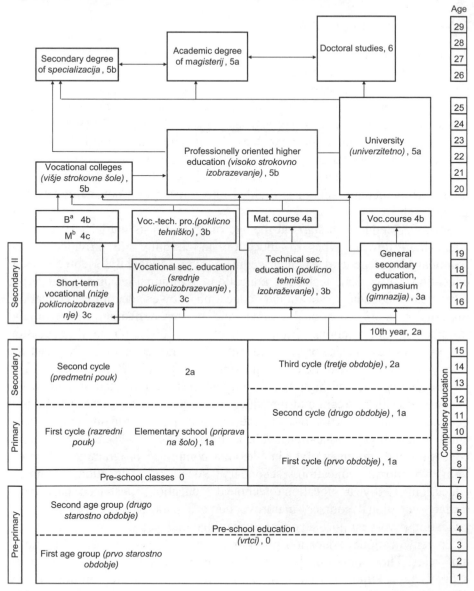

Note: [a]Bridging exam for admission to post-secondary vocational education; [b]Master craftsman preparatory course.
Source: ETF (2000)

Secondary vocational programmes last for three years and are intended to provide qualifications at the skilled worker level for work in the industrial, crafts and service sectors. Such programmes are offered by vocational schools and by a dual system in which theoretical education is provided by schools, while the majority of practical training is provided by employers. The dual system and the school-based programmes end with a final exam testing both theoretical and practical knowledge and skills. The qualifications provided by these programmes enable enrolment in two-year vocational/technical programmes.

Secondary technical education programmes last for four years. The certificate of completion, *spričevalo o zaključnem izpitu* or more recently *spričevalo o poklicni maturi*, allows entry into specific occupational fields and the possibility of continuing education in vocational colleges or in professionally oriented higher education. If students have also completed an additional maturity subject, they may also enrol in university studies.

Two-year vocational/technical programmes are continuing secondary education programmes that end with a vocational maturity degree. These programmes are meant to be a progression route especially for those finishing three-year vocational programmes. They lead to qualifications at the level of a secondary technical school and provide equal possibilities for continuation at the tertiary level.

A one year vocational course has been introduced to provide pupils from (general) secondary schools with a vocational qualification, thus enabling entry into the labour market.

Master craftsman, foreman and managerial examinations provide a vertical progression route within the dual system. They qualify people to run their own craft business as well as to be tutors of apprentices. As a condition for applying for master craftsman and foreman examinations, students are required to have at least a completed three-year vocational school and have a minimum of three years work experience.

Post-secondary vocational education in the form of vocational colleges was introduced by the Vocational and Technical Education Act of 1996. They offer two-year post-secondary vocational courses that are designed as a form of tertiary education but are markedly more practical in content than other forms of higher education. In these courses, practical training accounts for around 40% of the curriculum and is completed within companies. Post-secondary vocational education ends with a diploma exam, which enables students to start working in specific occupations.[7]

At the level of higher education, the reform enacted in 1993 introduced three-year higher professional education and four to five year university education. University education is oriented toward academic work. Completion of university education results in a university diploma (university degree) and enables direct enrolment in postgraduate studies, specialisation and master's programmes and, most recently, to doctoral studies. Higher professional education is intended for the labour market with an emphasis on the development of applied skills and competencies. Cooperation between institutions of higher education and enterprises in carrying out education programmes is underlined. Completion of higher professional education results in a higher education non-university diploma.

On the basis of the Bologna process, the following levels of higher education are enacted: (1) first stage including higher professional education and university education (undergraduate studies, BA, BS); (2) second stage encompassing master studies and unified master studies (MA, MSc); and (3) third stage representing doctoral studies (PhD).

Vertical dimension of the education system

Figure 13.2 displays the trends in educational enrolment in Slovenia starting as early as 1952. At that time, the vast majority of the school-aged population was enroled in basic elementary education, but the proportion of these pupils has been declining from about 85% in 1952 to slightly less than 50% in 2002.

Figure 13.2: Enrolment (% of total students enrolled) by type of school in Slovenia

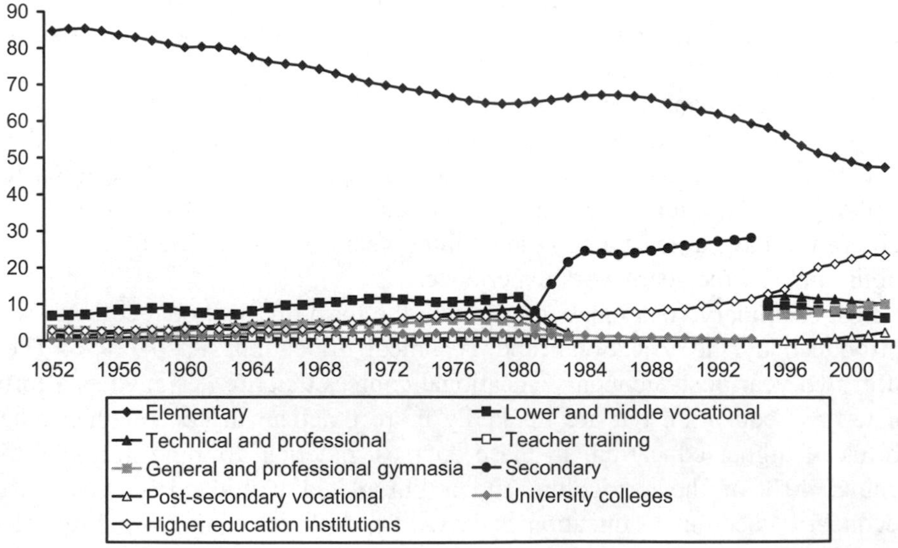

Source: Statistical Office Slovenia (1980-2004)

At the same time, an expansion in the enrolment in various tracks of secondary, as well as tertiary, education is clearly visible. Enrolment in lower and middle vocational education increased from 6.8% in 1952 to 7.7% in 1981, at which time this programme was terminated, and was reintroduced in 1995 with 9.6% of pupils enrolled. Since then, a decrease in enrolment can be observed. Similarly, a number of other education tracks were terminated between 1984 and 1995. These were technical and professional programmes and gymnasia that were replaced by comprehensive secondary schools. In 1995, the former were re-established with enrolment in technical and professional tracks at levels somewhat higher than before termination. University colleges with a relatively low proportion of students were also eliminated by 1995. At the same time, one can observe a dramatic increase in the number of students enrolled in academic education institutions from 2.7% in 1952 to 23.5% in 2002.

In 2003, women outnumbered men in almost all levels and education tracks except for three-year secondary vocational programmes, where 37% of those enrolled were women. Secondary technical schools exhibit an equal number of men and women, and women only slightly outnumber men (53% to 47%) in academic institutions of higher education (Statistical Office Slovenia, 2004).

In Slovenia, the Roma (which, according to the 2002 Census, represents only 0.2% of the total population) are the most marginalised ethnic group with regard to their participation in education at all levels and stages with 90% of Roma failing to complete basic education (Ministry of Education and Sports, 2004).

Secondary level of education

Stratification and track differentiation

Initial education decisions are made in Slovenia at the age of 15, which is similar to the timing of decision making in the Baltic countries and is somewhat later than in the Czech and Slovak Republics and Hungary. At the age of 15, pupils and their parents face the choice between continuing general education or opting for vocational training. In recent years, a general trend of increasing enrolment in secondary general education programmes is visible in Slovenia. After having completed general secondary education, the general maturity examination represents a universal entrance ticket to all tertiary programmes. On the other hand, vocational education and training programmes leading directly to employment have a lower value and usually represent the destination for those who do not reach the threshold for entering general and technical education. Accordingly, enrolment in these programmes has been in constant decline since 1994 (see Figure 13.3). In the school year 1995/96, approximately 36% of those enrolled in secondary programmes participated in two and three-year VET programmes, 36% in technical programmes and 27% in general programmes. The figures for the school year 2004/05 show a different picture: 21% were enrolled in VET programmes, 38% in technical programmes and 40% in general programmes. Moreover, more than 1% was enrolled in a maturity course, and almost 8% of those finishing three-year VET continued on to two-year vocational technical programmes to obtain the vocational maturity certificate.

Figure 13.3: Enrolment in initial secondary education by type of programme (%), 1994/95-2004/05

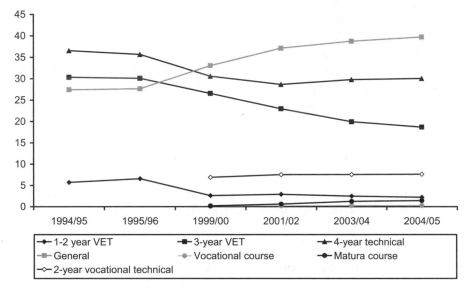

Note: VET = vocational education and training.
Source: Statistical Office Slovenia: Rapid reports: No 85/ 2006, Tables 2.2, 4.2; No 114/2006, Table 3; No 121/2005, Table 3; No 66/2004, Table 2.2; No 111/2004, Table 3; No 270/2002, Table 2.2; No 44/2002, Table 2; No 335/99, Table 1; No 75/1996, Table 2.2

There is a pronounced division between males and females in terms of type of secondary education and field of study. In the school year 2001/02, 34.2% of all women enrolled in secondary education were enrolled in general education and 75.8% in vocational and technical education; the corresponding percentages for men were 24.2% and 75.8%, respectively (Cek and Vranješ, 2002). Women far outnumber men in social sciences, business and administration, law, education, healthcare and personal services. On the other hand, natural sciences and technical programmes still largely remain male dominated.

Organisation of vocational training

Secondary vocational education and training is primarily organised in a dual system, in which the weight of theoretical (school-based) knowledge and practical training is 40% and 60%, respectively. Theoretical education is provided by schools while the majority of practical training is provided by trainers in enterprises. Although the dual system accounts for the majority of secondary vocational training, the existing school-based three-year vocational programmes have not been abolished; they continue to exist as a parallel alternative. The Chamber of Commerce and the Chamber of Handicrafts are responsible for practical training in enterprises within the dual system. They are in charge of the quality of training places and for organising practical examinations. Some evaluations suggest that the development of dual programmes has thus far been primarily supply-led, leading to an oversupply of programmes above the demand from both students and firms (Medveš, 2000).

Standardisation and quality differentiation of secondary education

Centralised and input-based quality control instruments have been complemented by attempts to modernise already existing output standards (through standards of knowledge and skills based on occupational standards). Pressure from the labour market and high drop-out rates from vocational education have led to attempts to decentralise and deregulate the education system starting in 2000. The following nation-wide elements of secondary education curricula reveal a still-high degree of standardisation: minimum standards of general education, professional theoretical and practical training defined in terms of percentages and numbers of hours, uniform duration of programmes at each stage, uniform examination catalogues and fully (general matura) or partly (vocational matura) externally conducted final examinations.

Tertiary level of education

Horizontal dimension

Figure 13.4 presents changes in enrolment in tertiary education by field of study in the school years 1995/96, 1999/2000 and 2003/04. The most popular fields in the 1990s and early 2000s were social sciences, business and law, with the number of enrolled increasing between 1995 and 1999 and then slightly decreasing. The number of students in agriculture, veterinary medicine, engineering, manufacturing and construction somewhat decreased in the observed period.

There is also a visible differentiation between female and male fields of study at the tertiary level. In 2002, in the fields such as education, humanities and arts, social sciences and health and welfare, the share of women enrolled ranged from 66% to 81%, while in the fields such as science, mathematics and computing, engineering, manufacturing and construction, women represented between 24% and 31% (Eurostat, 2005).

Figure 13.4: Enrolment in tertiary education by field of study (%)

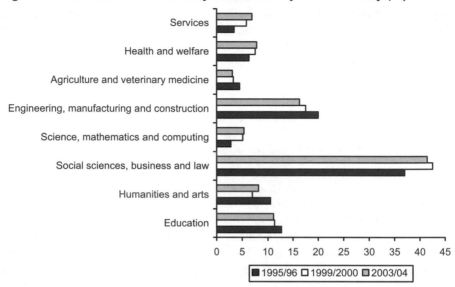

Source: Statistical Office Slovenia (1996, 2000, 2004)

Standardisation, quality differentiation and openness of tertiary education

Higher education institutions have autonomy in preparing their study programmes. Nevertheless, publicly recognised higher education programmes are regulated by the Higher Education Act. The structure of programmes and formal procedures for their accreditation are legally regulated. The accreditation body is also responsible for quality assurance in higher education (Higher Education Act, 2006). Higher education reform opened up the opportunity for the establishment of private higher education providers. In 2005, 13 independent private higher education institutions and four state universities were operating in Slovenia (see Higher Education Masterplan, 2006).

Tertiary education in Slovenia, especially university education, may be designated as exclusionary. Access is based on credentials obtained in a classical education route. Individual higher education institutions and programmes can specify some additional requirements such as the grades attained in maturity examinations, differential exams or aptitude tests. Young people who do not reach the criteria for enrolment as regular students tend to enrol as irregular students. About one quarter of all students enrolled in tertiary education is comprised of irregular students.

In Slovenia, education for students enrolled in full-time (regular) education in public education institutions at all levels is free; however, those enrolled in irregular (part-time) education must pay tuition fees.

Labour market

Economic development

An economic recession in Slovenia had already begun by the second half of the 1980s. At the start of transition, however, Slovenia's recession was rather weak compared to other CEE countries, Slovenia experiencing a maximum decline of –8.9% in GDP in 1991 (Figure 13.5).

Figure 13.5: GDP growth, 1991-2006

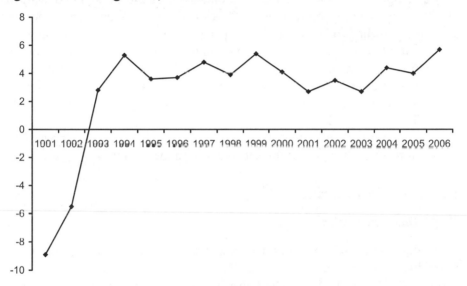

Source: ILO (2008); data for 2006 from Eurostat (2008)

After gaining its independence in 1991, Slovenia had to cope with three distinct transitions: from a socialist to a market economy, from being a part of SFRY to becoming an independent state and from a regional to a national-based economy. From an economic perspective, this last transition might have been the most difficult of all since Slovenia had to adjust to the loss of the former Yugoslav market. Nevertheless, the initial economic contraction was followed by rapid growth from 1993 onwards, reaching local peaks of 5.4% in 1994, 5.2% in 1999, and 5.7% in 2006. Slovenia quickly succeeded in regaining growth momentum and achieved one of the highest and least volatile growth rates among the CEE countries.

In contrast to the radical market reforms undertaken in some other CEE countries, Slovenia opted for gradual structural reforms and subsidises for state-owned enterprises. The capital market remained restrictively regulated such that foreign direct investments were limited. These capital restrictions protected Slovenia from the significant transitional crisis in former CEE countries, but they also prevented the economy from taking full advantage of the benefits of international integration. In general, the role of the state was considerably strengthened in the first years of transition. A number of state and quasi-state institutions were established with great authority and control over the economy. The pace of privatisation remained slow throughout the transition period. Most companies were privatised through the free distribution of vouchers that citizens could exchange for shares in the privatised enterprises. In addition, shares of each company were transferred to a quasi-governmental pension fund and to the Restitution Fund with the objective of covering future state liabilities toward the social pension system and former owners of nationalised property (Simoneti et al, 2004). In 1993, 85.7% of all firms were private, but only 9.5% of the entire employed population was employed in these firms. The slow pace of privatisation also negatively affected the restructuring of companies because business decisions and adjustments to extremely unfavourable economic conditions were delayed due to unclear ownership. As a consequence, the government adopted various intervention measures to help firms and enterprises in financial trouble, thus preserving social peace in the country.[8]

Labour market dynamics

Employment dynamics

At the beginning of the economic transition in 1990, 10.7% of employed individuals worked in agriculture, 44.1% in industry and only 45.1% in services (ILO, 2008). During the transition period, employment in agriculture remained fairly stable at around 10%, and the Slovenian agricultural sector has not experienced any significant modernisation or productivity improvement. The agricultural sector remains most prominent in less developed parts of Slovenia with an older, poorly educated population and very limited job opportunities. Agriculture still functions either as a supplementary economic activity, a way of socioeconomic subsistence or as a traditional form of settlement and activation in rural areas.[9]

In contrast to agriculture, employment share in industry and construction decreased slightly over the transition period to 37.2% in 2005 (ILO, 2008). The decline in industrial employment occurred principally in labour-intensive sectors such as textile and leather manufacturing and food processing. An increase was registered in sectors such as manufacturing of transport equipment, machinery and, to a somewhat lesser degree, chemicals and chemical products (Kovač, 2002: p 25). The service sector's share of total employment has been steadily increasing to 53.4% in 2005 (ILO, 2008), still a relatively low level compared to Western EU countries. According to the data for 2004, the highest increase of employment was in business services, public administration, health and social services and financial intermediaries (Kovač, 2002: p 25).

Structural changes in the economy and society also initiated changes in the demography of firms and enterprises in terms of size. The structure of business entities changed in favour of small and medium-sized enterprises (SMEs). In 2004, approximately 93% of all enterprises had less than 10 employees (62% of entities employed between zero and one employee), 1.5% represented mid-sized enterprises and only 0.3% were large enterprises with 250 and more employees. In spite of the large share of SMEs, the statistics show that the largest share of workers is employed in large enterprises.[10] About 40% are employed in large enterprises and about a quarter in micro firms (between one and nine employees) (Statistical Office Slovenia, 2006).

Labour force participation rates of the population aged 15-64 sharply declined from 70.1% in 1990 to 60.9% in 1993 (Figure 13.6). However, in contrast to many other CEE countries, the employment rate in Slovenia has increased since the mid-1990s, reaching a maximum of 71.1% in 2005.

Figure 13.6: Labour force participation rate (age group 15-64), 1990-2006

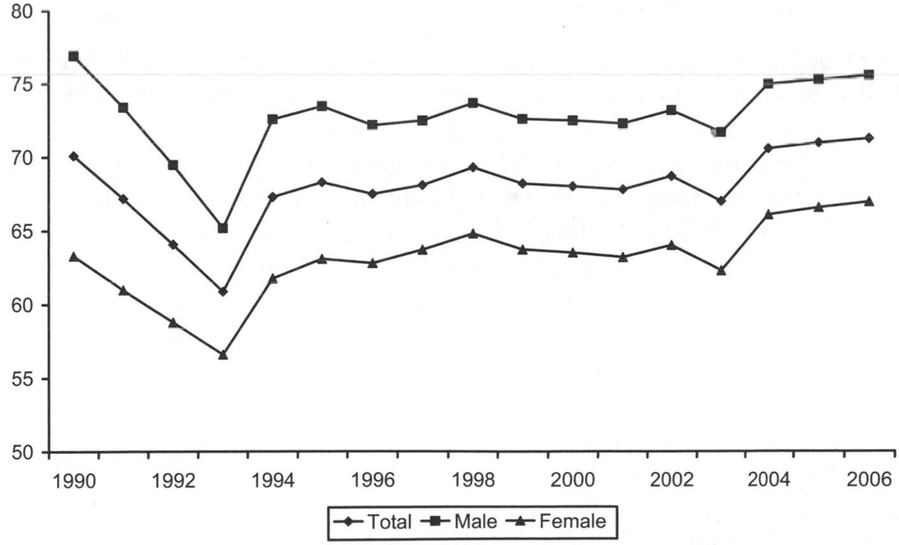

Source: ILO (2008)

Gender-specific labour force participation rates display the same time trend. The high rate of participation in the labour force may be a result of the increased economic growth during the last few years, the increased participation of students and the 1999 pension and disability insurance reform, which extended active life and postponed early retirement.[11]

The decline from 49.9% to 37.3% between 1990 and 2006 may be explained by prolonged education careers and increasing labour market integration problems of the young age cohort. In contrast, the middle-age cohorts achieved very high activity rates of approximately 88%-92% during the transition period. The participation rate of people aged 65 and over is relatively high at around 10%. In 2006, the youngest age cohorts (15-24 years) exhibited a low activity rate of 37.3% (Table 13.1).

Table 13.1: Labour force participation rate by age cohort, 1990-2006

	1990	1995	2000	2006
15+	61.8	59.0	58.1	60.0
15-24	49.9	41.0	38.7	37.3
25-54	87.9	88.9	87.9	91.9
55-64	29.3	24.3	23.7	28.8
65+	11.0	7.4	8.8	9.7

Source: ILO (2008)

Labour market flexibilisation

Even before the transition, a high proportion of first-time job seekers was forced to accept temporary employment. As a consequence, the majority of the unemployed population in the 1980s was represented by young people transitioning from school to work. To improve the employment opportunities for these young people, a system of internships lasting from six months to one year depending on the level of education was enacted at the beginning of the 1980s. An internship enables young people to gain the work experience necessary to access more stable employment. The renewed Employment Relations Act of 2002 left the regulation of internships to respective sectoral laws and collective agreements. As a consequence, the number of vacancies for interns began to decrease rapidly in 2002.

Young people transitioning from school to work currently represent the most important component of the flexible labour force. Their jobs mostly consist of temporary employment and some other forms of flexible work. In 2001, 10.5% of all newly employed workers had a temporary contract, but in the 15-24 cohort this share amounted to 42.9% (Kanjuo-Mrčela and Ignjatović, 2004: 247).

Unemployment dynamics

At the beginning of the transition in 1989, registered unemployment measured 2.9%, but the transition to a market economy caused a dramatic jump in unemployment to 14.4% in 1993 (Figure 13.7). The Labour Force Survey (LFS) unemployment rate is much lower than the registered unemployment rate due to the fact that the former captures all people who register whereas the latter is a self-assessed measure.

Figure 13.7: Unemployment rates, 1990-2006

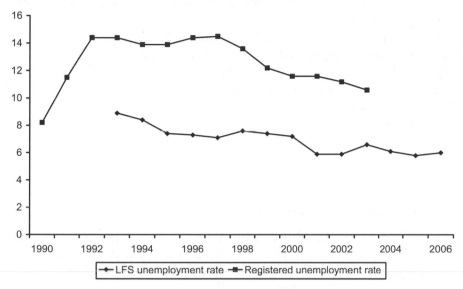

Note: Both unemployment rates refer to individuals aged over 15.
Source: ILO (2008); LFS unemployment rate for 2006 from Eurostat (2008)

However, as a result of labour market policies encouraging the unemployed population to actively deal with their unemployment, the difference between LFS unemployment and registered unemployment has been gradually decreasing. The remaining difference may largely be explained by the fact that the long-term unemployed are discouraged from actively seeking employment because they still have the possibility of working unregistered in the grey economy while continuing to receive social benefits such as health insurance and social assistance as well as still rather generous system of unemployment protection (Kajzer, 2006).

Labour market entrants, approximated as the youngest age cohort of 15- to 24-year-olds, are especially affected by unemployment. Their unemployment rate was about six times higher than the average unemployment rate for the whole adult population in 1993, but the ration decreased to approximately three times higher in 2004 (ILO, 2008).

In terms of gender, the female unemployment rate was somewhat lower than the male unemployment rate until 1996 (Statistical Office Slovenia, 2003, 2006). In 1997, female unemployment for the first time surpassed the overall unemployment rate, a trend which has continued and slightly increased since 1998. Industrial restructuring during the transition was concentrated in male-dominated industries, contributing to male unemployment. More recently, female-dominated industries such as textile and leather manufacturing have also undergone restructuring, which has endangered women's jobs. Moreover, to avoid the costs associated with pregnancy (leave) and family duties, employers discriminate against women in hiring processes.

With regard to educational level, unemployment is concentrated among the lowest education category and is lowest among the highly educated (Kajzer, 2006: 36). Individuals with no and only primary school education experienced an unemployment rate of 9.7% and 9.0%, respectively, in 2004. The unemployment rate of those with secondary education lay between 5.7% and 7.5%. Graduates of tertiary education have the lowest unemployment rates at around 3%.

Labour market institutions

Employment protection legislation

Decisive changes to the Slovenian Employment Relations Act took place while Slovenia was still part of SFRY. In particular, the 1988 Yugoslav Law on Enterprises transferred decision-making rights from workers to equity owners, thus formally ending the era of self-management. Furthermore, employers were equipped with the right to lay off workers, although exercising this option remained extremely costly for them (Vodopivec, 2004).

Regulations concerning regular and temporary employment are more restrictive in Slovenia than in other CEE countries and in EU countries (see Table 2.7 in Chapter Two of this book). Regulations concerning collective dismissals are rather similar. The Employment Relations Act of 2002 reduced both the rate of collective dismissals and regular employment (Tonin, 2005). The overall Employment Protection Legislation (EPL) index of 2.6 is slightly higher than the average of 2.3 in both CEE10 and EU15 countries.

Industrial relations

Prior to 1990, Slovenia's industrial relations were characterised by central political and managerial control exercised by the state, and its centralised wage-setting system was preserved during the transition. Wage bargaining usually takes place at national and sectoral level or to a lesser extent at company level (Visser, 2004: Table 1.8). Union membership sharply declined during the 1990s from the 100% coverage of the workforce registered at the beginning of transition. According to Van Gyes et al (2007: Figure 2), the

Slovenian unionisation rate decreased from 63% in 1995 to 44% in 2004. The decrease is primarily attributable to the shift towards free choice of union membership status, increased levels of unemployment, privatisation, growing numbers of small businesses and sectoral shifts. However, the degree of unionisation in Slovenia is still the highest in CEE countries. Even more important than the number of unionised workers is collective agreement coverage. Van Gyes et al (2007: Figure 4) estimate the percentage of employees covered by collective agreements in Slovenia to be 100% in 2002, representing the maximum level of union coverage. Furthermore, Slovenia exhibits the highest degree of union coordination compared to other CEE countries (Visser, 2004: Table 1.10). The same picture appears for the degree of centralisation, which is the highest in CEE countries (Visser, 2004: Table 1.9).

Welfare regime

Under socialist rule, the state assumed responsibility for comprehensive social protection of the population. A large share of social benefits for the employed was provided by firms and enterprises. Although the transition to a market economy has seen the state slowly withdraw from this area, Slovenia's Constitution defines the country as a social (welfare) state in which social security is regarded as a basic human right.

Labour market policy

Active labour market policy

During the early transition period, labour market policy was characterised by significant expenditures on active measures due to the major structural economic changes and increasing labour market problems. Different active labour market policy (ALMP) measures such as employment subsidies, self-employment promotion programmes, training and retraining of unemployed were introduced. As a percentage of gross domestic product (GDP), expenditure on ALMP programmes was highest in 1991 and 1992, at 0.83% and 1.17%, respectively; expenditure then declined to around 0.4%-0.5% of GDP in the late 1990s and 2000 (Vodopivec, 2004) and then to 0.34% of GDP in 2004/05 (Kajzer, 2006). In the late 1990s, ALMP expenditure was between 40% and 70% of expenditure on passive labour market measures, which is similar to the rate in Organisation for Economic Co-operation and Development (OECD) countries.

Public works are the most important ALMP measure targeted at young unemployed individuals. Compared to other CEE countries, expenditure on public works is relatively high in Slovenia. In the mid-1990s, a large share of

ALMP funds was also directed to subsidising employment in firms and enterprises, thereafter the share decreased (Kajzer, 2006: 54).

The first ALMP programme specifically targeting youth transition into the labour market was the state-subsidised internship introduced in 1991. In 1993, 88% of young people's first jobs were subsidised. The state-subsidised internship was abandoned at the end of 1996 (Trbanc, 2005: 174). Recently, subsidised internships have been reintroduced, mainly to support the employment of young people in less developed regions of Slovenia.

In general, young job seekers may participate in various ALMP programmes targeting the unemployed, the most popular of which are workshops for individual career planning and employment searching, job searching clubs, short training courses and apprenticeships. Among the most comprehensive ALMP measures addressing structural unemployment is the government's 'Programme 10,000+', adopted in 1997, which subsidises formal training among unemployed young adults, primarily targeting school drop-outs, those without formal qualifications and those with qualifications not in demand in the labour market.

Unemployment insurance

In 1991, Slovenia adopted the unemployment insurance scheme that was in force in the former socialist system. This system is based on an unemployment insurance system that comprises a compulsory and a voluntary element. All individuals in a regulated employment relationship are automatically insured against the risk of unemployment, while voluntary insurance is available to the self-employed and independent professions such as founders, owners and co-owners of enterprises who are not otherwise insured. The unemployment insurance system is characterised by two main benefits: the income restitution payment linked to individual earnings and to the duration of unemployment insurance, and the means-tested financial assistance available after expiry of the income restitution payment. The basic condition for eligibility for the income restitution payment is the duration of the unemployment insurance. The unemployed are entitled to benefits if they lose their job through no fault of their own and register with the unemployment office within 30 days after the termination of employment.[12]

The duration of the income restitution payment depends on the duration of unemployment insurance.[13] For example, between 1991 and 1998, 12 months in employment within the previous 18 months were sufficient to receive income restitution payments for three months (Table 13.2). The replacement rate of the income restitution payment within the first three months amounted to 70% of the basis, and to 60% later on.[14] The maximum amount of income restitution payment could not be higher than five times 80% of the legally guaranteed income. The payment was complemented with an additional financial allowance for dependent family members.

After the right to the income restitution payment expired, the unemployed person could apply for means-tested financial assistance, the maximum duration of which was three years.[15] The amount of the financial assistance corresponded to 80% of legally guaranteed income after taxes are deducted. Financial assistance was also granted to interns whose temporary internship, not shorter than nine months, was successfully completed and to apprentices who, after finishing their apprenticeship, were not required to do an internship and became unemployed. Those entitled to financial assistance were also entitled to the additional allowance for the dependents.

Table 13.2: Changing payment duration of income restitution payments

| | Required contribution period with breaks | |
	1991-98	1998-
3 months	12 months within last 18 months	1-5 years
6 months	50 months within last 5 years	5-15 years
9 months	5 years and more but less than 10 years	15-25 years
12 months	10 years or more but less than 15 years	above 25 years
18 months	15 years and more but less than 20 years	above 25 years and above 50 years of age
24 months	20 years and more	above 25 years and above 55 years of age

The amendments to the Employment and Unemployment Insurance Act that came into force in 1994 reduced the maximum amount of the income restitution payment to four times the minimum amount and decreased the maximum duration of financial assistance to six months and the allowance for dependents was abolished.[16] Complementary financial allowance for the dependent family members was abolished.

Further substantial changes in the unemployment insurance scheme were introduced by the October 1998 Act on Changes and Amendments to the Employment and Unemployment Insurance Act. Conditions for eligibility for income restitution payment have sharpened to at least 12 months of employment relationship within last 18 months with one or more employers. The basis for the calculation of the restitution was set to the average monthly income received by the unemployed person in the 12 months prior to termination of the unemployment insurance. The minimum benefit level was set at 100% of the legally guaranteed income (minus taxes). The maximum was fixed at three times the minimum benefit level.

Severe changes to the detriment of the unemployed were made in regard to the duration of the income restitution payment (Table 13.2). Payment duration was significantly reduced. The Act on Changes and Amendments of Employment and Unemployment Insurance also included a long list of situations in which the restitution payment would be reduced or terminated, such as availability for work, working for pay while receiving the restitution and the readiness to participate in ALMP measures. The definition of an adequate job was extended to one level below the qualification of the unemployed person. While restitution payment became less generous, the duration of entitlement to financial assistance was increased to a maximum of 15 months; however, interns and apprentices having paid less than 12 months of unemployment insurance were no longer eligible to receive financial assistance.

With the changes of the Employment and Unemployment Insurance Act introduced in 2006, the minimum payment was fixed to 45.6% of the minimum income and the maximum payment to three times the minimum. Given the eligibility criteria, unemployed youth seldom have the right to the income restitution payment. Hence, during the entire period of 1997-2003, this group represented only a very small share of all restitution recipients. On the other hand, at least until 1999, more than a third of unemployed youth received financial assistance (see Table 13.3). This development is probably connected with the right of temporarily employed interns and apprentices to financial assistance during unemployment spells. When this right was terminated, the percentage of youth receiving benefits decreased strongly. At the same time, the total number of financial assistance recipients increased markedly from 2818 individuals in 1998 to 6059 in 2005. The increase was particularly substantial among the oldest age group.

Table 13.3: Trends in the percentage of unemployed receiving financial assistance by age group, 1997-2005

	1997	1998	1999	2000	2001	2002	2003	2004	2005
18-25	37.0	33.1	37.4	24.8	22.5	16.6	16.2	13.5	13.4
26-30	16.0	17.1	18.9	16.3	18.4	20.2	20.2	19.5	20.2
31-40	24.3	21.1	22.8	23.9	22.1	24.3	27.0	27.8	26.9
41-50	18.5	22.0	15.9	23.9	21.3	22.1	23.5	24.3	22.7
51+	4.2	6.7	5.0	11.1	15.7	16.8	13.1	14.9	16.8
Total number	3,734	2,818	3,283	3,754	4,516	5,664	6,063	5,979	6,059

Source: National Employment Office (1995-2005)

Minimum wage

A legal minimum wage exists and is set at the national level. Compared to other CEE countries, a minimum wage comprises a relatively large share of the average wage in Slovenia. Schneider and Burger (2005) estimate that the minimum wage represents 58% of the average wage in 2001. This share is even higher than the OECD average of 45%-50% for the same period.

Family policy

Public childcare

Slovenia inherited a well-developed and organised childcare and pre-school system from the socialist regime. The most recent education reform removed daily childcare and pre-school education from the social protection sector and placed them in the education sector regulated by school legislation (Ministry of Education and Sports, 1996). Pre-school education is not compulsory.[17] Full-time, part-time and shorter pre-school education programmes are offered. Shorter programmes are meant for the children from three years of age to the time of enrolment in primary schooling. Pre-school education is not free of charge, but prices are set locally and means-tested subsidies for parents are available.

Of all children between one and six years, 51% were in pre-school in 1990; in 1995, the percentage rose to 56.9% and by 2005 had dropped slightly to 53%. Part of the decline after 2000 may be the result of the implementation of a nine-year primary school, which now starts at the age of six. At the beginning of the transition, 56% to 60% of children aged three to six were enrolled in organised child care, and the percentage increased steadily up until 1999 (see Table 13.4). After that, the rate declined slightly, until a significant drop was registered in 2002, which also corresponds to the introduction of the nine-year primary school. Table 13.4 also reveals a steady increase in the enrolment of two-year-old children in organised childcare from one-third in 1998 to one half in 2005. In both pre-schools and child care, the availability of places in these institutions closely corresponds to the rates of participation.

Table 13.4: Pre-primary enrolments (net rates, percentage of population aged 3-6) in organised childcare, 1989-2005

	1989	1993	1998	2002	2004	2005
3-6 years	56.3	60.3	68.3	64.2	76.9	–
2 years	–	–	33.1	43.3	48	49.9

Source: UNICEF (2007), Statistical Office of Slovenia (1990-2006)

Cash benefits

Child allowance is regulated by the Parent Protection and Family Allowance Act (1993/96). This financial support was originally intended for children from low-income families only, but in the last decade it has become virtually universal. Parents are eligible for the child allowance if the family income does not exceed 99% of the average salary in the Republic of Slovenia in the previous year. The amount is means-tested. Children older than 18 years are eligible for the child allowance if they are in regular education up to a maximum age of 26.

During parental leave, parents are entitled to one year of fully paid parental leave based on the parent's salary in the year prior to the birth of the child. The income replacement rate for the time of parental leave amounts to 100% of the average monthly income in the year before the maternity/parental leave took place. The duration of maternity leave is 105 days, and the remaining days may be shared by both parents. The unemployed are entitled to paid parental leave during the time of the entitlement to the income restitution payment and financial assistance in line with the Employment and Unemployment Insurance Act. Parents not eligible for paid parental leave are entitled to parental allowance. The duration of entitlement corresponds with the duration of paid parental leave. The amount is legally defined (€171 in 2006).

Social assistance

The Social Protection Act defines financial social assistance as a social right that enables one to meet basic needs for survival.[18] People earning an income that is less than the legally defined minimum wage are entitled to a reduced amount of financial assistance, and single parents are entitled to 30% more than the basic amount.

The duration of first-time social assistance amounts to three months and subsequently to a maximum of six months. It is paid from the first day of the month after the submission of the application. The unemployed receiving financial social assistance are obliged to accept any regulated, subcontracted, honorary or voluntary work available. After receiving social assistance for three months, individuals are also obliged to accept suitable temporary humanitarian or similar work (e.g. helping elderly people). If such work is refused, the right to social assistance is forfeited for the subsequent six months.

Notes

[1] In 1952, the faculty of theology was separated from the university.
[2] Two-year university colleges died out by the end of 1980.

[3] The section is based on Eurydice (1999) and ETF (2002) publications.

[4] A maturity course has been designed for graduates who have passed a final examination but who wish to enrol in more demanding academic programmes. This course prepares them for taking the matura (high school graduation examination).

[5] The matura is an external (state) certification exam for all students finishing high school. The maturity exam is run and controlled by the State Examination Centre. It consists of five subjects: three subjects are compulsory (the native language, mathematics and the first foreign language) and two are elective.

[6] Around 70% of the curriculum of professionally oriented high school programmes is the same as the general high school programme.

[7] Since the academic year 1998/99, vocational college graduates have gained the possibility to enrol in the second year of professional types of higher education programmes if the higher education institution providing this type of studies had made such an arrangement possible.

[8] Initially, the state measures were limited to passive and indirect interventions toward organisations that had fallen into financial troubles due to objective reasons; later on, the state played an active role through the nationalisation of some financially insolvent companies and through subsidies paid directly from the state budget.

[9] In addition to the difficult conditions, the main hindrance to greater production capacity, efficiency and production intensity is the unfavourable agrarian structure revealed by the small average size of agricultural holdings, the high degree of dispersion and the poor socio-demographic structure of the agricultural labour force. At the same time, due to the low mobility of production sources, land is not cultivated by more capable workers and unsuccessful agricultural holdings do not go bankrupt. All this results in low productivity and a large share of mixed holdings, i.e., farms that make their living also from non-agrarian activities (see Kovač, 2002: 8, 11).

[10] In Europe, the largest share (39.4%) of the employed is found in micro firms and enterprises (Žakelj, 2004: 42).

[11] Early retirement and disability retirement were the most common measures for coping with redundancies in the transition period. Within the state-financed programme of early retirement, 1,082 individuals were retired in 1990, 6,600 in 1991 and an additional 4,600 in 1992 (Ivančič, 1999: 95).

[12] In this case, the income restitution payment is paid from the first day of employment termination. If an unemployed person fails to register within 30 days after termination of employment, the entitlement is paid from the day the application was submitted.

[13] Only full-time and part-time employment and unemployment spells with the restitution payments are taken into account.

[14] The basis for the calculation of the payment was the average monthly salary received by the unemployed person during the three months prior to the termination of employment. If the salary in the fourth, fifth and sixth months prior to termination was higher, these months were used to make the calculation rather than the three months directly prior.

[15] Her/his average monthly income together with the monthly income of the family members in the months prior to applying for the financial assistance must not have exceeded 80% of the legally guaranteed personal income.

[16] The Employment and Unemployment Insurance Act from 1991 granted a maximum duration of three years for receipt of financial assistance, 12 months for interns and apprentices.

[17] The exception was the one-year pre-primary education prior to the enrolment in primary school (the so called 'mala šola' – small school) before the implementation of the nine-year primary education enacted by the 1996 educational reform (see also the section on the education system).

[18] This is provided by a legally set minimum wage adjusted once a year for inflation.

References

Cek, M. and Vranješ, P. (2002) *Vocational and professional education in Slovenia 2001*, Ljubljana: National Observatori for Vocational Education and Training.

ETF (European Training Foundation) (2000) *Vocational education and training in Central and Eastern Europe: key indicators*, Luxembourg: Office for Official Publications of the European Communities.

ETF (2002) *Vocational education and training and employment services in Slovenia*, Luxembourg: Office for Official Publications of the European Communities

Eurydice (1999) *Structure of education, vocational training and adult education systems on Europe*, Brussels: European Commission.

Eurydice (2007) *Eurybase: Czech Republic*, Brussels: Eurydice European Unit (www.eurydice.org/portal/page/portal/Eurydice/EuryCountry).

Eurostat (2005) *Europe in figures: Eurostat yearbook*, Luxembourg: Eurostat (http://epp.eurostat.ec.europa.eu/cache/ITY_OFFPUB/KS-CD-05-001-2/EN/KS-CD-05-001-2-EN.PDF).

Eurostat (2008) *Data: labour market*, Luxembourg: Eurostat (http://epp.eurostat.ec.europa.eu).

Ignjatović, M., Ivančič, A., and Svetlik, I. (2003) *The role of national qualification systems in promoting lifelong learning: Slovenia, country background report*, Paris: OECD (www.oecd.org/dataoecd/33/28/34258475.pdf).

ILO (International Labour Organization) (2008) *Key indicators of the labour market programme*, Fifth Edition, Geneva: ILO.

Ivančič, A. (1999) *Izobraževanje in priložnosti na trgu dela* (*Education and labour market opportunities*), Ljubljana: Faculty for Social Sciences and Slovenian Institute for Adult Education.

Kajzer, A. (2006) *Spremembe na trgu dela v Sloveniji v obdobju 1995-2005* (*Chances in the labour market in Slovenia in the period 1995-2005*), Working Paper No 5/2006, Ljubljana: Institute of Macroeconomic Analysis and Development.

Kanjuo-Mrčela, A. and Ignjatović, M. (2004) 'Neprijazna fleksibilizacija dela in zaposlovanja' ('Unkind flexibilisation of work and employment'), in I. Svetlik and B. Ilič (eds) *Razpoke v zgodbi o uspehu* (*Gaps in the story of success*), Ljubljana: Sophia, pp 230-58.

Kovač, M. (2002) *Primarna dejavnost: politika in stanje v Sloveniji v primerjavi z EU* (*Primary sector: policy and conditions in Slovenia in comparison to the EU*), Working Paper No 11/2002, Ljubljana: Institute of Macroeconomic Analysis and Development.

Medveš, Z. (2000) 'Kompatibilnost z evropskimi sistemi' ('Compatibility with European systems'), in Z. Medveš, I. Svetlik, M. Tome and J. Renko (eds) *Ocena reforme poklicnega in strokovnega izobraževanja ter predlogi za prihodnji razvoj* (*Evaluation of the vocational education and training reform and recommendations for future development*), Ljubljana: Ministry of Education, Science and Sports, Phare MOOCA.

Ministry of Education and Sports (1996) *School legislation*, Ljubljana: Ministry of education, Science and Sports.

Ministry of Education and Sports (2004) *Strategija vzgoje in izobraževanja Romov v Republiki Sloveniji* (*Strategy of education of the Roma in the Republic of Slovenia*), Ljubljana: Ministry of Education and Sports.

Ministry of Higher Education, Science and Technology (2006) *Nacionalni programm visokega šolstva v republiki Sloveniji* (Higher education masterplan in the Republic of Slovenia), Official Gazette of the Republic of Slovenia No 20/2006.

National Employment Office (1995-2005) *Annual reports 1995-2005*, Ljubljana: National Employment Office.

OECD (Organisation for Economic Co-operation and Development) (2004) *Employment outlook*, Paris: OECD.

Schneider, F. and Burger, C. (2005) 'Formal and informal labour markets: challenges and policy in the Central and Eastern European new EU members and candidate countries', *CESifo Economic Studies*, vol 51, no 1, pp 77-115.

Silva-Jáuregeui, C. (2004) 'Macroeconomic stabilization and sustainable growth', in M. Mrak, M. Rojec and C. Silva-Jáuregi (eds) *Slovenia: from Yugoslavia to the European Union*, Washington DC: World Bank.

Simoneti, M., Rojec, M., and Gregoric, A. (2004) 'Privatization, restructuring, and corporate governance of the enterprise sector', in M. Mrak, M. Rojec and C. Silva-Jáuregui (eds) *Slovenia: from Yugoslavia to the European Union*, Washington DC: World Bank.

Statistical Office Slovenia (1980-2006) *Statistical yearbooks*, Ljubljana: Statistical Office Slovenia.

UNICEF (United Nations International Children's Emergency Fund) (2007) *TransMONEE 2007 database*, Florence: UNICEF Innocenti Research Centre (www.unicef-icdc.org/resources/transmonee.html).

Tonin, M. (2005) *Updated employment protection legislation indicators for Central and Eastern European countries*, Working Paper, Institute for International Economic Studies, Stockholm: Stockholm University.

Trbanc, M. (2005) 'Zaposlovanje in brezposelnost mladih' ('Youth employment and unemployment'), in A. Černak-Meglič (ed) *Otroci in mladi v prehodni družbi* (*Children and young people in transitional society*), Maribor: Aristej, pp 161-88.

Van Gyes, G., Vandenbrande, T., Lehndorff, S., Schilling, G., Schief, S. and Kohl, H. (2007) *Industrial relations in EU member states 2000-2004*, Dublin: European Foundation for the Improvement of Living and Working Conditions.

Visser, J. (2004) 'Patterns and variations in European industrial relations', in European Commission (ed) *Industrial relations in Europe*, Luxembourg: Office for the Official Publications of the European Communities, pp 11-57.

Vodopivec, M. (2004) 'Labor market developments in the 1990s', in M. Mrak, M. Rojec and C. Silva-Jáuregi (eds) *Slovenia: from Yugoslavia to the European Union*, Washington DC: World Bank.

Žakelj, L. (2004) *Razvoj malih in srednjih podjetij v Sloveniji in Evropski uniji* (*The development of small and medium enterprises in Slovenia and the European Union*), Working paper No 6/2004, Ljubljana: Institute of Macroeconomic Analysis and Development. secondary education

Index

A

active labour market policy 86–89
Bulgaria 116–17
Czech Republic 143–4
Estonia 171–2
Hungary 202–3, 205
Latvia 232–3
Lithuania 261
Poland 287–8
Romania 313–14
Slovakia 341–3
Slovenia 369–70
apprenticeship 15, 18, 22
Czech Republic 124, 126, 129
Estonia 158
Lithuania 250
Poland 276, 286
Romania 296, 298–9, 301–2
Slovakia 324, 326–8, 330
Slovenia 370–1

B

Bulgaria
active labour market policy 116–17
child allowance 119
economic development 109–10, 114
education *see* education
education system *see* education system
employment *see* employment
employment protection 115
enrolment in pre-school education 120
family policy *see* family policy
gender *see* gender
industrial relations *see* industrial relations
labour force participation 111–12
labour market *see* labour market
minimum wage 116–19
minorities *see* minority ethnic groups
pre-school education institutions 120
privatisation 110, 116
secondary education *see* secondary education
social assistance 119
standardisation of education 105, 107–9

stratification of education 103–4
tertiary education *see* tertiary education
track differentiation *see* stratification of education
unemployment *see* unemployment
unemployment insurance 117–19
unions 116
vocational education and training 99–105

C

communism *see* socialism
Czech Republic
active labour market policy 143–4
apprenticeship 124, 126
dual system 132
economic development 134–6
education *see* education
education system *see* education system
employment *see* employment
employment protection 142
enrolment in pre-school education 146
family policy *see* family policy
gender *see* gender
industrial relations *see* industrial relations
labour force participation 137–8
labour law 141
labour market *see* labour market
liberalisation 135, 142
minimum wage 144–7
minorities *see* minority ethnic groups
pre-school education institutions 146–7
privatisation 135–6
secondary education *see* secondary education
social assistance 144–5, 147
standardisation of education 132–4
stratification of education 131–2
tertiary education *see* tertiary education
track differentiation *see* stratification of education
unemployment *see* unemployment
unemployment insurance 144–5
unions 142, 145

vocational education and training 124–33

D

dual system 21–2, 31
    Czech Republic 132
    Hungary 186, 191
    Romania 302
    Slovenia 356–7, 360–1

E

economic development 35–40, 66, 68, 75, 78, 90
    Bulgaria 109–10, 114
    Czech Republic 134–6
    Estonia 162–4
    Hungary 194–5
    Latvia 224–6
    Lithuania 253–5
    Poland 279–81, 285, 288
    Romania 305–7, 311
    Slovakia 333–5
    Slovenia 363–4
economic growth *see* economic development
education
    attainment 7–11, 13, 23, 73
        Hungary 197
        Lithuania 243
    curriculum 11
        Bulgaria 98
        Czech Rebublic 127
        Estonia 155
        Hungary 183–5
        Latvia 216–17, 221
        Lithuania 243, 246
        Romania 303
        Slovakia 325
        Slovenia 357
    drop-out 31
        Latvia 219
        Romania 298
        Slovakia 326
        Slovenia 361
    enrolment 18–20, 23–6, 46
        Bulgaria 99, 101–7
        Czech Rebublic 124
        Estonia 152, 155–6, 159–60, 164
        Hungary 188, 190–2, 196
        Latvia 216–23, 228
        Lithuania 243, 246–51
        Poland 270, 274–8, 283

Romania 295–6, 300–4
Slovakia 327–32, 336, 344
Slovenia 357–62
expansion 7–11, 23–4, 26–8, 31
    Bulgaria 98
    Czech Republic 124
    Estonia 151
    Hungary 185, 188–9
    Poland 269, 270
    Poland 279
    Romania 301
    Slovakia 324
    Slovenia 358
gender *see* gender
minority ethnic group *see* minority ethnic group
private 21, 23, 26–8, 98–9, 101, 107–9
    Czech Republik 127–8, 134
    Estonia 155, 162
    Hungary 193
    Latvia 216–17, 220, 223–4
    Lithuania 243, 252
    Poland 278
    Romania 304–5
    Slovakia 330, 332–3
    Slovenia 362
public 26, 27, 28–9
    Bulgaria 107–9
    Czech Republic 127, 134
    Estonia 155
    Hungary 193–4
    Latvia 223
    Lithuania 243, 252
    Poland 278–9
    Romania 298, 305
    Slovakia 332–3
    Slovenia 362
vocational *see* vocational education and training *or* secondary education
education level
    basic level 11–13
        Bulgaria 98–9
        Czech Republik 124–5, 130–2
        Estonia 152–8
        Hungary 183–6, 200
        Latvia 214–19
        Lithuania 242–3, 247
        Poland 270–1
        Romania 295–8, 300
        Slovakia 323–6
        Slovenia 355–6
    compulsory 8, 11, 31, 98–9, 103
        Czech Republik 124–5, 131
        Estonia 152–3, 158

Latvia 216, 221
Lithuania 243, 245, 248
Poland 271, 273
Romania 296–9
Slovakia 323–26
Slovenia 355
higher education *see* tertiary education
secondary level *see* secondary
education
tertiary level *see* tertiary education
education system 2, 4
Bulgaria 98–109
Czech Rebublic 124–34
Estonia 152–62
Hungary 183–94
Latvia 214–24
Lithuania 242–52
Poland 270–9
Romania 295–305
Slovakia 323–33
Slovenia 354–62
socialist 9–12, 15, 23, 28
Bulgaria 98
Czech Republik 124
Estonia 152, 158
Hungary 183
Lithuania 242–3
Poland 270–1
Romania 295–6
Slovakia 324
standardisation *see* standardisation of
education
stratification *see* stratification of
education
vertical dimension
Bulgaria 101–3
Czech Republik 129–31
Estonia 155–8
Latvia 218–19
Lithuania 246–8
Poland 274–5
Romania 300–1
Slovakia 327–8
Slovenia 358–9
employment
employment dynamics 41–3, 136–8
Bulgaria 110–12
Estonia 164–5
Hungary 195–8
Latvia 226–8
Lithuania 255–7
Poland 281–3
Romania 307–9
Slovakia 335–7

Slovenia 364–6
employment protection *see*
employment protection
part-time 47–9
Czech Republik 138
Poland 283
Slovenia 373
sectoral employment 41–3
Bulgaria 110–11
Czech Republic 136–7
Estonia 164
Hungary 195–6
Latvia 226–7
Lithuania 255–6
Poland 281–2
Romania 307–8
Slovakia 335
Slovenia 364–5
self- employment 47–50
Bulgaria 117, 118
Czech 138
Poland 284
Romania 309
Slovenia 369–70
temporary employment 47–9, 54–5,
286
Bulgaria 115, 117
Czech Republik 142
Estonia 166, 170
Hungary 198, 201
Latvia 231
Lithuania 260
Poland 284, 288
Romania 312
Slovakia 340
Slovenia 366
employment protection 53–6
Bulgaria 115
Czech Republik 142
Estonia 169–71
Hungary 201
Latvia 231
Lithuania 259–60
Poland 286
Romania 312
Slovakia 339–40
Slovenia 368
Estonia
active labour market policy 171–2
apprenticeship 158
economic development 162–4
education *see* education
education system *see* education system
employment *see* employment

employment protection 169–71
enrolment in pre-school education
175–6
family policy *see* family policy
gender *see* gender
industrial relations *see* industrial
relations
intergenerational transfers 177
labour force participation 164–5
labour law 169–70
labour market *see* labour market
liberalisation 151
minimum wage 174–5
minorities *see* minority ethnic groups
pre-school education institutions 175
privatisation 162–64
secondary education *see* secondary
education
social assistance 176–7
standardisation of education 152, 158,
162
stratification of education 158
tertiary education *see* tertiary
education
track differentiation *see* stratification
of education
unemployment *see* unemployment
unemployment insurance 172–4
unions 170–1, 174
vocational education and training 152–
8
EU accession 3, 38, 68–70, 77
Estonia 170
Lithuania 253

F

family policy 65
Bulgaria 119–20
cash benefits
Bulgaria 119
Latvia 290
Lithuania 264
Romania 317–18
Slovakia 346–7
Slovenia 374
child allowance *see* cash benefits
Czech Republic 146–7
enrolment in pre-school education
Bulgaria 120
Czech Republic 146
Estonia 175–6
Hungary 206–7
Latvia 236–7

Lithuania 264–5
Poland 290
Romania 316–17
Slovakia 346
Slovenia 373
Estonia 175–6
Hungary 205–7
Latvia 236–7
Lithuania 264–5
Poland 290
pre-school education institutions
Bulgaria 120
Czech Republic 146–7
Estonia 175
Hungary 205–6
Latvia 236
Lithuania 264–5
Poland 290
Romania 316
Slovakia 345
Slovenia 373
Romania 316–18
Slovakia 345–7
Slovenia 373–4

G

gender
education 23, 25, 31
Bulgaria 102–3
Bulgaria 106
Czech Republik 130, 133
Estonia 157–8, 160
Hungary 185, 192
Lithuania 251
Slovakia 332
labour 44
Bulgaria 111
Czech Republik 137
Hungary 196–7
Latvia 227–8
Poland 282–3
Romania 308
Slovakia 332
Slovenia 365, 367
guaranteed minimum income 68
Latvia 213
Romania 315, 318
Slovakia 347

H

Hungary

active labour market policy 202–3,
205
dual system 186, 191
economic development 194–5
education *see* education
education system *see* education system
employment *see* employment
employment protection 201
enrolment in pre-school education
206–7
family policy *see* family policy
gender *see* gender
industrial relations *see* industrial
relations
intergenerational transfers 209
labour force participation 196–8, 201
labour market *see* labour market
liberalisation 194–5
minimum wage 203–5, 208
minorities *see* minority ethnic groups
pre-school education institutions 205–
6
privatisation 194–5
secondary education *see* secondary
education
social assistance 207–8
standardisation of education 191, 193–
4
stratification of education 190
tertiary education *see* tertiary
education
track differentiation *see* stratification
of education
unemployment *see* unemployment
unemployment insurance 203–5, 208
unions 202
vocational education and training 184–
91, 193

I

industrial relations 56–9
Bulgaria 115–16
centralisation 57–9
Czech Republic 142
Poland 287
Slovakia 341
Slovenia 369
collective bargaining 56–9
Bulgaria 116
Czech Republic 142
Estonia 171
Hungary 202
Latvia 231

Lithuania 260
Poland 287
Romania 313
Slovakia 340
Slovenia 368
coordination 57–9
Czech Republic 142
Poland 287
Slovakia 341
Slovenia 369
Czech Republic 142
Estonia 171
Hungary 202
Latvia 231–2
Lithuania 260
Poland 287
Romania 312–13
Slovakia 340–1
Slovenia 368–9
unions *see* unions
inequality
poverty risks 73–5
regional 70, 72, 73
Bulgaria 114
Czech Republic 140–1
Hungary 200
Latvia 225, 230
Poland 285–6
Romania 311
Slovakia 339
unemployment risks 71–3
Bulgaria 114
Latvia 230
wage 67, 70–3, 75
Poland 269
intergenerational transfers
Estonia 177
Hungary 209
Poland 291
Slovakia 349

K

kindergartens *see* family policy

L

labour force participation 43–47, 51
Bulgaria 111–12
Czech Republic 137–8
Estonia 164–5
Hungary 196–8, 201
Latvia 227–8
Lithuania 256–7

Poland 282–3
Romania 308–9
Slovakia 335–7
Slovenia 365–6
labour law 53–6
  Czech Republic 141
  Estonia 169–70
  Latvia 231
  Lithuania 259
  Poland 286
  Romania 312
  Slovakia 339–40
labour market
  flexibilisation 47–50
    Czech Republic 138
    Estonia 165–6
    Hungary 198–9
    Poland 283–4
    Slovenia 366
  institutions *see* industrial relations
Latvia
  active labour market policy 232–3
  child allowance 290
  economic development 224–6
  education *see* education
  education system *see* education system
  employment *see* employment
  employment protection 231
  enrolment in pre-school education 236–7
  family policy *see* family policy
  gender *see* gender
  guaranteed minimum income 213
  industrial relations *see* industrial relations
  labour force participation 227–8
  labour law 231
  labour market *see* labour market
  liberalisation 224
  minimum wage 232–5, 238
  minorities *see* minority ethnic groups
  pre-school education institutions 236
  privatisation 224–6
  secondary education *see* secondary education
  social assistance 238
  standardisation of education 221, 223–4
  stratification of education 219–20
  tertiary education *see* tertiary education
  track differentiation *see* stratification of education
  unemployment *see* unemployment

unemployment insurance 233–5
unions 231–2
vocational education and training 214–21
liberalisation 36, 38–40, 67, 76
  Czech Republic 135, 142
  Estonia 151
  Hungary 194–5
  Latvia 224
  Lithuania 260
  Poland 280, 286
  Romania 305, 312
  Slovakia 335, 340
Lithuania
  active labour market policy 261
  apprenticeship 250
  child allowance 264
  economic development 253–5
  education *see* education
  education system *see* education system
  employment *see* employment
  employment protection 259–60
  enrolment in pre-school education 264–5
  family policy *see* family policy
  gender *see* gender
  industrial relations *see* industrial relations
  labour force participation 256–7
  labour law 259
  labour market *see* labour market
  liberalisation 260
  minimum wage 262, 264
  minorities *see* minority ethnic groups
  pre-school education institutions 264–5
  privatisation 253–5, 260
  secondary education *see* secondary education
  social assistance 291
  standardisation of education 250, 252
  stratification of education 248–50
  tertiary education *see* tertiary education
  track differentiation *see* stratification of education
  unemployment *see* unemployment
  unemployment insurance 261–3
  unions 260
  vocational education and training 242–50, 252
living standards 48, 59, 63, 68, 70, 75, 89
  Bulgaria 116
  Hungary 202, 209

Lithuania 252, 260
Poland 287
Romania 313, 315

M

minimum wage 81, 84–6
   Bulgaria 116–19
   Czech Republic 144–7
   Estonia 174–5
   Hungary 203–5, 208
   Latvia 232–5, 238
   Lithuania 262, 264
   Poland 289
   Romania 314–15
   Slovakia 344–5, 347–9
   Slovenia 373–4
minority ethnic groups
   education
      Lithuania 243, 248
   labour
      Bulgaria 114
      Czech Republic 140
      Estonia 169
      Hungary 200
      Latvia 230
      Romania 311
      Slovakia 339

P

PISA (Programme for International
   Student Assessment)
   Czech Republic 133
   Hungary 191
   Latvia 221
   Romania 303
   Slovakia 331
Poland
   active labour market policy 287–8
   apprenticeship 276, 286
   economic development 279–81, 285,
      288
   education *see* education
   education system *see* education system
   employment *see* employment
   employment protection 286
   enrolment in pre-school education 290
   family policy *see* family policy
   gender *see* gender
   industrial relations *see* industrial
      relations
   intergenerational transfers 291
   labour force participation 282–3

   labour law 286
   labour market *see* labour market
   liberalisation 280, 286
   minimum wage 289
   minorities *see* minority ethnic groups
   pre-school education institutions 290
   privatisation 280–1, 287
   secondary education *see* secondary
      education
   standardisation of education 276–9
   stratification of education 275–6
   tertiary education *see* tertiary
      education
   track differentiation *see* stratification
      of education
   unemployment *see* unemployment
   unemployment insurance 288–9, 291
   unions 287
   vocational education and training 270–
      7
poverty 65–78, 90
   Estonia 174
   Romania 295
   Slovakia 347
pre-school education *see* family policy
privatisation 21, 35, 38–40, 42, 49, 59,
   67–8, 76
   Bulgaria 110, 116
   Czech Republic 135–6
   Estonia 162–4
   Hungary 194–5
   Latvia 224–6
   Lithuania 253–5, 260
   Poland 280–1, 287
   Romania 307, 313–14
   Slovakia 330, 333–4
   Slovenia 364, 369

R

reform of social policy 76–80, 90
   Bulgaria 117
   Czech Republic 144
   Hungary 204
   Latvia 234–5
   Lithuania 261, 263
   Romania 314–15, 317–18
   Slovakia 341–4, 348
   Slovenia 373
Romania
   active labour market policy 313–14
   apprenticeship 296, 298–9, 301–2
   child allowance 317–18
   dual system 302

economic development 305–7, 311
education *see* education
education system *see* education system
employment *see* employment
employment protection 312
enrolment in pre-school education
    316–17
family policy *see* family policy
gender *see* gender
guaranteed minimum income 315, 318
industrial relations *see* industrial
    relations
labour force participation 308–9
labour law 312
labour market *see* labour market
liberalisation 305, 312
minimum wage 314–15
minorities *see* minority ethnic groups
pre-school education institutions 316
privatisation 307, 313–14
secondary education *see* secondary
    education
social assistance 315, 318–19
standardisation of education 302–5
stratification of education 301–2
tertiary education *see* tertiary
    education
track differentiation *see* stratification
    of education
unemployment *see* unemployment
unemployment insurance 314–16
unions 312–13
vocational education and training 295–
    303

S

secondary education 9–10, 13–22
    Bulgaria 98–105
    Czech Republic 124, 126–7, 129–33
    Estonia 152–8
    general 15–21
        Bulgaria 103–4
        Czech Republic 131–2
        Estonia 158
        Hungary 190, 193
        Latvia 219–20
        Lithuania 249–50
        Poland 275–77
        Romania 301–2
        Slovakia 329–30
        Slovenia 359–60
    Hungary 183–91
    Latvia 214–21

Lithuania 242–50
maturita/matriculation examination 18
    Bulgaria 104
    Czech Republic 131
    Latvia 220
    Lithuania 250
    Poland 270
    Slovakia 326–7, 330
Poland 270, 272–7
Romania 297–303
Slovakia 324–31
Slovenia 354–61, 368
standardisation *see* standardisation of
    education
stratification *see* stratification of
    education
technical 15–21
    Czech Republic 131–2
    Poland 276
    Romania 301
    Slovenia 359–60
vocational education and training *see*
    vocational education and training
shadow economy 46–7, 69–70, 76
Slovakia
    active labour market policy 341–3
    apprenticeship 324, 326–8, 330
    child allowance 346–7
    economic development 333–5
    education *see* education
    education system *see* education system
    employment *see* employment
    employment protection 339–40
    enrolment in pre-school education 346
    family policy *see* family policy
    gender *see* gender
    guaranteed minimum income 347
    industrial relations *see* industrial
        relations
    intergenerational transfers 349
    labour force participation 335–7
    labour law 339–40
    labour market *see* labour market
    liberalisation 335, 340
    minimum wage 344–5, 347–9
    minorities *see* minority ethnic groups
    pre-school education institutions 345
    privatisation 330, 333–4
    secondary education *see* secondary
        education
    social assistance 347–9
    standardisation of education 330–3
    stratification of education 329–30

tertiary education *see* tertiary
education
track differentiation *see* stratification
of education
unemployment *see* unemployment
unemployment insurance 341, 343–4
unions 340–1
vocational education and training 323–
31
Slovenia
active labour market policy 369–70
apprenticeship 370–1
child allowance 374
dual system 356–7, 360–1
economic development 363–4
education *see* education
education system *see* education system
employment *see* employment
employment protection 368
enrolment in pre-school education 373
family policy *see* family policy
gender *see* gender
industrial relations *see* industrial
relations
labour force participation 365–6
labour market *see* labour market
minimum wage 373–4
minorities *see* minority ethnic groups
pre-school education institutions 373
privatisation 364, 369
secondary education *see* secondary
education
social assistance 367, 374
standardisation of education 361–2
stratification of education 359–60
tertiary education *see* tertiary
education
track differentiation *see* stratification
of education
unemployment *see* unemployment
unemployment insurance 370–2
unions 368–9
vocational education and training 354–
61
social assistance 66, 68, 82–4, *see also*
guaranteed minimum income
Bulgaria 119
Czech Republic 144–5, 147
Estonia 176–7
Hungary 207–8
Latvia 238
Lithuania 291
Romania 315, 318–9
Slovakia 347–9

Slovenia 367, 374
social expenditure 51, 66, 78–80, 86–8,
90
Bulgaria 116–17
Czech Republic 143
Estonia 171–2
Hungary 202–3, 205
Latvia 232–3, 236
Lithuania 261, 264
Poland 287–8, 290
Romania 313–14
Slovakia 341–3, 345, 347
Slovenia 369
social policy under communism 64–8
paternalism 76
price subsidies 66
reforms 66–8
workplace benefits 76
socialism 21, 24, 38–9, 41, 59, 64–8, 70,
76–7, 98
Estonia 151, 153, 162–3
Hungary 184–5, 209
Latvia 213–14, 217, 227, 230
Lithuania 242–3, 255, 259
Soviet *see* socialism
standardisation of education 13, 22, 26–8,
see also secondary *or* tertiary
education
Bulgaria 105, 107–9
Czech Republic 132–4
Estonia 152, 158, 162
Hungary 191, 193–4
Latvia 221, 223–4
Lithuania 250, 252
Poland 276–9
Romania 302–5
Slovakia 330–3
Slovenia 361–2
stratification of education 13–15, *see also*
secondary *or* tertiary education
Bulgaria 103–4
Czech Republic 131–2
Estonia 158
Hungary 190
Latvia 219–20
Lithuania 248–50
Poland 275–6
Romania 301–2
Slovakia 329–30
Slovenia 359–60

T

tertiary education 8, 10–11, 14–15, 20–29, 71
  Bulgaria 100–103, 105–9
  Czech Republic 124, 126–30, 133–4
  Estonia 154, 155–62
  expansion 24
    Bulgaria 98
    Czech Republic 124
    Estonia 151
    Hungary 188–9
    Poland 279
    Slovakia 324
    Slovenia 358
  field of study *see* horizontal dimension
  horizontal dimension 24–26
    Bulgaria 105–7
    Czech Republic 133–4
    Estonia 159–61
    Hungary 191–2
    Latvia 221–3
    Lithuania 250–1
    Poland 277–8
    Romania 303–4
    Slovakia 331–2
    Slovenia 361–2
  Hungary 184–9, 191–4
  Latvia 214–15, 217–19, 221–4
  Lithuania 242, 244, 246–8, 250–2
  openness 29
    Bulgaria 107–9
    Czech Republic 134
    Estonia 162
    Hungary 193–4
    Latvia 223–4
    Lithuania 252
    Poland 278–9
    Romania 304–5
    Slovakia 332–3
    Slovenia 362
  Poland 272–5, 277–9
  private 23, 28
    Bulgaria 107–9
    Czech Republic 134
    Estonia 162
    Hungary 193
    Latvia 223
    Lithuania 252
    Poland 278–9
    Romania 304–5
    Slovakia 332–3
    Slovenia 362
  public 26–9
    Bulgaria 107–9
    Czech Republic 134
    Hungary 193–4
    Latvia 223
    Lithuania 252
    Poland 278–9
    Romania 305
    Slovakia 332–3
    Slovenia 278–9
  Romania 296–7, 299–301, 303–5
  Slovakia 324–5, 327–8, 331–3
  Slovenia 356–8, 361–62, 368
  standardisation *see* standardisation of education
  stratification *see* stratification of education
track differentiation *see* stratification of education

U

unemployment
  dynamics 52
    Bulgaria 112–14
    Czech Republic 138–40
    Estonia 167–9
    Hungary 199–200
    Latvia 228–30
    Lithuania 258–9
    Poland 284–5
    Romania 309–11
    Slovakia 337–9
    Slovenia 366–8
  long-term 52, 68, 73–5, 82, 84, 86, 88
    Bulgaria 114
    Estonia 168–9, 171
    Hungary 199
    Latvia 230, 233
    Lithuania 259, 261
    Poland 288
    Romania 311, 315
    Slovakia 323, 338, 344
    Slovenia 367
  youth 50–1
    Bulgaria 114
    Czech Republic 139
    Estonia 167, 169
    Hungary 199
    Latvia 230
    Lithuania 258
    Poland 284
    Romania 311
    Slovakia 338
    Slovenia 367

unemployment benefits *see*
    unemployment insurance
unemployment insurance 65, 80–86
    Bulgaria 117–19
    Czech Republic 144–5
    Estonia 172–4
    Hungary 203–5, 208
    Latvia 233–5
    Lithuania 261–3
    Poland 288–9, 291
    Romania 314–16
    Slovakia 341, 343–4
    Slovenia 370–2
unions 3, 56–9, 64
    Bulgaria 116
    Czech Republic 142, 145
    Estonia 170–1, 174
    Hungary 202
    Latvia 231–2
    Lithuania 260
    Poland 287
    Romania 312–13
    Slovakia 340–1
    Slovenia 368–9

V

vocational education and training 12, 13,
    14, 15–22, 26
    Bulgaria 99–105
    Czech Republic 124–33
    Estonia 152–8
    Hungary 184–91, 193
    Latvia 214–21
    Lithuania 242–50, 252
    Poland 270–7
    Romania 295–303
    Slovakia 323–31
    Slovenia 354–61